W9-BZQ-903
11.95

An Introduction to the Criminal Justice System and Process

Alan Coffey

Director, Staff Training
Santa Clara County Juvenile Probation Department
Instructor, De Anza College

Edward Eldefonso

Supervisor, Santa Clara County Juvenile Probation Department
Instructor, Law Enforcement Education Department, De Anza College

Walter Hartinger

Supervisor, Santa Clara County Juvenile Probation Department
Instructor in Corrections,
Law Enforcement Education Department, De Anza College

Prentice-Hall, Inc. Englewood Cliffs, New Jersey

Library of Congress Cataloging in Publication Data

COFFEY, ALAN.
An introduction to the criminal justice system and process.

(Prentice-Hall series in criminal justice)
Includes bibliographical references.
1. Criminal justice, Administration of—United States. I. Eldefonso, Edward, joint author. II. Hartinger, Walter, joint author. III. Title.
HV8138.C58 364 73-14900
ISBN 0-13-481127-5

Prentice-Hall Series in Criminal Justice
James D. Stinchcomb, Editor

Printed in the United States of America

10 9 8 7 6 5 4 3 2 1

Prentice-Hall International, Inc., *London*
Prentice-Hall of Australia, Pty. Ltd., *Sydney*
Prentice-Hall of Canada, Ltd., *Toronto*
Prentice-Hall of India Private Limited, *New Delhi*
Prentice-Hall of Japan, Inc., *Tokyo*

Contents

3

Law Enforcement in a Democratic Society, 50

PART TWO

THE POLICE ROLE, FUNCTION, AND POWER IN DEALING WITH CRIMINAL BEHAVIOR

4

Law Enforcement and Scope of Criminal Law, 77

5

Legal Aspects of Law Enforcement and the Judiciary Process, 94

6

An Introduction to Theories Relating to Crime and Delinquency, 133

PART THREE

SPECIAL ENFORCEMENT PROBLEMS AND THE POLICE ROLE IN COURT

7

Social Problems: Impact on Law Enforcement, 149

8

The Prosecution, 179

9

The Defense, 200

PART FOUR

SCOPE OF JUVENILE AND ADULT CORRECTIONS

10

The Justice System and Juveniles, 213

Preface

Criminal justice in America is rapidly approaching a crisis—or may now be in a crisis. Crowded court calendars and other impediments to "speedy trial," rioting outside and inside correctional institutions, increasing violence in general, and a host of other "symptoms" signal the approach of a crisis in the criminal justice system's ability to remain effective. And this crisis affects every segment of the criminal justice system: police, courts, prosecution-defense, and corrections.

We cannot fully understand any one segment of criminal justice without concern for all the other segments. Police procedures clearly affect the courts, prosecution, and corrections. Courts in turn affect police. Prosecutors affect both police and corrections. There is no longer any doubt that these relationships have profound influence upon the entire *system* of criminal justice.

For this reason, we wrote this book about these relationships and the functions of those involved in the relationships—about those who cope with the crisis facing criminal justice. But more important, because this book is about the *system* of criminal justice, it concerns human will, human freedom, and the societal system of integrating the will and freedom of many men.

The American system of criminal justice may prove to be the only hope of integrating the diverse freedom and will of so many people within a complex society. With this is mind, the introductory chapter focuses exclusively on the concept of systems and systematic relationships. Through this method of introduction, the relationships between various criminal justice segments will hopefully remain clear even though each will be isolated and presented separately in later chapters—chapters covering a wide range of subject areas.

With regard to these subject areas, there are entire volumes and even series of volumes in the literature for every subject area we have presented. For example, the subject of *evidence,* presented in Chapter 8, The Prosecution, could comprise a virtual library. With this in mind, the authors judge the "depth" of discussion of any given subject solely by its relation to the *overall* system of criminal justice. An annotated reference list at the conclusion of each chapter affords "greater depth" if the reader desires it.

ACKNOWLEDGMENTS

In a subject as diversified and challenging as the administration of criminal justice, countless obligations are necessarily incurred in developing a text. Therefore, with the usual proviso that they cannot be held accountable for either errors of omission or commission, the authors express their gratitude for the encouragement, advice, and counsel tendered by B. Earl Lewis, Director of the Department of Law Enforcement Education, De Anza College, and the Administration and Staff of the Santa Clara County Juvenile Probation Department, San Jose, California: Richard W. Bothman, Chief Probation Officer and his assistant, Michael Kuzirian. Staff members such as Michael Johnson, Michael McDonald, Susan Compolong and Thomas Slatten were quite helpful in obtaining many of the photos in this text. Others who were helpful in this area were James Geary, Sheriff, Santa Clara County; Philip D. Guthrie, Chief, Community Relations and Information, California Department of Corrections; Frank Furnaw, Campbell Police Department; Phil Crawford, San Jose Police Department; Carl Cieslikowski, Santa Cruz Probation Department; and Leonard Pacheco, Public Information Officer, Santa Clara County.

Acknowledgments, as far as the authors are concerned, are incomplete without some mention of our wives, Beverly May Coffey, Mildred Ann Eldefonso (specifically for working on the indexing), and Patricia B. Hartinger, whose firm support, encouragement, and understanding do not go unappreciated.

ALAN COFFEY
EDWARD ELDEFONSO
WALTER HARTINGER

PART ONE

Crime, Justice, and Society

Systems of law and systems for the determination of guilt do not spring forth full grown. Our present system of justice is the product of centuries, and perhaps millennia, of trial and error. In addition to the experience of history, the complexity of civilization must determine the methods by which men determine codes of conduct and execute sanctions for disobedience of those codes.

P. B. WESTON AND K. M. WELLS,
Law Enforcement and Criminal Justice: An Introduction

1

An Introduction to the Criminal Justice System

There has never been a civilized society that did not find itself continually coping with crime. Great differences exist between the philosophies of various societies and between the criminal theories and activities of various cultures. It cannot be said, however, that any society, including the United States, has devised a method to avoid coping with crime on a continuing basis. This book is about the approach to crime in the United States.

The American method of dealing with crime is commonly known as the criminal justice system. Later chapters will question the term *criminal* and the term *justice;* this chapter will question the term *system.* This book in general is about the *criminal justice system.*

GOVERNMENT POWER AND THE INDIVIDUAL

Although this book is about the criminal justice system, it is also about people. Criminal justice is a societal method of doing things for and to people; but the things done for and to people are also done by people. This observation is crucial because a discussion of the complex facets of the criminal justice system tends to obscure the fundamental roles played by the people both directly and indirectly, involved in criminal justice. For this reason, stress will be placed on the human implications of a systems theory even in this somewhat technical introductory chapter.

Put another way, the only rationale for exploring the criminal justice system as a *system* is to make possible greater understanding of its impact on *people*—people both inside and outside the system itself.

THE CRIMINAL JUSTICE SYSTEM

The criminal justice system has many segments, each of which will be covered in depth in the eleven chapters that follow. Police, courts, prosecution-defense, corrections, and the law itself will all be discussed in many different contexts. Moreover, the interrelationships between these various segments will be presented, along with the social considerations that affect each functioning unit. Above all else, the criminal justice system will be presented as a system.

Criminal justice can function systematically only to the degree that each segment of the system takes into account all other segments (Figure 1-1). In other words, the system is no more systematic than the relationships between police and prosecution, police and court, prosecution and

Figure 1-1 Once the crime is reported, the criminal justice process goes into effect. Arrest of the suspect hopefully follows immediately. Photo courtesy of Ambassador College, Pasadena, Ca.

corrections, corrections and law, and so forth. In the absence of functional relationships between segments, the criminal justice system is vulnerable to fragmentation and ineffectiveness. Consider, for example, the relationships depicted in the following flow chart.

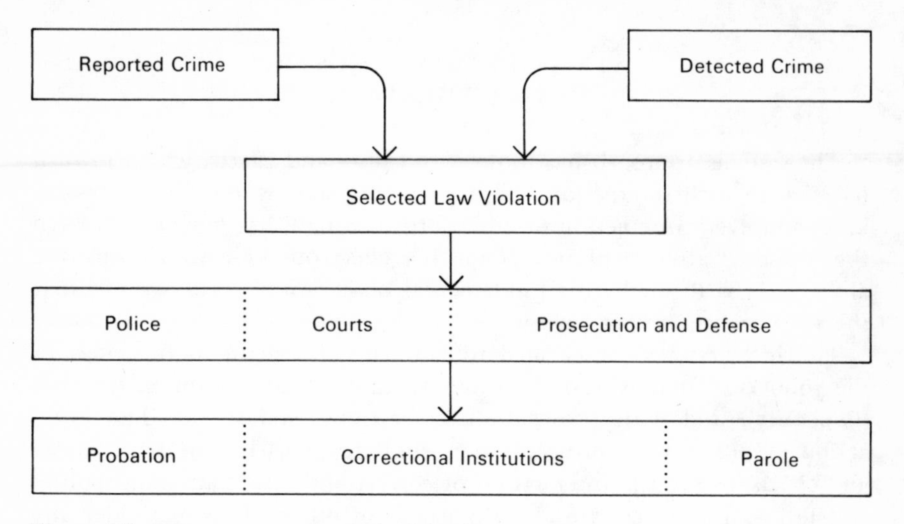

Figure 1-2 Flow process of criminal justice.

Fragmentation

Fragmentation and ineffectiveness can be measured simply in terms of crime rates that are not reduced, and by law violators that continue to offend. If we assume that fragmentation produces ineffectiveness, then we must conclude that the American society is not coping *effectively* with crime when its criminal justice system is fragmented.

It is worth noting, however, that the precise manner in which the criminal justice system suffers fragmentation can vary from one part of the United States to another. Ineffective criminal justice through fragmentation may have many causes. For example, when the police operate without regard to prosecution, the syste m is clearly fragmented. Another example elsewhere in the system might be the court showing indifference to corrections or to the police.

The point is that when any segment of the system functions in isolation from the rest of the system, the resulting fragmentation reduces the effectiveness of the system. Effectiveness in this case is the measure of the success of society's approach to crime in general.

In the eleven chapters that follow, both the segments that are potentially subject to fragmentation and the factors that influence fragmentation will be discussed. In order to evaluate potential fragmentation, this chapter will present what might be called a "systems approach." Once again, attention is directed to the vital role played by *people* in their actions and reactions inside and outside the system.

SYSTEMS–CRIMINAL JUSTICE AND OTHERWISE

The systems approach has to do with causes and effects, which in turn have to do with interaction. All human interactions are effects of some kind, and every interaction whether large or small, has some effect. Even the supposed absence of interaction has effect on those who notice the absence. It is through this fundamental observation about systems that the vital role of *people* emerges.

The interaction of an armed robber with the victim is the effect of the robbery, but it is also the cause of another interaction with police (hopefully), and with prosecution, corrections, and so on. The interaction of police with prosecution is similarly a variety of both causes and effects, as are the interactions of corrections with courts and police.

The limitless effects are also the causes of other effects. Consider any possible reaction to police making an arrest. The arrest is an interaction which itself is an effect, but any reaction to this effect is the cause of another effect. And so the endless cycle goes. A system is simply a chain of these causes and effects. The system may or may not cause favorable effects; indeed, many effects tend to cause unfavorable effects (or results).

This chapter has already noted the need to relate each segment of the criminal justice system to all other segments. When fragmentation prevents this relationship, it should not be surprising that the system produces extremely unfavorable effects (or results) despite the fact that the effects are still causes. A system that produces *unfavorable* effects may continue to work but with little or no *effective* impact on the problem for which it was intended. And consistent effective impact is the measure of the success of any system.

System Consistency

To clarify how a systematic chain of interactions can be designed to provide consistently desirable effects, we might use the analogy of heating a house. If a home is equipped with an efficient furnace controlled by a thermostat, it can be said that a heating *system* is available. Of course the relationship between a heating system and the criminal justice system is somewhat obscure unless it is recalled that both systems can be made to operate systematically—*systematically* implying predictable, controllable causes and effects.

The reason that both criminal justice and heating a home can be systematic is that both have consistent chains of causes and effects. The specific causes and effects are different in each system but are related in the same manner. The consistency of these chains provides a desirable range of production—a desirable range of warmth on a predictable basis in the case of the heating system, and a desirable range of crime reduction in the case of criminal justice. In the case of a heating system, desirable results are produced on a self-adjusting basis; this basis is also desirable in criminal justice.

Complaints about the degree of heat are not required to get the furnace turned down or up in the heating system. Sensitivity to the problem which the *system* is intended to solve insures consistent and proper adjustments of the system on an on-going basis. The thermostat measures the temperature inside the house and then controls the furnace accordingly. This interaction of causes and effects produces the desirable result of a healthy indoor climate.

Compare this system of sensitivity to temperature changes to a "system" where one waits for complaints about the heat before running to the basement to adjust the furnace. Then consider the overall system. Does any single part function independently to the degree that it is not directly related to the overall purpose of the system? Clearly the system that adjusts itself to change produces better results, requires less effort, and necessarily becomes the only definition of a desirable system.

In regard to criminal justice as a system, the individual functions of police, sheriff, prosecution, court, probation, parole, and corrections *can* (in the ideal) function in much the same manner as the heating system. Moreover the systematic manner in which various criminal justice functions occur could make possible the allowance for variations of many kinds. In other words, while the heating system responds to the single variable of heat, the criminal justice system can and does respond to a great number of variables. For example, social change, legal change, and economic change impinge directly upon police, courts, prosecution–defense, and corrections through a number of "thermostats." The criminal justice system, then, has potentially much more flexibility than does the heating system analogy.

Consider, for example, the flexibility required of criminal justice in terms of *change*—particularly social change. Although this view is tremendously oversimplified, changes during the history of the world might be thought of in terms of the thousands of years man has spent farming compared to the couple hundred years of "blue-collar work" that accompanied the Industrial Revolution. With this background of suddenly accelerated change, man now faces an uncertain future with automation, cybernation, and an explosion of knowledge that creates more knowledge in one day than was created during the thousands of years prior to the twentieth century.

The social problems that result from this accelerating change are an integral part of the chain of causes and effects that constitute criminal justice. This ever-accelerating pace of social change which has direct impact on the causes and effects within the criminal justice system itself, requires an incredible degree of flexibility in order for criminal justice to survive as a *system.*

What Makes a System Systematic?

When we combine the idea of social change with a number of other variables that require great flexibility, we can begin to clarify the nature of a functioning system. We gain greater clarity, however, by further consideration of cause and effect within the system. More precisely, knowing *how* significant an interaction is and to what degree it affects the system is probably the key to understanding criminal justice as a system.

For example, the interaction between two policemen may or may not be as significant to the overall system of criminal justice as one policeman interacting with a judge or prosecutor. To organize all of the complicated possibilities, the idea of a system (at least a linear system) can be thought of as having three essential parts: *input, process,* and *output.*

Input, Process, and *Output.* Before elaborating on these three component parts of a system, it may be worthwhile for us to note that this particular configuration is not the only way to conceive of a system. For example, most dictionaries define *system* merely in terms of an arrangement that is in some way interrelated.

Even the technical definitions of *system* vary somewhat. Consider the following examples:

> . . . general-systems model is one that brings together in an ordered fashion information on all dimensions of an organization. . . .[1]
>
> . . . the term system covers an extremely broad spectrum of concepts. . . .[2]
>
> . . . system is a network of related procedures developed according to an integrated scheme for performing major activity. . . .[3]

[1] B. M. Gross, "What Are Your Organization's Objectives? A general Systems Approach to Planning," *Human Relations,* Vol. 43, No. 4 (April, 1964), p. 205.

[2] R. A. Johnson, F. E. Kast, and J. E. Rosenzweig, "Systems Theory and Management," *Management Science,* Vol. 10, No. 5 (January, 1964), p. 368.

[3] R. F. Neuschel, *Management by Systems* (New York: McGraw-Hill, 1960), p. 10.

> . . . system in general can be defined as an established arrangement of components which leads to the attainment of particular objectives according to plan. . . .[4]

Of course, many other varying definitions are correct. But in order to approach the concept of criminal justice as a system and to do so on a consistent basis, the three main component parts of a linear system will be used: input, process, and output.

Among the advantages of this approach is the ease with which this particular systems concept can be adopted. Indeed, the single configuration of:

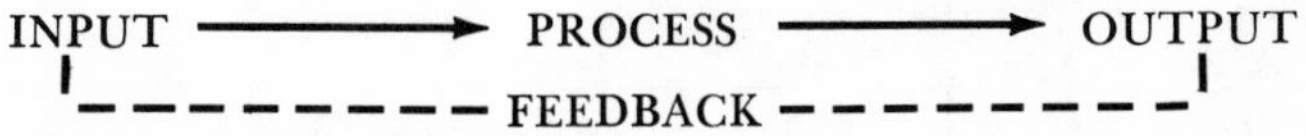

INPUT ——→ PROCESS ——→ OUTPUT
- - - - - - - - - FEEDBACK - - - - - - - - -

will be utilized for the sake of consistency in every context in which reference is made to system. The input is what the system deals with; the process is *how* the system deals with the input; and the output is the *results* of the process—results that may or may not be desirable in criminal justice.

CRIMINAL JUSTICE AS A SYSTEM

Using the distinctions between input, process, and output, we can see the criminal justice system in its major systematic parts. The input of the criminal justice system is selected law violations. The number of *unreported* crimes, as will be seen later in this volume, is mere conjecture. Thus, "selected" law violations refer only to the reported crimes which become input and which bring one or more segments of the criminal justice system into contact with the victim or the violator, or both.

The process of the system refers to the many activities of police, attorneys, judges, probation and parole officers, and prison staff. Process therefore is the most visible part of the system—and perhaps the most significant.

Why Include Output?

The output of the criminal justice system includes the results obtained or not obtained from the process—in other words, the success or failure of society to cope with crime. Output, or results, is extremely relevant.

[4] L. J. Kazmier, *Principles of Management,* 2nd ed. (New York: McGraw-Hill, 1969), p. 349.

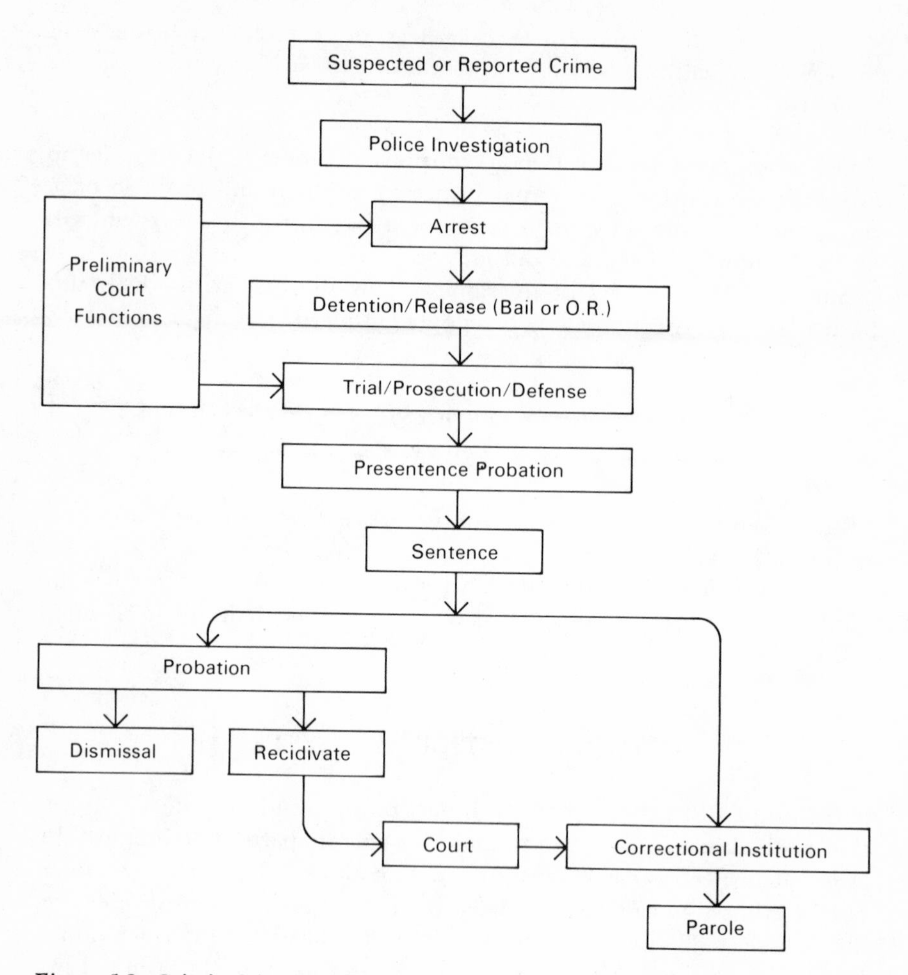

Figure 1-3 Criminal justice parts.

A system that is unable to provide a process which can change input into *desirable* output is not an effective system; it is a system destined to have changes made (either willingly or unwillingly) in its process.

The achievement of results can come either from the workings of the entire criminal justice system, or from any given subsystem such as police, probation, parole, and so on. Consider again the overall system of justice:

Now consider any one subsystem that helps make up the process of criminal justice; take the probation subsystem of corrections as an example.

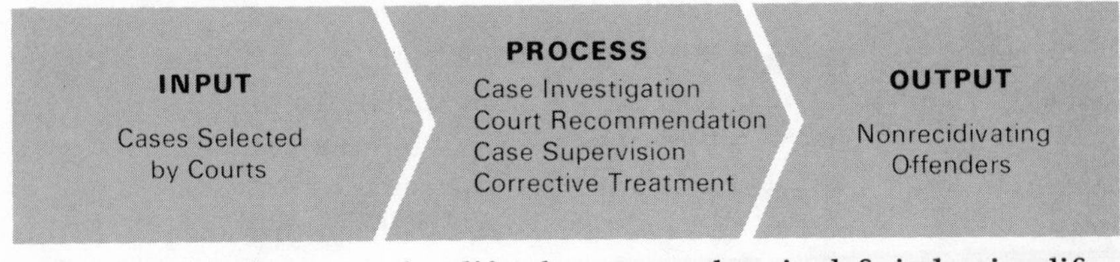

Of course this does not simplify the system, but it definitely simplifies the *concept* of criminal justice as a system. It is from this frame of reference that the efficiency or the effectiveness of this system can be considered.

EFFECTIVENESS VERSUS EFFICIENCY

Again with the use of an analogy, we can clarify the distinction between an effective criminal justice system and an efficient criminal justice system. Consider, for example, an automobile as a total system. In terms of efficiency, the engine may be well tuned, the transmission and power column may be perfectly synchronized; and the torque pounds of wheel turning power delivered to the rear axle may be optimal. All these elements may be in sufficient harmony to consider the automobile *efficient.*

Now consider this extremely "efficient automobile" when it is stuck in the mud. Regardless of the efficiency of the machine, *effectiveness* is not forthcoming until the automobile is pulled from the mud. This analogy, when applied to the people involved in criminal justice, says even more.

The efficiency of the police dispatcher has little impact if the offender subsequently overpowers the policeman who is dispatched. The efficiency of the reports of the parole officer have little effectiveness if the offender continues to offend. Indeed, the efficiency of any part of the criminal justice system has little effect if the output goals are not met. Thus, we must include output in our consideration of the system. Many systems, when functioning without regard to output, become extremely "efficient" —they are efficiently accumulating, storing, and distributing records or other paperwork which may or may not influence the accomplishment of specific results. Criminal justice as a system requires the ultimate combination of efficiency with effectiveness. Having noted the implications of criminal justice input and the crucial significance of output, let us now consider process.

THE FUNCTIONS OF PROCESS

We have already noted the problems of possible fragmentation between system segments that make up process. Functional, working relationships between all segments are absolutely necessary for any segment to succeed. Isolating police from prosecution or courts, isolating courts from police or corrections, or isolating any other segments from one another is dysfunctional; this is scientific fact.[5]

In reality, every segment of process is a subsystem, a system-within-a-system.[6] These subsystems, when combined, form the overall system of criminal justice. In the chapters that follow, each segment or subsystem of criminal justice will be presented in terms of the area of responsibility—police, judicial, prosecution, or the various correctional responsibilities. To explore the unfragmented interrelationships necessary for continuity within criminal justice, the function and role of each subsystem will be discussed. Particular emphasis will be placed upon the *function* of each of these subsystems. We shall also present several contexts from which to consider the interrelationships between functions.

In Chapter 2 a policeman's views of criminal justice and of the functions that make up the criminal justice process will be discussed. The functions of enforcing law will be presented in Chapter 3. Chapters 4 and 5 cover a variety of law enforcement considerations with emphasis on the functions of legal aspects that relate to the criminal justice process. Chapter 6 considers many of the theoretical matters on which the functions of criminal justice are based.

The various social problems that relate directly to both criminal justice input and to the functions that form criminal justice process are the subjects of Chapter 7. Chapters 8 and 9 deal with the prosecution-defense function—recognizing of course that the specific function of criminal defense is somewhat removed from other areas of criminal justice process. Finally, the entire range of correctional functions will be presented in the last three chapters.

In dealing with the specific functions of the various subsystems, the reader may reduce the risk of losing sight of how each subsystem relates to the others by approaching a discussion of various functions in terms of the overall criminal justice system. Consider, for example, the open-

[5] T. W. McRae, *Analytical Management* (New York: John Wiley & Sons, 1970), Chaps. 1, 2, 8, 10, and 18.

[6] Rocco Carzo, Jr., and John W. Yanouzas, *Formal Organization: A Systems Approach* (Homewood, Ill.: Dorsey Press, 1967), pp. 235-54.

ing sentence of Chapter 4 which reads: "The primary responsibility of law enforcement is not technical legalities but the provision of personal safety and property security for members of society who conform to the law." Since the chapter is entitled "Law Enforcement and Scope of Criminal Law," this statement accurately introduces the function of the enforcement subsystem. But here, and in all such examples throughout this text, the reader is asked to bear one critical factor in mind. Those functions of criminal justice that *are* concerned with the legal technicalities actually have no immediate responsibility for "personal safety and property security," which is the responsibility of the law enforcement segment. Nevertheless, personal safety and property security, legal technicalities, and every other responsibility of *any* segment of the entire criminal justice system are crucial parts of the picture as a whole. Every segment carries specific responsibilities but does not forget that successful discharge of that responsibility depends upon the successful discharge of all other responsibilities in the system.

SUMMARY

In this chapter, the criminal justice system of the United States has been presented as the American society's method of coping with crime. The human factor, or the role of *people,* is crucial even in a technical discussion of the overall system.

It was noted that the terms *criminal justice* and *system* would be further clarified. Segments of the criminal justice system were dealt with in terms of the interrelationships between police, prosecution-defense, courts, corrections, and the law itself.

The problem of system fragmentation was shown to interrupt continuity and reduce effectiveness. The "systems approach" was introduced and further classified into its three components: input, process and output. Input was defined as selected law violations (of *reported* nature); process was presented as the function of police, courts, prosecution-defense, and corrections; and output was defined as the results of coping with crime within society.

Flexibility and sensitivity to social change were also seen as crucial to a *functional* system of criminal justice. The *function* of each criminal justice system segment was distinguished from the relationships between segments. The functions of various segments make up the theme of this book, but this focus does not exclude consideration of interrelationships. Indeed, an appreciation of the interrelationships between segments is a virtual requirement to understanding the overall approach to crime within the United States.

QUESTIONS

1. Discuss the notion of *complexity* in terms of the rationale for presenting a "systems approach" to understanding criminal justice in America.
2. Why is the risk of "forgetting" the role of *people* increased in a comprehensive discussion of a complex system?
3. In what way does the observation that no society has been able to avoid coping with crime related to the additional observation that *people* are the crucial consideration in criminal justice?
4. Contrast efficiency and effectiveness in terms of the criminal justice system.
5. Discuss fragmentation within the criminal justice system in terms of: (a) effectivenes, (b) continuity in dealing with crime.
6. How does human interaction relate to causes and effects?
7. How do causes and effects relate to systems?
8. Discuss system flexibility and social change.
   (a) input, (b) process, (c) output.
10. What is the process of the criminal justice system?
11. Discuss any two roles in criminal justice process.

ANNOTATED REFERENCES

BARNES, H., and TEETERS, N. *New Horizons in Criminology*. Englewood Cliffs, N.J.: Prentice-Hall, 1960. Chapter 1 covers in great detail the concept of crime in society in the context used to introduce this chapter.

COFFEY, A.; ELDEFONSO, E.; and HARTINGER, W. *Human Relations: Law Enforcement in a Changing Community*. Englewood Cliffs, N.J.: Prentice-Hall, 1971. Chapter 1 presents a broad picture of system input.

COFFEY, A.; ELDEFONSO E.; and HARTINGER W. *Police-Community Relations*. Englewood Cliffs, N.J.: Prentice-Hall, 1971. The first three chapters succinctly elaborate how system input and process interact outside the immediate sphere of reported crime.

ELDEFONSO, E.; COFFEY, A.; and GRACE, R. *Principles of Law Enforcement*. New York: Wiley & Sons, 1967. Chapter 1 elaborates upon criminal justice system input for the reader wishing extra clarity in this regard.

TAPPAN, P. *Crime, Justice, and Correction*. New York: McGraw-Hill, 1960. Chapters 1 and 2 elaborate in great depth the "selected law violation" presented here as input.

WINSLOW, R. *Crime in a Free Society*. Belmont, Calif.: Dickinson Publishers, 1968. Chapters 11, 12, and 13 clarify segments of process.

2

The Policeman's View of the Criminal Justice System

The federal government's detailed report, *Task Force Report: The Police,* points out that the police are the part of the criminal justice system that is in direct daily contact both with crime and the public. They comprise some 420,000 people, working for approximately 40,000 separate agencies that spend more than $2.5 billion a year. The entire system—courts and corrections as well as the police—is charged with enforcing the law and maintaining order. What is distinctive about the responsibility of the police is that it is largely a policeman's judgment which determines whether the criminal justice process is invoked against an individual. Theoretically, his judgment is based upon the statutory definition of the crime, but it is abundantly clear that there are many situations in which a violation has in fact occurred and is known to the police, but no effort is made by the police to make an arrest. Among the factors accounting for this exercise of discretion are a large volume of violations, the limited resources of the police, the overgeneralization of legislative enactments defining criminal conduct, and various local pressures reflecting community values and attitudes.

Because the police have the responsibility for dealing with crime or violence where and when it occurs, there is a tendency on the part of the public, and often the police themselves, to think of crime control almost exclusively in terms of police work. One response to the recent increases in crime has been the charge that the police lack the competence or the will to keep crime within bounds. A far more common response has been the assertion that the police could keep crime down only if the appellate courts, or civilian review boards, corrupt politicians, or an uncooperative public allow them to do so. "Take the handcuffs off of police" is a cry familiar to everyone.[1]

It is indeed unfortunate that even under the most favorable conditions, the ability of the police to respond to criminal activities is limited. The police did not create and cannot resolve the social conditions that stimulate crime. They did not start and cannot stop the convulsive social changes that are taking place in America. They do not enact the laws that they are required to enforce, nor do they dispose of the criminals they arrest. It has been the misfortune of law enforcement to inherit those problems of our society which no other agency of government can immediately cope with or control. In addition to myriad duties and public service functions, the police are expected to supervise the whole spectrum of the law and to stand accountable if it is wrong or unacceptable. The police are only one part of the criminal justice system; the criminal justice system is only one part of the government; and the government is only one part of society.[2] M. Canlis, the sheriff of San Joaquin County, in California, puts it this way:

> The whole gamut of the system of criminal justice has not been geared to today's interpretation of constitutional requirements of the police service. As a matter of fact, almost the entire system of criminal justice breaks down at night and on week-ends, when you'll find that every other part of the system provides either limited service or is entirely unavailable. I refer now to the District Attorney, the Public Defender, the Probation Office, the Parole Services and generally, the members of the Bar. The police then becomes the catch-all for all kinds of inquiries concerning the other government and private services by the mere fact that we are always available every minute of every hour, seven days a week, 365 days a year.[3]

According to Sheriff Canlis, the availability of the policeman makes him the front line instrument for government, and especially for the system of criminal justice.

[1] *Task Force Report: The Police,* A Report by The President's Commission on Law Enforcement and the Administration of Justice (Washington, D.C.: U.S. Gov't. Printing Office, 1967), p. 1.

[2] *Task Force Report: The Police,* p. 1.

[3] M. N. Canlis, "The Police and Criminal Justice," *Youth Authority Quarterly,* Vol. 20, No. 3 (Fall, 1967), p. 12.

THE ADMINISTRATION OF THE CRIMINAL JUSTICE SYSTEM

Any criminal justice system is an apparatus, which society uses to enforce the standards of conduct necessary to protect individuals and the community. It works by apprehending, prosecuting, convicting, and sentencing those members of the community who violate the basic rules of group existence. The action taken against law breakers is designed to serve three purposes beyond the immediate punitive one. It removes dangerous people from the community; it deters others from criminal behavior; and it gives society an opportunity to attempt to transform law breakers into law-abiding citizens. What most significantly distinguishes one country's system from that of another is the extent and the form of protections it offers individuals in the process of determining guilt and imposing punishment. Our system of justice deliberately sacrifices much in efficiency and even in effectiveness in order to preserve local autonomy and to protect the individual. Sometimes it may seem to sacrifice too much. For example, the American system was not designed with Cosa Nostra type criminal organizations in mind, and it has been notably unsuccessful to date in preventing such organizations from preying on society.[4]

The criminal justice system has four (if prosecution and defense are viewed as separate entities from court) separate organized parts—the police, the court prosecution, the defense, and corrections—and each has distinct tasks (refer to Figure 2-1). However, these parts are by no means independent of each other. The courts must deal, and can only deal, with those individuals the police arrest. The business of corrections is with the persons delivered to it by the courts. (Refer to Figure 2-2.) The success of the correctional system determines whether the offender will once again become police business, and it influences the sentences that judges pass.

Police activities are subject to court scrutiny and are often determined by court decisions; the most significant of which (Mapp, Mallory, and Miranda) we shall discuss later in this chapter. (See Appendix B.) Fur-

[4] W. Hartinger, E. Eldefonso, and A. Coffey, *Corrections: A Part of the Criminal Justice System* (Pacific Palisades, Calif.: Goodyear Publishing Co., 1972), Chap. 1; see also: *The Challenge of Crime in a Free Society,* A Report by The President's Commission on Law Enforcement and the Administration of Justice (Washington, D.C.: U.S. Gov't. Printing Office, 1967), p. 7.

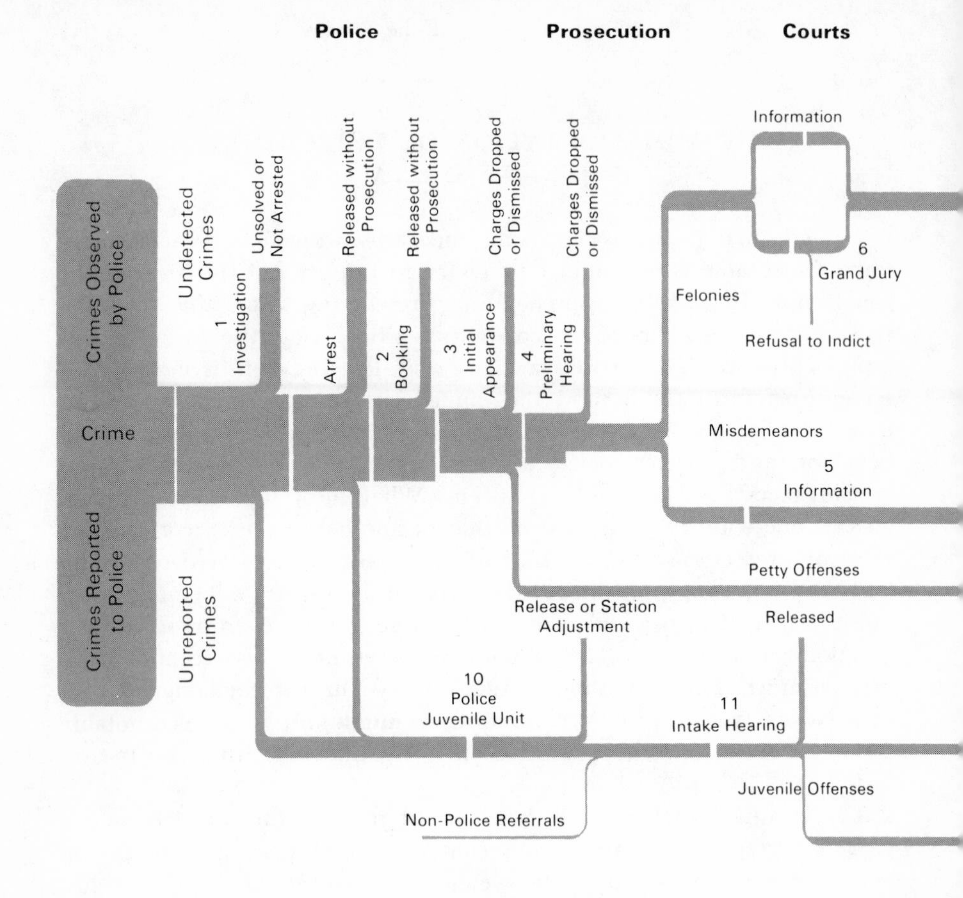

1 May continue until trial.

2 Administrative record of arrest. First step at which temporary release on bail may be available.

3 Before magistrate, commissioner, or justice of peace. Formal notice of charge, advice of rights. Bail set. Summary trials for petty offenses usually conducted here without further processing.

4 Preliminary testing of evidence against defendant. Charge may be reduced. No separate preliminary hearing for misdemeanors in some systems.

5 Charge filed by prosecutor on basis of information submitted by police or citizens. Alternative to grand jury indictment; often used in felonies, almost always in misdemeanors.

6 Reviews whether Government evidence sufficient to justify trial. Some States have no grand jury system; others seldom use it.

Figure 2-1 A general view of the criminal justice system. This chart seeks to present a simple yet comprehensive view of the movement of cases through the criminal justice system. Procedures in individual jurisdictions may vary from the pattern shown here. The differing weights of line indicate the relative volume of cases disposed of at

Corrections

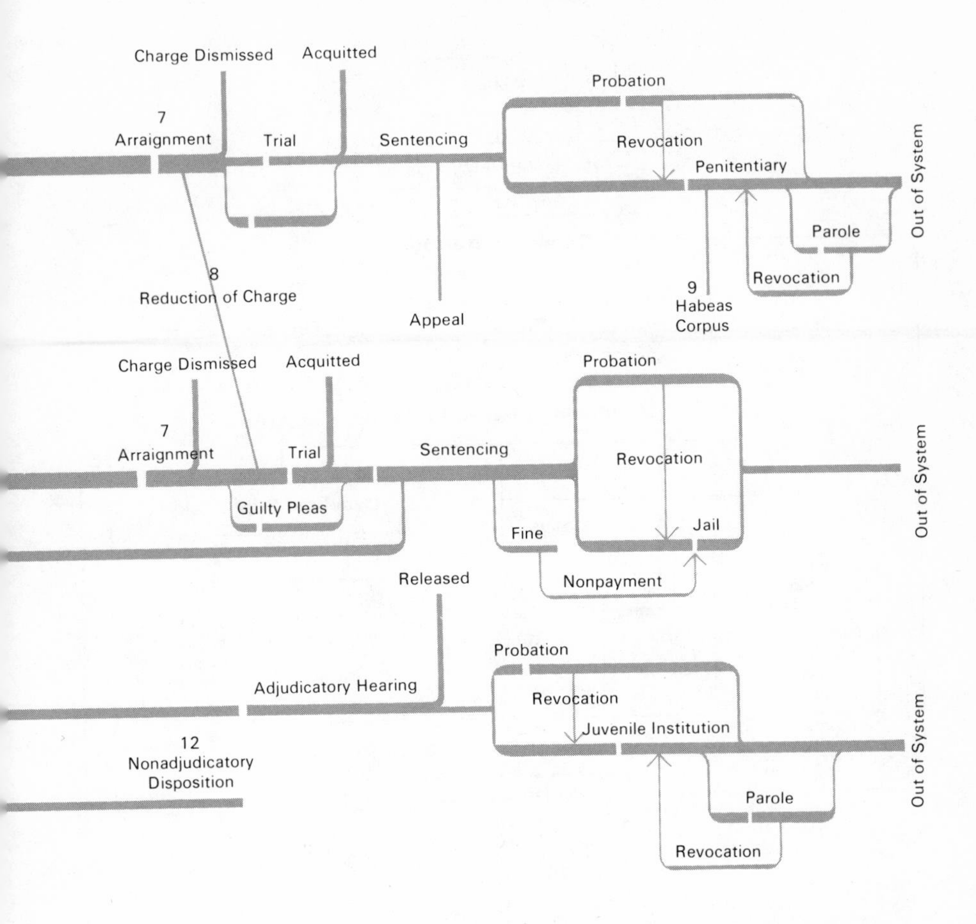

7 Appearance for plea; defendant elects trial by judge or jury (if available); counsel for indigent usually appointed here in felonies. Often not at all in other cases.

8 Charge may be reduced at any time prior to trial in return for plea of guilty or for other reasons.

9 Challenge on constitutional grounds to legality of detention. May be sought at any point in process.

10 Police often hold informal hearings, dismiss or adjust many cases without further processing.

11 Probation officer decides desirability of further court action.

12 Welfare agency, social services, counseling, medical care, etc., for cases where adjudicatory handling not needed.

various points in the system, but this is only suggestive since no nationwide data of this sort exist. This chart is taken from pp. 8–9 of The President's Commission on Law Enforcement and the Administration of Justice, *The Challenge of Crime in a Free Society* (Washington, D.C.: U.S. Government Printing Office, 1967).

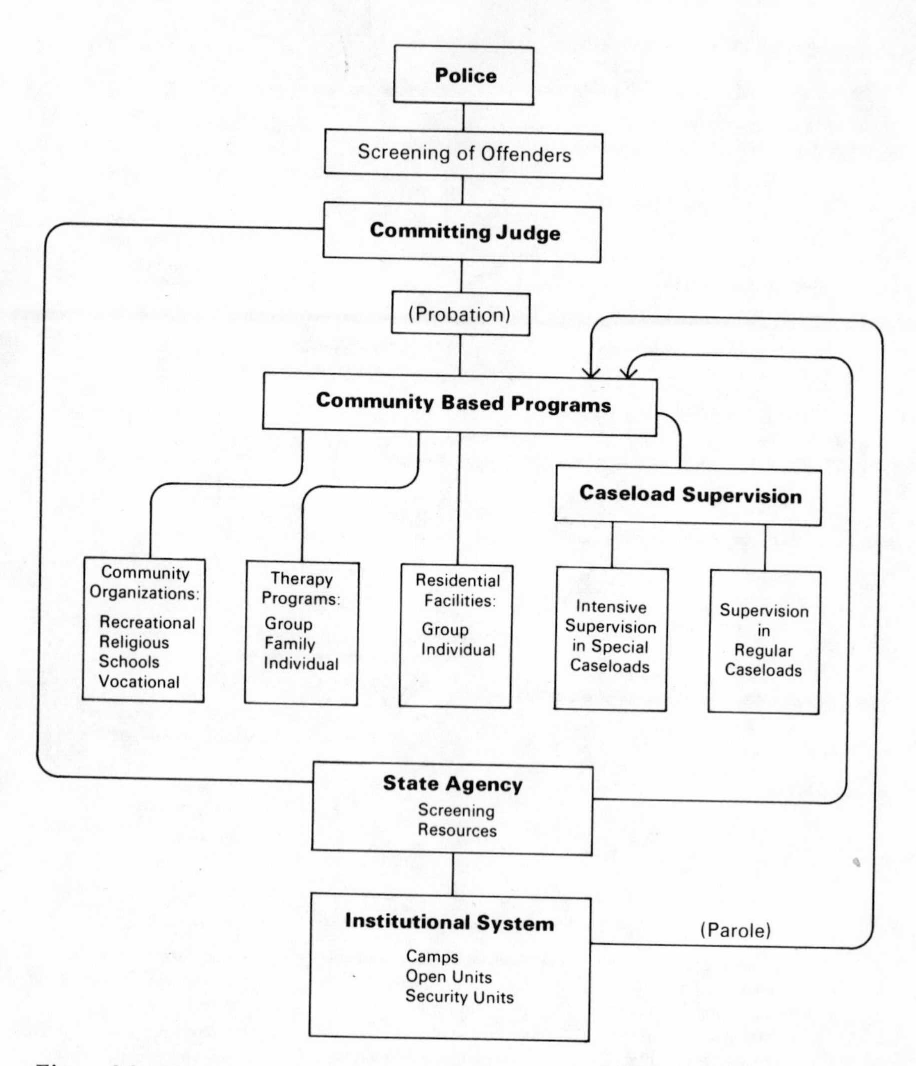

Figure 2-2 Elements of a modern correctional system. From *The Challenge of Crime in a Free Society,* The President's Commission on Law Enforcement and the Administration of Justice (Washington, D.C.: U.S. Government Printing Office), p. 182.

thermore, the criminal process, the method by which the system deals with individual cases, is not a hodgepodge of random actions. It is rather a continuum—an orderly progression of events—some of which, like arrest and trial, are highly visible and some of which, though of great importance, occur out of public view. A study of the system must begin by examining it as a whole.

The Administration of Justice and Due Process of Law[5]

The *administration of criminal justice* is a term which seeks to describe a complicated process that is designed by our society to deal with the problems of crime and delinquency. Some of the implications of this term become apparent when one considers the large number of formal agencies which deal with different aspects of the problems of crime and delinquency. The police, the prosecutor, the courts, and other agencies are formally organized to operate an area of the process of justice. In addition, large numbers of unofficial agencies or community organizations are organized to give assistance and to have a role in the process.

Justice, therefore, is not easily achieved. Each of the agencies—official or unofficial—which takes part in the process of administering criminal justice may have either a functional or dysfunctional effect upon the entire system. The task of one agency may be assisted or hampered by the policies and procedures followed by another agency. The actions of any one of these agencies may have unintended consequences for the planned programs and goals of another agency or for the process as a whole.

In the United States, it is assumed that the courts will occupy a prominent position in the administration of criminal justice. The courts, in particular the appellate courts, interpret the meaning and the scope of such principles as *due process of law, presumption of innocence,* the reasonableness of *searches* and *seizures,* and so on. Few of our citizens, however, come into any contact at *any* time during their lives with the functioning of our appellate courts. If most citizens have dealings with any of the agencies of justice at all, then this contact usually results from their dealings with lower, magistrate-level courts or with the police.

Justice, for the most part, can be measured by the actual contact which the average citizen has with the police or lower courts. The enunciations of the higher courts notwithstanding, the content of justice, the real meaning of justice, is determined by the types of relationships the individual can consistently expect to experience when he deals with these two lower-level agencies. If the average citizen—one without personal power or influence—can reasonably expect to receive fair and sympathetic treatment from the police and from the lower courts, then

[5] Adapted from J. D. Lohman, and G. E. Misner, *The Police and the Community: The Dynamics of Their Relationship in a Changing Society,* Sections I and II, Vol. 2. A Report prepared for The President's Commission on Law Enforcement and the Administration of Justice (Washington, D.C.: U.S. Gov't. Printing Office, 1966), pp. 132-33.

justice to him is both fair and sympathetic. If he cannot expect this treatment, then to him justice is neither fair nor sympathetic. It is for this reason, therefore, that the operating policies and procedures of the police are of crucial importance. Contacts with the police, more than any other public agency, determine citizen evaluation of the administration of criminal justice as a whole. Justice, in fact, consists of those rights which the average citizen enjoys "on the streets."

The role of the police in the administration of criminal justice can be divided basically into six parts. These are:

1. The prevention of crime
2. The detection of crimes which have been committed
3. Identification of the person or persons responsible for crimes
4. Apprehension of the person or persons responsible
5. Detention of the person for processing by the judiciary
6. Presentation of the evidence to the prosecutor

Throughout the performance of these functions, any attempt to deprive any person of any of the rights guaranteed him by law represents a violation of due process.

Police violation of due process may take the form either of technical legal violations; or they may, in fact, be more subtle violations of the "spirit" of due process. Technical legal violation of due process may take a variety of forms. The police may, through sloppy investigative techniques,[6] inadvertently cause "prosecution problems" which delay presenting the case in court. The district attorney, once again because of "legal technicalities" (illegal search, neglecting to advise suspects of rights, and so forth), may find it necessary to accept a plea to a lesser offense (plea bargaining). Therefore, poor police work may cause insurmountable problems on the prosecution level—something all police agencies are trying to eliminate by better training.

FOUR PHASES OF THE ADMINISTRATION OF CRIMINAL AND JUVENILE JUSTICE

The law enforcement field represents the system by which our society deals with adults who violate the law and with youthful law violators or those who show delinquent tendencies. The police is one of *four* distinct, interrelated phases of the administration of criminal and

[6] According to the presiding judge, this occurred in the Juan Corona case, handled by the Sutter County Sheriff's Department.

juvenile justice. A continuum representing the broad sweep of this process would be in this sequence: the police; the court (included here is the prosecution and defense); and corrections.

The Police

Law enforcement is basically concerned with the collection of evidence about reported offenses and with the detection and arrest of suspected offenders. This particular profession is concerned about dealing with the criminal in an objective and expedient manner. Law enforcement's approach to crime is legalistic and practical. Expediency is a virtue, and the peace officer is well aware that he does not have a great deal of time in dealing with the arrestee. In other words, the policeman's role in an integrated society such as ours, by definition and by law, is expressly concerned with: *control, apprehension,* and *support.* The basic philosophy relating to law enforcement responsibilities specifies that the police are charged with the protection of lives and property, the safety and well-being of all citizens through the detection and apprehension of criminals, the prevention of crime, and limited control of nonviolent behavior. The police responsibility to the people of the community involves taking aggressive and technically competent action to solve crimes committed by adults or juveniles. Police are expected to protect the people from crimes committed by anyone, regardless of age.[7]

Therefore, many law enforcement agencies are designed to deal with the crime problem by giving due consideration to the underlying causes. The police cannot ignore the causes of crime, but in performing their appointed tasks of law enforcement, police officers must often dismiss the causative factors. At the very beginning of the process—or more properly, before the process begins at all—something happens that is scarcely discussed in law books and is seldom recognized by the public: law enforcement policy is made by the policeman.[8] Policemen cannot and do not arrest all the offenders they encounter. It is doubtful that they arrest most of them. The criminal code, in practice, is not a set of specific instructions to policemen but a more or less rough map of the territory in which policemen work. How an individual policeman moves around the territory depends largely on his personal discretion.

[7] E. Eldefonso, A. Coffey, and R. C. Grace, *Principles of Law Enforcement* (New York: John Wiley & Sons, 1968), pp. 4-5. See also: W. Hartinger, E. Eldefonso, and A. Coffey, *An Introduction to Corrections,* Chap. 2.

[8] *The Challenge of Crime in a Free Society,* A Report by The President's Commission on Law Enforcement and the Administration of Justice (Washington, D.C.: U.S. Gov't. Printing Office, 1967), p. 10; See also: *Task Force Report: The Police,* p. 10.

A policeman's duties obviously compel him to exercise personal discretion many times every day. As one writer stated:

> How they do their job may well decide whether or not the city as we know it will survive.
>
> The policemen who patrol the streets of our cities have to deal not only with over-eager drivers, drunks, thieves, and muggers, but also with unruly or abandoned children, bickering adults and disturbed persons. What is more, we ask him to handle all the tasks they encounter—from accidents and violent crimes to personal problems that were once thought to be private and personal affairs—with the wisdom of Solomon, the concern of a social worker, and the prompt courage of the combat soldier.[9]

Crime does not look the same on the street as it does in a legislative chamber. How much noise or profanity makes conduct "disorderly" within the meaning of the law? When must a quarrel be treated as a criminal assault: at the first threat, at the first shove, at the first blow, after blood is drawn, or when a serious injury is inflicted? How suspicious must the conduct be before there is "probable cause," the constitutional basis for an arrest? Every policeman, however complete or sketchy his education, is an interpreter of the law.

Every policeman, too, is an arbiter of social values; he meets situation after situation in which invoking criminal sanctions is a questionable line of action. A boy throwing rocks at his school's windows is obviously committing the statutory offense of vandalism, but it is not at all obvious whether a policeman will better serve the interests of the community and the boy by taking the boy home to his parents or by arresting him. Who are the boy's parents? Can they control him? Is he a frequent offender who has responded badly to leniency? Is vandalism so epidemic in the neighborhood that he should be made a cautionary example? With juveniles especially, the police exercise great discretion.

Finally, the manner in which the policeman works is influenced by practical matters: the legal stress of the available evidence, the willingness of victims to press charges and of witnesses to testify, the temper of the community, the time and information at the policeman's disposal. Much is at stake in how the policeman exercises this discretion. If he decides that conduct is not suspicious enough to justify intervention, the chance to prevent a robbery, rape, or murder may be lost. If he overestimates the seriousness of a situation or his actions are controlled by panic or prejudice, he may hurt or kill someone unnecessarily. His actions may even touch off a riot.[10]

[9] G. Edwards, *The Police on the Urban Frontier: A Guide to Community Understanding* (New York: Institute of Human Relations Press, 1968), p. 4.

[10] *The Challenge of Crime in a Free Society,* p. 10.

The Court: Prosecutor and Defense

In discussing the court, we bring in the invaluable role of the prosecutor and defense. Although the court remains an integral part of the administration of the criminal justice system, the policeman customarily does not deal with the magistrate as often as he deals with the prosecuting and defense attorneys. Therefore, we will consider the prosecuting *district attorney* and the *defense attorney* as two of the distinct interrelated phases of the administration of criminal justice. The court will be considered as the foundation upon which these attorneys work.

In direct contrast to the policeman, the magistrate before whom a suspect is first brought usually exercises less discretion than the law actually allows. He is entitled to inquire into the facts of the case, into whether there are grounds for holding the accused, but he seldom does or can. The more promptly an arrested suspect is brought into the magistrate's court, the less likelihood there is that much information other than the arresting officer's statement will be available to the magistrate. Moreover, many magistrates, especially in big cities, have such congested calendars that it is almost impossible for them to subject any case but an extraordinary one to prolonged scrutiny.

In practice, the most important things by far that a magistrate does are to set the amount of a defendant's bail and in some jurisdictions to appoint counsel. Too seldom does either action get the careful attention it deserves. In many cases the magistrate accepts a waiver of counsel without insuring that the suspect knows the significance of legal representation.

Bail is a device to free an untried defendant and at the same time make sure he appears for trial. That is the sole stated legal purpose of bail in America. The Eighth Amendment to the Constitution (refer to Appendix A) declares that the bail must not be "excessive." Appellate courts have declared that not only the seriousness of the charge against the defendant, but also the suspect's personal, family, and employment situation, must be weighed before the amount of bail is fixed. Yet according to a research study conducted by Sam Ervin, in 1971, more magistrates than not set bail according to standard rates: so many dollars for a certain offence.[11]

The persistence of money bail can best be explained, not by its stated purpose, but by the belief of police, prosecutors, and courts, that the best way to keep a defendant from committing more crimes before trial is to set bail so high that he cannot obtain his release.

[11] S. J. Ervin, *Preventive Detention* (Chicago: Ill.: Urban Research Corporation, 1971), p. 26.

Bail and the Poor. Some studies have proved that bail is a method of punishment rather than insurance. In setting bail, magistrates have confused prevention of crime with the nature of the crime charged. Satisfactory evidence has been obtained to indicate that most people released on bail have no intention of violating bail and will appear for trial. Courts should assume that all defendants will return to the time and place of trial rather than assume that the individual defendant will flee the jurisdiction to avoid prosecution and punishment. Obviously, the former position is compatible with the presumption of innocence. Unfortunately, in order to appease the community, the courts often fail to consider essential elements relating to the defandant's roots in the country and state where he lives. The Federal Rules of Criminal Procedure now urge this more logical and consistent method of analysis in setting bail.

The persons who suffer the most from any type of bail process are those without money. The facts are that about half of all criminals are indigent and that defendants released on bail are placed on probation three times as often as defendants who come into court from a detention jail; these facts seem to indicate that it is easier to rehabilitate a man who has been released pending proof of his guilt than a man who has been incarcerated without determination of his guilt. With greater awareness of the importance of civil liberties and increased cries for equal justice, the bail system should be given first priority for reform throughout the country.

In the case of sentencing indigents, equal financial justice has been attained as an alternative to the payment of a fine. Normally the court used to impose a fine as the sentence for certain offenses. Instead of paying this fine, the defendant could spend one day in jail for every $10 not paid by a certain date. Obviously, under this method of sentencing, a rich man never saw the inside of a jail. In order to make the rich man and the poor man equal the court now must either impose a fine or a jail sentence *at the outset.* (This is not to say the court cannot imprison a defendant if he is convicted of a particular offense.) This type of rationale should be applied to the bail system today.

It should be noted that such "preventative detention" also lessens the person's chance of clearing himself. A person who has money can supply the bail required and then be free to assist his lawyer in the preparation of his case. But the person who is destitute cannot afford bail, much less hire a competent attorney. Discussing the subject of bail, Senator Sam J. Ervin has stated: "A man's chance of being convicted was increased at least 20 percent by his being deprived of his liberty pending trial of his case."[12] L. T. Empey, discussing the same topic, stated:

[12] Ervin, *Preventive Detention,* pp. 29-30.

The appearance and demeanor of a man who has spent days or weeks in jail probably is not conducive to a good presentation in court. Confined idleness and isolation are destructive of his self-concept. He is nervous and unsure of himself. He may even be unwashed and unkempt. His appearance under guard further destroys his image and is far less different than if he presents it himself along with his counsel, neatly dressed and more self-confident. Neither judge nor jury can fail to be influenced by these factors.[13]

A New York study concluded that being in jail operates to the disadvantage of the defendant at every stage of the proceedings. This is suggested by statistical comparisons of bail and jailed cases at the grand-jury level, in terms of court disposition and in the sentencing process.[14]

The Prosecutor. The key administrative officer in the processing of cases is the prosecutor. The President's Commission on Law Enforcement reported:

Before a formal information or indictment is lodged in court, the prosecution has the opportunity to consider not only which charges to press but also whether to press toward conviction at all. The decision whether to file formal charges is a vitally important stage in the criminal process. It provides an opportunity to screen out cases in which the accused is apparently innocent, and it is at this stage that the prosecutor must decide in cases of apparent guilt whether criminal sanctions are appropriate. The decisions the prosecutor makes influence and often determine the disposition in all cases brought to him by the police. The prosecutor's decisions also significantly affect the arrest practices of the police, the volume of cases in courts, and the number of offenders cleared through the correctional system. Thus the prosecutor is in the most favorable position to bring about the needed coordination among the various law enforcement and correctional agencies in the community.[15]

Theoretically the examination of the evidence against a defendant by a judge at a preliminary hearing and the reexamination of the evidence by a grand jury are important parts of the process. These practices, however, are usually not very important because a prosecutor seldom has any difficulty in making a *prima facie* case against a defendant. In fact, most defendants waive their rights to preliminary hearings, and, much more often than not, grand juries indict precisely as prosecutors ask them to. The prosecutor wields almost undisputed sway over the pretrial progress of most cases. He decides whether to press a case or drop it, and he deter-

[13] L. T. Empey, *Alternatives to Incarceration* (Washington, D.C.: U.S. Gov't. Printing Office, 1966), pp. 17-18.

[14] J. S. Campbell, *Law and Order Reconsidered* (Washington, D.C.: U.S. Gov't. Printing Office, 1970), p. 7.

[15] *The Challenge of Crime in a Free Society,* pp. 10-11.

mines the specific charge against a defendant. When the charge is reduced, as occurs in two-thirds of all cases in some cities, the prosecutor is usually the official who reduces it.[16]

The Defense Counsel. The important role of defense counsel in helping to achieve the most appropriate disposition of his client was forcibly expressed by the Supreme Court of the United States more than 30 years ago in *Powell* v. *Alabama,* in which the court stated:

> The right to be heard would be, in most cases, of little avail if it did not comprehend the right to be heard by counsel. Even the intelligent and educated layman has small and sometimes no skill in the science of law. . . . Left without the aid of counsel he may be put on trial without a proper charge and convicted upon incompetent evidence, or evidence irrelevant to the issue or otherwise inadmissible. He lacks both the skill and knowledge adequately to prepare his defense, even though he may have a perfect one. He requires the guiding hand of counsel at every step in the proceedings against him. Without it, though he be not guilty, he faces the danger of conviction because he does not know how to establish his innocence.[17]

The right of a criminal defendant to be represented by counsel is a fundamental protection for individual liberty in our system of criminal justice. The importance of counsel proceeds from values transcending the interests of any individual defendant. Counsel is needed to maintain an effective criminal justice. Our particular system is an adversary system of justice which depends for its vitality upon rigorous and proper challenges to assertions of governmental authority and accusations of crime. It relies upon the judge or prosecutor to protect the interests of defendants and is an inadequate substitute for the advocacy of conscientious defense counsel.[18]

Judicial process means determining and ruling upon legal issues and evidence and then rendering appropriate decisions. From the beginning of the criminal process to its end, from police work to correctional work, there is a tension between efficiency (protecting the community from crime) and fairness (protecting the rights of individuals). If these opposing poles are not kept in balance, the process tends to become either excessively arbitrary, perfunctory, and hasty—or deliberately excessive, cumbersome, and dilatory.[19]

16 *The Challenge of Crime in a Free Society,* pp. 10-11.

17 Powell v. Alabama, 287 U.S. 45, 68-69, 1932.

18 *Task Force Report: The Courts,* A Report by The President's Commission on Law Enforcement and the Administration of Justice (Washington, D.C.: U.S. Gov't. Printing Office, 1967), p. 52; See also Hartinger, Eldefonso, and Coffey, *An Introduction to Corrections,* Chap. 2.

19 *The Challenge of Crime in a Free Society,* p. 154.

In the juvenile justice system, the court attempts to keep the hearing informal and nonadversary. In most states, although the district attorney and defense counsel play a prominent part in the hearing, the judge still stresses informality and nonadversary decorum as much as possible. The deputy probation office (sometimes referred to as the intake office or screening office) decides whether a case should be the subject of formal court proceedings. If the intake officer decides it should, he draws up a petition, describing the offense. In very few places is bail a part of the juvenile system; a youth whose case is referred to court is either sent home with orders to reappear upon a certain date or remanded to custody by a juvenile court referee who handles the detention care and process in most cases and in most communities. Thus, though these officials work in quite different environments and according to quite different procedures than those of magistrates and prosecutors, they in fact exercise the same kind of discretionary control over what occurs before the facts of the case are adjudicated.

Corrections

The correctional process is the final interrelated phase of the administration of criminal and juvenile justice. Corrections involves implementing the orders that the court gives to probation departments or parole agencies and institutions. Corrections—America's prisons, jails, juvenile training schools, and probation and parole machinery—is the part of the criminal justice system that the public sees the least of and knows the least about. It seldom gets into the news unless there is a jail break, prison riot, or a sensational scandal involving corruption or brutality in an institution or by an official. The institutions which house about one-third of the corrections population are situated for the most part in remote rural areas or in the basements of police stations or courthouses. The other two-thirds of the corrections populations are on probation and parole and thus are invisibly dispersed in the community. The elements of a modern correctional system are presented in Figure 2-3.

The most striking fact about the correctional apparatus today is that, although the rehabilitation of criminals is presumably its major purpose, the custody of criminals is actually its main task. On any given day, there are well over a million people being "corrected" in America, and, as previously stated, two-thirds of them are on probation and parole and one-third of them in prisons or jails. However, prisons and jails are where four-fifths of correctional money is spent and where nine-tenths of correctional employees work. Furthermore, fewer than one-fifth of the people who work in state prisons and local jails have jobs that are not essentially either custodial or administrative in character. Many jails have nothing but custodial and administrative personnel. Of course many jails are

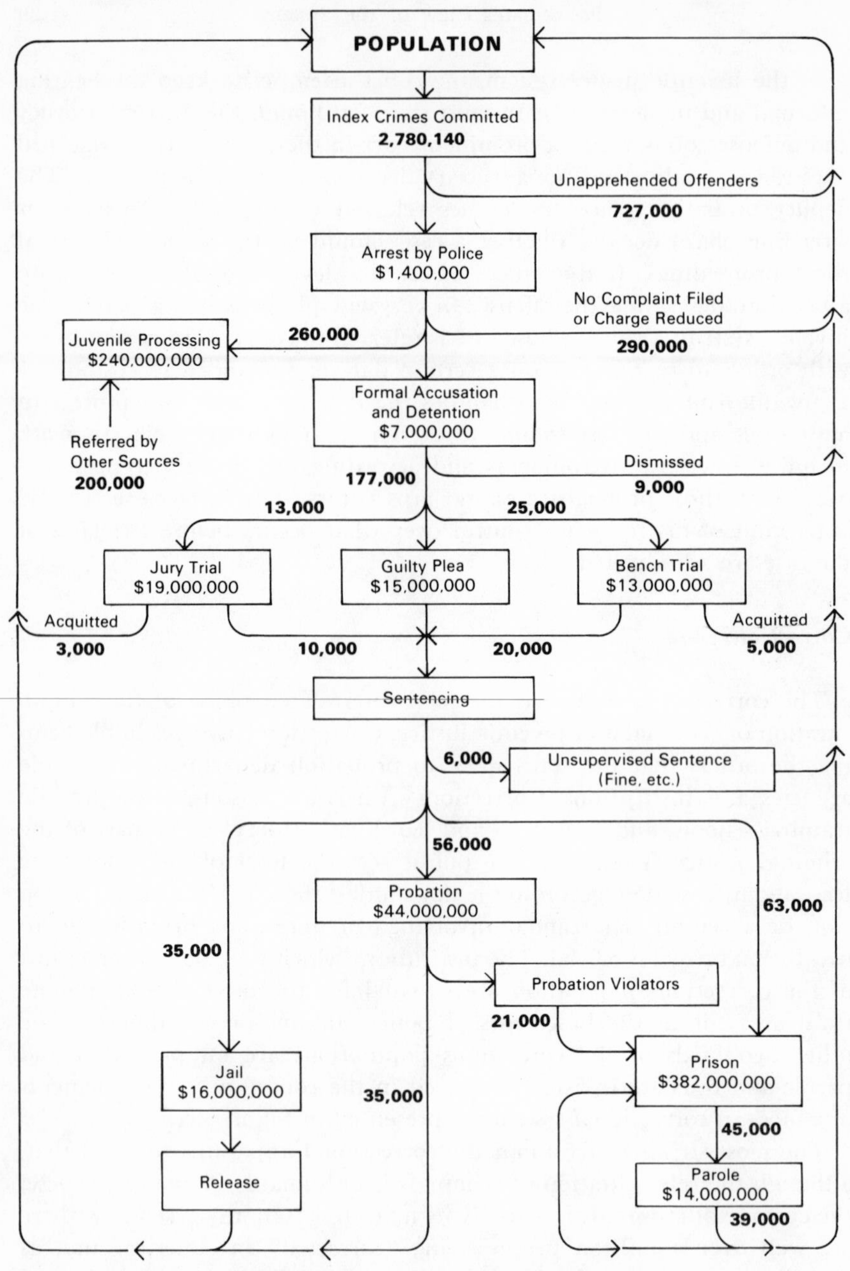

Figure 2-3 Criminal justice system model with estimates of offenders and direct operating costs for index crimes in the United States in 1965. From pp. 262–63 of The President's Commission on Law Enforcement and the Administration of Justice, *The Challenge of Crime in a Free Society* (Washington, D.C.: U.S. Government Printing Office, 1967).

crowded with defendants who have been unable to furnish bail and who are not considered by the law to be appropriate objects of rehabilitation because it has not yet been determined that they are criminals who need it.

In practice, this emphasis on custody means that the enormous potential of the correctional apparatus for making creative decisions about the treatment of convicts is largely unfulfilled. This applies both to offenders in custody and to offenders on probation and parole. Most authorities agree that, although probationers and parolees need varying degrees and kinds of supervision, an average of no more than thirty-five cases per officer is necessary for effective attention; 97 percent of all officers handling adults have larger caseloads than that. In the juvenile correctional system the situation is somewhat better. Juvenile institutions, which typically are training schools, have a high proportion of treatment personnel, and juvenile probation and parole officers generally have lighter caseloads. However, these comparatively rich resources are very far from being rich enough.

Except for sentencing, no decision in a criminal process has more impact on the convicted offender than does the parole decision, which determines how much of the maximum sentence a prisoner must serve. This again is an invisible administrative decision that is seldom open to attack or subject to review. It is made by parole board members who are often political appointees. Many are skilled and conscientious, but they generally are able to spend no more than a few minutes on a case. Parole decisions that are made in haste and on the basis of insufficient information are necessarily imperfect decisions. And since there is virtually no appeal, these decisions can be made arbitrarily or discriminatorily. Just as carefully formulated and clearly stated law enforcement policies would help policemen, charge policies would help prosecutors, and sentencing policies would help judges, so parole policies would help parole boards perform their delicate and important duties.

THE POLICEMAN'S VIEW OF THE CRIMINAL JUSTICE SYSTEM

By the very nature of our present criminal justice system, it is essential that police cooperate with courts and corrections. Unfortunately, we have found that cooperation between these interrelated systems has been diminishing steadily during the last decade, thus resulting in a confused conglomeration of separate entities, each having its own function and separate ways of performing tasks. The interrelated systems seldom consult with each other and quite often are at odds with one another.

The fragmented criminal justice system directly affects the amount and type of crime that exists. Thus, the failure of our system to involve all functions simultaneously is to the detriment of everyone concerned. The administration of criminal justice in America is, according to a special report by *Newsweek,* in serious trouble. This prominent magazine paints a rather vivid picture:

> America's system of criminal justice is too swamped to deliver more than the roughest justice—and too ragged really to be called a system. "What we have" says one former government hand, "is a non-system in which the police don't catch criminals, the courts don't try them and the prisons don't reform them." The system, in a word, is in trouble—and Americans have only slowly awakened to the urgency of putting justice right.
>
> The trouble has been neglect—"astonishing neglect" Attorney General John Mitchell's phrase—and the decade just made it painfully clear that neglect is a luxury the U.S. can no longer afford. The paralysis of the Civil Courts, where it takes five years to get a judgment in a damage suit, has long been well known. But now events have thrown criminal justice into a sharper focus. The causes and crazes of the '60s—civil rights, peace, draft resisting, pot—brought about arrests by the thousands and exposed the middle-class to a ramshackle justice that the poor had always known.[20]

The numerous problems confronting the criminal justice system have had a devastating effect on the police and their function. Thus, police often have a very cynical view of the correctional and the court process, and frequently hardly believe in their value.

> The failure to involve the courts, prosecutors, and corrections officials in the training of police, the failure to involve police in the orientation of newly chosen judges and prosecutors and in the training curricula for newly appointed probation and parole officers, and even more general failure to consult police in the planning stages of executive and legislative decision making in areas which may directly or indirectly affect their responsibilities or operations—all further compound this already difficult situation.[21]

Evidence of the fractures that exist between corrections and law enforcement can be documented by systematic data collected in a number of comparative studies of control agents. One particular study [22] investi-

[20] "Justice on Trial: A Special Report," *Newsweek,* March 8, 1971, p. 16. Reprinted by permission.

[21] J. S. Campbell, J. R. Sahid, and D. P. Stang, *Law and Order Reconsidered* (Washington, D.C.: U.S. Gov't. Printing Office, 1968), p. 288.

[22] P. G. Garabedian, "The Control of Delinquent Behavior by Police and Probation Officers," Paper read at the annual meeting of the Society for the Study of Social Problems, Montreal, Canada, August, 1964.

gated the attitudes of law enforcement officers and juvenile probation officers. A major aim of the study was to determine what these two groups perceived to be the causes of juvenile delinquency. When asked about the causes of juvenile delinquency, seven out of ten police officers felt that delinquents are capable of knowing the difference between right and wrong, are capable of controlling the situation that might lead them to commit crime, are capable of understanding the consequences of their behavior, and therefore should be held accountable for their actions. However, only two out of ten juvenile probation officers endorsed this particular ideological orientation. They were oriented more toward a psychological position of delinquency causation.[23]

When the sample was asked whether a juvenile probation officer who made the delinquent "toe the line" got better results than one who was more lenient, the results were again in the "expected" direction. Almost 60 percent of the police officers responded that tougher officers got better results, while only about 30 percent of the probation officers agreed. When the sample was asked whether the policeman should restrict his activities to the investigation of delinquency complaints and not try to reform juveniles who come to his attention, four out of ten probation officers agreed, while only about one out of ten police officers agreed. Not surprisingly, probation officers see themselves as professional treatment agents, and they see law enforcement officers as just that—enforcers of the law and not treatment agents. These data clearly suggest that there is a lack of concensus regarding the appropriate role of each of these control agents; further, the misconception is perpetuated that police and probation officers are autonomous and therefore should operate independently of each other.

Another study collected data from police and probation officers and also from judges and court psychiatrists.[24] These officials were asked to rank various occupational groups (probation officers, police, judges, clergy, psychiatrists, school guidance counselors, and social workers) according to how the attitudes of the members of each occupational group compared to their own attitudes toward delinquency. The findings are consistent with those mentioned previously. Police chiefs and juvenile officers ranked the police as being most similar to themselves in attitude; and probation officers saw themselves as more similar in attitude to members of their own group than to any of the other groups.

Taken together, the findings from these studies document the lack of

[23] P. G. Garabedian, "Challenges for Contemporary Corrections," *Federal Probation*, Vol. 33, No. 1 (March, 1969), pp. 7-8.

[24] S. Wheeler, E. Powacich, M. R. Cramer, and I. S. Wheeler, eds., *Controlling Delinquents* (New York: John Wiley & Sons, 1968), pp. 31-60.

communication and coordination between the various segments of the criminal justice system. At the present time there is no way of determining whether the system *as a whole* is achieving its overall aims. The lack of statewide integration remains the most crucial problem confronting the police and the criminal justice system.[25]

POLICE AND THE FRAGMENTED CRIMINAL JUSTICE SYSTEM

The President's Commission on Law Enforcement and the Administration of Justice reminds us that the American system of criminal justice is not monolithic or even a consistent system. It was not, according to the Commission's report, designed or built in one piece at a time. The transition from rural to urban and thence to metropolitan conditions has been met, not by intelligent reconstruction, but by patching and addition. Its philosophic core is that a person may be punished by the government if, and only if, it has been proven by an impartial and deliberate process that the person has violated a specific law. Around that core, layer upon layer of institutions and procedures, some carefully constructed and some improvised, some inspired by principle and some by expediency, have accumulated. Parts of the system—magistrates' courts, trial by jury, bail—are extremely antiquated. Other parts—juvenile courts, probation and parole, *professional policemen*—are relatively new. The entire system represents an adaptation of the English Common Law to America's peculiar structure of government which allows each local community to construct institutions to fill its own needs. Every village, town, county, city, and state has its own criminal justice system, and there is a federal one as well. All of them operate somewhat alike. No two of them operate precisely alike.[26]

Needless to say the police are hampered by the fragmentation of services they must depend on. In one county alone, there may be twenty different police departments, plus twenty sets of records. Laboratory services, records, communications, and field operations are all part of this confused conglomerate, all being uncoordinated. There is an almost universal need for better coordination between the various facets of the criminal justice system.[27]

There is a definite need to eliminate the long delays in bringing a de-

[25] Garabedian, "Challenges for Contemporary Corrections," pp. 7-8.

[26] *The Challenge of Crime in a Free Society,* p. 7.

[27] H. Ohmart, "The Challenge of Crime in a Free Society," *Youth Authority Quarterly,* Vol. 21, No. 3 (Fall, 1968), 2-11.

fendant before the court. Such delays make law enforcement completely ineffective and make a mockery out of justice—particularly since the courts are supposed to serve as a deterrent to crime. Also, when the defendant does appear before the court, law enforcement effectiveness is further lost if the courts are unable to deal properly with the defendants brought before them. These particular areas will have to be ameliorated in order to assist the police officer in promoting definitive actions within a particular community. In validating the complaints of police personnel regarding the courts, a study conducted in 1971 brought forth the following comments regarding the judiciary process:

> The courts are in desperate repair—badly managed, woefully undermanned and so inundated with cases that they have to run fast just to stand still. "Oliver Wendell Holmes could not survive in our criminal court," says NYU Law Professor Harry I. Subin. "How can you be an eminent jurist when you have to deal with this mess?" Many of the jurists are considerably less than eminent. Most still come up through politics, elective or appointive, with little criminal-court experience except for those who apprenticed as prosecutors and who sometimes never shake the habit of presuming defendants guilty. Some learn their business competently and even brillantly; some don't.
>
> The system often is at its worst at precisely the point where it ought to be best—in the juvenile and misdemeanor courts where at least some fraction of the new offenders might still be turned around. Half the nation's juvenile judges don't have college degrees; 4 out of 5 have no psychiatrist or psychologist regularly available; many practiced a sort of closed-door authoritarian folk-law until the Supreme Court held four years ago that the fact that offenders are children "does not justify a kangaroo court" and began ordering some reforms. The lowest adult courts are a worse shambles still. They sit in shabby, noisy courtrooms, shoveling cases through at rates running up to 300 a day or more. "The poor mope hardly gets out of the bull-pen, and he's got 90 days" says one Chicago lawyer. The complaint is nearly universal. "The lower courts have never functioned well anywhere in my lifetime" says former New York judge Bernard Botein. He is 70 years old.
>
> Courts at every level are mired in delay—a situation now so critical that one Christmas Day, Chief Justice Warren Burger wrote a memo to all Federal judges urging a speed-up; "public patience is running out, and we must respond." [28]

The study goes on to report that the delaying tactics of defense attorneys motivates the district attorney to become involved in bargaining for a plea to a lesser offense. Such pleas conducted between the defense attorney and the district attorney are not unusual. The reason for such bargaining is quite simple; most courts, particularly in the urban areas,

[28] "Justice on Trial," p. 18.

would be unable to handle all the cases if the DA decided to prosecute rather than bargain with the defense attorney to achieve a guilty plea without an extensive court hearing. Although the aforementioned practice is acceptable, it is by no means infallible; quite occasionally, such bargaining results in the imprisoning of a person who is really innocent or who lacks an appropriate defense. On these occasions, the defendant may feel that he "stands a better chance" if he pleads guilty to an offense with the understanding that he will not be incarcerated for an excessive period of time. As a matter of fact, the bargain may allow the individual to return to the community on probation.

Some cases are dismissed or settled in a matter of a few minutes; or the district attorney makes a negotiated plea. To the police officer, this is a difficult process to understand. Police officers often become quite disenchanted and thoroughly disgusted when it becomes necessary to arrest the same person several different times during the course of the year. Thus, the faith in courts and corrections is ultimately diminished, and often the incentive to protect and serve is jeopardized.

Police must look to corrections as a means of rehabilitating the offender. But here again, like the courts, corrections have failed to a large extent. The recidivism rate is phenomenal, the parolee or probationer often makes an unsatisfactory adjustment and once again finds his way back to the point of arrest (Figure 2-4). There are many reasons for this difficulty; perhaps the most significant are lack of personnel and the fact that agencies are chase-oriented rather than reference-oriented. Also, only a small proportion of the persons employed in corrections are concerned with actual treatment or rehabilitation; the majority are guards or maintenance personnel.

Since our new concept of reform has changed from the corporal techniques to the parole or probation technique, it has become necessary to shift our attention. Incidentally, progressive rehabilitation techniques were not solely responsible for the shift in emphasis. Rather, it was accomplished by the economic facts that probation and parole are indeed more inexpensive than prisons or jails. We must now ask why the prisons have not stimulated the inmates to keep recidivism at a minimum and, more importantly, to eventually lead viable lives. Part of the reason for these problems is the lack of transition emphasis given to the inmate prior to his release. For example, after an inmate spends ten years in prison, at an expense to the state of approximately $30,000, the state gives the parolee a remarkably small sum of money to begin his life anew. This becomes a real problem when one considers that this man has been stamping license plates for ten years, and that is basically all he knows. The reality of this statement becomes evident when recidivism rates are analyzed. A new prison in New Jersey, theoretically a landmark in its own

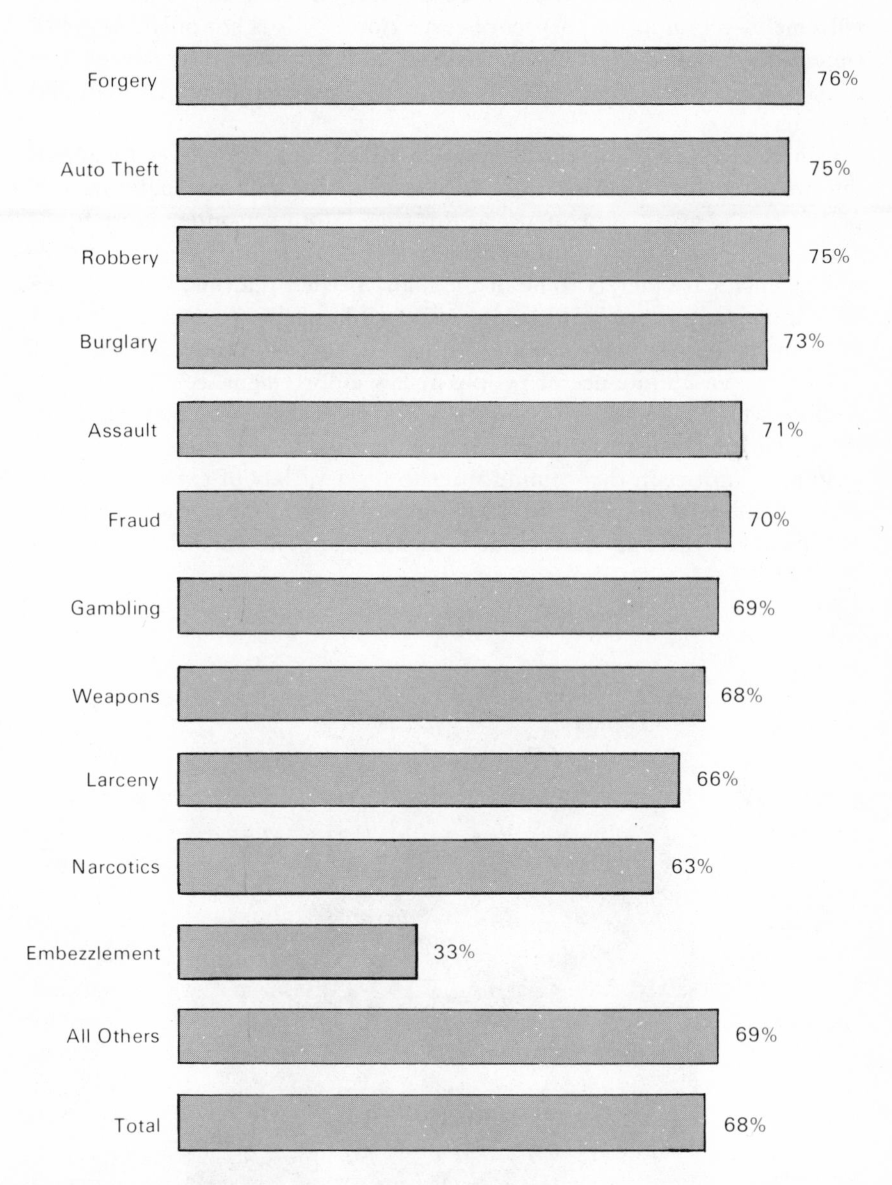

Figure 2-4 Percent repeaters by type of crime (persons arrested in 1971). From the *Uniform Crime Report,* 1971, p. 37.

time, was recently opened with progressive techniques being utilized. However, this prison was erected miles away from the community in an isolated backwoods area, where there was no provision for community involvement—an important aspect of corrections. This is not only a waste of community resources but also a waste of the tax dollar. Average cost per inmate was estimated at $34,000 annually, far exceeding the national average.

Courts and corrections can be of great assistance to the police by adopting and reevaluating their roles in regard to the police. Analyzing our priorities is of great consequence at this time. More personnel, more funds adequately placed, new statutes, and greater cooperation between responsible agencies are merely some of the many needed reforms. Probably the most important asset would be for responsible parties to take a personal stake in their work, which would ultimately affect the total system.

We have an abundance of people in law enforcement, courts, and corrections who have both the goodwill and intelligence to be a strong force in preventing crime or rehabilitating the criminal. Also there are numerous opportunities in our communities to try a variety of experiments for effective cooperation. The determination to take advantage of these opportunities is the only force that is lacking, and we should tolerate no

Figure 2-5 Motorcycle patrol is *one* method utilized by large municipal police agencies. Photo courtesy of Officer Phil Crawford, City of San Jose Police Department, San Jose, Ca.

more delays. There will then be validity in the premise that the affirmative task initiated by the policeman is complimented by the work of the courts and corrections.

LAW ENFORCEMENT: A PERIOD OF UNCERTAINTY

It has been said that the American courts function as social controls of values and attitudes toward law, while at the same time reconciling grievances—grievances between either the state and the individual or between individuals.[29]

Although for the past fifty years the press has carried prominent articles about the need for strong judicial measures on behalf of the state, only recently has general concern focused on the court reconciliation of grievances between the state and individuals.[30] Currently, law enforcement agencies are finding themselves caught in a period of unusual uncertainty. Primarily, this uncertainty can be attributed to two separate but interdependent developments. The first is directly related to the United States Supreme Court; the second development, which is just as important, is that law enforcement is experiencing a series of civil disturbances associated with a wide range of efforts to upgrade minority groups.

Supreme Court Decisions

In constitutional forms of government, the traditional role of law enforcement is in *apprehending* law violators, while leaving *punishment* to the judicial process. Philosophically, at least, such a role permits crime prevention to be a mutual, although secondary, responsibility of both police and courts. But in recent times, police and courts are increasingly faced with "crimes" stemming from growing demands for social reform, rather than from the violation of criminal statutes. One apparent reaction of the courts, particularly the Supreme Court, has been to pass down a number of decisions which have great impact on police procedure in general and on the relationship of police to social change in particular. In effect, the Supreme Court has handed down rulings that are judgments not only of the functions of the lower courts but also of the police as well.

Much of the basis of the increasing Supreme Court assessment of police practice is the Fourth Amendment and to some degree the Fifth and Sixth Amendments. The implications of the Fourth Amendment to the police

[29] H. Freeman, *Society on Trial* (Springfield, Ill.: Charles C. Thomas, 1965), Preface.

[30] R. W. Winslow, *Crime in a Free Society* (Belmont, Calif.: Dickerson, 1968).

function have received more than adequate concern in the literature.[31] Nonetheless, a brief review of the highlights of the more significant court decisions may serve to clarify these implications.

In 1914 the United States Supreme Court ruled in *Weeks* v. *United States* that a federal court could not accept evidence that was obtained in violation of search and seizure protection, which is guaranteed by the Fourth Amendment. In 1963 the Supreme Court ruled on the appeal case of *Gideon* v. *Wainwright.* The effect of this ruling was that a new trial could be demanded by anyone convicted of a crime who did not have legal counsel. Moving closer to the function of the police, in 1964 a decision was handed down in the case of *Escobedo* v. *Illinois.* This decision, based on a five to four majority, held it a constitutional right (Sixth Amendment) that a person be provided with legal counsel at the time of police interrogation. In June, 1966, again by a five to four majority (Fifth Amendment), the Court ruled in the case of *Miranda* v. *Arizona.* The Miranda decision had the effect of providing legal counsel during police questioning for persons suspected of crimes. This decision was based on "custodial interrogation," meaning that prior to questioning the suspect must be warned that he has a right to remain silent, that any statement he makes may be used as evidence against him, and that he has a right to the presence of an attorney, either retained or appointed. Since this and the previous rulings were made on the basis of "constitutional rights," law enforcement found itself compelled to regard many traditional investigative methods as unconstitutional. If constitutional rights are violated by former police methods, the question becomes one of alternate approaches. Yet, alternate approaches are at best difficult to discern when the overall function of the courts is undergoing change, as a result of Supreme Court interpretations of the United States Constitution. The following is one definitive assessment of the court role in an era marked by social change.

> Some constitutional limitations on the criminal court are based on principles common to most civilized criminal systems. One is that criminal penalties may be imposed only in response to a specific act that violates a pre-existing law. The criminal court cannot act against persons out of apprehension that they may commit crimes, but only against persons who have already done so. Furthermore, the basic procedures of the criminal court must conform to the concepts of "due process" that have grown from English Com-

[31] E. L. Barrett, "Personal Rights, Property Rights, and the Fourth Amendment," *1960 Supreme Court Review* (Chicago, Ill.: University of Chicago Press, 1961), p. 65. See also, C. R. Sowled, ed., *Police Power and Individual Freedom* (Springfield, Ill.: Charles C. Thomas, 1962); and W. H. Parker, "Birds Without Wings," *The Police Yearbook, 1965,* International Association Chiefs of Police.

mon Law seeds. Unquestionably, adherence to due process complicates, and in many instances, handicaps the work of the courts. But the law rightly values due process over efficient process. And by permitting the accused to challenge its fairness and legality at every stage of his prosecution, the system provides the occasion for the law to develop in accordance with changes in society and society's ideals.[32]

After elaborating these points, the report goes on to state:

> Nevertheless, these limitations on prosecution are the product of two centuries of Constitutional development in this country. They are integral parts of a system for balancing the interests of the individual and the state that has served the nation well.[33]

If the goal of the judicial process is to become "a system for balancing the interests of the individual and the state," then the definition of what these interests actually are becomes important. The particular importance of such a goal to law enforcement is clearly implied in the evolution of Supreme Court decisions geared to relieve social problems—relief frequently requiring police to abandon traditional police methods. Defining interests is important, but such a task cannot be easy in an era of divergent interests. The difficulty is increased still more by Supreme Court decisions that influence not only the definition of *due process* but also the definition of the *interests* served through due process. Nevertheless, defining interests remains crucial to law enforcement.

Needless to say, the decisions by the Supreme Court have elicited a great deal of "hot debate." They have been attacked as placing restraint on the police by coddling the law violator. Furthermore, according to some, the police are placed in a position where they must fight by "Marquis of Queensberry Rules," while the criminals are not bound by such rules. Others have received the decisions as evidence that the Supreme Court has finally become more concerned with human liberty than with the protection of property rights.

Civil Disturbances

The strategies and nonviolent techniques of civil rights groups are creating unusual problems for law enforcement agencies because exploiting excessive use of police coercion is one of their major weapons. *This nonviolent method is the explicit and knowing violation of a particular*

[32] *The Challenge of Crime in a Free Society,* Section entitled "The Courts," p. 125.
[33] *The Challenge of Crime in a Free Society,* p. 125.

law by persons who are quite ready to accept, without resistance, the penalty attached to that specific law violation. By utilizing the nonviolent resistance method, minority groups dramatize certain laws as unjust. Furthermore, the use of police coercion is invited (and welcomed) as an opportunity to identify peace officers as "the intimidators or aggressors" against "peaceful demonstrators." It is not unusual to use children, women, ministers, and other responsible persons to gain a favorable public image as "victims" of police "aggression." Nonviolent resistance has its ideological genesis in the values of Christian morality and humanitarianism; the premise is that minority groups have a moral obligation *not* to cooperate with the forces of "evil."

> In essence, the non-violent resistance is a form of passive aggression, in that it frustrates its opponents by enveloping them in a cloud of "Christian love" for one's enemies. The established power structure of the community is to be forced into the role of "bad guys." . . . Non-compliance with carefully selected laws creates a community crisis, but, by refraining from violent resistance the law violators make application of police coercion an opportunity to present social protest as consistent with the highly prized values of humanitarianism and concern for the under-dog.[34]

The problems of crime control, in general, and law enforcement, in particular, are always related to changes in the social scene. The dimensions and substance of community life are undergoing such wholesale and radical transformation in our time that it behooves us to pause and reflect upon the influences that are sharply modifying the conditions of contemporary community life and posing new problems for the agencies of law enforcement.[35]

THE POLICEMAN: A SYMBOL OF THE SYSTEM

The police officer is such a visible embodiment of the law that neither he nor the public find it easy to differentiate between the law and the enforcement of such law. The public for the most part is confused and unable to recognize the broad concept of the police officer. As one writer pointed out:

[34] E. H. Johnson, "A Sociological Interpretation of Police Reaction and Responsibility to Civil Disobedience," *The Journal of Criminal Law, Criminology and Police Science*, Vol. 58, No. 3 (September, 1967), p. 407.

[35] A. Coffey, E. Eldefonso, and W. Hartinger, *Human Relations: Law Enforcement in a Changing Community* (Englewood Cliffs, N.J.: Prentice-Hall, 1971), p. 28; See also: D. J. Lohman, "Race Tension and Conflict," *Police and the Changing Community* (Washington, D.C.: International Association Chiefs of Police, 1965), pp. 42-47.

> Relatively few citizens recall ever having seen a judge; fewer still a prosecutor, coroner, sheriff, probation officer or prison warden. The patrolman is thoroughly familiar to all. His uniform picks him out from the crowd so distinctly that he becomes a living symbol of the law—not always of its majesty, but certainly of its power. Whether the police like it or not, they are forever marked men.[36]

Any officer of the law is partly a symbol, and to some extent law enforcement work includes creating in persons a response to these symbolic attributes. Thus, an unoccupied police vehicle can slow down turnpike traffic or motivate drivers to stop at designated intersections, and the presence of half a dozen officers can control a large crowd.[37]

The uniform of the police officer is viewed as a symbolic license to judge and punish. It does so not only by representing the right to arrest but also by connotating the role of a disciplinarian. Unfortunately, it is for this reason that parents may make small children behave through repeated and pointed references to policemen. Needless to say, this "punishing role" does not lend itself to the promotion of any social role other than that of "enforcer." [38]

Joseph Fink, Deputy Inspector of the New York City Police Department, pointed out in a recent article that the police are encountering strong resistance in their attempts to rectify deteriorating public support.[39] Conflict between the police and the residents of the city slums and ghettoes—the very neighborhoods that need and want effective policing the most—has, on occasions, broken out into open warfare. In these areas there is much distrust of the police, especially among boys and young men, who are the people police deal with most often. It is common in those neighborhoods for citizens to fail to report crimes or refuse to cooperate in investigations. Often policemen are stared at or insulted on the beat. Indeed, everyday police encounters in such neighborhoods can set off riots, as many police departments have learned.

It may be ironical that the same people who are most victimized by crime are most hostile to the police, but it is not remarkable. It is not remarkable because the policeman is the symbol of middle-class society and values. He generally comes from a middle-class community in the suburbs where he lives a well-regulated life according to middle-class

36 B. Smith, "Municipal Police Administration," *Annals of the American Academy of Police and Social Science,* Vol. 40, No. 5, p. 22.

37 H. H. Toch, "Psychological Consequences of the Police Role," *Police,* Vol. 10, No. 1 (September-October, 1965), p. 22.

38 Toch, "Municipal Police Administration."

39 J. Fink, "Police in a Community—Improving a Deteriorating Image," *Journal of Criminal Law, Criminology and Police Science,* Vol. 59, No. 4 (December, 1968), p. 624.

standards of ethics and morality. But he works in an area populated largely by people who are alien to him. He finds the language, customs, and resentments of Puerto Ricans, Mexicans, blacks, and other minority groups strange, hostile, and aggravating. Undoubtedly, both the people of the community and the police find themselves misunderstood, mistreated, and much maligned. Under such circumstances, it is no wonder that antagonisms develop to the point that distrust and dissatisfaction on both sides replace logical thinking and conduct.[40]

It is wrong, however, to define the problem solely as hostility to police. In many ways, the policeman merely symbolizes much deeper problems. Apathy or disrespect for law enforcement agencies would be more appropriately attributed to "a social system that permits inequities and irregularities in law, stimulates poverty and inhibits initiative and motivation of the poor, and regulates low social and economic status to the police while concommitantly giving them more extraneous, non-police duties than adequately can be performed." [41]

To a considerable extent, then, the police are the victims of community problems which are not of their making. For generations, minority groups and the poor have not received a fair opportunity to share the benefits of American life. The policeman in the ghetto is the most visible symbol of a society from which many ghetto residents are increasingly alienated.

> At the same time, police responsibilities in the ghetto are greater than elsewhere in the community since the other institutions of social control have so little authority: The schools because so many are segregated, old and inferior; religion, which has become irrelevant to those who have lost faith as they lost hope; career aspirations, which for many young Negroes are totally lacking; the family, because its bonds are so often snapped. It is the policeman who must deal with the consequences of this institutional vacuum and is then resented for the presence and the measures this effort demands.[42]

The policeman, furthermore, has unfortunately become a symbol, not only of law, but of the entire system of law enforcement and criminal justice as well. As such he becomes the tangible target for grievances against shortcomings throughout the system. When a suspect is held for long periods because he cannot make bail, when he is given inadequate counsel or none at all, when he is assigned counsel that attempts to

[40] Fink, "Police in a Community."

[41] R. L. Derbyshire, "The Social Control Role of the Police in Changing Urban Communities," *Excerpta Criminologica*, Vol. 6, No. 3 (1966), p. 319.

[42] *Report of the National Advisory Commission on Civil Disorders* (Washington, D.C.: U.S. Gov't. Printing Office, 1968), p. 157.

extract a financial settlement from him or his family even though he is indigent, when he is paraded through the courtroom in a group or is tried in a few minutes, when he is sent to jail because he has no money to pay a fine, when the jail or prison is physically dilapidated or its personnel brutal or incompetent, or when the probation or parole officer has little time to give him, the offender will probably blame, at least in part, the police officer who arrested him and started the process.[43]

The policeman assigned to the ghetto is the symbol of increasingly bitter social debate over law enforcement. The Commission on Civil Disorders noted that one side of the community, disturbed and perplexed by sharp rises in crime and urban violence, exerts extreme pressure on police for tougher law enforcement. Another group, inflamed against police as agents of repression, tends to defy what it regards as order maintained at the expense of justice. Because the police are a symbol of social ills, it is incumbent upon them to take every possible step to allay grievances that flow from a sense of injustice and increased tension and turmoil.

Reducing Influences on Bad Police Image

Since public attitudes toward the police are mostly the result of personal contacts rather than knowledge of police methods, the public is not only ill-informed concerning the general caliber of its police, but it also lacks appreciation of the conditions under which the police must operate. It is therefore of great importance to police departments to spend considerable amounts of time in the area of public relations, building of a favorable image. It must be remembered, however, that only in a utopian society would every citizen feel respect and friendliness toward the police. A certain amount of resentment on the part of the public is natural and must be expected. James J. Skehan paints a word picture of the crux of the whole problem:

> A police force gains the respect of the community it serves by carrying out its functions in a spirit of tolerance, human kindness and good will toward all men. This is a difficult task, because people in every community have many standards of morality, and although they are willing to obey some of our laws, they are determined to violate others. Therefore, the policeman is never popular with all classes of persons. He is, of course, looked upon by the vicious and lawless as their natural enemy. He is considered to be an obstructionist by every arrogant and selfish citizen who desires to indulge in his own self-seeking whims and inclinations, to the annoyance or disadvantage

[43] *Report of the National Advisory Commission on Civil Disorders.*

of others. He is often and will be continued to be used as a footstool by every crack-brained reformer whose ideas are born of emotionalism. And the reputation of the fine, manly, decent men who comprise the overwhelming majority of police organizations will probably continue to be besmirched by the bad conduct of the comparatively few in police organizaions who prove false to the trust placed in them.[44]

Policemen, then must be realistic; they must realize that the people they serve will not universally like or respect them.

Today's policemen are the heirs of that frightful legacy of ill will built up over many years—the man who walks the street bitter at the police may still be harboring a grudge of 40 years' standing. The policeman who embittered him then may long ago have gone to his reward, but his successors may suffer the consequences.[45]

The problem thus becomes one of creating the most favorable image possible, being the finest law enforcement officer possible. It is extremely difficult, however, for police organizations to construct codes or rules dictating the specific manner in which all police tasks shall be performed. As Don Kooken, in his book *Ethics in Police Service* pointed out, "The problems of police service are many and they are subject to the influences of the constant development of public administration.[46] Furthermore, police officers are continually deluged with new orders, directives, and advice, much of it conflicting and confusing. "Be firm but fair." "Use caution." "Assert yourself and be consistent." "Address everyone as Mr., Miss, or Mrs." "You'll be expected to attend community-relations classes." In view of the importance, complexity, and delicacy of police work, it is necessary that police administrators develop and articulate clear policies aimed at guiding and governing the way policemen exercise discretion on the street.

SUMMARY

Although the entire criminal justice system is charged with enforcing the law and maintaining order, the police have a distinctive responsibility. This responsibility, not associated with the courts and correctional

[44] J. J. Skehan, *Modern Police Work* (New York: Francis M. Basuind, 1951), pp. 8, 9.

[45] E. Adlow, *Policemen and People* (Boston: William J. Rockfort, 1957), p. 17.

[46] D. Kooken, *Ethics in Police Service* (Springfield, Ill.: Charles C. Thomas, Publisher, 1957), p. 6.

process, is the discretion a policeman must use in deciding whether to initiate the criminal justice process. In other words, the distinctive responsibility of the police is to judge whether the criminal justice process will be invoked against an individual.

The criminal justice system in the United States, and for that matter in most countries, is used to enforce standards of conduct necessary to protect individuals and the community. The action taken against law breakers is designed to serve three purposes: (1) it removes dangerous people from the community; (2) it deters others from criminal behavior; and (3) it gives society an opportunity to attempt to transform law breakers into law-abiding citizens. In discussing these areas, we have pointed out the significant distinguishing characteristic of the criminal justice system in the United States as compared to other countries—that is, the extent and the form of protections offered to individuals in the process of determining guilt and punishment.

The administration of justice is a process involving not only the three formalized agencies (police, courts, and corrections) but also unofficial agencies of the community organized to give assistance and to have a role in the process. Thus, the criminal justice system may fragment, and the process of justice may have either a functional or dysfunctional effect upon the entire system.

Police are involved in all phases of criminal justice. The role played by police in court (including prosecution and defense) and in corrections is an extremely important one. In conjunction with a discussion of the policeman's role in court, we have also touched upon the role and function of the *prosecutor* and *defense counsel.* Corrections is the final interrelated phase of the administration of justice. Corrections is defined as a process which is responsible for the implementation of orders of the court. The elements of a modern correctional system have been presented. Perhaps the most striking fact about the correctional apparatus today is that, although the rehabilitation of criminals is presumably its major purpose, the custody of criminals is actually its main task. Statistical information has been introduced to support this statement.

The last part of the chapter deals with the incohesive and fragmented criminal justice system. It is pointed out that such fragmentation tends to have a direct result on the amount and type of crime, as well as law enforcement's ability to control lawlessness in a democratic society. This portion of the chapter details the problems of the criminal justice system—particularly as it relates to crowded court calendars, prisons, and jails. The policeman's view of the criminal justice system is negative; the reasons for such disenchantment have been pointed out.

QUESTIONS

1. How does the criminal justice system work in the United States, and what is the distinguishing characteristic?
2. Discuss the administration of justice and due process of law as analyzed by the authors.
3. Discuss the *four* interrelated phases of the administration of criminal and juvenile justice.
4. What do the authors mean by, "Law Enforcement: A Period of Uncertainty"?
5. Police serve as symbol of social ills within our society. What is meant by this statement?

ANNOTATED REFERENCES

BARRETT, E. L. "Personal Rights, Property Rights and the Fourth Amendment," *1960 Supreme Court Review*. Chicago: University of Chicago Press, 1960. A fine discussion on decisions (Miranda, Gault, and so on).

ELDEFONSO, E.; COFFEY, A.; and GRACE, R. C. *Principles of Law Enforcement*. New York: John Wiley & Sons, 1968. Chaps. 1, 2, and 8 cover areas such as: police role and function; philosophy of law enforcement and police-community relations. For similar information see also: Derbyshire, R. L. "The Social Control Role of the Police in Changing Urban Communities." *Excerta Criminologica* 6 (1966); Toch, H. H. "Psychological Consequences of the Police Role." *Police* 10 (September-October, 1965).

COFFEY, A.; ELDEFONSO, E.; and HARTINGER, W. *Human Relations: Law Enforcement in a Changing Community*. Englewood Cliffs, N.J.: Prentice-Hall, 1971. Chapter 3 covers the problem of the deterioration of police image in the community, particularly the symbolic attributes discussed in this volume.

GARABEDIAN, P. G. "Challenges for Contemporary Corrections," *Federal Probation* 33 (March, 1962). Garabedian, a noted educator and writer, discusses the attitude of law enforcement officials and probation officers as it relates to leniency and punishment.

"Justice on Trial: A Special Report." *Newsweek*. March 8, 1971. An excellent discussion of the problems confronting the entire administration of criminal justice system.

OHMART, H. "The Challenge of Crime in a Free Society." *"Youth Authority Quarterly* 21 (Fall, 1968). Ohmart analyzes the incohesive and fragmented criminal justice system to support his argument. A concise article well worth reading.

RUBIN, S. *Crime and Juvenile Delinquency: A Rational Approach to Penal Problems.* New York: Oceana Press, 1970. Amplifies the institutional problems discussed in Chapter 2 of this volume.

TAPPAN, P. W. *Crime, Justice and Correction.* New York: McGraw-Hill, 1960. Chapters 10 through 13 orient enforcement of law in the legally defined judicial process.

3

Law Enforcement in a Democratic Society

Criminal justice has thus far been discussed as a system made up of three parts: input, process, and output. The input of criminal justice, is comprised of selected law violations. These law violations in turn systematically produce a process that involves some or all of the criminal justice subsystems: police, presecution-defense, courts, and corrections.

This chapter deals with one subsystem of the criminal justice system: the subsystem of law enforcement, or the role of police. Specifically, this chapter explores the police role in a democratic society. The implications of human rights, of man's will, and of the complexity of enforcing law in a democracy are also the subjects of this chapter.

One approach to exploring the subsystem of law enforcement is through the "comparative visibility" of police in relation to other subsystems of criminal justice. Police receive more public attention than any other subsystem; they are more visible for many reasons, one of which is numerous public contacts.

POLICE ROLE

Police Visibility

Law enforcement is in some way involved with nearly all law violations that are "processed" by *any* part of the criminal justice system. Much, if not most, of the overall public image of the system may be largely "police image." Law enforcement is involved in virtually all violations that constitute system input, whereas other subsystems handle comparatively few offenses. For example, the prosecution does not and cannot process every police arrest. Clearly, the courts and the defense are involved in fewer law violations than are the police. And since the correctional subsystem of probation, institutions, and parole function primarily after court handling (and in only certain cases) they of course have still fewer involvements with law violations than do the police.

The disproportionately high police involvement in criminal justice processing of law violations is probably the least troublesome aspect to the role of police in a democratic society. Nevertheless, this very disproportionate involvement magnifies all other police difficulties by increasing the "visibility" of the police role. (See Figure 3-1.)

In effect, the role of processing far more law violations than any other criminal justice subsystem tends to invite attention to the responsibility of police to *select* the law violations that can be processed by other subsystems. With relatively few exceptions, the overall system deals with law violations that are selected by police. This remains true despite many arguments to the contrary. It is in the context of this *primary* responsibility for enforcement that we shall examine the major difficulties of law enforcement in democracies.

Prevention of Crime

By casting the role of police in the overall context of criminal justice, the vital police function of *preventing* crime might appear less significant. Preventing the offenses processed by the overall system should be the most important part of the police role in democracy. Thus, emphasizing that part of the police role which deals with *processing* law violations in no way diminishes the value of crime prevention. Such emphasis is solely for the purpose of relating law enforcement to the overall system of criminal justice.

ENFORCING LAW IN DEMOCRACY: A TOUGH TASK

The following line from Anatole France's *Crainquebille* says a great deal about law and implies even more about *enforcing* law, particularly in democracy:

> The law, in its majestic equality, forbids the rich as well as the poor to sleep under bridges, to beg in the streets, and to steal bread.

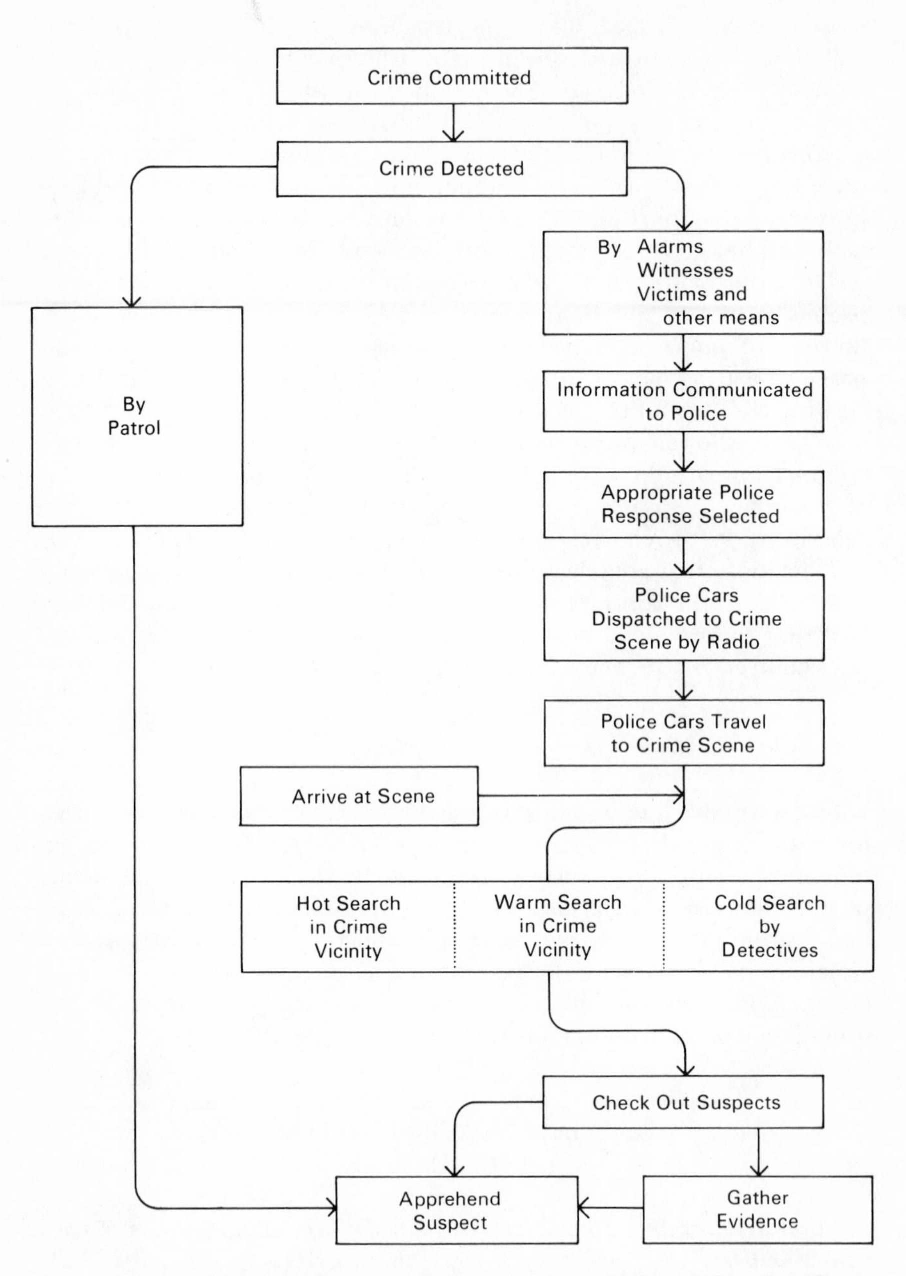

Figure 3-1 Criminal apprehension process. From pp. 58–57 of The President's Commission on Law Enforcement and Administration of Justice, *Task Force Report: The Police* (Washington, D.C.: U.S. Government Printing Office, 1967).

Figure 3-2 In a democracy, police have the difficult job of being responsive to the law, while also remaining sensitive to the social implications of enforcing laws that discriminate unfairly. Photo courtesy of the President's Commission on Law Enforcement and the Administration of Justice, Superintendant of Documents, Washington, D.C.

Police must remain responsive to laws that forbid sleeping under bridges or in alleys, begging, or bread stealing. (See Figure 3-2.) After all, law is law. But at an ever increasing pace, the police role in democracy includes sensitivity to the social implications of enforcing laws that by their nature discriminate unfairly. A traffic law against excessive speeds for Cadillacs may be enforceable but is certain to generate problems for police which are not likely to be restricted to hostility from citizens owning Cadillacs. Indeed, every one wishing to demonstrate the unfairness of police practice has "the Cadillac situation" at his disposal in a democratic society.

This kind of situation steadily increases the pressure on those who enforce the law to consider the social implications of law as a function of *democratic* government. In another context, the authors have pointed out that this growing pressure has broadened the definition of the term *enforcement:*

> The complexity of enforcing law has increased steadily with the advent of Magna Carta, Bill of Rights, and Fourth Amendment, all of which have molded the foundation of modern Constitutional government.

But complex or not, law enforcement has one function that has remained consistent in all governments throughout history: the promotion of an orderly environment. In meeting this governmental function, Constitutional government more than any other government form, must take into consideration the relationship between societal power and the power of man's will. Most of what is called "the wisdom of the ages" probably deals with this very relationship in one way or another. So also does this very relationship define most of our "social" problems. For in the final analysis, the individual power of the person is equal whether in support of or in dissent from the provision of an orderly environment—"orderly environment" being increasingly defined in terms that transcend the mere provision of personal safety and property security.[1]

Orderly Environment and Mobile Population

Pressures to broaden the definition of . . . enforcement must be in the context of "order"—and "orderly environment." Democracy, particularly the Constitutional government form of democracy, *assumes* an orderly environment. The assumption of order is based on the obvious requirement that *all* governments survive only to the degree that order is maintained. But in the case of democracy, the very distinction between democratic and undemocratic government hinges on the orderly participation of people in governing their own society—the kind of order "that transcends the mere provision of personal safety and property security."

Population mobility is one of the more salient features of societal order in democracy. But it is also one of the major problems confronting the enforcement of law. Population mobility is a problem relating to orderly environment to the degree that society permits *mobility* to be *freedom* as well. In other words, if a society regiments the mobility of its population, then enforcing law is greatly simplified—at least from a technical viewpoint. In societies that regiment mobility, enforcing law is relatively simple because the single goal of *government security* is substituted for the double goals of personal safety and property security. Thus, the problems involved in providing an orderly environment are increased because of individual freedom to move. Police problems that flow from population mobility can include witnesses leaving the jurisdiction "at will" or crime suspects becoming "lost" in the vast mobility of the society in general.

The population mobility is only one of many problems of enforcing

[1] A. Coffey, E. Eldefonso, and W. Hartinger, *Police-Community Relations* (Englewood Cliffs, N.J.: Prentice-Hall, 1971), p. 28.

At least one function of police, then, is to regulate human behavior —a singularly difficult function in a democratic society as already noted. And because of the difficulty involved in regulating behavior in a democracy, the power of police and how that power is defined, becomes crucial.

Police Power

In regulating human behavior, police are empowered to arrest suspected law violators. *Arrest is simply taking a person into custody as specified by law.* The actual specifications of the law of arrest are extremely complex and are subject to constant change through court decisions and legislative acts. But the power to arrest remains essentially the core of police ability to regulate human behavior after other approaches fail. This *power* is essential to maintain the social control necessary to regulate human behavior. Of course this power is not the sole influence that police have on behavior. Hopefully, police power is the last government alternative to social control and is used only after all else fails. Ultimately, however, if everything else does fail, then police power is the only means of social control.

Social Control

Social control is actually both *formal* and *informal* enforcement of law. But whether the control is formal or informal, the power to arrest is fundamental. Indeed, there are ever-increasing pressures for police to restrict the use of power even under severe stress—particularly the use of lethal force. Moreover, sophisticated police training now focuses more and more on innovative alternatives to using power. Again, however, the formal and informal police powers of arrest underpin virtually *all* applications of law as an instrument of social control.

One approach of exploring police powers is to compare the power of police to the established folkways, mores, and social institutions of a democratic society. It is also helpful to at least briefly consider the "nature of man." One group of authors made the following observations.

> If we considered the question, "What is man?" our answers will tend to infer that "man is *merely matter*," or that "man is a *spiritual being*." If we consider the question, "What is meant by spiritual?" our answers will tend to infer that "spirituality denotes the *supernatural*, the *mysterious*, the *irrational*," or that *"spirituality connotes intransic independence of matter."*
>
> How one answers the question, "What is man?" is important to one

> interested in law enforcement, for much of what is considered *good* or *bad* in law enforcement is judged so in terms of the nature of man.[3]

For purposes of discussing formal and informal social control, then, the *nature of man* as expressed through folkways, mores, and social institutions must be considered. That part of the police role which involves the formal and informal use of power in effect hinges on the definition of the nature of man.

Folkways and mores might be thought of as degrees of conformity. For example, most societies (democratic and otherwise) have a "folkway" of arriving at a motion picture performance "on time." The "penalty" for violating the folkway of arriving at the motion picture on time is at worst little more than angry glances from those interrupted.

In an instance where arriving late may be met by a more severe penalty, "arrival behavior" then becomes one of society's mores. When arriving late for an airplane departure, for instance, the penalty is more severe (the departure is missed). In other words, the severity of penalty determines the category of formal or informal.

Now when the society adds *formal* sanctions through law to the folkways or mores of "arrival behavior," a *social institution* is formed which further implies *enforcement.* Arriving late for a scheduled court appearance carries the possibility of a *formal* penalty—which in some cases can be severe.

The formality and informality of police power functions in a similar manner. For instance, like folkways and mores, the warnings that many motorists receive from policemen are "degrees of informality." The policeman regards the nature of man as being sensitive to this kind of informal control. When the offense is serious enough for *formal* arrest, a more severe penalty implies another police interpretation of man's nature—in other words, the individual in question requires the formality of a social institution. Of course, police role includes sensitivity to the human factors involved in a formal penalty, even though the formal penalty immediately introduces the further involvement of the entire criminal justice system.

The actual gradations and distinctions between informal and formal power are not clear. But in a democratic society, a great deal of the distinction between informal and formal power rests with the judgment of the officer enforcing the law; this is *police discretion,* which we shall define as an individual police officer making a personal judgment regarding the amount of power required to handle a given situation.

[3] A. C. Germann, F. D. Day, and R. R. Gallati, *Introduction to Law Enforcement* (Springfield, Ill.: Charles Thomas, 1966), p. 11.

Force

In discussing police authority and democracy, Eleanor Johnson states:

> In establishing the basis for our democratic institutions, the Constitution gave the individual guarantees against arbitrary and authoritarian government. The original text included protections against being held for a crime without cause (writ of habeas corpus); being punished for an act that was not illegal when performed (ex post facto law), being singled out for punishment by an Act of Congress (Bill of Attainder), being convicted of treason except for offenses and by procedures spelled out in the Constitution. The protections were supplemented by the Bill of Rights which included prohibition against "unreasonable searches and seizures" of persons, houses, papers, and effects; guarantee of "due process of law" with respect to life, liberty, and property; guarantee of rights of the accused, including trial by jury and the right to counsel; and prohibition of excessive bail or fines or cruel and unusual punishments.[4]

Implicit in virtually all of the guarantees is that police power, and particularly police force, is of constitutional concern. Police discretion in a democratic society, as it relates to the use of force, has been put into the following context:

> The term *enforcement* and the very nature of man implies a potential use of force. This potential to wield the force, then, is necessarily a part of the police image. And the public's opinion of how the police use this potential largely determines whether its image of the police is good or bad. The ramifications of bad image in itself provide considerable motivation for acquiring a good image. Additionally, a good police image and similar influences tend to promote in indivduals a willingness to observe the law voluntarily; this is a singularly practical consideration in the understaffed police organizations charged with the responsibility for nonvoluntary law observance. So the question becomes: What can be done to promote the understanding and use of social influences to encourage voluntary law observance? [5]

In terms of the nature of man, the discretion of police in distinguishing between formal and informal use of power or force relates to the *degree* to which police are able to achieve voluntary law observance. Obviously,

[4] E. H. Johnson, *Crime, Correction, and Society* (Homewood, Ill.: Dorsey Press, 1968), pp. 361-62.

[5] A. Coffey, E. Eldefonso, and W. Hartinger, *Human Relations: Law Enforcement in a Changing Community* (Englewood Cliffs, N.J.: Prentice Hall, 1971), p. 224.

with voluntary law observance the need to use force is eliminated. But the police must also use discretion in judging this variable.

Police Discretion

Reports of police discretion functioning without regard to human relations date back many years. Specific, partially documented assertions of mutual hostility between police and public began as early as 1964.

> Criticism of the way a big-city police department was run was largely confined to the younger, most recently promoted sergeants, but "alienation" —an acute sense of citizen hostility or contempt toward officers—was found in almost all age groups. Over 70 percent of the over 800 officers scored high on an index of perceived citizen hostility—more, indeed, than thought the force was poorly run (though these were over half the total).[6]

The mere possibility that the foregoing assertion accurately describes any part of police discretion poses major difficulties for the police role. In the context of mutual hostility, the public may well perceive police power and ability to use force solely as a threat. The implication of the public view of police discretion is reflected in the title (and partially in the substance) of the book, *Justice Without Trial: Law Enforcement in a Democratic Society*.[7] The relationship between police and the public becomes more tense when "urbanized anonymity" impinges upon public acceptance of the police role. Public support of police discretion may ultimately affect the philosophical implications of a police officer's judgment far less than the practical applications.[8]

Both informal and formal police power entail police discretion that must be measured in the context of "man's nature" in a democratic society. Let us now move from an examination of police power functioning by discretion from the informal through the formal to a discussion of structure or level of *jurisdiction*.

[6] J. Q. Wilson, "Police Attitudes and Citizen Hostility," unpublished paper, Harvard University, September, 1964.

[7] J. Skolnick, *Justice Without Trial: Law Enforcement in a Democratic Society* (New York: John Wiley & Sons, 1967).

[8] T. F. Adams, "The Philosophy of Police Discretion," *Criminal Justice Readings* (Pacific Palisades, Calif.: Goodyear, 1972), pp. 218-31; See also: J. Q. Wilson, "Police Discretion," *Criminal Justice Readings,* ed. T. F. Adams (Pacific Palisades, Calif.: Goodyear, 1972), pp. 213-17.

Figure 3-3 It is incumbent upon police agencies to develop community relations programs relevant to the youth in their community. Photo courtesy of Los Angeles Police Department.

JURISDICTION: FEDERAL, STATE, AND LOCAL

Thus far we have discussed matters relating to law enforcement at the local level of jurisdiction. A brief discussion of the various levels of law enforcement might now be in order. This discussion is intended merely to clarify the distinctions between: federal, state, and local law enforcement. (Law enforcement is defined as encompassing both security and investigative functions.)

Federal Law Enforcement

The police role in a democratic society becomes diversified precisely *because* the society is democratic. Of course defining law enforcement as including security and investigation introduces additional diversity. But the main point here is that those governments that function in terms of state security alone (to the exclusion of individual rights) have little reason to create "police levels" (except for state security reasons). When individual rights *are* guaranteed by government, enforcement of law theoretically *doubles:* first there is enforcement of laws protecting the state, and second there is enforcement of laws protecting the individual. Both kinds of laws require enforcement in a genuine democracy. Add to this the "federal concept" of guaranteeing these rights in all jurisdictions regardless of any other laws. This diversity then is a partial explanation of how federal courts and federal law enforcement emerge.

Of course the role of federal law enforcement encompasses much more than investigation, security, and the enforcement of laws dealing with individual rights. There are numerous federal agencies that readily qualify for consideration in any discussion of the broadly defined police role in democracy. Some of these agencies are: the Federal Bureau of Investigation, the Bureau of Narcotics and Dangerous Drugs, several divisions of the Treasury Department, Federal Marshalls, and the Immigration and Naturalization Agency.

The agents of the FBI and the various law enforcement arms of the Treasury Department perform many of the governmental security tasks necessary in all modern societies. These tasks include enforcing such areas as treason, smuggling, and other crimes of national scope.

Federal Marshalls are often publicized for activities that cover *all* federal law enforcement concerns. Specialized intelligence services such as the CIA also diversify at least the investigative segment of federal efforts to police the national interests. Though considerably removed from the civil police role, the Military Intelligence made up of all branches of the services are clearly a facet of security.

The authority and jurisdiction of any federal agency is either *explicitly* defined by federal law *or it does not exist.* Law enforcement jurisdiction, in the absence of specific federal law to the contrary, becomes a matter for the state—regardless of the offense. Of course agencies such as the FBI are authorized and equipped to assist state and local agencies *upon request.* This "requested assistance" usually involves technical matters relating to the criminalistic science of police investigation (fingerprints, ballistics, and so forth). Federal agencies also provide sophisticated training for state and local law enforcement—the FBI Academy being an outstanding example of this kind of service.

State Law Enforcement

Variations in the pattern of law enforcement practiced at the state level range from simple traffic control (Highway Patrol) of major traffic arteries to virtual operation of most law enforcement activities within a state. As in the case of federal agencies, the question of jurisdiction is crucial in determining the involvement of state law enforcement in any given situation or location. And again, legislation customarily determines jurisdiction. Also, investigative or training assistance is frequently made available by the state to the local levels of law enforcement.

Local Law Enforcement

Local law enforcement can refer to a sheriff, a city police department, a "constable," or a justice of the peace. In certain instances, investigative staff of the local prosecutor or even the coroner can be considered local law enforcement; certainly, the discretion used by such persons frequently impinges upon man's will, nature, or freedom. However, the distinguishing characteristics between levels of law enforcement jurisdiction is likely to be the *directness* of public influence on law enforcement practice. Examining this directness of impact more readily clarifies the various levels than a comparison of the precise activities of federal, state, and local jurisdictions.

In many cases, the city police department must remain sensitive to local political issues that have little impact on state-level law enforcement and virtually no impact on federal law enforcement. City councils, mayors, county boards of supervisors, along with a host of local groups directly influence the police department or sheriff—at least far more directly than the same group might influence a state law enforcement activity or a federal law enforcement function. This is not to say that higher jurisdictional levels are politically insensitive. It is to say, however, that operational survival of law enforcement programs are far less insulated at the local level. Put another way, public concern over law enforcement is more easily focused at the local level.

Police role, then, varies somewhat by jurisdictional level. But in terms of the relationship between law enforcement and other criminal justice subsystems, the enforcement segment of the police role, regardless of level, usually overshadows any operational differences.

POLICE ROLE IN A SYSTEM OF CRIMINAL JUSTICE

Thus far we have focused on the specific implications of enforcing law in a democratic society. The relationship of law enforcement to social problems will be presented in Chapter 7. In the remainder of this chapter we shall attempt to integrate police role in a democracy with the police view of the criminal justice system as discussed in Chapter 2.

In the preface to their book, *The Police Officer and Criminal Justice,* Gene Wright and John Marlo state:

> Historically the police officer and the criminal justice system have operated as separate entities, coming together only at the apex of a criminal case and separating again during the post-trial procedures. This operational system, though not altogether ineffective, has resulted in some rather wide gaps of understanding and philosophy regarding justice as an American institution. Today we are seeing the emerging roles in the entire system of criminal justice developing a closer relationship and demanding that such gaps be narrowed through more cooperative efforts from arrest to release of all suspected criminal offenders.[9]

This says a great deal about police role in the democratic society. And it says even more about police function in the criminal justice system. (See Figure 3-3.)

The virtual "blizzard" of seemingly contradictory legal opinions and regulations tends at times to distort not only police function in a democracy but also police functions in criminal justice. Despite this, the criminal justice system is demanding such gaps be narrowed through more cooperative efforts from arrest to release.

As noted earlier in this chapter, law enforcement bears the awesome responsibility of "selecting" practically all of the law violations processed by the overall system. Integration of this facet of police role with the roles of other criminal justice subsystems is not optional—at least not optional if criminal justice in America is to become truly effective The law enforcement activities flowing from the police role in democracy make up volumes of individual topics. Nevertheless, clarification of the relationship of police role to the criminal justice system requires at least brief consideration of specific police activities.

[9] G. Wright, and J. Marlo, *The Police Officer and Criminal Justice* (New York: McGraw-Hill, 1970). Preface.

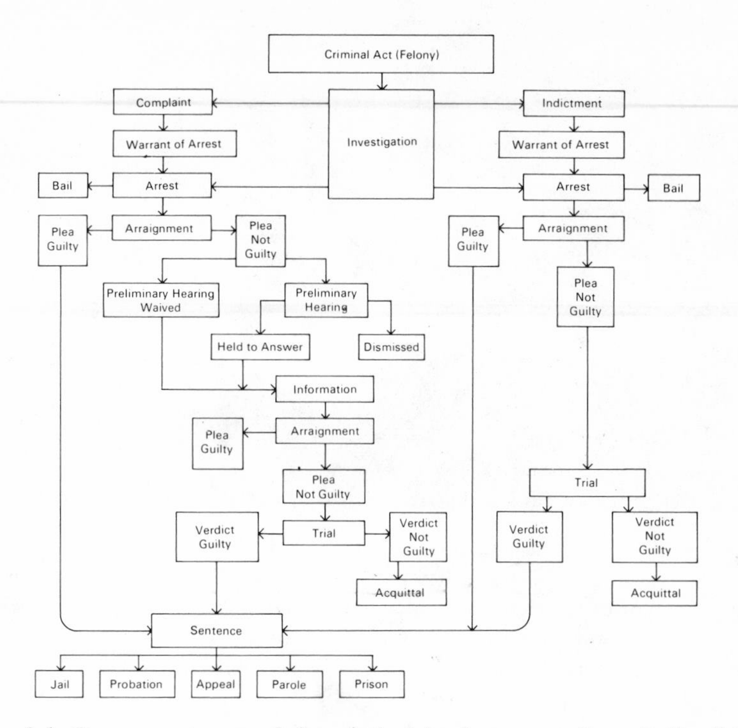

Figure 3-4 Component parts of the criminal justice system. From Police Science Division, West Valley College, Campbell, Ca.

Technical Facets of Police Operation

Police Patrol. A former Chief of Police, August Vollmer, is often quoted as having once observed that citizens expect police officers to have the wisdom of Solomon, the courage of David, the strength of Samson, the patience of Job, the leadership of Moses, the kindness of the Good Samaritan, the strategical training of Alexander, the faith of Daniel, the diplomacy of Lincoln, the tolerance of Jesus, and an intimate knowledge of every branch of the natural, biological and social sciences. If he had all these, he might be a good policeman. Of course a great deal of controversy surrounds how realistic any of these expectations might be, but few would argue that at least some of them actually reflect the views of a large number of American citizens. These expectations probably developed during the steady increase in property crime that accompanied the growth of American cities during the latter part of the nineteenth century and first half of the twentieth century. More often than not, the expecta-

Figure 3-5 One effective and much used method of patrolling both urban and rural areas is the police patrol car. Photo courtesy of Sgt. Frank Furnaw of the Campbell Police Department, Campbell, Ca., and Michael Johnson, Santa Clara County Juvenile Probation Department, San Jose, Ca.

tions, both reasonable and unreasonable, confront those responsible for police patrol.

The patrol division of any size agency is customarily considered the one police activity that cannot be eliminated under any circumstances.[10] The other activities discussed as police operations in this chapter—along with transportation, custody, communications, and maintenance—are also vital to the modern police agency. Nevertheless, with very few exceptions, police patrol is considered the most vital of all police activities. In the United States, over 35,000 city police departments and over 3,000 sheriff's offices provide a patrol function in one form or another—a function of vital concern to the criminal justice system.

Foot Patrol. Historically the most common form of patrol has been patrol on foot. The advent of the automobile, however, has virtually eliminated the foot patrol as a major method of performing this police function in the nearly 40,000 law enforcement agencies of the United States. Considerable discussion about once again "walking-a-beat" seems to be emerging in many areas where there is concern with police problems. Until a change occurs, a consistent use of the foot patrol appears

[10] Eldefonso, Coffey, and Grace, *Principles of Law Enforcement,* p. 179.

limited to areas of extremely dense population, usually business districts and/or slum districts.

The perplexing problem facing police administrators customarily involves (1) insufficient staff for the population of a community, weighed against (2) considerable evidence that an individual officer "walking-a-beat" stands a far greater chance of achieving law enforcement objectives. The foot patrolman will be particularly successful if he is equipped with modern radio communication to summon help from patrol cars or even helicopters.

Patrol Car. A considerable amount of the entire police "image" in the United States relates to the "prowl car" or "cruiser." Again, this image is formed because the most consistent contact that occurs between police and the public involves the patrol car. The police patrol function is carried out almost entirely with the use of patrol cars, and patrol programs are almost invariably conceived of in terms of automobiles. The efficiency, the high mobility, and (when necessary) the speed of the automobile are extremely persuasive arguments to police administrators.

Additionally, the police automobile serves as "equipment" in the sense that it carries first-aid items, riot guns, tear gas, extra clothing, blankets, flares, fingerprint equipment, fire extinguishers, and a host of other items simply unavailable to a patrolman on foot. Transportation of prisoners, other officers, and similar advantages leave little doubt that the police vehicle will continue to be a major consideration not only to the patrol functon but also to the entire police activity.

Motorcycle, Bicycle, and Horse. In attaining effective and efficient police patrol, the implications of population, geography, terrain, and even climate become immediately apparent. Prevention of crime, protection of lives and property, enforcement of laws, preservation of peace, detection and apprehension of criminals, and even courteous performance are obviously subject to influences such as the size of the city, the people in the population, the terrain, and the weather. Thus, due to certain types of terrain (large city parks, for example), motorcycles, bicycles, and even horse patrols readily lend themselves to achieving law enforcement goals.

Specialized Control

The complexity of urbanized crime continues to impinge heavily on the entire criminal justice system, but the patrol function of law enforcement will probably require the greatest sensitivity to new problems. Various adaptations such as "canine control" (use of police dogs for a wide variety of activities) have already emerged. Airplanes and helicopters have increasingly been adopted for many police patrol activities. Harbor and marine patrols are by no means new but are increasingly called upon to serve in innovative ways for the criminal justice system. Above all else, however, detection and apprehension of criminal violators is the primary "connection" between the public and the criminal justice system; and it is the patrol function, in whatever form it takes, that initiates this "connection."

INVESTIGATION

The role of the prosecution and of the defense will be discussed in Chapters 8 and 9 of this text. The relationship between police and the prosecution-defense exists primarily through the apprehension of accused law violators *and* in the accumulation of evidence. Police investigation is customarily the basis of criminal complaints resulting in prosecution-defense. The role of the investigative process, then, cannot be ignored in an introduction to the overall criminal justice system. Initially, police investigations customarily are directed toward determining whether a law has been violated. This can occur within the patrol function, or it may be the function of the detective division specializing in investigation. In either event, police assume the responsibility in most instances to determine whether other parts of the criminal justice system need be brought to bear. Once a determination is made that the law has in fact been violated, police investigation serves to collect evidence. (This will be discussed further in Chapter 8.) The investigative process has the responsibility of *preserving* evidence after it is obtained, but the collection of evidence itself is of far more importance in making the criminal justice system a viable method to deal with crime.

Methods

The entertainment media has for years acquainted the general public with a wide range of investigative methods. Undercover surveillance, fingerprints, ballistics, and interrogation of suspects and witnesses are included. The general public has been made keenly aware of police use of "stake-outs," informants, file checks on motor vehicle registrations, and a host of other methods of collecting information geared to apprehending alleged law violators.

A law enforcement specialty referred to as *criminalistics* has grown steadily in the American criminal justice system during the last twenty or thirty years. Crime laboratories and the investigative process have steadily merged in their functional application in police work since J. Edgar Hoover founded the FBI laboratory in 1932. Among the many valuable contributions made by criminalistics to law enforcement have been methods to produce irrefutable tests in blood, urine, ballistics, hair, voice, and many other scientific tests every bit as valid as the fingerprint. Police investigative use of photography along with handwriting analysis and similar innovations have made the investigative process a science unto itself, which combines limitless use of scientific principles with the sharp intuitive powers necessary for all investigations. Although the role of the polygraph (lie detector) has failed to attain the scientific status attributed to many other police investigative methods, this method does demonstrate the wide range of innovation emerging in twentieth century police practice. At any rate, the relevance of police investigation necessarily rests upon the *combination* of apprehending an accused offender and acquiring and preserving the evidence necessary to the judicial process.

JUVENILE

The relationship between police and juvenile offenders may not at first appear to be extremely relevant to a consideration of the overall criminal justice system. For one thing, a delinquent is not customarily considered a criminal—even though the status of delinquent may be the result of an act that may have been defined as a crime had it been committed by an adult.

One method of clarifying the relationship between police and juveniles might be through the concepts of *accountability* and *responsibility*. A five-year-old boy who plays with matches and burns down his neighbor's home would not be considered, by most, to be *responsible* for his act. Depending upon evidence of his maturity, some might consider him slightly *accountable* for the arson even though they would acknowledge that he could not be *responsible*.

A fifteen-year-old boy who burns down the neighbor's home in most jurisdictions is still not criminally *responsible* for the arson. In terms of *accountability*, however, the 15-year-old boy presumably would be much more "accountable" than the five-year-old boy for the same act. To clarify further, a 21-year-old who burns down a house would be presumed both *accountable* and *responsible* (except for the various criminal defenses to be discussed later in this volume).

The point here is that the police exercise considerably more latitude in discretion when they have reason to believe a child perpetrated the offense. In coping with the horrendous volume of reported crime, the police function is to apprehend "criminals" and develop evidence needed for the judicial process. When the reported crime has been perpetrated by a juvenile, however, the police take on the additional responsibility of dealing with the juvenile in a way that *prevents* the child from becoming an adult criminal—even though the offense may be precisely the same act for which an adult would be apprehended and prosecuted.

Put another way, the criminal justice system in its entirety and the police segment in particular have the purpose of *preventing* children from growing into adults who will be dealt with by the criminal justice system. Police operations that deal with juveniles, then, are unique but also worthy of consideration in any discussion of the overall criminal justice system.

Juvenile Procedures

Police involvement with juveniles falls into two distinct categories: *delinquent* and *dependent.* (Dependent children are those who have been *battered, abused, molested,* or *neglected.*) Since police involvement with *dependent* children is primarily focused on parents or guardians who are processed by the criminal justice system, juvenile procedures will be discussed here primarily in terms of *delinquency.*

Figure 3-6 Delinquent minors taken into custody by police officers of the Campbell Police Department, Campbell, Ca. Photo courtesy of Michael Johnson, Santa Clara County Juvenile Probation Department, and Campbell Police Department, Campbell, Ca.

Juvenile Delinquency

The first concern of anyone seriously discussing delinquency should be the *definition,* but delinquency is not even well defined in law.[11] Great variations exist from state to state between juvenile court laws. An offense handled by a juvenile court of one state may, in another state, be brought by polic to the attention of the adult court.[12] State laws more or less uniformly define the *delinquent* as a minor who has been adjudged delinquent by a juvenile court. Such a definition fails, however, to account for children who violate the law but who are not brought before the court or perhaps not even apprehended.[13]

The behavioral sciences have failed to completely clarify juvenile delinquency. There is very little agreement as to what delinquency *is* or *how* it is caused. This is not to say that academic research is without a classification system of juvenile delinquency. Indeed, numerous and sophisticated methods of delinquency classification systems have emerged over the years —one noted example being that of Sellin and Wolfgang.[14] The problem with classification systems, however, is their dependence on a definition of delinquency—a definition which in turn depends on behavior that may or may not be called delinquent by the police in a given jurisdiction.

Amazingly enough, virtually everyone retains an individual conception of juvenile delinquency along with the assumption that this conception represents the bulk of juvenile problems. For our purposes and with the recognition of many inadequacies, we shall define delinquency as simply "the violation of law by juveniles"—apprehended or not.

Another concern of police in dealing with juvenile problems is in the area known as "pre-delinquency." Runaway kids and a host of family problems customarily make up this segment of police efforts. Of course, whatever inadequacies occur in a definition of delinquency will also necessarily weaken the definition of *pre-delinquency.* One approach to clarify-

[11] U.S. Department of Health, Education, and Welfare, Children's Bureau, *A Look at Juvenile Delinquency,* pamphlet No. 380 (Washington, D.C.: U.S. Gov't. Printing Office, 1966), p. 1.

[12] P. W. Tappan, *Crime, Justice and Correction* (New York: McGraw-Hill, 1960), pp. 392-93.

[13] T. Sellin, "The Significance of Records of Crime," *Law Quarterly Review,* 47 (October, 1951), 495-96; See also: "Measurement of Crime in Geographic Areas," *Proceedings of the American Philosophical Society* 97:163-167 (April, 1953).

[14] T. Sellin and M. E. Wolfgang, *The Measurement of Delinquency* (New York: John Wiley & Sons, 1964), pp. 145-64.

ing pre-delinquency, however, might begin with considering offenses that are law violations only for children. Law violations entailing police action—whether committed by an adult or a juvenile—may seem "more delinquent" to some and "less delinquent" to others than do offenses that are illegal only for children. Assault, robbery, auto theft, and perhaps drug abuse may seem somewhat different than truancy, runaway from home, curfew violations, or ungovernable behavior. Certainly in terms of the danger posed to the community, there is a difference; and perhaps here the notion of *pre-delinquency* may gain a degree of clarity. The offenses that are illegal only for children occur "before" criminal offenses per se. That is, in terms of a scale of increasing danger to the community juvenile offenses would come before crime in general. Thus, law violations that are offenses only for children might be thought of as pre-delinquency.

It should be stressed that many if not most children classified by such criteria do not progress into more serious offenses—a fact readily acknowledged by most experienced policemen. Indeed, many such pre-delinquents never violate a law that would constitute a crime if committed by an adult.

TRAFFIC CONTROL

Much of traffic control occurs in many (if not most) law enforcement agencies as part of the patrol function. The overwhelming complexity of this police function, however, appears to justify a separate consideration of traffic control. In most of the fifty states, even those traffic violations considered serious enough to take to court are at least philosophically (and sometimes by law) separated from what is defined as *crime*. Even in severe cases involving the entire criminal justice process of law enforcement, courts, prosecution-defense, and even corrections, traffic offenders are usually processed as being distinctively different from "ordinary criminals." Only in rare instances when evidence exists that a vehicle was used as a weapon in premeditated homicide do these distinctions break down. Traffic control, however, is both a major problem to police operations and a major activity of the criminal justice system throughout the United States.

Though somewhat incidental to the function of traffic control, another significant consideration is the public image that is generated by the traffic control peace officer. Indeed, even though the general public has its greatest contact through the patrol function of a police agency, in the eyes of most citizens the criminal justice system is probably most often personified by the "traffic cop." He represents the most frequent contact of the criminal justice system with the widest range of the population.

SUMMARY

This chapter presented the role of police in a democratic society. The will and the nature of man was provided as the context for examining the relationship of law enforcement to the overall criminal justice system. The higher proportion of law violations dealt with by police was isolated as a significant variable for two reasons: the focus upon police activities, and the virtual "selection" of law violations processed by the other criminal justice subsystems.

The necessity of maintaining an orderly environment was discussed as part of police work in democracy; this was discussed from the broad scope of recognizing the social implications of enforcing specific laws.

The mobility of population was presented as posing one of many difficulties for law enforcement in maintaining an orderly environment in a democracy. An orderly environment was in turn presented as a requisite in any form of government. Another difficulty presented was the "urban paradox"—the conflict between retaining individual freedom and remaining anonymous.

Police power and the use of force were dealt with in the specific context of man's will and man's nature. Power and force were discussed as the least desirable approach to maintaining order but were also presented as the only alternative available when all other methods failed.

The formal and informal applications of police power in democracy were compared to folkways, mores, and social institutions from the nature-of-man perspective. Great emphasis was placed on police discretion in determining the degree of formality of power. This discretion was also discussed in terms of man's nature.

The various levels of police role in democracy (federal, state, and local) were discussed with emphasis on jurisdiction and authority. A discussion of the relationship between police role in democracy and the overall criminal justice system preceded an examination of specific police activities such as foot patrol, the patrol car, and the use of motorcycles and horses.

Noted early in the chapter was the extreme significance of *preventing* crime even though this subject was not discussed because of the emphasis on *relationship* to criminal justice in general in democracy.

QUESTIONS

1. Discuss the significance of the proportion of law violation dealt with by police as compared to other subsystems of criminal justice.

2. Contrast the simple responsibility to enforce law with the quote from Anatole France.
3. Relate "orderly environment" and "population mobility." Relate both to the police role in democracy.
4. How do mobility and freedom differ?
5. What is the "urban paradox"? How does it relate to the police role in democracy?
6. What is police power?
7. Why is police power necessary?
8. What is the priority for determining the use of power?
9. Contrast the theory of police power with the concept of force.
10. Contrast formal and informal power.
11. Discuss police discretion.
12. Discuss any three "local" police activities.

ANNOTATED REFERENCES

ADAMS, T. F., ed. *Criminal Justice Readings*. Pacific Palisades, Calif: Goodyear, 1972. Section 1 entitled "The Police Role" contains fine articles of significance to the serious student of law enforcement in a democratic society. See pages 3 through 50.

COFFEY, A; ELDEFONSO E.; and HARTINGER, W. *Human Relations: Law Enforcement in a Changing Community*. Englewood Cliffs, N.J.: Prentice-Hall, 1971. Chapter 4, "The Problem of the Police Image in a Changing Community," outlines many of the difficulties encountered by police in adjusting to gross social change in democracy (pages 67 through 100). See also: Coffey, Eldefonso, and Hartinger's *Police Community Relations* in its entirety for full range of this topic.

ELDEFONSO, E.; COFFEY, A.; and GRACE, R. *Principles of Law Enforcement*. New York: John Wiley & Sons, 1968. Chapter 2 affords the student both historical perspective and the philosophy of police role (pages 35 through 52).

SKOLNICK, J. *Justice Without Trial: Law Enforcement in a Democratic Society*. New York: John Wiley & Sons, 1967. Although somewhat oriented to the specific period of publication, this work is valuable to any student interested in the subject area of the title. See Chapter 1 in particular.

WRIGHT, G., and MARLO, J. *The Police Officer and Criminal Justice*. New York: McGraw-Hill, 1970. For elaboration of police role in democracy as it relates to court process, this entire volume is recommended because of its brevity. For deeper elaboration of this concept, see: Eldefonso, E.; Coffey, A., and Sullivan, J. *Police and the Criminal Law*. Pacific Palisades, Calif.: Goodyear, 1972.

PART TWO

The Police Role, Function, and Power in Dealing with Criminal Behavior

The efficiency of law enforcement is determined to a large degree by the extent that community mores support the legal norms. Whereas the community mores support police action against traditional crimes such as murder and theft, the attitudes are less universal in respect to laws regulating morality. In a pluralistic culture, the treatment of immoralities as crimes invites the imposition of the morality of a politically powerful minority on all groups. When the criminal law runs counter to the traditions of minorities, administration of justice becomes entangled in the difficulties of coercing substantial numbers of respectable citizens to conform to rules they regard as unnatural and unreasonable.

E. H. JOHNSON,
Crime, Correction and Society

4

Law Enforcement and Scope of Criminal Law

The primary responsibility of law enforcement is not with technical legalities but with the provision of personal safety and property security for those members of society who conform to the law. A noted publication on this subject painted a vivid picture of the "philosophy of enforcing laws":

> Regulating behavior is necessary because individuals striving for survival and other needs tend to jeopardize each other's personal safety. How striving for survival might jeopardize personal safety might be illustrated by the activities of an imaginary tribe of mythical "cave men." Younger cave men striving to survive and meet other needs by slaying saber-toothed tigers might have little patience and perhaps open hostility toward older, less agile "cave men" —particularly when the older hunters sought division of hunting rewards without correspondent hunting effort. But society, "recognizing" the combat wisdom of these older survivors of earlier tiger fights would likely protect the personal safety of the tribe's elders by "regulating" the behavior of the younger "cave men." In short, this prehistoric society's very existence probably depended upon enforcing a rule that older men offer leadership and share fighting secrets with younger men in exchange for protection, skins or meat, and of course, women. In return for observing these rules, society offers personal safety.
>
> * * *
>
> Another consideration in the philosophy of enforcing laws concerns the freedom permitted the individual by society. Personal safety is provided by all societies to individuals who observe the rules (although some rules in cer-

tain societies appear virtually impossible to observe). But in those societies permitting greater freedom, individuals usually are permitted to acquire property rights. This differs from a society in which the state retains all property rights. Control of property rights is a matter of "degree rather than kind," inasmuch as no society actually retains *all* property rights but many societies attempt to control all *significant* properties.[1]

PRIMITIVE LAW[2]

Human beings persistently struggle for control over human beings. Such endeavor may be centered solely on self, or directed toward another living person, or aimed at coalitions of human beings. The relationship may also be that of coalitions to coalitions, or group to individual. But regardless of direction, group to individual or contrariwise, the control has been, and currently is, sought through the use of cults, practices, disciplines, and institutions. Ideals, symbols, and weapons, in series, alternately, or in combination, are utilized to achieve the desired goal. Moreover, when human actors take measures in effectuation of this desideratum they are influenced by the anticipated reactions of other human beings against whom that effort is directed. A corresponding state of anticipation is similarly engendered in those human organisms for whom the control would be prescribed.

Whatever notions of jurisdiction are evolved there must be some authority called forth in support of it, procedural devices to execute it, and methods for sustaining it. Accompanying a structure for a social control is the need for persuasive authority to shore up the framework. In the earlier stages this was probably entirely physical force; and in the later stages, as today it consists of some clusters of rationale plus brute force, if necessary. However, some of the external standards first launched by human beings, assembled together in crude forms of social units, are unfathomable since the incompleteness of man makes him partially unpredictable.

Information about primitive men depends upon intervening human conduct. Each succeeding reporter translates such data by his own experience, training, and background. Consequently, presuppositions lie at the bottom of all writings pertaining to the past. It is here that one must recognize that there is a pyramiding of inferences, for examiner and examinee each bear mental scars of their respective pasts and environments. Conjecture, seemingly, displaces deduction in regard to the remote historical period under study in this section. That hordes of human beings did manifest some crude forms of institutions is still clearly traceable through the indelible impres-

[1] E. Eldefonso, A. Coffey, and R. C. Grace, *Principles of Law Enforcement* (New York: John Wiley & Sons, 1968), p. 36.

[2] This section has been reprinted from W. L. Clark and W. L. Marshall, *A Treatise on the Law of Crimes* (7th ed.), Callaghan and Company, 6141 N. Cicero Ave., Chicago, Ill., pp. 11-17, by courtesy of the publisher.

sions left on the minds of modern men. For this reason those incipient stages require even this short examination.

Taboos, totems, and customs constituted the social regulation of tribal life in early civilizations.[3] Protection of the community, its leaders, and individual members was one of the chief aims of both the taboo and totemic systems. Those people who were dominated by such beliefs apparently assumed a taboo to be self-activating and self-executing; they believed that punishment automatically followed upon breach of such tribal rules. Consequently, violations of taboos were punishable without regard to an offender's state of mind.[4]

AN INTRODUCTION TO THE CRIMINAL AND COMMON LAW SYSTEMS

Although the primary responsibility of law enforcement is the provision of *personal safety and property security,* there is a general expectation that policemen also understand laws to which there is general conformity. After all, these are the very laws that policemen enforce. Police agencies respond to this expectation by requiring police officers to know enough law to *recognize* crime. But rare is the police officer who claims extensive knowledge of the complex variety of statutes clogging court calendars. Of course it can be argued that policemen have little need for the working attorney's legal knowledge to enforce laws concerned primarily with immediate safety and security. The complex courtroom nuances of several, probate, corporate, appeal, and even some criminal laws are thought by many to fall outside the sphere of a peace officer's concern. Therefore, an effort has been made in this chapter to *limit* discussion pertaining to criminal law. (See Chapter 5, "Legal Aspects of Law Enforcement and Judiciary Process," for a detailed discussion on the court process.) In this chapter, we shall be concerned with the areas which have a definite effect on a peace officer's ability to perform his daily tasks. We shall focus on two major divisions of law—the *common law* system derived Germanic territories and from

[3] See Freud, *Totem and Taboo* (Strachey transl 1952); Kelsen, *General Theory of Law and State* 16 (Wedberg transl 1945); Maine, *Ancient Law 67* (Everyman's Library ed 1954); Maine, *Early History of Institutions* (1878); Sumner, *Folkways* (1940).

[4] Attributing guilt and taint to inanimate physical objects and animals involved in the death of a human being is part of the theory of deodand. The significance, here, lies in the theory of responsibility. See e.g., 1 Hawkins, *Pleas of the Crown* 75 (Curwood ed 1824); Holmes, Common Law 24-26; 1 Blackstone, Commentaries 301; 3 Holdsworth, History of English Law 276-277, 311 (3rd ed 1923). The modern theory of contraband objects (i.e., proceedings in rem) bears vestiges of this type of thinking.

England, and the *civil law* system derived first from Roman influence and then from France.

> The Common Law system is a process of developing law "continuously" by reference to precedence, whereas *Civil Law* is based on *specific codes* that are written and legislated. Put another way, Common Law seeks to "remain common" by using court rulings from similar cases in the past as a guide for current dispositions. Civil Law, on the other hand, concerns itself with precise interpretations of an appropriate, but legislated statute. A further distinction might be made in the "accusatorial" nature of Common Law, and the "inquisitional" nature of Civil Law. Yet another and far more "practical" distinction would be made in the case of "Civil cases" later in this chapter.[5]

Since it would be difficult—if not impossible—to fully comprehend Part Three of this volume without some understanding of the common law system and the distinctions between civil and criminal laws, it would be appropriate at this time to discuss these areas.

The Common Law System

Our common law is itself inherited in part from the common law which originated among Germanic and English peoples. The principles of the common law of England are still applied in some of our states; to some extent, however, this common law has been changed by statute or modified by the interpretations of our own courts. The common law system is a process of developing law "continuously" by reference to *precedence.* As such, the development of common law is the result of judicial decisions; certain accepted principles were then more fully developed, qualified, and expanded by the magistrates. Common law, therefore, is a constantly growing body of material, evolving through usage and custom. Certain rules come to be accepted for settling ordinary disputes or controversies between man and man and for dealing with those who commit crimes. Thus, a complicated set of rules, principles, concepts, and standards have developed and are enforced by the courts even though they have never been adopted by legislative action. Furthermore, the authority of these doctrines are almost completely based upon their general reception and continual usage. The only method of proving that a particular doctrine is a rule of common law would be to show that it has always been used in the past.

[5] Eldefonso, Coffey, and Grace, *Principles of Law Enforcement,* pp. 75-76.

> This, however, pictures its beginning rather than its later stages. In its maturity the development of the Common Law is largely, if not wholly, the result of judicial decisions. Somehow, no one can say precisely how, certain principles came to be accepted as the law of the land. The judges held themselves bound to decide cases which came before them according to those principles, and as new accommodations of circumstances threw light on the way in which they operated, the principles were in such cases more and more fully developed and qualified.[6]

It was fairly obvious that laws developed in this manner were inadequate and unsatisfactory; they were not meeting the demands of the rapidly changing American culture and were thus producing a "cultural lag." It was therefore necessary to make additions or changes by legislative enactment.

> Legislation itself, however, became a new source of Common Law growth. In cases applying the words of the statute to a multitude of widely varying factual situations, there came to be a body of authoritative material not found in the statutes themselves but only in judicial decisions, and this is also regarded as part of the Common Law.[7]

It would be proper, therefore, to say that all segments of authoritative instruments which are used to control, guide, and direct the judiciary and administrative machinery of the state in carrying out its official tasks and which lack the "blessing" of constitutional authority or legislative enactment are referred to as common law.

Federal Common-Law Crimes. The question is often asked: "Are there any crimes punishable by the federal courts merely because they are recognized as common law crimes?" In response we refer to the Constitution of the United States and a decision handed down by the United States Supreme Court in 1812 *(United States* v. *Hudson and Goodwin).* No crime, according to the Supreme Court's interpretation of the Constitution, may be punishable by the federal courts merely because the violation was viewed as a common law crime. This decision does not mean, however, that there is no federal common law of crimes. Although this may appear to be contradictory, a closer analysis reveals that unless Congress actually declares a particular act a crime, there can be no punishment under federal statute. However, if Congress declares an act to be a crime and provides a specific penalty for the violation of the act (civil rights laws and other laws relating to consumers goods), the

[6] R. L. Perkins, *Criminal Law* (Mineola, N.Y.: The Foundation Press), p. 23.

[7] Perkins, *Criminal Law,* p. 23.

Federal courts will resort to the common law in the interpretation and application of these statutes.[8] Furthermore, if the statute violated makes use of a common law crime without definition, the common law definition will apply.[9]

Although common law crimes are not punishable or recognized in California, same states adhere to the federal rule previously mentioned. (In California, no act or admission is criminal unless prescribed by the California Penal Code or other statute, ordinance, or municipal, county, or township regulation.) Still, in other states, common law crimes are prosecuted although the act may not be codified. Perkins has stated: "Other statutes purport to define certain offenses, but many of these definitions are so general that they would be practically meaningless without elaborate modern common law explanations without the words and phrases employed."[10] Terms such as *murder* (with malice aforethought), *malice, battery, assault,* and many others would be incomprehensible if it were not for judicial decisions and definitions passed along through decades of "common usage."

Civil and Criminal Laws Distinguished

A fundamental division splits the legal roles of our society into two classes: *criminal* and *civil.* Civil action concerns itself with torts. Criminal law is concerned with crimes—*wrongs committed against society as a whole.* The criminal law does not take into consideration offenses against the moral order unless such acts are prohibited by statute as well. Criminal Law, in general, attempts to rectify private and public wrongs. *A "tort" or "civil injury" is a private wrong done to other persons, property, or reputation by another.* A person suffering this harm must show that the party inflicting it had a duty to do or refrain from doing it. Furthermore, he must show that this duty was violated in a *neglectful* manner and that such an act was the approximate cause suffered.

> A *public* wrong or crime is a breach and a violation of the public rights and duties due to the whole community considered as a community, in its social aggregate capacity. It is a wrong that affects the *whole community and not merely individual members of the community,* and therefore, the public good requires the State to interefere and punish the wrong-doer. The punishment

[8] Perkins, *Criminal Law,* pp. 24-25.

[9] Eldefonso, Coffey, and Sullivan, *Police and the Criminal Law* (Pacific Palisades, Calif.: Goodyear Publishing Co., 1972), pp. 97-98.

[10] Perkins, *Criminal Law,* p. 25.

is imposed for the protection of the public, and not because of the injury to the individual. The latter may seek redress in a Civil action.[11]

It is conceivable, therefore, that in *almost* every crime there is a possibility of a tort action when the victim suffers some harm. If the victim is injured deliberately, the wrong-doer is liable for *criminal* action; if property is stolen and not recovered, civil action will apply; or, if an automobile is stolen and subsequently recovered, *civil* action will also apply. As indicated in Figure 4-1, prosecution, theory and compensation differ according to the crime. Damages in terms of monetary compensation will usually be awarded for the *actual* loss suffered. Also, in some states, punitive damages are awarded (recovery of damages for the sake of example and by way of punishing the wrong-doer) to "teach the wrong-doer a lesson." One writer has stated, however,

> This division which seems so simple at first glance, is in fact exceedingly complex. In the first place, many acts designated as crimes clearly involve a wrong committed against individuals. Typical crimes, such as assault and rape, obviously injure a particular person and only indirectly do they threaten society as a whole. In the second place, many illegal acts may be treated as either crimes or torts, depending on the circumstances of the case. Adultery, for example, may be prosecuted by the State as a crime (although in fact, it is so handled) or it may form the basis for Civil proceedings.[12]

Separate Actions. The two actions—civil and criminal—are separate and distinct. (See Table 4-1.) In a civil court the action is brought by different parties, with different causes of action, and with different types of judgment than would occur in a criminal court. The *criminal* court is "the people against the defendant," while the *civil* action is a "remedy by the victim for loss suffered." A criminal conviction *does not* cancel out the civil action for money damages, however.

Example: A person steals an automobile. The wrong-doer may be prosecuted in criminal court for auto theft; the victim may sue the wrong-doer in civil court for damages in a tort action.
Example: A person strikes another; the injured party may sign a complaint and have the wrong-doer prosecuted for battery in a criminal court; he may also sue in civil court for money damages in a tort action.

[11] Clark and Marshall, *A Treatise on the Law of Crimes;* See also, M. E. Wolfgang, L. Savitz, and J. Johnston, eds., *The Sociology of Crime and Delinquency* (New York: John Wiley & Sons, 1962), pp. 14-18.

[12] G. M. Sykes, *Crime and Society* (New York: Random House, 1956), pp. 15-16.

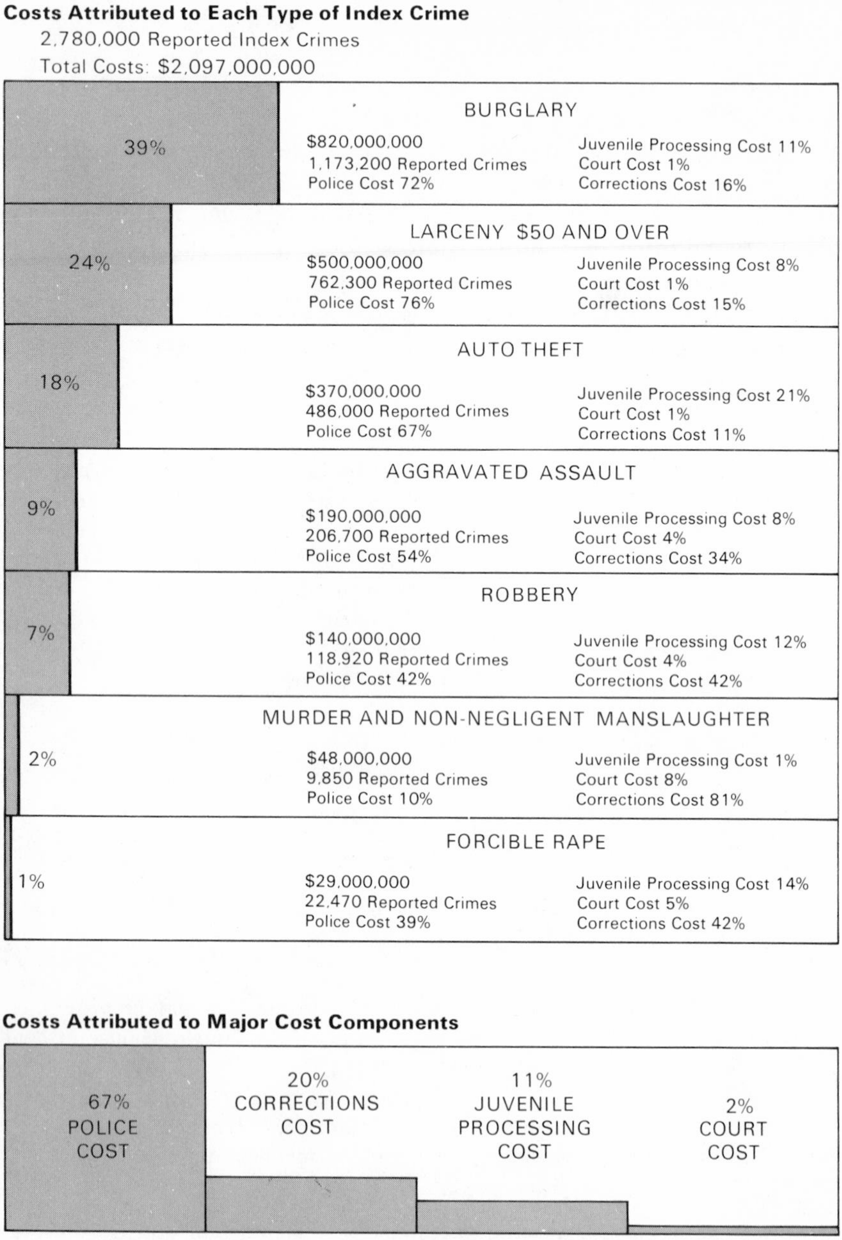

Costs Attributed to Each Type of Index Crime

2,780,000 Reported Index Crimes

Total Costs: $2,097,000,000

39%

BURGLARY

$820,000,000
1,173,200 Reported Crimes
Police Cost 72%
Juvenile Processing Cost 11%
Court Cost 1%
Corrections Cost 16%

24%

LARCENY $50 AND OVER

$500,000,000
762,300 Reported Crimes
Police Cost 76%
Juvenile Processing Cost 8%
Court Cost 1%
Corrections Cost 15%

18%

AUTO THEFT

$370,000,000
486,000 Reported Crimes
Police Cost 67%
Juvenile Processing Cost 21%
Court Cost 1%
Corrections Cost 11%

9%

AGGRAVATED ASSAULT

$190,000,000
206,700 Reported Crimes
Police Cost 54%
Juvenile Processing Cost 8%
Court Cost 4%
Corrections Cost 34%

7%

ROBBERY

$140,000,000
118,920 Reported Crimes
Police Cost 42%
Juvenile Processing Cost 12%
Court Cost 4%
Corrections Cost 42%

2%

MURDER AND NON-NEGLIGENT MANSLAUGHTER

$48,000,000
9,850 Reported Crimes
Police Cost 10%
Juvenile Processing Cost 1%
Court Cost 8%
Corrections Cost 81%

1%

FORCIBLE RAPE

$29,000,000
22,470 Reported Crimes
Police Cost 39%
Juvenile Processing Cost 14%
Court Cost 5%
Corrections Cost 42%

Costs Attributed to Major Cost Components

67% POLICE COST

20% CORRECTIONS COST

11% JUVENILE PROCESSING COST

2% COURT COST

Figure 4-1 Estimated criminal justice system direct operating costs for United States index crimes in 1965. From pp. 262–63 of The President's Commission on Law Enforcement and the Administration of Justice, *The Challenge of Crime in a Free Society* (Washington, D.C.: U.S. Government Printing Office, 1967).

Table 4-1 *Differences between Criminal and Civil Actions*

Crime	*Tort (Civil Wrong)*
A. Prosecutor is "people."	A. Prosecutor is victim.
B. Damages (fines) go into the people's fund.	B. Victim receives damages as compensation.
C. Theory of prosecution is punishment.	C. Theory of prosecution is redress for injury.
D. Few settlements allowed out of court.	D. Most settlements made out of court.
E. Contributory negligence is no defense.	E. Contributory negligence is a good defense.
F. Prosecution cannot usually appeal.	F. Either party may appeal.

As the examples demonstrate, a recovery in civil action for a tort *does not* bar criminal action for the same act.

Distinguishing Characteristics. As previously indicated, the same act may constitute two violations—civil and criminal. Therefore, the act alone (or tendency) does not necessarily dictate whether the act in question is a crime and whether the proceeding therefore is a criminal prosecution. According to Marshall and Clark, "the purpose and nature of the proceeding must be considered." [13]

There is no denying that in the great majority of cases presented to the courts, crimes and torts are very seldom confused. The confusion is eliminated since the methods utilized to initiate court action differ. An offense that is pursued at the discretion of the injured party, or his representative, is a civil injury. An offense which is pursued by the state, or by a subordinate of the state, is a crime. In other words, *civil* proceedings usually commence with a "complaint" by a private person and conclude with an order by the court to make restitution. *Criminal* proceedings are initiated with a grand jury indictment or action by the district attorney, at least in the more serious cases; and the conclusion reached is a "conviction" (guilty) or "acquittal" (not guilty). The confusion, then, between crime and civil tort does not appear in proceedings conducted by the court. Instead, the confusion derives from legislative acts. In other words, what acts will be state designated crimes? As an example:

> If a person enters another person's property wrongfully without committing a breach of peace, the intruder commits a *tort* which does not affect the other members oı the community to such an extent as to require the state

[13] Marshall and Clark, *A Treatise on the Law of Crimes.*

> to punish him. The intruder is merely liable in an action for damages by the individual whose rights the intruder infringed upon. The is *not* a public wrong or a crime, but a mere private wrong (tort).
>
> Reflecting on an identical situation, we see that an incident is a private wrong *if* the intruder maintains a nuisance which disturbs a single individual only, or a Common Law, if the intruder obtains another man's property by merely lying or by intentionally breaking a man's glasses.
>
> If, however, the intruder enters upon another person's property under such circumstances as to render him guilty of breach of public peace, or if the intruder maintains a nuisance on or about a public highway, so as to affect all who pass, or in a thickly settled community, so as to affect the entire community, it is a *public wrong or a crime.* In aforementioned cases the wrong affects the entire community to such an extent that the welfare of the community requires the state to intercede and punish the wrong-doer.

It is important to be cognizant of the distinction between criminal acts and civil torts—many important principles of law are based on it.

> Thus, by reason of the fact that a crime is punished for the protection of the public, and not merely because of the injury to the individual, there are many acts which render the doer criminally responsible, notwithstanding the consent of the individual against whom they are committed. For the same reason, it is ordinarily no defense in a criminal prosecution to show that the individual particularly injured was himself committing, or attempting to commit, an offense, or that he was guilty of negligence, or that he was guilty to contributory negligence, or that he has settled with the wrong-doer, or condoned the offense, or recovered damages in a civil action.[14]

SCOPE OF CRIMINAL LAW

The designation of a particular act as a crime by legislative action within a particular state is more than a matter of applying an official label; it is a social process of far-reaching significance. Sir Henry H. Maine, in his book *Ancient Law,* adamantly stated that a great majority of illegal acts were originally thought of as private wrongs in primitive society and gradually redefined in "discretionary" stages as misdeeds directed against the community.[15] Research in this area has been critical of this theory. The socialist state that the criminal law is merely an additional weapon of the ruling classes for the exploitation of the working class, particularly with reference to criminal law involving property.

[14] Wolfgang, Savitz, and Johnson, *The Sociology of Crime and Delinquency,* pp. 15-16.

[15] Sykes, *Crime and Society,* p. 17.

Still others allege that much of our criminal law is "emotionally" packed; rather than being a stabilizing factor in our society, it is alleged that our criminal law is irrational and serves as a "catalyst" inviting and relieving the emotions of society in legalized retribution. In the words of Professor Robert Park, "We are always passing laws in America. We might as well get up and dance. The laws are largely to relieve emotion, and the legislators are quite aware of that fact." [16]

Although inadequate, all the theories pertaining to origins of law are relatively correct. As previously stated, in order to survive, the community must regulate disagreements and divisiveness. (How often do we hear this term used today?) Yet, the requirements of social survival can hardly rationalize the inordinate amount of acts we now designate as crimes—gambling, cruelty to animals, prostitution, homosexuality, drunkenness, and so forth. Conceivably, influential individuals in society enlist the aid of the state in protecting their vested interests by means of the criminal law. Yet, there are arguments against the belief that the wealthy and affluent protect their 'plunder" by using the "judiciary machinery" to suppress the envious. In the opinion of the noted author and lecturer, Gersham M. Sykes:

> . . . it may be true that many criminal statutes are emotional gestures of an aroused community. Yet much law is created in sober reflection. In short, we cannot be satisfied with any easy, global explanation of why a certain act comes to be designated as crime by the state . . . and bears the imprint of the historical epochs in which it was developed; and the acts which men are willing to view as injurious to the state change as the social structure changes.[17]

As has been said, criminal law exists to maintain social interests as such; but the social interests in the general security, on the one hand, and individual life, on the other hand, continually come into conflict. In criminal law, as everywhere else in law, the problem is one of compromise—of balancing conflicting interests and securing as much general safety as possible with the least sacrifice of other interests. The most insistent and fundamental social interests are involved in criminal law.

In the process of adjusting human relations and conduct in order to eliminate friction and waste, the legal order often deals with controversies between individuals. Where their claims or wants or desires overlap, the legal order seeks some sort of reconciliation through a system of rules and principles administered in tribunals. It also has to

[16] Originally quoted in E. H. Sutherland, *Principles of Criminology,* rev. by D. E. Cressy (Philadelphia, Penn.: J. B. Lippincott, 1955), p. 10.

[17] Sykes, *Crime and Society,* p. 17.

deal with certain acts or conduct which run counter to the interests of a functioning, civilized society. To restrain these persons and to deter others who might follow their example, to correct antisocial modes of conduct as far as possible and to further the social interests, the law imposes a system of duties upon all persons in society and enforces these duties through the penal system. *The part of the legal system that defines these duties and prescribes how they shall be enforced through prosecution and penal treatment is criminal law.*

Effectively Enforced Laws

Laws are effectively enforced when they represent the moral concensus of the society. When there is a general lack of agreement, effective enforcement is unlikely. One need only refer to the classic illustration of the Eighteenth Amendment which made it illegal to manufacture, sell, or transport alcoholic beverages in the United States. Needless to say, this particular law did not reflect the mores of the majority of the citizens—certainly moral concensus was lacking. Liquor was considered, by the majority, to be an important part of our society, and it was not difficult to locate a source of supply. Thus, as one author has put it:

> Law is more or less a systematic body of generalized rules, balanced between the fiction of permanence and the fact of change, governing specifically defined relationships and situations, and employing force or the threat of force in defined or limited ways. The body of rules which make up law in some varying measure secures the compliance of a national society, or some jurisdictional heart of it by means of concept of legitimacy. *In other words, law must be regarded by a clear majority as the ultimate and repository of social control for their total society.*[18]

Of course, no specific law ever achieves universal compliance; there are rebels, criminals, reformers, and subverters in every society. However, although a law with *no* moral backing would almost certainly fail to be enforced, a law can be enforced with far less than unanimous moral support if the dedication of its supporters exceeds that of its evaders. Since crime is an act which the group views as threatening to its fundamental interests, society makes the following assumptions, thus justifying a formal reaction to restrain the violator:

1. *Criminal laws derived from or are a part of the larger body of cultural norms.* The character and interests of special groups within the popula-

[18] A. W. Green, *Sociology: An Analysis of Life in Modern Society* (4th ed.) (New York: McGraw-Hill, 1964), p. 532. Italics added.

tion influence criminal legislation. Therefore, the subjects selected for legal sanctions and the nature of the sanctions directed against the transgressors are a reflection of the identical social pressures whereby the group's feelings are "molded" into rules of behavior and, subsequently, into group resistance to the violator.

2. In contrast to the legal definition, crime—utilizing the social concept—is defined rather *broadly*. The *social concept* views crime as anti-social behavior that runs against the group interest which rules of group behavior —including codified law (penal law in each state)—aren't designed to support. Such a definition, needless to say, includes behavior (variety and quantity) beyond the scope of criminal law (as legally defined).
3. *There is only limited interest (directly) in the phenomenon of crime per se, but a great deal of attention is focused on its implications for personality or social deviations.* If the characteristics of the criminal personalities and their social situations are to be studied effectively, the scientist must be free to select and qualify the data appropriate to his specific research.[19]

The Object of Crime: Person, Property, and State

We tend to assume that most crimes are perpetrated against the *person* —he is the victim. It is true that most violent and most serious crimes, which are therefore the most publicized, are those against a person—homicide, assault, rape, and battery being the principal crimes. By far, however, the largest number of crimes each year are not against the person but against property—including robbery, burglary, arson, auto theft, and the like. According to the latest statistics (Uniform Crime Reports, 1973), crimes against property "far outdistance" crimes against the person in both the acts committed and property offenses "not cleared by arrests." Finally, there is a rather small but very important class of crimes against the state or government—treason, subversion, or sedition, and other forms of interference with government authority.

SUMMARY

In this chapter, we have discussed the primary responsibility of law enforcement, which is the provision of personal safety and property security for those members of society who conform to "the law." This chapter further indicates that, although law enforcement agencies are expected to carry out their primary responsibilities, peace officers are

[19] E. H. Johnson, *Crime, Correction, and Society* (Homewood, Ill.: The Dorsey Press, 1968), p. 13. Italics added.

Figure 4-2a & b During the past five years, law enforcement has been made more difficult because of mass disturbances. Protection of life and property during riots has placed a great deal of pressure on police agencies. Photos courtesy of the San Francisco Police Department, San Francisco, Ca.

also expected to understand laws to which there is conformity. Since peace officers are responsible for enforcing society's laws, they should know enough about such laws to determine violations and recognize the divisions.

We have noted that it would be impossible to discuss enforcement and criminal law without referring to the *common law* system. Accordingly, the principles of common law, initially developed in England, were explored. The common law system, as pointed out in this chapter, is the process of continuously developing law by reference to precedent. As such, the development of common law is a result of judicial decisions. The distinguishing characteristics of common law have been compared to tort or civil injury. As indicated here, criminal law is concerned with crimes—wrongs committed against society as a whole. The criminal law does not take into consideration those offenses against the moral order unless such acts are prohibited by statutes as well. A tort or civil injury is a private wrong done by another to one's person, property, or reputation. Differences regarding the process for court action in criminal law and in tort or civil injury were discussed.

In the area of criminal law the designation of a particular act as a crime by legislative action within a particular state is more than a matter of applying an official label; it is a social process of far-reaching significance. This particular social process is discussed in this chapter under the caption "Scope of Criminal Law." In this chapter, we have also presented the philosophy of enforcing laws. The law enforcement philosophy expressed here is that individuals conforming to society's regulations are entitled to *personal safety.* This philosophy also entitles the conformer to *property security,* but only to the degree that a given society permits the individual to acquire rights. Laws are effectively enforced when they represent the moral concensus of the society. When there is a general lack of agreement, effective enforcement is unlikely. An example of this is the Eighteenth Amendment which made it illegal to manufacture, sell, or transport alcoholic beverages in the United States. This particular law did not reflect the mores of the majority of the citizens, and, therefore, the particular law was ineffective.

The *social definition* of crime involves the concept that criminal activities are threatening to society's fundamental interests; this attitude justifies a formal reaction to restrain the violator. Along these lines, society assumes that (1) criminal laws are derived from or are a part of the larger body of cultural norms; (2) in contrast to the legal definition, the social concept of crime is defined rather broadly; and (3) there is only limited interest in the phenomena of crime *per se,* but a great deal of attention is focused on its implications for personal or social deviations. These areas have received attention in this chapter since the authors feel it is pertinent to an understanding of the legal and social components in the definition of crime.

The latter part of this chapter reviewed the object of crime. It is mentioned that although crimes against a *person* is perhaps the most publicized and brings forth the greatest degree of wrath on the part of society, in actuality the largest number of crimes each year is brought against *property*.

QUESTIONS

1. Discuss the common law system.
2. Describe the manner in which civil and criminal actions are brought into court. What are the differences?
3. In this chapter, Arnold W. Green gives a general definition of law. In your own words, describe the definition.

ANNOTATED REFERENCES

CAHN, E., ed. "Criminal Guilt" in *Social Meaning of Legal Concepts,* Vol. 2. New York: N.Y. Univ. Press, 1966. A new, concise, and up-to-date work on the law and judicial and postjudicial systems of justice in the United States.

CLARK, W. L., and MARSHALL, W. L. *A Treatise on The Law of Crimes,* 7th ed. Chicago, Ill.: Callaghan & Co., 1967. Chapter 1 discusses primitive law in depth as well as the scope of criminal law. Presented in nontechnical language.

ELDEFONSO, E.; COFFEY, A.; and GRACE, R. C. *Principles of Law Enforcement.* New York: John Wiley & Sons, 1968. The chapters pertaining to "Scope of the Crime Problem" and "Legal Aspects of Law Enforcement" introduce the student to legal terminology and criminal law in a clear and concise fashion.

JOHNSON, E. H. *Crime, Correction, and Society.* Homewood, Ill.: The Dorsey Press, 1968. This book draws on theory to promote understanding of crime causation, the modes of societal responses to crime, and the relationships between crime and patterns of legitimate society.

MICHAEL, J., and WECHSLER, H. *Criminal Law and Its Administration.* Chicago, Ill.: Foundation Press, 1940. Excellent resource for cases, statutes, and commentaries.

PERKINS, R. M. *Criminal Law.* Brooklyn, N.Y.: Foundation Press, 1957. Chapter 1 on "Scope, Purpose, Definition, and Classification" is a classic in introducing the student to the field of criminal law.

Skolnick, J. H. *Justice Without Trial: Law Enforcement in a Democratic Society.* New York: John Wiley & Sons, 1966. An excellent discussion of police attitudes toward criminal law. See Chapter 9.

Tappan, P. W. *Crime, Justice and Correction.* New York: McGraw-Hill, 1960. Chapter 1 discusses "Elements of Crime" (pp. 10-14). Chapters 10 through 13 orient enforcement of law in the legally defined judicial process.

Westbrook, J. E. "Mens Rea in the Juvenile Court." *Journal of Family Law,* Vol. 5. University of Louisville School of Law, 1965. This article (pp. 121-29) discusses *mens rea* in its historical perspective and introduces the reader to the concept of free will.

5

Legal Aspects of Law Enforcement and the Judiciary Process

Within recent times, there has been a tremendous expansion of the area of human conduct regulated by the criminal law. In early days this law concerned itself only with seriously antisocial conduct. Social institutions such as the church and the home were relied upon to regulate conduct in other respects. The present tendency is to place the entire burden upon the criminal law and the judiciary process; and while this shift has been taking place, changes in the socioeconomic structure of the community have created many new conflicts. The result has been a constant increase of public interest in the *administration of criminal justice.* With this increased interest, however, the average layman still has no idea of the criminal justice system—specifically, he has little idea of the purpose of criminal law and the American judiciary process.

> The tremendous growth of the nation in population and industrial development and the accompanying changes of urbanization, problems are created more rapidly than solutions could be found. Other processes of government, particularly in the area of administrative control, have developed much more rapidly than the processes of administering our system of criminal justice. The great trend toward centralization of governmental authority and particularly the increasing impact of the power of the federal government have brought forth almost revolutionary legal controls over commerce, industry, labor, and almost every other aspect of our national life. In fact, the ad-

ministration of criminal justice can be described as the unique exception to this general trend.[1]

In this field of government we find a system whose most notable characteristic is its decentralization. It is a system which has remained static and almost completely unchanged in many of our jurisdictions since its early beginnings. Obviously, this stunted development has impaired the efficiency of the system and has left our society with inadequate defenses against crime.

Unlike the controls designed to restrain it, crime does not remain static. It has grown and expanded until, in some of its most extreme developments, those engaged in it have been able to challenge the authority of government itself.

> On the other hand, it is not correct to assume that the failure of the administration of criminal justice to adequately cope with crime has meant that its processes must bear lightly on the individual citizen. Unfortunately, whether or not the law keeps pace with modern developments, any government must fulfill its function of law and order. In doing so it necessarily employs the tools that are at hand. If they are inadequate, the result is improvisation, the adoption and continued use of extra-legal methods, and the use of administrative procedures which often afford scant protection for basic human rights.[2]

Punishment is often considered the purpose of criminal law and the judiciary process, but this is quite erroneous. *The purpose of criminal law and the subsequent judiciary process is to define socially intolerable conduct and to hold conduct within limits which are reasonably acceptable from the social point of view.*

THE INFLUENCE OF JUSTICE ON LAW

A chapter dealing with the legal aspects of law enforcement and the judiciary process requires at least some mention of the influence of the consequences of law violation—such "consequences" frequently serving as a limited definition of "justice." In the nineteenth century the trend in penology shifted from punishing the individual to reforming the individual. Changes in the past two centuries have evolved the reformatory, and ultimately, the notion of parole. Moving further from the early tra-

1 *The Administration of Criminal Justice in the United States, Plan For Survey* (Chicago, Ill.: American Bar Foundation, 1955), pp. 2-3.

2 *The Administration of Criminal Justice . . .*, pp. 2-3.

dition of transporting criminals to the American colonies or to Australia as punishment, England and the United States and, indeed, most of the world are seemingly appraching an era of rehabilitation that virtually excludes the concept of punishment.

Although the specific origins of parole, pardons, restoration of prisoners' rights, and probation appear to have little direct effect on enforcing criminal law and the judiciary process, collectively these processes appear to greatly influence the interpretation of the laws to be enforced. It is noted that underlying the confusion of frequently conflicting codes and statutes is the additional confusion of conflicting interpretation—conflicts often pivoting on the consequences of law violation rather than on the codified violation itself. The influence of "consequences" is a subtle, yet significant influence on the relationship between criminal law, its enforcement, and the judiciary process.

DEFINITION OF CRIME

The matter of definition is of the major importance in the whole field of criminal law. It is important simply because our criminal philosophy does not permit a conviction for what was not clearly recognized as a crime at the time it was committed. A statute which purports to provide for punishment without making sufficiently precise just what is punishable is held to be "invalid for vagueness." It is therefore important to start with a clear understanding of what constitutes a true definition.

The two major divisions of law are the *common law* and *codified law* (see Chapter 4). It would be difficult—if not impossible—to discuss the essential elements of crime without reference to common law. Thus, at the risk of being repetitive, a review of this system seems appropriate in order to help the student grasp the significance of a thoroughly integrated code of laws.

As previously stated, our criminal law is inherited in part from the common law which originated in Germanic territories and then expanded in England. The principles of the common law of England are still applied in some of our states, although some changes have been made by statute or through the interpretations of our courts. Common law is the process through which law continuously develops by reference to precedent. This development is the result of judicial decisions; certain accepted principles or combinations of principles are accepted and then developed, qualified, and expanded further by the magistrates.

Keeping this description in mind, we could also cite R. M. Perkins' definition:

> All of that part of the authoritative materials, used to guide and direct the judicial and administrative organs of the state in the performance of their official functions, which is not found in legislative enactment or written constitution is called the common law.[3]

In the course of time, the law developed in this manner; as it was felt to be inadequate or unsatisfactory, additions and changes were made by legislative enactment.

Under the Constitution of the United States, as interpreted by the Supreme Court, no misdeed is punishable by federal courts merely because it is recognized as a common law crime. This does not imply that there is no federal common law of crimes. Nothing is to be punishable as a federal crime unless the appropriate authority can be found in some act of Congress; but if Congress has declared some misdeed to be a crime and has provided penalty for such an act, the federal courts will resort to the common law in the interpretation and application of the statute. The rule in some of the states is similar to the federal rule in that most common law offenses are included in the statutes of the states. At times, a statute merely specifies a penalty for an offense. With the exception of determining the punishment, the courts must rely upon the common law as if criminal laws had never been adopted. Other statutes purport to define certain offenses, but many of these definitions are so general that they would be practically meaningless without elaborate explanations of the words and phrases employed.

What, then, is the legal definition of crime as it has been employed in practice, not only in our courts of law, but in criminology as well? A true definition is made up of three parts: (1) *the term,* (2) *the genus,* and (3) *the differentia.* The term is the subject of the definition—the word or phrase to be defined; the genus is a category of classification—a class or group ranking beneath a family and above species; the differentia is the attribute or characteristic by which one species or genus is distinguished from the other.[4] In other words, true definition must give: (1) the word or phrase to be defined—the term; (2) the placement of this thing in a group of like things—the genus; and (3) the peculiarity which distinguishes it from other like things—the differentia.

In essence, a crime is any act or admission prohibited by public law for the protection of the public and made punishable by the state in a judicial proceeding in its own name. Crime may also be defined as "an intentional act or admission in violation of criminal law (statutory and

[3] R. M. Perkins, *Criminal Law* (Mineola, New York: Foundation Press, 1957), p. 23.

[4] Perkins, *Criminal Law,* p. 6.

case law), committed without the offense or justification and sanctioned by the state as a felony or misdemeanor."[5]

Criminal law does not represent the final moral judgment of society. It does, however, restrict and regulate behavior—social behavior compounded in the heat of passion, emotions and cool rationality—sometimes creating what most men find morally reprehensible and sometimes subject to bitter dispute.[6] Criminal law usually strives to protect the safety and welfare of the community as a whole. On occasion, it serves a limited interest group. It should not surprise us that a crime—a violation of these rules—is complex and difficult to explain.

It is important to note that, to warrant public prosecution, the legal definition given above assumes the violation of a previously existing law. This principle of *nullum crimen sine leg* or *nulum poena sine lege* (the coordinate principle) prohibits sanctions in the absence of penal law and implies that penal statutes should be precisely construed.

As indicated by the legal definition, crime concerns transgressions against the public order rather than against moral or private orders. It will soon be seen that mere criminal intent is not punishable, although it is believed to be punishable under the general theory of Christian morality. Even an act, or an admission to act, accompanied by criminal intent is still not a crime unless it offends the general public rather than a private person. After considering definitions of crime, let us next examine the principles of criminal law.

Principles of Criminal Law

Despite the ultimate influence of cultural change, law is, in fact, more conservative than some other forms of social control. There has been much criticism of lags in legal standards. Such conservatism is generally characteristic of the common law, since it is based upon judicial decisions; state and federal constitutions which express well-established rules of social policy are also conservative in character.[7] It is possible, in the Anglo-American system of criminal justice, to distinguish certain principles of criminal law which stand out as standards of conservatism. These have remained fairly constant for many decades but are still considered essential to a fair system of law. Tappan and Taft have written extensively about conservatism and the principles of criminal law:

[5] P. Tappan, *Crime, Justice, and Corrections* (New York: McGraw-Hill, 1960), p. 10.

[6] G. Sykes, *Crime and Society* (New York: Random House, 1956), p. 21.

[7] Tappan, *Crime, Justice, and Corrections,* pp. 22-24.

1. The doctrine of *nullum crimen sine lege or no ex post facto* legislation still exists. There can be no crime without a statute that quite specifically forbids the behavior involved. It is considered a basic right that acts which are forbidden and which can lead to retribution shall be *known* and that no person can be punished at a later stage for behavior which was not criminal when committed.
2. A person is presumed to have some knowledge of the law. However, whether or not he is familiar with the statutes—within a system of justice according to law—the individual must be held accountable for violations. In fairness, however, the rules must be reasonable, stable, and clear as guides to conformity. This principle, pertaining mainly to statutory law, is strengthened by the Common Law rule of precedent that guides court decisions, the doctrine of *stare decisis* (let the weight of decisions stand and not disturb settled things).
3. The principle of *equality before the law* is intended to eliminate discrimination based on race, religion, and social class.
4. *Extenuating circumstances:* There are certain obvious situations or circumstances that directly relate to the violation which may be considered by the court and influence its disposition of a case.
5. *An attempt to commit crime* is viewed (all circumstances being equal) as less serious than a crime consummated. Therefore, punishment for an attempt is not as severe.
6. *Complicity:* Although an accomplice may be as guilty of the law violation as the principal party, certain specific relationships are essential to complicity.
7. In sentencing a criminal who has been involved in a multitude of offenses prior to his arrest, it is usually customary to punish him for the most serious one of which he is convicted. *Recidivism* (repeated convictions) may, however, under the "habitual criminal" acts result in punishment of greater severity.
8. Finally, the principle of the *Statute of Limitations* has remained fairly constant for many years. In essence, the "limitation statute" in criminal law provides that, except for serious crimes (murder or other capital offenses), prosecution may not be initiated after certain specified periods (usually dictated by law) has elapsed.[8]

Sources of Law

In the United States there is a specific separation of powers which emanates from the federal Constitution. The separation of powers

[8] D. R. Taft, *Criminology* (New York: Macmillan, 1956), pp. 6-8 and 377-78. See also Tappan, *Crime, Justice, and Corrections*, p. 23.

doctrine prescribes the duties of each major branch of government. The *legislative branch* makes the law; the *executive branch* administers and enforces the law; and the *judicial branch* interprets the law. Whenever the law must be changed because of the changing desires or needs of society, the machinery for change is readily available through the representation of the populace by federal and state legislators. If the law is not changed when society demands it, the populace may either take the law into its own hands or totally disregard the law. However, law is the only basis upon which an orderly society may be built.

The basic law of the United States is the federal Constitution. Congress enacts statutes which provide guidelines and/or sanctions for activities which involve federal crimes and other activities which directly or indirectly affect areas over which the government has jurisdiction. This authority and power stems from the Constitution. The basis for any *state law* is its constitution. Unfortunately, some constitutions are overburdened with provisions which should be codified rather than placed at the constitutional level.

The legislature of each state has the power and authority to enact statutes. Probably the most difficult task of any legislature is to codify the laws into separate headings. Thousands of laws flow from the floor of the legislature every year to be recorded and printed as matters of public record. Codification is the procedure by which statutes are placed into codes. These codes represent most of the written law in any given state. Aside from the written law, judges make "new law" by interpreting statutes when deciding cases. Actually, *the court does not make law.* That power and authority is reserved for the legislative body. However, the court may announce its interpretation of a given statute and that interpretation will, if given at the appellate level, constitute the basis on which the populace may conduct its activities.

Stare Decisis. Stare Decisis is the rule which requires a judge to follow precedent. Otherwise the defendent in a civil or criminal case would never know whether or not his activities were lawful. However, the time may come when the demand for change requires a reversal or modification of prior case law. In those instances, the appellate courts have overruled prior decisions.

Administratice Law. Other types of law exist which stem from administrative agencies. *An administrative agency is a unique body which makes, interprets, and enforces the law.* Most of these agencies are subject to judicial review. If an administrative body feels the need to make a ruling, it will give public notice of its intention to make the proposed change or addition. After public hearings, the administrative body adopts the rule. The administrative body may also make policy decisions, not normally subject to judicial review, establishing health or safety standards or minimum working rights. After the administrative body has made either type of law, it acts as a court in interpreting and applying its own law. After interpretation of the law by the administrative body, the same body may enforce the law by contempt citations which carry as much weight as a formal court proceeding.

CLASSIFICATION OF CRIMES

The common law of England divided crime into three major groups: (1) treason, (2) felony, and (3) misdemeanor. Treason, in turn, has been divided into: (1) high treason and (2) petty treason.

High treason, in the words of Blackstone, is a term applied when "loyalties arrears its crest to attack even majesty itself." [9] In the ancient common law it consisted of killing the king, promoting revolt in the kingdom or the armed forces, or counterfeiting the great seal. A tendency to enlarge the scope of the offense by analogy led to such uncertainty that an act of Parliament was required to define it. The Senate of Treason enacted in 1350 specified exactly what should constitute high treason including among certain other wrongs a manifested intent to kill the king, queen, or prince; levying war against the king; or adhering to his enemies, giving them aid and comfort.

Petty treason was based upon grave breach of an inferior allegiance. Examples would have been malicious homicide such as killing a husband or wife, a servant killing a master or mistress, or a clergyman killing a prelate. The purpose of distinguishing this offence from high treason was to evoke a particularly brutal punishment. Petty treason, however, was abolished in England in 1828.

Felony, in the general adaptation of English law, comprised every species of crime which occasioned the forfeiture of land and goods. Under the theory of English common law a felon had forfeited life and member and all that he had. But, it is "better to define a felony in terms of an offense punishable by forfeiture." [10] Although the list of felonies recognized by the English common law was very small, it was greatly enlarged by statute. And although the true criteria of a felony was forfeiture, enlargements by acts of Parliament in the early days tended to emphasize capital punishment as the chief punishment of felony.

[9] W. Blackstone, *Commentaries on the Laws of England* (Dobbs Ferry, N.Y.: Oceana, 1966).

[10] J. Michael and H. Wechsler, *Criminal Law and Its Administration* (Mineola, N.Y.: The Foundation Press, 1940), p. 12.

Misdemeanor was the label ultimately applied to all offenses other than treason or felony. Acts *malum in se* included, in addition to all felonies, all branches of public order, injuries to persons and property, outrages concerning public decency and morals, and breaches of official duty when done willingly and corruptly. Acts of *mala prohibita* included any matter forbidden or commanded by statute, but not otherwise wrong.

Two comments are in order at this point: first, this distinction is limited to the misdemeanor group and has no application to treason or felony. Second, an offense *malum prohibitum* does not represent social harm which has been defined and made punishable by law, but rather is forbidden even though it is not otherwise wrong. It represents a situation in which a regulation was deemed wise and a penalty was imposed for purpose of enforcement.[11]

Statutes in this country today currently divide crimes into two classes: 1) felonies, and (2) misdemeanors. Usually the detriment is the nature of the penalty that may be imposed. Distinguishing felony from misdemeanor generally follows one of two patterns; the distinction is based upon either type of institution in which the offender may be incarcerated or the length of term which may be imposed.

Elements of a Crime: Act and Intent

It is a basic principle of the American system, as well as most other systems of criminal justice, that every crime is composed of two elements —a *criminal act* and *criminal intent.* Neither an act alone or an intent alone is sufficient to constitute a crime. *The two must concur to establish criminal responsibility.* It would be futile and dangerous for the state to attempt to punish individuals merely for a subjective state of mind or for conduct engaged in by mistake. Deeply ingrained in human nature is a tendency to distinguish intended results from accidental happenings. This is the everyday experience of the man on the street. One who has been greatly benefited by the act of another person will have different feelings toward the other person depending on whether the good act was accidental or intentional. Similarly, one who has been injured by another's actions will not have the same feeling of resentment if the act was accidental rather than intentional. "I didn't mean to" is used so frequently that it is often one of the early sentences of small children.

[11] Michael and Wechsler, *Criminal Law and Its Administration,* p. 11.

A mental element is required in all crimes. *Mens rea* is the term commonly given to the necessary mental element. This state of mind is called intent, and intent must be present. The specific intent obviously differs with the crime involved. It is important, when considering this term, not to confuse it with motive. *Motive* is not an element of a crime, although it may be used as evidence in deciding whether the defendant committed the act.

Many crimes require a *specific intent* to do an act in a certain manner or with a certain objective. This specific intent must be proved as a fact and cannot be proved from the doing of the act. Where specific intent is required, it must be particularly designed in the definition of the crime itself. An example might be the case of burglary; in such instances, the defendant must enter the structure with the intent to commit a felony therein. This is a specific intent; unless the defendant entered the structure with the intent to commit a felony therein, he is not guilty of the crime of burglary.

General intent is the name applied to the mental element of the crime when no special state of mind is required. General intent is of two types. (1) Crimes requiring *mens rea;* this crime requires that the state of mind and the intent are elements of the crime and must be proved. This has been called *malum in se.* In the absence of proof of this bad state of mind, the defendant cannot be found guilty of a crime. (2) Crimes not requiring *mens rea* are called *malum prohibitum.* The defendant may be entirely innocent of any intentional wrong but may still be guilty of the crime simply because he has done the act in question. It is important to remember that these so-called crimes are all statutory in origin. They derive from the power of the legislature (police power) to regulate certain types of conduct in the public interest.[12] These concepts may be better amplified with the following example. A statute states that anyone who has in his possession an automobile with the motor serial numbers taken off for the purpose of concealment is guilty of a misdemeanor. A defendant acquired an auto from person A, who had removed the numbers for the purpose of concealment. The defendant was found guilty of this crime even though he did not intend to commit the crime because this statute requires only the completion of the act and does not require a bad state of mind. The following is a second example. Defendant Jones was driving his automobile on the highway and believed the speed limit to be 65 mph. In reality, however, the speed limit was only 55 mph. The defendant was stopped by the Highway Patrol and given a ticket for speeding. He was found guilty be-

[12] Holmes, *The Common Law,* Vol. 3, ALR, 1881, p. 743.

cause this type of police regulation does not require *mens rea* and doing the act is sufficient to constitute a crime.

The area of intent can be examined even further with the handling of the *doctrine of transferred intent.* Whenever the accused undertakes the prohibited act with the requisite wrongful state of mind, but the act results in the evasion of an interest which was not intended or forseeable, the accused will remain criminally liable—if, and only if, the injuries inflicted require a different *mens rea.*[13] Thus, in general, it may be said that if A intends to injure B and in the effort inflicts injury on person C, A is guilty of the same kind of act (involving the same *mens rea* requirement as if his aim had been more accurate).

In certain crimes, negligence may be substituted for the general *mens rea.* Criminal liability may thus be imposed if the act was done nonvolitionally but with such lack of care as to constitute criminal negligence. The most frequent examples of crimes in which criminal negligence may be a basis for criminal conviction are assault and battery, murder, and manslaughter.

In essence then, intent includes those consequences which (1) represent the purpose for which an act is done (regardless of likelihood of occurrence) or (2) are known to be fairly certain to result regardless of desire.

THE JUDICIARY PROCESS AFTER AN ARREST

The field of criminal law would be superfluous if there were no method of bringing the violator to the attention of the authorities to answer for his offense. The key to this segment of the system is an efficient judiciary process. Insofar as criminal procedure is concerned, the process of bringing a criminal to justice is set in motion by an *arrest.* An arrest, as the term is used in criminal law, signifies the apprehension or detention of a person in order that he may be forthcoming to answer for an alleged or supposed crime. An arrest on a criminal charge may be made up upon a warrant, although a warrant may not be necessary. In most situations an arrest is usually made without a warrant. Any peace officer or private person to whom a valid warrant is lawfully directed may arrest the person named in the warrant.

Prosecution for a felony commences by *grand jury indictment* or by *information.* Prosecution for a misdemeanor is normally commenced by the issuance of a complaint.

[13] Holmes, *The Common Law,* p. 822.

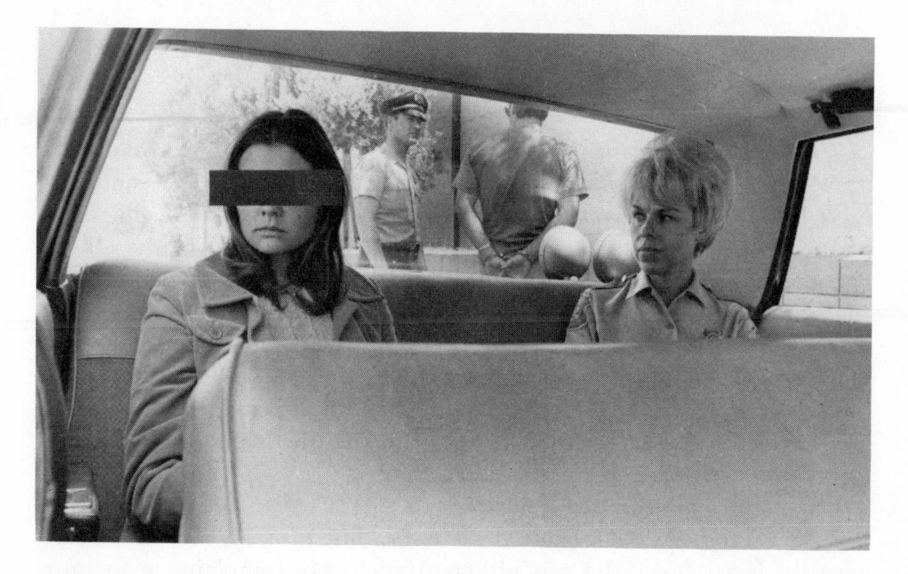

Figure 5-1 An arrest initiates the process of criminal justice. Photo courtesy of the Santa Clara County Sheriff's Department, San Jose, Ca.

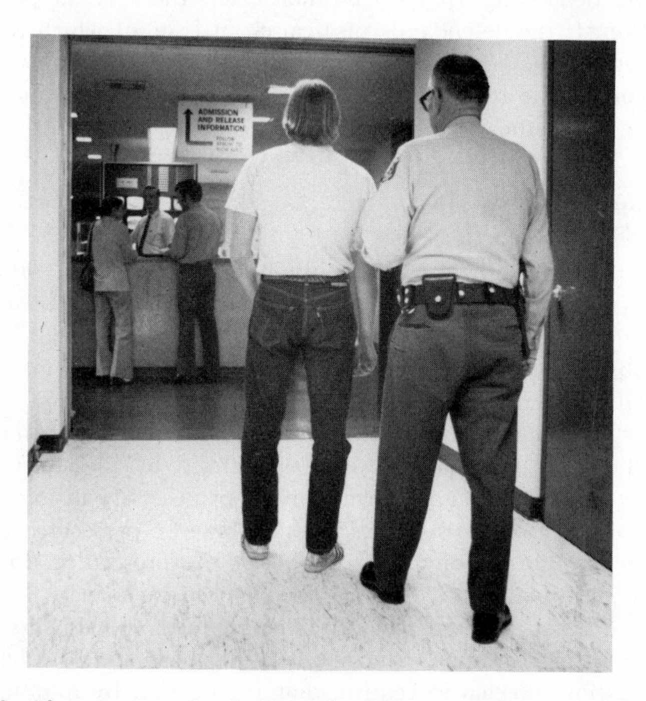

Figure 5-2 After an arrest has been made, suspects are usually transferred to a holding facility, i.e., jail or juvenile hall. Photo courtesy of the public Information Office, Santa Clara County, Len Pacheco.

Misdemeanors and Complaints

When the defandant has allegedly committed a misdemeanor, the basis for prosecution after arrest is a written complaint. The complaint must be in writing, sworn to and signed by the complainant. The complaint must allege the commission of an offense, the aim of the alleged defendant, and the time, place, and jurisdiction of the court from which the complaint issues. A complaint is normally made by a citizen. However, the district attorney's office issues the complaint against the defendant. The victim of the crime *is not* the party who alleges commission of the crime by defendant. The *people of the state* are the proper plaintiffs in a criminal prosecution. The victim of the crime can only be a complaining witness.

A misdemeanor complaint justifies the arrest of the defendant so he can be arraigned and required to enter his plea. When the misdemeanant is arraigned, he may either plead to the complaint or demure. A demurer is a legal attack on the face of the complaint arguing that the complaint does not state facts sufficient to constitute a cause of action against the defendant. In misdemeanor cases, there is no preliminary examination. If the defendant's plea raises an issue of which reasonable men may disagree, a trial is conducted in a municipal court or other inferior court. The defendant is then either acquitted or found guilty and sentenced by the same court.

Misdemeanors and Felonies

The prosecution may also begin by an information. *An information applies to misdemeanors which do not require the return of an indictment.* The information is normally signed by the state attorney and sworn to by him or by any member of his staff. The information must comply with the same requirements as the indictment.

Under the common law an information was used in misdemeanant cases. (All felony prosecutions were commenced by indictment.) However, under modern law, an information is not necessary in misdemeanor cases. In fact, in twenty-two states, felonies may be prosecuted by either indictment or information at the option of the prosecutor. In most of these states, criminal proceedings are commenced exclusively by information. A few states and the federal system require indictments to commence felony prosecutions. The majority of those states which utilize the information alternative require that prosecution by information be commenced only after preliminary examination.

Figure 5-3 Arraignment of a misdemeanor in a municipal court. Photo courtesy of the District Attorney's Office, Santa Clara County and Dick Cox, Public Information Office, Santa Clara County, Ca.

Felonies which are tried in superior court must be prosecuted by indictment or information. If the district attorney elects to proceed by information, formal criminal procedures are commenced by filing the complaint in the inferior court in the county where the offense was committed. In the great majority of cases, the police officer gives a copy of the police report and arrest report to the deputy district attorney who prepares written felony complaints. If the facts as stated would support a felony prosecution, the complaint is prepared and filed with the magistrate. Technically, the complaint is not a plea. It is only a deposition of facts submitted by an informant and sufficient to constitute the basis for a felony prosecution. After the complaint is filed with the magistrate or judge in an inferior court, the magistrate or court judge may issue an arrest warrant if he concludes that a crime has been committed and that there is reasonable cause to believe the defendant committed it.

Felonies

The district attorney may not wish to proceed with a felony prosecution on the basis of the information. He has the right to proceed by indictment. An indictment is an accusation in writing, returned by a *grand jury* to the superior court, charging a person with a criminal offense. Theoretically, an indictment is a formal charge brought by the state acting through the *grand jury.*

Function of the Grand Jury. In order to fully understand the nature of an indictment, the student must realize the function and purpose of a grand jury. A grand jury is an investigative body which is part of the judicial system. Its primary function is to initiate prosecution by indictment when the district attorney elects that method of prosecution. The grand jury *does not* determine the guilt or innocence of a defendant. The only question it must answer is whether the defendant should be brought to trial. The grand jury hears all the evidence placed before it, and it must return an indictment when, in its collective judgment, a conviction by the trial jury would result. This does not mean the jury trial must return a guilty verdict. The grand jury must determine *only* that the defendant should stand trial because there is reason to believe he has committed a felony. If an *indictment* is returned before the defendant has been taken into custody, a *bench warrant* is issued for his arrest. If the defendant is already in custody, no secrecy surrounds the grand jury proceedings. If substantial cause exists, the state may desire to arrest the defendant before the indictment. If this is so, it must follow the complaint procedure described previously. A bench warrant is issued by the court, and the court determines bail. However, the grand jury may make a recommendation as to the amount of bail that should be set for a particular offense. The court then uses its own discretion in following the recommendation.

The grand jury is a branch of the judicial system. It must act consciously and without fear of the state or court interfering with its duties and obligations. Neither the court nor the state can limit its investigation. It has the power to remove defendants from public office, to inquire into the condition and maintenance of public prisons within the county, to examine the books and records of all county offices and make reports of its findings, to issue subpoenas for the attendance of witnesses, and to require the presentation of books, documents, and other evidence as aids in the discharge of its duties. The grand jury does not have to wait for the prosecuting attorney to commence the proceeding. It may bring to trial anyone against whom the state has neglected to commence proceedings. Grand juries also have the power to grant general or special immunity to witnesses who refuse to testify. If the witness still refuses to testify after the grand jury grants immunity, he is held in civil contempt. This means the witness is jailed until he decides to comply with the order and answer the questions put to him. Criminal contempt is an affront to the court itself and commands an independent sentence regardless of compliance after sentencing.

It is not unusual for law enforcement officers to be called before the grand jury to testify. Under the *federal system,* an indictment may be based entirely on hearsay. But the majority of state courts follow the rule that the evidence presented must be legally competent (admissable in a criminal trial). Witnesses, including police officers and in some instances defendants, do not have the right to counsel. The grand jury is an investigative body, not an adjudicative body; nevertheless, the privilege against self-incrimination is available to any witness, including the accused.

Arraignment

If a complaint has been filed against a person and it is decided that he is to be prosecuted, he must be arraigned. *The purpose of an arraignment is to accord the accused an opportunity to know the nature of the charge against him and to answer whether he is guilty or not.*

One group of courts maintains that failure to arraign a defendant and to take his plea of guilt or innocence at or before the beginning of his trial invalidates the trial and a new trial must be granted. Others maintain, however, that the trial, the verdict or conviction, and the judgment stand regardless. Under the former view, failure to arraign a defendant accused of a felony precludes conviction. When the charge is for a misdemeanor, it is usually held that arraignment is unnecessary.

Preliminary Examination

The preliminary examination is often referred to as a judicial inquiry directed toward the determination of the existence, validity, and sufficiency of probable cause.[14] Depending upon the procedure, either a judge or a prosecutor will preside over the proceedings, and an inquiry will be made of the defendant in order to determine the probability of his having committed the crime. This is a stage at which all the material facts are gathered and tested and subsequently reported by the judge who prepares the case for trial. The court then determines the credibility and truthfulness of the matters discovered. It must be determined if the state's evidence against the accused is strong enough to warrant holding the man for further proceedings.

The purpose of a hearing is essentially to advise the person of his

[14] M. C. Bassiouni, *Criminal Law and Its Procedures* (Springfield, Ill.: Charles C. Thomas, 1969), p. 437.

right to remain silent and his right to assistance of counsel at trial. It also serves the following purposes:

1. To determine the existence of probable cause for which a warrant was issued for arrest.
2. To inquire into the reasonability of the arrest and search, and the compliance of the executing officer with the command of the warrant.
3. To afford the magistrate who issued the warrant the opportunity to hear the accused and determine whether probable cause still exists after the hearing of witnesses or examining evidence presented by the accused.
4. To release the accused on bail.

Should evidence prove substantial the defendant will be indicted.

The Trial

When a person is formally charged and prosecution is commenced either by indictment, information, or complaint, the accused is called into court before trial and informed of the charges against him and is given the opportunity to make a plea. Arraignment is not a trial, and the court does not examine any matters pertaining to the accused's guilt or innocence.

Upon representation by counsel the accused is asked to enter a plea. The plea entered is either guilty, not guilty, not guilty by reason of insanity, or *nolo contendere*. If no plea is offered the court will offer a plea of not guilty for the accused. A plea of guilty will not be accepted by the court at arraignment until the nature and consequences of such a plea and the maximum penalty that may be imposed by law for such an offense has been fully explained to the defendant.

A criminal trial in the United States is always conducted by a *judge*. In direct contrast to the policeman, the *judge* before whom a suspect is first brought usually exercises less discretion than the law allows him. The judge is entitled to inquire into the facts of the case and as to whether there are grounds for holding the accused; in practice, however, he seldom does this. The more promptly an arrested suspect is brought into the courts, the less likelihood there is that much information about the arrest other than the arresting officer's statement will be available to the judge. Many judges, especially in urban areas, have such congested calendars that it is almost impossible for them to give any case except the most extraordinary ones prolonged scrutiny.

In practice the most important things a judge does are to set the amount of the defendant's bail and in some jurisdictions to appoint counsel. Too seldom does either action get the careful attention it deserves. In many cases the magistrate accepts a waiver of counsel without insuring that the suspect is aware of the significance of legal representation.

Jury, Prosecutor, and Defense Counsel. The defendant has the right to trial by *jury* in certain cases. The jury is the finder of facts. All guilty pleas are tried by a judge with no jury since no contradictions exist for jury to decide. The defendant may elect to be tried by the bench without a jury. Should the defendant choose a trial by jury, he is entitled to a speedy trial by his peers.

The jury is usually composed of twelve men and women (juries may have varying members according to a recent Supreme Court decision) and is drawn to represent a cross-section of the community within the jurisdiction of the court. The method and standards of selection are established by law in each state but must satisfy the minimal standards of due process which call for fair and impartial procedures. No state can set standards which discriminate against its citizens by reason of race, religion, or national origin.

Serving as a juror is deemed a duty of citizens of a certain age, unless they are exempted by law. In addition, persons who qualify for jury service may be temporarily excused for some valid reason. The selection of jury is generally made by drawing from the official list of voters or taxpayers of the county or state. Any impropriety, prejudice, or discrimination in the selection of jury will constitute a denial of due process and grounds for a mistrial.

In a criminal proceeding, the *prosecution* always has the right and the duty of opening the case and offering evidence in support of the defense irrespective of the nature of the defense. The purpose of the opening statement is to explain to the jury the issue or issues to be tried. An interesting example of an opening statement is set forth in the Santa Clara County *District Attorneys' Procedural Manual.*

> Ladies and gentlemen, the evidence in this case will show that Mr. Jones, who lives here in San Jose on Fruitdale Avenue, arrived home after dark one Thursday night in January, after working late at the office. As is his practice, he parked his car in the apartment carport slot assigned to him and locked the doors. Being rather tired, he went to bed around 10 P.M. Although he was soundly asleep at midnight, Mr. Thief was not (pointing and looking directly at the defendant). No, he was up and around, and in fact he was in the very neighborhood of Mr. Jones. Seeing Mr. Jones' car sitting unattended in the dark secluded carport, he crept up to it, silently unlocked the driver's door by use of a coathanger, and then proceeded to rewire the ignition so that the car could be driven without a key. In his haste, however, he inadvertently dropped an envelope from his pocket, which ultimately led in part to his undoing.

> Once inside the car, he started it up and hurriedly backed out of the driveway and drove away. A neighbor, Mr. Stevens, who happened to be in the kitchen getting a drink of water for his 4-year-old daughter, looked up out of his kitchen window in time to see the car drive off. Although he recognized the car, he had no reason to suspect at the time that the car was being driven by anyone other than Mr. Jones.
>
> Although it was only a day or so later that Mr. Thief was caught, he got clear to Los Angeles with the car and was driving down the freeway towards Santa Ana when spotted and stopped by the California Highway Patrol. Upon being arrested for auto theft, Mr. Thief gave the classic explanation for possession of a stolen car: he "borrowed" the car from a friend, a friend whose name he "couldn't remember." [15]

The prosecuting attorney has a right to state in his opening what facts the prosecution intends to prove, but he cannot site facts for which he has no competent evidence.[16] Following the opening statement by the prosecuting attorney a motion to allow the defendant to make his opening statement is addressed to the court. Counsel for the defendant is properly restricted from stating in his opening statement matters which would be inadmissible in evidence. He has a right, however, to state his theory of the legal principles applicable to the entire case.

Disputes on issue of fact arising in a criminal prosecution are determined on the basis of evidence offered and admitted at the trial. For the most part, this will be the testimony of persons who witnessed the facts, and such testimony will be given in open court. In addition to the written or spoken word, tangible objects and tests may be admissible as evidence. Tests can be conducted by both prosecution and the counsel for the defense in order to prove their case of guilt or innocence.

The presentation of his defense by argument to the jury, by himself or by his counsel, is a constitutional right of the defendant which may not be denied, however clear the evidence against him may seem. As pointed out by the American Bar Association, the general posture of defense counsel is that he undertakes his function with built-in handicaps arising out of the reality that by the time he undertakes his main task a series of events has placed his client under a cloud which is very real, notwithstanding the presumption of innocence.[17] In a typical case, the first event is an arrest on *warrant* or by a police officer who witnesses

[15] *District Attorney's Procedural Manual* (San Jose, Ca.: Santa Clara County District Attorney's Office, 1972).

[16] R. A. Anderson, *Whorton's Criminal Law and Procedures,* Vol. 4 and 5 (Rochester, N.Y.: Lawyers' Co-Operative Publishing, 1957).

[17] Anderson, *Whorton's Criminal Law and Procedure,* p. 2081. See also: "The Prosecution Function" and "The Defence Function," in *American Bar Association Project on Standards for Criminal Justice,* tentative draft, pp. 141-51.

the act or flight following the act. Thereafter the accused is processed through the magistrate hearing and charged on information or by indictment. Between presentation to the magistrate and submission to the grand jury or the filing of an information, it can be assumed that police investigation has tended to confirm the participation of the accused and that the prosecutor has screened the evidence and concluded to proceed. If the police and the prosecutor as well as the magistrate and the grand jury are performing their respective functions properly, the charge has a solid basis by the time defense counsel begins preparation for the trial. This is not simply a matter of the cliche that an accused has "all the forces of government arrayed against him." The accused often has a large array of facts and adverse evidence against him which neither he nor anyone can alter except by motions to suppress evidence when there is a legal and factual basis for such course.

The *primary* role of counsel is to act as champion for his client. In this capacity he is the equalizer, the one who places each litigant as nearly as possible on an equal footing before the substantive and procedural law under which he is tried. Of course, as a practical matter counsel does this, not by formally educating the client on every legal aspect of the case, but by taking those procedural steps and recommending those courses of action which the client, were he an experienced advocate himself, might fairly and properly take. A lawyer cannot be timorous in his representation. Courage and zeal in the defense of his client's interests are qualities which are necessary in order to perform as an advocate. And, since the accused may well be the most despised of persons, this burden rests more heavily upon the defense lawyer. Against a "hostile world" the accused, called to the bar of justice by his government, finds in his counsel a single voice on which he must be able to rely with confidence; through his counsel, his interests will be protected to the fullest extent consistent with the rules of procedure and the standards of professional conduct.

The order of summing up varies somewhat in different jurisdictions and is largely controlled by statute. The prevailing practice gives the prosecution the closing argument to the jury first. The court decides whether to hear closing arguments at the close of the evidence or at recess, or whether to adjourn for the purpose of physical rest. The court also decides the time allowed for the summation of each argument, and abuse of time is error.

During the prosecution's rebuttal, the prosecutor attempts to show that the statement of the witness as to what occurred is not true. At all stages of the trial, evidence may be introduced during the rebuttal of evidence by the defense.

The court will instruct the jury on its duties under the law and on the law applicable to the case. It will then ask the jury to return verdict which is arrived at by applying the relevant law to the facts and evidence presented at the trial. The court also instructs the jury on the nature of the presumption of innocence and on the burden of proof which is necessary to return a conviction. If the evidence presented by the state is insufficient to support a guilty finding, the court may direct the jury to return a not-guilty verdict.[18]

After being instructed by the court, the jury retires to deliberate in secret, and an officer of the court may be appointed to keep the jurors together and prevent communication with persons not on the panel. The court may order the jury to be confined and isolated until a verdict is rendered. Any external influence or contacts which could prejudice any member of the panel can be grounds for a mistrial. During the deliberations, jurors may take with them the court's instructions and the record of the trial. Under the law in some states they may also take exhibits presented in evidence at the trial.

Following deliberation, the jury must return a general verdict of guilty or not-guilty. Some states allow less than unanimity of jurors for a verdict. If the jury cannot reach agreement, the court will enter an order for a mistrial, and a new trial will take place before a new jury. The jury returns its verdict either verbally or in writing at the next session of court. A verbal verdict is given by the foreman of the jury in open court. A written verdict can be returned in the same manner and read by the foreman or by the court.[19] A mistrial will also be declared by the court if, after adequate deliberation, the members of the jury are unable to reach a verdict. In common legal phraseology, a jury that cannot agree is called a "hung" jury.

Should the jury reach a guilty verdict the defendant is bound over for sentencing. Such sentencing shall be imposed without unreasonable delay. Before imposing sentence, the court will offer counsel an opportunity to speak on behalf of the defendant and shall address the defendant personally and ask him if he wishes to make a statement in his own behalf. Once the sentence has been imposed, the court advises the defendant of his rights to appeal and of the right of a person unable to pay the cost of an appeal to apply for leave to appeal in *forma payseris*. If the defendant makes such a request, the clerk of the court will prepare and file a notice of appeals on behalf of the defendant.

While awaiting action on the appeal, a writ of *habeas corpus* may be served. There are different types of writs of habeas corpus. However, insofar as a postconviction remedy is concerned, a writ of habeas corpus

[18] Bassiouni, *Criminal Law and Its Procedures,* p. 489.

[19] Bassiouni, *Criminal Law and Its Procedures,* p. 492.

ad respondendum may be sought. Such a writ would be issued when one party has a claim against another person who is in custody under process of an inferior court; the writ is issued in order to remove the prisoner and prefer the claim against him to higher court.[20] Habeas corpus is, by nature, a civil rather than criminal proceeding even though sought in behalf of one charged with or convicted of a crime.

Statutes commonly confer upon the trial judges the authority to suspend sentence and place a defendant on probation. During the period of suspension, the court may place the defendant on *probation* and may impose such conditions as it deems proper. A *parole* in criminal law is the release of a convict from imprisonment with the stipulation that certain conditions be observed by him. A parole by the court, pursuant to statutory authority and on conditions, is not a pardon; parole does not release the convict from legal custody and control. Further, a parole may be granted upon any terms or conditions that the granting power sees as fit. Failure to comply to these terms and conditions is grounds for termination of parole and recommitment of the offender to prison.

PROSECUTION AND POLICE DISCRETION

The prosecuting *district attorney* not only possesses a great deal of responsibility in enforcing the criminal law but *also exercises a fantastic degree of discretion in the manner in which efficient and fair law enforcement is achieved.* The decisions that he must make are numerous and often difficult; some of the most important decisions he makes occur when he exercises his power to charge or refrain from charging an individual with a crime. The decision to charge an individual with a crime and thereby subject him to the processes and sanctions of the criminal adjudication system is a very important one—especially to the person who is charged. His reputation and standing in the community are at stake; the process will be time consuming and expensive; and the result may ultimately involve deprivation of his physical liberty. Thus, the decision must be made with care, intelligence, and good judgment. It is impossible to set forth systematically and categorically all the factors and criteria which enter into the decision of charging an individual with a crime. However, a few of the considerations that enter into that process will be discussed in the following paragraphs.

In most jurisdictions four tests are applied in every case to determine whether a criminal complaint should be prepared. These are:

[20] Anderson, *Whorton's Criminal Law and Procedure,* p. 2227.

1. Has a public offense been committed?
2. Is the identity of the perpetrator known?
3. Can the offense be proved beyond a reasonable doubt?
4. Should there be a prosecution under all the circumstances of the case?

No complaint should be authorized unless each of the four questions can be answered in the affirmative.

The elementary considerations are important but are easily overlooked. It must be obvious from the police report that all the elements of the crime can be proven and that the identity of the perpetrator can also be proven. This includes such elements as knowledge, willfulness, or specific intent, which have to be proven from the circumstances presented in the evidence. Furthermore, not only must the elements be present, but the proof of such elements must also be admissable into evidence. Thus, if a crucial portion of the evidence was obtained by an illegal search and seizure, and the deputy's analysis of the case law is correct in this respect, it would be useless and a waste of valuable resources to proceed any further.

In practice, a great deal of discretion has already occurred by the time the police officer or agent from another law enforcement body presents a report to a deputy district attorney for approval. The liaison officer already has a good understanding of whether a case is likely to result in criminal prosecution because of his frequent contact with the district attorney. Cases which clearly do not merit further proceedings are disposed of at the police level and are never reviewed by the district attorney's office. The same principle applies to cases which originate in governmental agencies other than police departments. Thus, a substantial portion of the cases which are presented to deputy district attorneys are cases which merit prosecution, and a complaint is in fact issued. It is not unusual, however, for the police department to present a case to the district attorney's office with the express purpose of obtaining objective and disinterested, discretionary review of the matter by that office. This happens mainly in cases of significant public interest and in cases involving very serious crimes.

The prosecuting attorney is not the only party who uses discretion in bringing a criminal to justice. The frequency and type of arrests to be made are questions of priority. These priorities are established by local law enforcement officials. It is obvious that policemen do not arrest all people who commit offenses. Why? *Because at the grass-roots level the policeman is the party who uses discretion in deciding whether to arrest an individual.*

The policeman's job cannot be summarized as simply enforcement of the law. He is placed on the street for the purpose of preventing crime. Although the arresting officer like any other citizen is biased and prejudiced by his religious, ethnic, and social backgrounds, he must draw the thin line between morality and law in an objective manner. When the officer takes the stand under oath, he must be able to say at what point he believed he had probable cause to make an arrest. He must indicate which facts and circumstances led him to believe there was probable cause to make the arrest. The police officer, then, is an interpreter not only of *local* policy but also of the *constitutional* quagmire which protects the criminal defendant. This use of discretion is never more evident than in domestic squabbles. Also, physical and emotional restraint must be exercised during riots and insurrections. The police officer must weigh his right to arrest a trespasser against the possibility that such an arrest will cause the death or injury of numerous persons.

Courtroom Testimony

The very nature of law enforcement virtually assures the need for police to be called not only as witnesses but in many instances as "star witnesses." For this reason, it becomes necessary for police to understand the nature of courtroom testimony. *Truth,* as called for by the court, is the object of the trial. Attorneys are officers of the court and as such are charged with responsibility in seeking truth in much the same way that police are charged with keeping the peace. There are many complicated rules that govern evidence and testimony, but each rule exists for the purpose of developing truth as called for by the court. The use of these rules, however, frequently gives the impression that witnesses are being tripped up or forced to contradict themselves. But regardless of how the questions are phrased, the witness responding to cross-examination with the truth has little cause for anxiety "Clever questions" pose relatively little threat—particularly in view of the judge's responsibility to protect the witness from the "have-you-stopped-beating-your-wife" variety of questions.

The truth, however, often incorporates far more than the question calls for—or for that matter far more than the court requires. This being the case, the witness is expected to define truth as being honest in specific answers to equally specific questions. The judge may allow a question to be asked because it does not call for answers that violate rules of evidence. The witness who gives an answer containing more information than called for may then prejudice a jury or even force the acceptable segments of testimony to be removed from evidence. This is possible even when the total response is completely true. This embarrassment, like most courtroom embarrassments, occurs primarily when uncalled-for information is volunteered by a witness forgetting that the judge and the attorneys are trying the case—not the witness.

Questions stress facts rather than opinions, and opinions will be acceptable only when the judge specifically allows. Chances are that the witnesses have been thoroughly "briefed" by the attorney in advance, thus making preparation possible. Preparation for testimony is usually not difficult, but it is always important. Fellow police officers are entitled to the good impression afforded law enforcement by a well-prepared and well-groomed police witness.

Once an officer is aware that he will appear in court, good preparation requires a careful review of notes and records relating to the case on trial. The majority of facts to which police testify are in police reports or notes. Although reference to these sources is acceptable during testimony, a better impression is made when "first-hand" responses are forthcoming. Some police confer with the prosecutor immediately prior to the court date in order to ensure sharp, concise, and straightforward testimony that inspires the court's confidence. The confident (not cocky) police witness is less likely to be subjected to prolonged or confusing cross-examination and is better able to deal with this eventuality if so subjected.

Personal appearance is another important part of preparation. Whether in uniform or civilian attire, clean, neat, and conservative clothing makes a favorable impression—as, of course, does well-trimmed hair and a clean-shaven face. Erect posture contributes further to the favorable impression. Personal conduct and demeanor becomes even more important in the court than "on the job," if that is possible. Clearly, an officer of the law who comes to court carrying a newspaper to read while waiting to testify or who causes disturbances implies disrespect for the dignity of the court. Registering surprise and disbelief at the testimony of other witnesses along with "natural" but unprofessional mannerisms do little to assure the court that police are as objective as possible.

Preparation may also entail rehearsing anticipated responses to ensure concise testimony. Deliberate effort to appear poised and impartial helps to remove the feeling that police are anxious to seek convictions no matter what. A part of such poise is an unemotional but audible and clear voice which delivers concise answers. A few examples of responsive, concise answers to an attorney's questions may prove helpful. The following suggestions may be an aid to the officer.

Testifying about Conversations. The matter of testifying in regard to conversations requires particular notice. The law requires that before a conversation can be related, the time, place, and parties present must be shown. Thus, the attorney must ask preliminary questions such as "Did you have a conversation with so and so about some matter?" Here you must not make the mistake of considering this the cue to go ahead and state the conversation; remember to state "Yes" or "No." The attorney then must ask questions to find out when and where the conversation took place and who were present. When it is finally asked that the conversation be stated, you are not to state your conclusions as to the result of the conversation; merely state what each party said as nearly as you can remember. It is realized, of course, that no witness has a photographic memory, and therefore no one is expected to state the exact words of a conversation that occurred some time in the past.

Telling Only Facts—Not Opinions. You should know that the court is only interested in facts, not opinions, conclusions, or arguments. To illustrate this point, the following are typical examples of the right and wrong ways of answering questions. *Question:* What was said concerning the Buick automobile?" *Wrong Form of Answer:* "We agreed that Mr. Jones would pay the cost of repairing the Buick." *Right Form of Answer:* "I said, 'The accident was your fault and you should pay the cost of repairing the Buick'; and Mr. Jones said, 'It was my fault and I will be glad to pay whatever it costs you to get it fixed.' "

Etiquette. A few suggestions as to courtroom etiquette might be helpful. Courts are the institutions which give effect to our constitutional rights and liberties and the laws of the state and nation. Without such laws and without the courts to make them effective, we would be completely uncivilized. It is, therefore, appropriate that courts should function in a dignified and somewhat formal manner; by their conduct, persons in the courtroom show and foster a feeling of respect for the laws and institutions of our state. A few little things to remember along these lines are: While court is in session, do not smoke, chew gum, eat candy, read newspapers, knit, or indulge in similar conduct which shows a casual or disrespectful attitude. Also, do not indicate by grimaces, shaking of the head, or the like reaction to a testimony of other witnesses. In conclusion, if you are a witness, remember:

Don't be nervous.
Tell the truth.
Only answer the questions.
Do not state opinions or arguments, only facts.
Speak up so you can be heard.
Be courteous.

DUE PROCESS

Throughout this volume we will refer to constitutional cases and, more specifically, to the due process clause of the Fourteenth Amendment. It is therefore appropriate to analyze the *due process.* In serving community needs, the Supreme Court cannot close its eyes to the archaic methods employed in the administration of justice. The courts must guarantee the protections which stem from the Constitution and specifically from the Bill of Rights. Constitutional protections are not static.

The community does not require unwavering standards and guidelines, which restrict rather than guarantee the rights of the accused. The utopia of justice is determination of the truth. If standards and procedures must be violated to achieve such a result, the courts must forge ahead toward a system of perfect justice by disregarding such standards. Throughout history, and especially in the 1960s, the Supreme Court has opened the door for protection of the criminally accused, which has long been overdue.

Inherent in the Constitution and the Bill of Rights are certain substantive guarantees which protect the accused against excessive governmental power and restrictions. As early as 1833, the Supreme Court decided that the Bill of Rights (consisting of the first eight amendments) was originally enacted to protect persons against actions of the federal government only. Today, through the application of the Bill of Rights in the Fourteenth Amendment, the individual is protected against actions of the state government. The Fourteenth Amendment provides in part: "No state shall make or enforce any law which shall abridge the privileges or immunities of citizens of the United States; nor shall any state deprive any person of life, liberty, or property without due process of law; nor deny to any person within its jurisdiction the equal protection of the laws." The critical question which faces the courts in modern times is the extent to which the *due process clause* of the Fourteenth Amendment incorporates the Bill of Rights. The courts are in disagreement over this question.

Arguments have been advanced that the Bill of Rights should be incorporated entirely to protect the individual against state infringement. However, the Supreme Court ultimately followed *the doctrine of selective incorporation.* Under this doctrine, the restrictions contained in the Bill of Rights limit state infringement only on a selective basis. In *Bloom* v. *Illinois* the court held the Bill of Rights is incorporated by the Fourteenth Amendment due process clause only on a *limited* basis.[21] The Supreme Court has determined that the guarantees and protections under the Bill of Rights are so fundamental and inherent to the basic rights of the individual that they should be protected against both federal and state interference.

A question arises as to how the court determines that a protection is so fundamental that it must be guaranteed against governmental infringement. The court reviews such rights on a case-by-case basis and

[21] Bloom v. Illinois, 391 U.S. 194 (1968).

defines these rights under only the most general of terms: "those principles implicit in the concept of order or liberty," or "the principles of justice so rooted in the traditions and conscience of our people as to be ranked fundamental." It is a simple task to give a definition in such broad terms, but it is difficult to apply that definition to any particular situation. Intangible guidelines cause confusion and apprehension.

Justice Frankfurter, in *Rochin* v. *California,* recognized the lack of concrete guidelines when he stated:

> A gloss of some of the verbal symbols of the constitution does not give them a fixed technical context, but it exacts a continuing process of application. . . . In each case "due process of law" requires an evaluation based on a disinterested inquiry pursued in the spirit of science, on a balanced order of facts exactly and fairly stated, on a detailed consideration of conflicting claims.[22]

Violations of constitutional rights resulting in the denial of life, liberty, and property have not only caused the Supreme Court to look to the due process clause but also to the *equal protection clauses* of the Fourteenth Amendment to protect the rights of the criminal accused. For our purposes here, however, our discussion can be limited to the due process clause.

Result. The law enforcement officer must look not only to the Constitution and the Bill of Rights for protection of the individual, he must now also investigate the various shades of meaning of the Bill of Rights to guide his actions. The student cannot limit himself to cases which already have established guidelines and safeguards for the criminal accused; he must also search his own conscience for the "fundamental fairness essential to the very concept of justice." [23] We can no longer adjudicate the guilt or innocence of an individual without assuring him the rights guaranteed by the Constitution. It is necessary for the law enforcement officer to understand the difficulties surrounding marginal cases when facts must be tested against such nebulous and flexible guidelines as those dicussed above. The only certainty is that change is inevitable, but individual rights cannot be disregarded during the process of change.

Reflection. During the 1960s, the "Warren Court" restructured and clarified the major areas in the field of criminal procedure. As a result, federal and state courts were made aware of constitutional limitations and, more importantly, of *the constitutional rights, protections, and privileges of the individual.* The most important question facing law enforce-

[22] Rochin v. California, 342 U.S. 165 (1952).

[23] Lisenba v. California, 314 U.S. 219 (1941).

ment agencies today is whether recent decisions of the Supreme Court have hindered law enforcement officials in their investigation and pretrial procedures.

The Supreme Court has, in essence, concluded that the constitutional rights of the individual can only be protected when all federal and state officials comply with the constitutional protections called for in *Mapp* v. *Ohio,* the case we shall refer to throughout this chapter. Before *Mapp* v. *Ohio,* the police officer, as an agent of the state, could obtain evidence which would be excluded in the *federal* court system but which was admissible in *state* court.[24] As a result, the defendant preparing for his execution or serving his sentence in a state penitentiary had the right (not a very gratifying privilege) to sue the state law enforcement agency because of misconduct which might have amounted to trespass, assault, battery, false imprisonment, or some other type of constitutionally prohibited state actions. The court sought to extend the protections against illicit federal action to the states. This was accomplished through a broad interpretation of the due process clause of the Fourteenth Amendment.

Unfortunately, there is a great gap between the rights afforded the criminal defendant and the reality of unlawful police practices. Only when the defendant is protected by court processes do these rights become a reality. The need to study and understand basic constitutional limitations imposed on police officials cannot be underestimated.

The desire of the Supreme Court to provide equal justice regardless of wealth, race, or religious background is tantamount to the theoretical goal of pure federalism. The states (though theoretically the "ball park of experimentation") should not be given the privilege of testing the constitutional rights of a criminal defendant. If the federal system of justice is the ultimate criteria, we must ask ourselves whether our country and society would not, in fact, benefit from such a course of action.[25]

Whenever the Supreme Court renders a decision which imposes more restrictive limitations on law enforcement agencies in arresting and convicting criminal defendants, peace officers typically feel indignant. Peace officers feel these limitations frustrate and impede the utopian goal of peace and tranquility. Without question, constitutional limitations make working conditions for the peace officer more difficult. The late Justice Black, on a national television interview show, stated emphatically that the police officer's role *should be a difficult one to fulfill.* The ultimate answer is a proper balance of interests. Can law enforcement agencies be burdened with the duty of preventing crime and, at the same time, be

[24] See: Mapp v. Ohio, 367 U.S. 643 (1961).

[25] K. Pye, *The Warren Court and Criminal Procedure,* 67 Mich. L. Rev. 249 (1968).

effectively restrained from obtaining evidence with which to prosecute the criminal defendant?

The duty of the peace officer is to arrest, prosecute, and convict criminals. He cannot be given an independent forum to carry out those goals. In order to protect the rights of the individual against the minority of police officers who violate constitutional guarantees, the Supreme Court recognizes the need for preventive rather than retributive control of law enforcement agencies.[26]

The student may well conclude that the peace officer is restricted in his duty and hampered in his goal of bringing about law and order. However, the opposite is true especially with respect to enforcement of minor statutes. It is a strange horse society rides when the greatest latitude and discretion is given to officials located in the most insignificant branch of a complex bureaucracy. Although we could not cover every criminal statute in every state, the *enforcement* of these "minor" statutes lies almost totally within the discretion of the lowest ranking police officer. Social values, backgrounds, formal education, and religious training vary from one police officer to the next. The unfortunate result is unequal enforcement of minor statutes, not only from county to county but from policeman to policeman.

The decision to arrest without a warrant is in the hands of the policeman. If the policeman bases his action on conduct which he believes transgresses his own personal values, he may decide to arrest an individual after a breach of some minor statute. It is doubtful prosecution or ultimate conviction will result if he does not act because his failure to make the original arrest usually terminates further investigation. In making such a value judgment, the police officer has assumed the role of prosecutor, public defender, judge, jury, and legislature. Because of this discretion, the officer's awareness must be clothed in due process reasoning.

CONSTITUTIONAL PROTECTIONS AND THEIR SIGNIFICANCE TO THE LAW ENFORCEMENT OFFICER[27]

The United States Constitution is of great importance to law enforcement officers not only because it sets out general standards and protects personal liberties, but also because a misunderstanding of its separate

[26] J. Skolnick, *Justice Without Trial* (New York: John Wiley & Sons, 1966), pp. 224-29.

[27] Adapted from *Handbook on the Law of Search and Seizure* (Washington, D.C.: U.S. Gov't. Printing Office, 1957), pp. 11-20.

parts will hinder the law-enforcement officer's proper performance of his duty. Nowhere is this more evident than in the area of search and seizure. The rules and procedures in this area, which have developed from the Fourth and Fifth Amendments, require careful study to insure that the individual's rights are protected while the criminal element is denied the opporutnity to evade or escape conviction because of a technical mistake. With the ever-improving competence of law officers throughout the country, there should be fewer instances of criminals being set free because of a technical error in law enforcement.

The purpose of this section is to develop some understanding of the constitutional protections against illegal search and seizures. The Fourth Amendment states:

> The right of the people to be secure in their persons, houses, papers, and effects, against unreasonable searches and seizures, shall not be violated, and no warrants shall be issued, but upon probable cause, supported by oaths of affirmation, and particularly describing the place to be searched, and the persons or things to be seized.

Clearly, the Fourth Amendment is designed for the protection of the individual's privacy. This means security for both his person and his property. This amendment allows the individual to conceal himself and his property from the view of his government—local, state, and federal. However, the framers of the Constitution recognized that this right must, at times, give way to other needs of society. The three words or phrases that are most important for police officers are "unreasonable," "probable cause," and "particularly." It is around these terms that most cases and problems arise.

The Fourth Amendment prohibits "unreasonable" searches and seizures, not *all* searches and seizures. Reasonable searches and seizures are permitted. The problem is in deciding what is "reasonable." While the search is usually deemed reasonable if a valid search warrant is first obtained, the courts have allowed searches without a warrant when consent was given by the subject, when the search was incident to a lawful arrest, and when only vehicles were searched. Such tests are, at best, general and there are many facets to each type of search. Through dealing with these difficult factors, the validity of the search is determined.

"Probable cause" raises further problems for law-enforcement officers. Determinations as to the reasonableness of a search can be categorized to some extent according to the methods officers use; but the question as to whether there is probable cause to justify a search must be decided on the basis of each specific set of facts. The standard for determining whether there is probable cause to justify a search has been established by the Supreme Court. The Court defined probable cause as: "A reasonable ground of suspicion, supported by circumstances sufficiently strong in themselves to warrant a cautious man in the belief that the party is guilty of the offense with which he is charged."

The Court has viewed probable cause as a nontechnical standard. It has judged the problem in the light of everyday experience and not on the basis of a legal formula. Also, reasonableness is not tested according to what an ordinary citizen would consider to be probable cause. The test is whether an *experienced officer* would consider that probable cause exists. This allows persons involved in law enforcement to weigh the circumstances in the light of their training and expertise. The rule is helpful since it ties the legal standards to the policeman's trained instincts.

The last key word which must always be considered by officers engaged in searches and seizures is "particularly." Unlike the problems involved in testing and evaluating reasonableness and probable cause, problems relating to the particularity of the person seized or the premises searched generally arise under a search warrant. The warrant must be specific—not only as to whom or what is to be searched, but also as to the items that are to be seized. *People* v. *Rainey* supports the rule of "specifics" or "particularity":

> Defendant was convicted of forgery and receiving stolen goods. On appeal, defendant contended that the trial court erred in denying his pretrial motion to vacate a search warrant and to suppress evidence, and in receiving as evidence, over his objection, material seized pursuant to a defective search warrant. The Court of Appeals of New York *reversed* the conviction and dismissed the indictment. Since the search warrant described an entire building, one part of which (for which probable cause was shown) was occupied by defendant and another part (for which probable cause was not shown) by an innocent third party, the warrant was obviously constitutionally deficient for not *"particularly describing the place to be searched."* The Court noted that the innocent third party's failure to complain about the search of her apartment was immaterial, since the pertinent issue was whether or not the warrant was constitutional when issued.[28]

The requirement of particularity not only restricts the items or places which may be searched, but also limits the type of search that may be conducted. A search of "Warehouse A, 1000 Jones Street, for illegal liquor stills" restricts officers to that location and that purpose. They cannot go into the warehouse and search file cabinets in the office because the specific items in the warrant are stills which could not be built in a file drawer. To search the file drawer would violate the rule of particularity.

In obtaining a search warrant, particularity as to what people and

[28] People v. Rainey, 197 N.E. 2d 527 (NY, 1964).

objects are sought is perhaps the most technical of the three standards. It is also the standard most directly under the control of the police officer. It should be carefully thought out in advance to insure correctness of the address, the person's name, the items sought, and the factual basis for seeking the warrant. If there is sufficient time to obtain a search warrant, there is sufficient time to insure that it is validly drawn up to cover the situation believed to exist.

This brief introduction to the effect of the Fourth Amendment on the law of searches and seizures should be kept in mind at all times. In conducting a search, the guidelines of *reasonableness* of the search, *probable cause* to warrant the search, and *particularity* as to the items seized or persons searched must all be tested in the officer's mind to insure that his actions are lawful and that any arrest or seizure of property will stand up in a court of law.

The Exclusionary Rule

The American colonies followed the English rule that evidence obtained by illegal search and seizure is nevertheless admissible in a criminal trial if it tends to prove an issue in the case. This rule is still followed in England, Canada, and various nations whose system of law is based on Anglo-Saxon sources. When the Constitution of the United States was written, the Fourth Amendment was added to guarantee against searches like those carried out under the notorious Writs of Assistance during colonial times. The language of the Fourth Amendment as well as the Fifth Amendment has been held by the Supreme Court to work in the area of search and seizure. Both amendments were adopted as part of the Bill of Rights in 1791. The Fifth Amendment reads:

> No person shall be compelled in any criminal case to be a witness against himself, nor be deprived of life, liberty, or property, without due process of law.

From these amendments, the Court has evolved several basic principles. *First,* searches may only be made for certain classes of materials, specifically: (1) the tools of the crime, (2) the fruits of crime, (3) contraband goods (things forbidden by law to be possessed), and (4) goods on which an excise duty is due.[29] *Second,* American courts have held that searches may only be carried out (1) with the consent of the person to be searched or the proprietor of the premises to be searched; (2) with a search warrant that conforms to the requirements of the Fourth Amendment (and a few

[29] Warden v. Hayden, 387 U.S. 394 (1967).

other requirements that have been added by rules of criminal procedure); and (3) incident to a valid arrest. The Constitution clearly forbids the use of "general warrants" or dragnet searches which were so odious to the American colonies before the Revolution.

In 1914, the Supreme Court unequivocally rejected the common law rule and substituted for it the so-called "exclusionary rule" that evidence obtained by an unreasonable search and seizure will be excluded from court. In 1961 the Supreme Court extended the exclusionary rule to every court and law enforcement officer in the nation.[30] In this decision handed down in June, 1961, the Supreme Court held that henceforth evidence obtained by procedures which violate federal constitutional standards will no longer be admissible in state courts. The Fourth Amendment guarantee against unreasonable searches and seizures is an essential part of the Fourteenth Amendment, which restrains the actions of the states and their officers. Evidence seized in an unreasonable search must be excluded since there is no other effective way to enforce the guarantees of the Fourth Amendment—and the Fourteenth Amendment—against unreasonable searches and seizures.

The wisdom of the exclusionary rule has not gone unquestioned. Michigan, which has long followed the rule, twice amended its constitution to provide that illegally seized evidence of certain violations (concealed weapons and narcotics) may nevertheless be used in court. The change in Michigan was a response to serious crime problems. In California, it has been suggested that the exclusionary rule followed in the state courts be relaxed to permit the use of evidence seized illegally in narcotic cases. The fact remains, however, that the exclusionary rule is now the law in both federal and state courts. That the exclusionary rule plays a vital part in the gathering of evidence for successful prosecution is a fact established by practitioners in the field:

> The police play a vital part in the process of prosecution in that they are in the best position to assure that evidence needed by the prosecutor will not be excluded by the court because it was obtained by improper methods. In the area of search and seizure, recent decisions have greatly increased the necessity of obtaining a search warrant. The decisions in Chimel *(Chimel* v. *California,* 1969) and Morales *(Morales* v. *California)* complement each other in requiring and then providing a workable warrant system. In terms of police work load, this imposes an added burden on the officer. . . . In the contacts of prosecution, however, the warrant requirements encourage the police officer to fulfill his role in providing dependable, admissible evidence.[31]

[30] Mapp v. Ohio, 367 U.S. 643 (1961).

[31] T. J. Gardner, "Aspects of Probable Cause," *Police Work: Concerning Criminal Evidence* (December, 1969), pp. 10-11.

Although knowledge of the Constitutional provisions will not solve all the everyday problems a law-enforcement officer must face when he conducts a search or makes a seizure, it is the starting point from which he must determine the legality of his acts. *Reasonableness, probable cause,* and *particularity* should be the principal headings for any mental check lists he uses in guiding his methods and actions. The federal standards on search and seizures *now* applicable to the states would be very difficult to treat definitively in this chapter. There have been hundreds, probably thousands, of judicial opinions attempting to do just that since the federal exclusionary rule went into effect a half-century ago. The case law is sufficient to fill several volumes at least, and it would be impossible to outline that body of law in the short space available here. The reader who needs further information about federal search and seizure law will find references at the conclusion of this chapter.

CONSTITUTIONAL LIMITATIONS

The Constitution was based on the common law of England. The common law consists of principles rather than a specific set of rules. The basis for the existence of the common law became the foundation for enforcement of the law. As society grew, common law grew. Law is expanded by constitutional interpretations. It is a living being, predicated on civil, social, economic and moral concepts which provide guidelines for the destiny of man.

During the era of the Warren Court, the gap between the dream and the reality of constitutional protection came into focus. Although the Court has a long way to go in enforcing constitutional protections for each defendant, it has effectively controlled police abuses which were considered routine at one time. The *Criminal Justice Act of 1964* has, for the most part, codified opinions handed down by the Supreme Court. Occasionally, the legislature does not entirely agree with the trend the Supreme Court has followed. It has the opportunity, and the right, to enact laws to deal with the problems of inequality, disparity of basic protections, and discrimination based on economics, religion, or race.

Unfortunately, the Supreme Court may, at times, overstep its boundaries and in effect "create law." Perhaps this activist course was prompted by the *inactivity* of federal and state legislatures in guaranteeing protections to the criminal accused. When the accused can rely on the Fourth Amendment guarantees against unreasonable searches and seizures, the Fifth Amendment right to *silence,* and the Sixth Amendment right to counsel and to confrontation of witnesses, respect for the law and policies of our system of jurisprudence will significantly improve.

Critics of the Warren Court do not give any credit to the Court for adopting procedures or guidelines which help the law enforcement agency. The right to eavesdrop, stop and frisk, use nontestimonial evidence, and, recently, to use statements made by the accused without having followed the *Miranda* procedures have all contributed to the battle against crime. The Court, however, does not take sides; it sits as a referee to interpret the law. In the future, the Court will make important decisions, but these decisions will probably be refinements and explanations of the primary decisions already rendered. The goal of the Court is to create a fair and impartial system of justice. We can best understand and realize the significance of the Supreme Court decisions when we comprehend the rationale upon which these decisions are based.

The rationale behind the *exclusionary rule* is that police officers will check their illegal practices if the result of violation is always inadmissibility of illegally acquired evidence. But, according to law enforcement authorities, the deterrent theory has been an overreaction. The exclusionary rule has had only mediocre success in eliminating illegal police practices. This conclusion is evident from the persistence of stop and frisk conduct which, to some degree, may violate the Fourth Amendment.

The deterrent theory is based on the assumption that law enforcement officers deliberately and willfully disobey constitutional guidelines and that the objective of their actions is a successful trial and conviction. Unfortunately, the police officer sometimes does not know his conduct is illegal until six months or sometimes two years after an arrest is made. There are no adequate, concrete guidelines which inform the policeman how he should have acted. If the police officer cannot understand the nature of the conduct which is declared unconstitutional, there is no basis for the exclusionary rule because the element of intent is lacking. The Supreme Court is the court of last resort, and much time passes before its decisions are handed down. Unfortunately, the police officer can only learn what is expected of him through an event which may have occurred months before. His memory is often vague, and he may have little desire to adjust his techniques in a case which is many months old.

There are many alternatives to the deterrent doctrine. One obvious course is to punish the wrongdoer. The theory expounded by judges throughout the country is that it is better to free ten guilty parties than to incarcerate one innocent party. In response to that argument, others have said that the innocent party should be compensated with money which is saved from lower insurance losses due to decreased theft, robbery, and embezzlement throughout the country. Obviously, this is not a clear-cut problem, but with the rising crime rate which the Court is unable to curb, other alternatives must be considered.

SUMMARY

Chapter 5 concerns itself with the criminal law and the judiciary process. In dealing with these areas, the authors have taken the logical step of defining crime and the essential elements of common law. The two major divisions of law previously introduced in Chapter 4 have been reviewed. A true definition of criminal law is made up of three parts: (1) the *term,* (2) the *genus,* and (3) the *differentia.* These terms are extensively discussed but briefly may be classified as follows: The *term* is the subject of the definition—the word or phrase to be defined; *genus* is a category of classification—a class or group ranking beneath a family and above species; the *differentia* is the attribute or characteristic by which one species or genus is distinguished from another.

The principles of criminal law have remained constant for many decades, and they are still considered essential to a fair system of law. The principles, as discussed in Chapter 5, are: (1) the doctrine of *nullum crimen sine lege* (no ex post facto legislation); there can be no crime without a statute that specifically forbids the behavior involved; (2) the presumption that a person has some knowledge of the law (he must be held accountable for violations); (3) the principle of equality before the law; (4) extenuating circumstances may be considered by the court; (5) an attempt to commit a crime is considered less serious than one consummated—all things considered equal; (6) specific relationships are essential to complicity; (7) it is customary to punish a law violator for the most serious offense; and (8) the statute of limitations principle, which has remained fairly constant for many years.

Regarding the "sources of law," the Constitution prescribes the duties of each major branch of government: the *legislative* branch makes the law; the *executive* branch administers and enforces the law; and the *judicial* branch interprets the law. The basic law for any state law is its constitution, and the legislature of the state has the power and authority to exact statutes. "Codification" is the procedure by which most statutes are placed into codes; these codes represent most of the written law in any given state. Aside from the written law, judges make "new law" by interpreting statutes when deciding cases. Although the court does not make law (this right is reserved for the legislative body), the court may influence the interpretation of a given statute and this interpretation will, if given at the appellate level, constitute the basis upon which the populace conducts its activities.

The common law divides crime into these major groups: (1) treason, (2) felony, and (3) misdemeanor. Statutes in the United States classify crimes into two classes: (1) felonies and (2) misdemeanors. Every crime is composed of two elements, a criminal act and a criminal intent—there must be concurrence of both to establish criminal responsibility. In this chapter, we have also discussed mental element of *mens rea,* motive (and how it differs from *mens rea*), and specific and general intent. In discussing these elements of crime the reader is introduced to Latin terms such as: *malum in se* (proof of intent and "state of mind") and *malum prohibitum* (crime not requiring a "state of mind"—*mens rea*). The area of *transferred intent* is also examined with examples provided.

In the remaining sections of the chapter, we discussed the legal aspects of police work—sociologically, the bases for arrest. We also considered misdemeanors and complaints, misdemeanors and felonies, grand jury indictments, preliminary hearings, arraignments, the trial, bail and the poor, the functions of the prosecutor and defense counsel, and constitutional protections.

QUESTIONS

1. Discuss the common law process.
2. Define the following terms as used in Chapter 5: the term, the genus, the differentia; *nullem crimen sine lege, stare decisis, malum in se,* and *malum prohibitum.*
3. List the common law division of crimes and the classification of crimes in the United States.
4. Discuss the elements of crimes.
5. Discuss the procedure for a felony prosecution.
6. What is the function of the grand jury?

ANNOTATED REFERENCES

Block, H. A., and Geis, Gilbert. *Man, Crime, and Society.* New York: Random House, 1962. Covers overall relationships of criminal justice to society.

Bristow, A. P., and Williams, J. B. *Criminal Procedure and the Administration of Justice.* Rev. ed. Beverly Hills, Calif.: Glencoe Press, 1966. A new, concise, and up-to-date work on law, judicial, and post-judicial system of justice in the United States. An excellent reference.

The Challenge of Crime in a Free Society. A report by the President's Commission on Law Enforcement and Administration of Justice. Washington, D.C.: U.S. Government Printing Office, 1967. An overview of same information covered in Chapter 5.

COHN, E., ed. "Criminal Guilt." In *Social Meaning of Legal Concepts,* Vol. 1. New York: New York University Press, 1950. A clear statement regarding the isolated subject of legally defined guilt.

CUMMING, E.; CUMMING, I. M.; and EDELL, L. "Policeman as Philosopher, Guide and Friend." *Social Problems,* Vol. 12 (Winter, 1965). Excellent coverage on responsibilities and role of police.

DAY, F. D. "Criminal Law Enforcement in a Free Society." *Journal of Criminal Law, Criminology and Police Science,* Vol. 54 (September, 1963). Covers scope of problems confronting law enforcement in a democratic society.

ELDEFONSO, E.; COFFEY, A.; and GRACE, R. C. *Principles of Law Enforcement.* New York: John Wiley & Sons, 1968. Chapter 4 covers the legal aspects of law enforcement in nontechnical language. An excellent resource for the beginning student in police science.

HALL, L., and KAMISOR, Y. *Modern Criminal Procedure.* 2nd ed. St. Paul, Minn.: West Publishing, 1966. An excellent reference of correct procedure, legal terms, definitions, and implications applicable to all systems of justice in the United States. This reference is a must for every student and law enforcement officer.

TAPPAN, P. W. *Crime, Justice and Correction.* New York: McGraw-Hill, 1960. Chapters 10 through 13 orient enforcement of law in the legally defined judicial process.

6

An Introduction to Theories Relating to Crime and Delinquency

Criminal and delinquent behavior do not just happen. They are the products of circumstance and chance, culture and environment, and most importantly, sociological and psychological conditioning. Criminal behavior usually grows from one or more of these factors. We shall take a brief look at each of these causes.

Criminal behavior often results from *circumstance* and *chance.* A small number of adults and juveniles acquire the label of criminals by circumstance. These individuals require neither the skilled help nor the extensive treatment that individuals in the other categories may need. Given temporary assistance and guidance, they will return to patterns of normal and acceptable behavior. Frequently, the person who commits a criminal act under these circumstances is a member of a group that temporarily engages in unlawful behavior. It is the presence and pressure of friends that helps this person to commit an act which he knows is wrong. If one would want to formulate a comparison between the juvenile and the adult offender, it could be said that more juveniles fall into the "circumstance and chance" category than adults. The reason is quite apparent; youngsters are naive and impulsive and therefore more easily influenced.

A second category of criminal behavior results from the influences of *culture* and *environment.* There are persons involved in criminal behavior who learn to esteem lawlessness and who engage in crime and delinquency because it is the acceptable thing to do. In these areas, *some* persons are trained to value those things that the greater society rejects. This individual is not maladjusted in the usual sense. He sees nothing wrong with the values he holds; hence he is unable to grasp the significance of his illegal behavior. In this group, all of the values held by an individual may not be at odds with the greater society; it may well be that only a few important values are inconsistent and unacceptable.

The criminal so influenced by his culture also has a greater opportunity to get into trouble. He not only lives with crime and vice but is subject to greater chance for apprehension by the larger concentration of law enforcement officers in *his* community. Even if this youth holds to the values that the greater society accepts, his opportunity for antisocial activities is enhanced by the area in which he resides. His potential for criminality is higher. Even if his other characteristics fall within the normal range of behavior.

Another cause of delinquent or criminal behavior is the *psychological* factor. In this classification (which primarily pertains to juveniles), we find children who have been psychologically conditioned to have high delinquency potentials. These children often become delinquents long before they are officially labeled by the police and courts. In this group, we find children who have received disapproval for everything they have said or done. Every effort has been made to make them feel inferior. Their parents have denied them admiration, appreciation, and affection, while permitting boredom to be a constant companion. Many of these children have been permitted to express their desires and have even had them stimulated by responsible adults who later squelched them. In addition to having been denied much, this group of children has usually been punished for or accused of deeds they did not do. Adults have taken every opportunity to show suspicion and disbelief. As a rule, these youths have had parents who demanded absolute obedience without giving an explanation and who prevented self-expression on the part of their children. These parents usually never allow their children to forget who's boss. Psychogenic delinquency has its roots in such unhealthy relationships between children and parents or other adult figures. The child who becomes antisocial because of such relationships tends to show marked characteristics as a potential delinquent. He is socially aggressive and shows extremes in defiance, suspicion, and destructiveness. His emotional ups and downs fluctuate without apparent cause. Most children are adventurous; but the delinquent is overly adventurous and extremely outgoing, demanding, and aggressive in his social relationships. He is susceptible and easily lead by children in his own group when he accepts them as his authority. When with adults and others in authority, he is frequently stubborn.

All children exhibit these symptoms at some time or another. Growing up is an uneven process with many ups and downs. In the case of the delinquent child, the symptoms are exaggerated and become established patterns for doing business with adults. It is the extent and duration of these deviations that establish delinquency—not just a single, unusual or illegal action by a child. Because of his psychological conditioning, a child may possess a high delinquency potential. Overt delinquency, however, may never be expressed unless certain necessary conditions exist—for example, the opportunity and ability to engage in unacceptable behavior. Offenders who exhibit the initial characteristics of delinquency are, therefore, the product of *situations, environments,* and/or *families* whose carelessness and lack of concern provide the fertile soil in which criminal behavior thrives.

CRIME AND DELINQUENCY: CONTRADICTORY VIEWPOINTS

Of all the social ailments which plague American society, none has aroused more deeply felt concern—and more anguished but misled editorial and official comment—than the phenomenon of crime and delinquency. And in none of the many sectors of social problems (including divorce, labor-management conflict, ethnic and racial prejudice, suicide, alcoholism, and drug addiction) have more heated and contradictory viewpoints been so vigorously expressed. Who are the adult and juvenile offenders? Why are they offenders, and what can be done about them? These are the basic queries to which this chapter shall address itself.

Deviate behavior has been seen in many different lights throughout history. In general terms, the explanation of deviate behavior has been reduced to three categories: (1) *deterministic deviance,* (2) *self-determined deviance,* and (3) *a combination of self-determined and deterministic deviance.* Put another way, a person either has no control over his behavior and is grossly influenced by external or internal forces (determinism); or a person has complete control over his behavior (moralistic self-determinism); or, finally, a person is influenced by external or internal influences but only exercises a degree of self-control.

From these three basic positions numerous "explanations" of deviate behavior have evolved. Explanations based on self-determined deviance can generally be reduced to a belief that insufficient punishment is the "cause" of deviance. Insofar as deterministic deviance is concerned, there is a wide variety of explanations. For purposes of this discussion, these explanations will be classified as either *sociological, psychological* (sometimes viewed as personality disorders), or *physiological* (also viewed as a biological causation). There is, of course, a problem in explaining why some individuals who are seemingly subjected to precisely the same influences as criminals and delinquents are not involved in criminal behavior. Because of this, there is actually considerable overlap between the different explanations for deviant behavior. In our discussion, however, the three categories will be treated as being mutually exclusive.

SOCIOLOGICAL EXPLANATIONS

Many of the deterministic explanations of deviance are based upon either a cultural or sociological approach. The *cultural approach* would include influences of various social values, status, roles, social structures, and so on. The *social approach* would include factors dealing with family and marital status, education, recreation, religion, occupation, and the like. For the sake of simplicity, all of these approaches will be discussed under the broader classification of *sociological explanations.*

Cultural Approach

Perceptive observers contend that the United States is in many respects the oldest country on earth because it has had the most experience with the complexities of modern industrial society. This experience has included the development of a "youth subculture" that remains, for the time being at least, more or less peculiar to the United States. This notion of referring to a given age group as a subculture suggests the need to define the term *culture* itself. Some 160 social science definitions of the term *culture* have been reduced, by the authors, to the following:

> Culture consists of patterns, explicit and implicit, by symbols, constituting the distinctive achievement of human groups, including their embodiment and artifacts; the essential core of culture consists of traditional ideas and their attached values; culture systems may on the one hand be considered as products of action, on the other hand as conditioning elements of further action.

Subculture then, could simply be a group at variance (or deviance) with the broad culture's patterns, artifacts, and traditional ideas. Of course, there could be subcultures that were not necessarily at variance (or deviant). A subculture at considerable variance with the larger culture was what criminologist Albert Cohen had in mind when he wrote his book, *Delinquent Boys.* The variance (or deviance) of the gang's subculture is in part attributed by Cohen to the "significantly different social worlds" between middle-class children and working-class children as they grow up.[1] As the working-class child experiences frustration in achieving culturally desirable goals, the readily available alternatives emerge.

The frustration of working-class children is identified by many cultural theorists as a struggle between means and ends. Put another way, the highly competitive struggle for material wealth eventually narrows the number of possible "victors" when "victory" is only attainable through *legitimate means.* It follows then that persons without the cultural advantage of legitimate means (often acquired through neighborhood and family status) are likely to experience frustration when they are competing with those who are fortunate enough to have legitimate means. One reaction of those who are culturally denied in this manner (the "have-nots") is to develop *illegitimate means* which in turn become defined by the broad culture as deviance.

An interesting extension of this theoretical explanation of deviance was posed by criminologist Edwin H. Sutherland. It is not the individual criminal who is sick, said Sutherland, but society.[2] A sick society is one that is in process of disorganization and eventual disintegration—it is coming apart at the seams. Cultural conflict exists in such a society because, as the value systems and mores disintegrate, whole subcultures come to adopt new norms and deny the old ones still held by the dominant culture. When these subcultures with opposing values exist side-by-side or intermingle, a child growing up in their midst is subjected to pulls and pressures from small primary groups of both the legal and illegal subcultures. According to Hardman, whether he becomes delinquent is a simple mathematical function of the amount of time he spends in each group and the intensity of their pressures and indoctrination. So in the final analysis, criminality or conformity is learned in the primary groups of peers.[3] Calling his theory *differential association,* Sutherland concluded that deviance flows from excessive exposure to social codes that prove conducive to misconduct. A person constantly exposed to deviance and rarely exposed to cultural conformity

[1] A. K. Cohen, *Delinquent Boys: The Culture of the Gang* (Glencoe, Ill.: Free Press, 1955), p. 25.

[2] Edwin H. Sutherland and Donald R. Cressy, *Principles of Criminology* (5th ed.) (Philadelphia: J. B. Lippincott, 1955).

[3] D. G. Hardman, "The Case for Eclecticism." Reprinted, with permission of the National Council on Crime and Delinquency, from *Crime and Delinquency,* July 1964, pp. 207-8.

may well come to conceive of deviance as "normal." Another criminologist, Walter Reckless, elaborates certain implications of differential association; he notes that a child who grows up learning the techniques and justifications for deviant behavior will respond to these influences in the same manner as a middle-class child responds to the influences of culturally accepted patterns of behavior. Reckless contends that the process of acquiring either the culture or the subculture is identical—only the *content* differs.[4]

There have been additional elaborations on differential association as it relates to middle-class deviance, but the actual process remains essentially the same—stress is laid on the frequency and the intimacy of social influence.

Social Approach

The family, particularly the parent, is a crucial aspect in the corrective treatment of the Juvenile Probation Department. By acknowledging the importance of the family unit, we imply that an intact marriage supports juvenile corrective goals. The earliest juvenile courts, noted that nearly 50 percent of delinquents came from broken homes; they were not long in blaming divorce and desertion for the problem of juvenile delinquency. Many studies were made in an effort to estimate the proportion of broken homes in the general population as compared to families of delinquents. Criminologists Shaw and McKay concerned themselves with broken homes and found only 42.5 percent of delinquent children came from broken homes. Shaw and McKay interpreted their findings as evidence that broken homes, although significant, were not a main "cause" of juvenile deviance.[5] Later studies of the relationship between broken homes and juvenile deviance, however, tended to support the contention that broken homes and delinquency are related. Indeed, a study of some 44,448 Philadelphia delinquents found a definite and continuous decline in the percentage of delinquents who live with both parents.

The nature of the parental separation has also been studied; such studies have concluded that desertion, divorce, and separation while one parent is in prison tend to be associated with juvenile delinquency. Where separation is due to a death or the serious illness of one parent, there is statistically less incidence of juvenile deviance.

[4] Walter Reckless, *The Crime Problem* (2nd ed.) (New York: Appleton-Century-Crofts, 1955), pp. 224-25.

[5] C. R. Shaw and H. D. Mckay, *Juvenile Delinquency in Urban Areas* (Chicago: University of Chicago Press, 1942), p. 55.

Another social variable thought to be related to juvenile deviance is recreation—or perhaps, more properly, the lack of recreation. Studies have indicated that delinquents seek exciting diversions which often lead them to dark streets, vacant lots, and railroad yards. Delinquent acts themselves become recreation for the youths involved; some criminologists, however, believe that engaging in delinquent activities as recreation is merely a stage of transition to delinquency for profit. In their volume, *Unravelling Juvenile Delinquency,* Sheldon and Eleanor Glueck found that delinquents are more outgoing and active than the nondelinquent; their findings suggest that recreational diversion is at least one variable in juvenile deviance.[6]

Economic status and the national economy itself is another variable thought by many criminologists to at least partially explain deviance.

> If someone were looking for the missing link between Marx and Durkheim, I believe he would find it in W. G. Bonger. Because of the pressures of the capitalistic system, he says, crime originates in the proletariat. This seems to be the essential theme of the current writers—Miller, Cloward and Ohlin, Cohen, Kobrin. In fact, I get the feeling in reading them (though they don't openly state this) that there should be little or no crime in middle-class society. Yet, offhand, I can name six or eight studies which indicate that crime is as much a middle-class, as a lower-class phenomenon. Both Cohen and Porterfield found 100 percent of college students studied involved in offenses serious enough for court action if known. Kenneth Polk found no correlation between economic status and delinquency. Wallerstein and Wyle, after questioning 1,700 middle-class adults, found that 99 percent admitted offenses punishable by one year imprisonment. About two-thirds of the men and one-third of the women admitted felonies. Several studies indicate a class differential in type of offense though no overall class differences. Wattenberg and Balistrieri found more ganging and gang delinquency in the lower class, more auto theft in the middle-class. This is of interest in view of Cohen's position that status-seeking lies at the root of lower-class delinquency. With the possible exception of cash-in-hand, nothing in our culture symbolizes adolescent status as does the automobile. Logically, then, most auto theft should be found in the status-deprived lower class. Cohen regards vandalism as a symbolic protest of the deprived classes against the propertied class: "It is an attack on the middle-class where their egos are most vulnerable." However, following the wave of swastika-painting in 1960, the American Jewish Committee found that 86 percent of the vandals came from middle-class homes. F. Ivan Nye found no overall class differences in delinquency but found some differences in type of offense—more sex delinquency in the lower class, more vandalism in the middle class. This was further confirmed by James Short, in Chicago, and by the New York City Youth Board. Elsewhere, Short summar-

[6] Sheldon and Eleanor Glueck, *Unravelling Juvenile Delinquency* (New York: Commonwealth Fund, 1950), p. 102.

ized his findings: "The traditional assumption of a higher incidence of delinquent behavior among members of the lower socioeconomic group, based on official statistics, is not substantiated." Numerous writers have believed that official records of arrest and prosecution discriminate against lower-class youth, but it was not until 1957 that anyone tried to test this. Short and Nye found little difference between lower- and middle-class boys in the amount of delinquency they reported in anonymous questionnaires. However, the official record (e.g., commitment rate) was several times as high for lower-class boys as for middle-class.[7]

The late Paul Tappan tended to question the relationship between deviant behavior and the national economy by noting the vast majority of economically impoverished families who did not become involved in deviant behavior. The social forces relating to economic and prestige nevertheless continue to gain prominence in efforts to reduce deviant behavior.

PSYCHOLOGICAL EXPLANATIONS

Many psychiatrically oriented criminologists consider criminality as a product of *personality maladjustment*. The socialization process is regarded as producing healthy or unhealthy personalities, and crime and delinquency is considered a correlate of the latter.

The outstanding name in this field is not as clearly identifiable as Lombroso's in the biological theories; however, I would nominate William F. Healy as the central figure of the psychological theorists. Briefly, he hypothesized that delinquency stems from emotional disturbance, which in turn stems from parental rejection and emotional deprivation in childhood. The delinquent child is basically a sick child. About 91 percent of the delinquents he examined, as compared with about 13 percent of his control groups, showed "major emotional disturbances." Since his initial investigations, literally hundreds of studies have been made comparing delinquents and nondelinquents on various measures of adjustment. In fact, if you devise a new adjustment test, it is almost approved behavior to standardize it by trying it out on delinquents and nondelinquents, as though it were a foregone conclusion that delinquents are shook up; and if your test is any good, it should reveal this.[8]

It is the contention of Dr. Franz Alexander, a celebrated psychoanalyst, that the human being enters the world as a criminal—in other words, socially not well adjusted. "The criminal," Alexander contends,

[7] Hardman, "The Case for Eclecticism," pp. 7-8.

[8] Hardman, "The Case for Eclecticism," p. 5.

"carries out in his actions his *natural,* unbridled, but instinctual drives; he acts as the child would act if it only could." "The only difference between the criminal and the normal individual," he concludes, "is that the normal man partially controls his criminal drives and finds outlets for them in socially harmless activities." [9]

If we start with such a conception of human nature, then our problem is not to explain crime, but rather, to explain its *absence.* Psychiatrist David Abrahamsen writes, for example: "We must now ask what, if any, are the reasons why some individuals have enough inhibitory mechanisms to refrain from transgressions while others lack these prohibitory functions?" [10] Most of the psychoanalytical writers acknowledge the relevance of the "social fact," but they tend to see it as a circumstance which triggers or precipitates a delinquent impulse which is already fully formed, but latent (lurking beneath the surface). Such inborn or instinctual antisocial impulses are commonly referred to as the *id;* most people, in growing up, acquire a capacity for controlling these id forces; this controlling force is known as the *ego.* The *super-ego* constitutes something akin to the conscience—an inhibitor of the id drives.

A number of personality disorders are thought by some to have very little bearing on criminal behavior; others consider these disorders to be somewhat casual in nature. Mental deficiency is probably one such disorder. The mentally deficient person is subnormal in that his mind has failed to develop normally. Other disorders such as psychotic conditions are *abnormal* in that disease or other malfunctions affect the working of the mind. Various forms of pathology and deterioration may produce mental deficiency. But mental deficiency itself probably explains very little deviance with the exception that the feeble-minded person is placed in an unfavorable position in a competitive society. Most psychoses or psychoneuroses are rarely considered explanations of crime and delinquency. However, the personality disorder known as *psychopathy* (or sociopathy) is thought by many criminologists to be the cause of a great deal of deviant behavior.

A psychopathic personality can be defined in terms of four criteria: (1) a lack of conscience (or a lack of Freudian super-ego) which in turn reduces or eliminates guilt feelings regarding misconduct; (2) most or all aggressive feelings directed outward towards the world rather than inward towards one's self; (3) infantile demand for immediate rather than postponed satisfaction of basic drives; and (4) inability or unwillingness to form affectional bonds to others. The actual development of

[9] P. Tappan, *Contemporary Correction* (New York: McGraw-Hill, 1951), p. 21.

[10] Tappan, *Contemporary Correction.*

psychopathy is complex but may be examined in terms of child-discipline technique. Discipline, more often than not, seeks to inhibit the id drives in order to produce a "civilized socialization." But to inhibit basic drives requires first a consistency in discipline and then a consistency in affection. Consistency in affection is needed to insure that guilt feelings occur when id impulses go unchecked. A kind of "bribery" is involved in which the parent (often mother) threatens withdrawal of love if the child fails to relinquish his id drives. But the child *without* feelings of maternal love is unlikely to feel threatened by the withdrawal of something he does not feel in the first place. The guilt feelings needed to control behavior are, therefore, not forthcoming, and the psychopathic personality begins to emerge.

The problems of *alcoholism* and, perhaps, *drug dependence* (as avenues of escape from painful reality) are thought by some to demonstrate personality disorders uniquely vulnerable to deviance. There is little agreement on how alcoholic problems develop, but a common explanation has evolved: The alcoholic tends to be self-pampering, and he resists unpleasant states of mind while insisting on self-expression. He is not willing to work toward attaining self-expression but tends to assume a *right* to self-expression. This assumption of self-expression, however, is not associated with *responsibility*. Instead he is extremely reluctant to assume responsibility, and responds in a childish manner. This immaturity produces a somewhat imitative characteristic, tending to develop and encourage excitement, which in turn provides a feeling of power and self-importance.

PHYSIOLOGICAL EXPLANATIONS

Additional "deterministic" theories or explanations of deviance might be called the *anthropological approach* and the *hereditary approach*. Each of these will be considered as a segment of the broader classification of physiological explanations.

Anthropological Approach

The great philosopher, Aristotle, commented on the relationship between behavior and body type: "There was never an animal with the form of one kind and the mental characteristic of another." Even before Aristotle, medicine's ancestor, Hippocrates, described two body types relating to specific diseases. But in terms of deviance, it wasn't until the nineteenth century that the Italian physician and criminologist, Cesare Lombroso, attempted to correlate physical features and misconduct.

Drawing heavily on phrenology (a belief that bumps on the head determine personality) and Darwin's theory of evolution, Lombroso sought to demonstrate what he called a "stigmata of degeneration" in which observable, asymmetric physical characteristics indicated the probability of deviance. The Lombrosian belief that "lantern jaws and pointed ears" might relate to deviance continued for some time to command the interest of criminologists.

In 1925, a book by Ernest Kretchmer proved to be the foundation of criminologist William H. Sheldon's systematic efforts to relate deviance to the shape of bodies. Delinquents were classified by Sheldon as either *endomorphic* (i.e., rotund with excessive fatty tissue); *mesomorphic* (muscular); or *ectomorphic* (lean and angular).[11] Sheldon theorized that the fatter endomorphs were gregarious and affectionate and less of a problem in so far as deviate behavior is concerned. The muscular mesomorphs were seen as delinquency prone by virtue of an excessive amount of physical energy. Finally, the tall, lean, often nervous ectomorph was seen as shy and aloof and, therefore, not prone to deviance. Later research by Sheldon and Eleanor Glueck tended to corroborate Sheldon's reasoning, which to this day is considered by many to account in part at least for deviance.

> In a massive study aimed at measuring all known dimensions of delinquency, the Gluecks found a small but significant tendency in support of Sheldon's hypothesis: his delinquents were definitely stockier, stronger, and more muscular than the controls. When we find a correlation between two variables, we are never justified in assuming that a cause-and-effect relationship exists—in this case, assuming that delinquency is causally related to body type. For instance, most crimes against persons—assault, bullying, strong-arm robbery, and rape—require better-than-average physique. The string-bean ectomorph and the roly-poly endomorph are not physically qualified for these offenses or for skylight burglary, which may require shinnying down a rope and up again, or for robbing boxcars on a moving train, or for removing a 500-pound safe. Further, social factors operate in selection of offenders. Recall your own childhood when you were choosing up sides for a game. Who was chosen first: the string beans, the roly-polys, or the muscle-and- blood boys? Since a sizable portion of our delinquency is gang delinquency, members may well be selected much the same way as play-group members. Social psychologists have demonstrated that strong, athletically inclined boys are given preferential group status and are selected as leaders. And finally we must take into

[11] G. B. Vold, *Theoretical Criminology* (New York: Oxford University Press, 1958), pp. 28-59.

account the cultural stereotypes that roly-poly people are jovial and jolly and big, burly, and bruiser go together like damn and Yankee. In short, because we expect people to behave in this manner, says Cooley, they tend to fulfill our expectations; thus we see a neat example of Merton's self-fulfilling prophecy. If we could accurately measure the effect of these three factors—the physical requirements of certain offenses, group selection of the more athletic, and our cultural expectations—I believe we could account for all of Glueck's correlations without assuming a direct causal relationship between body and behavior.[12]

Hereditary Approach

Students of criminology are invariably confronted with studies made of three seemingly criminal families: the Jukes, the Kallikaks, and the Nams. The legendary criminology of the Jukes and Kallikaks is customarily cited as evidence of the deviance being inherited like other family characteristics. The sociological "environmentalists," of course, posed the traditional argument that the very process of being reared in a criminal atmosphere helps perpetuate deviance and has little to do with lines of heredity.

Biologist Ashley Montague seems to combine the environmental and the heredity influence by acknowledging both "cultural factors" along with "the genetically determined, nervous, methological individual." Somewhat surprisingly for a biologist, Montague acknowledges *culture* as being possibly more significant than heredity in determining behavior patterns.

George N. Thompson, a biological psychiatrist, provides a new Lombrosian direction. He holds that organic brain damage is a prerequisite for habitual criminality. A defective environment, he says, provides only the soil wherein the seed may grow. The seed itself lies in the brain cells. He bases his assertion on his own studies (whose design he does not outline). He states that in a group of 280 delinquents or psychopaths (he uses the terms interchangeably), 93.6 percent had one or more symptoms of neural damage, compared with 28.5 percent of nondelinquents. He further showed high incidence of abnormal electroencephalograms and of abnormal psychological tests among his psychopaths.

Three years ago, one of my students became interested in Thompson's findings and resolved to duplicate his study as far as possible. He took a group of 43 diagnosed psychopaths in a Missouri state hospital and compared them with control groups according to Thompson's three criteria—neurological exam, psychological test, and electroencephalogram. In none of the three criteria did he find any significant difference between the psychopaths and the

12 Hardman, "The Case for Eclecticism," p. 3.

> controls. However, there is still room for concern. Thompson points to the similarity between certain forms of encephalitis and forms of delinquency. Encephalitic children are hyperactive, aggressive, destructive, sadistic, malicious, profane. Punishment has little effect. They show short-lived regret and soon return to their wild behavior. They "drive their environment to despair." Now this is practically a verbatim description of some of the delinquents you and I have handled. Further, another syndrome of wild, impulsive, unpredictable outbursts of maliciousness, aggression, and vandalism is known to be related to a type of brain damage associated with the Rh factor in parents. Note how closely this fits with Glueck's description of his delinquents' temperaments: restless, energetic, impulsive, adventurous, aggressive.[13]

The field of criminology in general continues to reserve judgment on hereditary considerations in deviate behavior.

SUMMARY

Who are the criminals and delinquents? Why are they involved in criminal or delinquent behavior? What can be done about them? These are the basic queries to which this chapter has addressed itself. Delinquent behavior has been classed into three general categories: *sociological, psychological,* or *physiological.*

Some of the theories relating to these areas were: Albert Cohen's theory of the *gang subculture;* Edwin Sutherland's *differential association* (expanded upon by Walter Reckless); Sheldon and Eleanor Glueck's findings in their volume *Unravelling Juvenile Delinquency;* and Paul Tappan's theory regarding the relationship between deviant behavior and the national economy. Contributions by Franz Alexander, the celebrated psychoanalyst, and David Abrahamsen, a noted psychiatrist, were also included in this chapter. These approaches strive to cut through the morass of confusion and conflict regarding the phenomenon of crime and delinquency. In this chapter, we have tried to integrate the contemporary contributions of several diverse social scientific disciplines—most notably sociology, cultural anthropology, social psychology, clinical psychology, criminology, and social psychiatry.

QUESTIONS

1. Discuss the psychological approach to crime and delinquency.
2. Discuss the sociological approach to crime and delinquency.

[13] Hardman, "The Case for Eclecticism," pp. 3-4.

3. Sutherland's theory of "differential association" is presented in this chapter; briefly critique the theory.
4. In what manner does economic status and national economy relate to crime and delinquency? Discuss briefly.
5. Sheldon classified delinquency into certain body types. What were these classifications?

ANNOTATED REFERENCES

BARNES, H. E., and TEETERS, N. K. *New Horizons in Criminology*. 3rd ed. Englewood Cliffs, N.J.: Prentice-Hall, 1959. Chapters 1 through 5 give the reader an excellent overview of criminal behavior in nontechnical language.

BARRON, M. *The Juvenile in Delinquent Society*. New York: Knopf, 1954, Chapter 4. An excellent discussion of the subject title.

BLOCH, H. A., and FLYNN, F. *Delinquency: The Juvenile Offender in America Today*. New York: Random House, 1956, pp. 205-19. Presents a thorough discussion of delinquent behavior in our society.

BORDUA, D. "Delinquency." *The Annals of the American Academy of Political and Social Science*, Vol. 338 (November, 1961), pp. 119-36. The author discusses *classic theories* relating to gang delinquency and impact on children.

ELDEFONSO, E.; COFFEY, A.; and GRACE, R. C. *Principles of Law Enforcement*, New York: John Wiley & Sons, 1968, Chapter 3. Theoretical approaches to criminal behavior are presented. The areas discussed are psychological, sociological, and physiological.

GLUECK, S., and GLUECK, E. *Unravelling Juvenile Delinquency*. New York: Commonwealth Fund, 1950. The authors present a classic study, covering many years of research, about the psychological, sociological, and physiological aspects of delinquent behavior.

HARDMAN, D. G., "The Case for Eclecticism," *Crime and Delinquency*, July 1964, pp. 3–8. The article discusses theories presented in this chapter in nontechnical language.

RECKLESS, W. C. *The Crime Problem*. 2nd ed. New York: Appleton-Century-Crofts, 1955. An introductory study of criminal behavior and the control, treatment, and prevention of crime in the United States.

TAFT, D. R. *Crimonology*. 3rd ed. New York: Macmillan, 1956. The first section (Part One) of this volume discusses the "Background of Criminal Behavior" in nontechnical language. An extremely interesting and classical volume by a noted author and scholar in the field of criminology.

PART THREE

Special Enforcement Problems and the Police Role in Court

Historically the police officer and the criminal justice system have operated as separate entities, coming together only at the apex of a criminal case and separating again during the post-trial procedures. This operational system, though not altogether ineffective, has resulted in some rather wide gaps of understanding and philosophy regarding justice as an American institution. Today we see the emerging roles in the entire system of criminal justice developing a closer relationship and demanding that such gaps be narrowed through more cooperative efforts from arrest to release of all suspected criminal offenders. . . .

We think it especially important that the police officer of today be thoroughly acquainted with the criminal procedure responsibilities of the entire court system and be able to identify his role in this system.

G. R. WRIGHT AND J. MARLO
The Police Officer and Criminal Justice

7

Social Problems: Impact on Law Enforcement

Law enforcement is intimately and primarily involved with social problems since crime and delinquency are defined as such. Specifically, law enforcement was created to deal with these particular social problems, but there is ample evidence that the problems of crime and delinquency are interrelated to most other social problems. Consequently, the impact of social problems on law enforcement is such that every person associated with the criminal justice system needs to be cognizant of its implications and ramifications.

The social and behavioral scientists have defined social problems in a number of ways. A review of some of these definitions might be helpful in reaching a fuller understanding of social problems *per se.*

SOME DEFINITIONS OF SOCIAL PROBLEMS

Four definitions of social problems will follow. Each definition shares many things in common with the other definitions but stresses a particular point about social problems. These different points should be pondered by the student interested in criminal justice. The first definition to be considered is by R. C. Fuller and R. R. Myers:

> A social problem is a condition which is defined by a considerable number of persons as a deviation from some social norm which they cherish. . . . *Social problems are what people think they are,* and if conditions are not de-

fined as social problems by the people involved in them, they are not problems to those people, although they may be problems to outsiders or scientists.[1]

A second definition of a social problem comes from P. B. Horton and G. R. Leslie:

> A social problem is a condition affecting a significant number of people in ways considered undesirable, about which it is felt something can be done through collective social action.[2]

The third definition of a social problem was expressed by R. R. Bell as follows:

> A social problem is . . . the result of a discrepancy between values of a society and the actual state of that society. Therefore, a primary motive for the study of social problems has been to look for ways to prevent, control, and ameliorate (them) . . . Social problems . . . exist when they are so defined (by) . . . one broad spectrum of society.[3]

The fourth definition of social problems to be presented here is that of J. Bernard. This long definition has been shortened with the important points preserved.

> Social problems (have) . . . three types of criteria . . . which (can be) . . . applied in determining (them). . . . One (is) . . . a humanitarian-sentimental criterion. One (is) . . . a utilitarian criterion, and one (is) . . . a criterion (called) . . . dysfunctionality.
>
> 1. The humanitarian-sentimental criterion of whether or not any stress situation should be reformed is whether or not it causes actual pain or suffering. According to this point of view, pain and suffering are intrinsically bad and therefore anything which produces them should be reformed, changed, or (abolished).
> 2. The utilitarian criterion specifies that a situation is a social problem not because it creates pain and suffering—physical or social—but because it imposes expense upon the rest of society, either officially in the form of taxes or unofficially in the form of voluntary contributions.
> 3. The criterion of dysfunctionality defines social problems in the societal sense. The functioning, or even survival, of groups, societies, or of cultures as a whole, is the central concern here.[4]

[1] R. C. Fuller and R. R. Myers, "The Natural History of a Social Problem," *American Sociological Review,* Vol. 6 (June, 1941), p. 320 (italics ours).

[2] P. B. Horton and G. R. Leslie, *The Sociology of Social Problems,* 4th ed. (New York: Appleton-Century-Croft, 1970), p. 4.

[3] R. R. Bell, *Social Deviance* (Homewood, Ill.: The Dorsey Press, 1971), p. 3.

[4] J. Bernard, *Social Problems at Midcentury* (New York: Holt, Rinehart and Winston, 1957), pp. 104-06.

Fuller and Myers' definition indicates that social problems are deviations from a norm. Norms are a statistical concept, and therefore this definition indicates that the intensity of a social problem can be measured. The ability to measure a problem, be it social or otherwise, can be most important in its solution. Horton and Leslie's definition states that a social problem affects a significant number of people in ways considered undesirable. This definition effectively separates social problems from individual problems.

Bell's definition, as well as Horton and Leslie's, implies that social problems can be eliminated, prevented, or controlled. This definition leaves one with the idea that something can be done to affect a social problem in a positive manner—certainly, an important concept. Bell's definition also suggests that social problems may be the result of discrepancies between the values of society and the actual state of that society. This idea relates to problems such as gambling.

Finally, Bernard's definition indicates that social problems impose expense on the rest of society. This definition of a social problem concerns itself with the huge economic cost of these problems, and certainly cost is a most important ingredient in social problems. Armed with these definitions and some ideas as to why these definitions were selected, one can examine certain specific social problems in a broader perspective. The first social problem to be examined will be poverty.

POVERTY

The definition of poverty cannot be given in absolute terms because it varies from one society to the next. For example, minimum economic standards in a highly industrialized country may be almost utopian standards in underdeveloped nations. Some light can be shed on this situation by checking the definitions of social problems. The idea that a social problem is a problem so defined by society is most helpful in defining poverty. Lewis A. Coser, put it quite succinctly by saying: "The poor are men who have been so defined by society and have evoked particular reaction from (society)." [5] In the United States at this time it is generally felt that being poor means not having enough money to live in a decent manner; people in these circumstances exist in a condition of want or near want.

By and large the poor live in slums or ghettoes. Generally speaking, slums are make up of ramshackle houses, inhabited by the poor.[6] On the

[5] L. A. Coser, "The Sociology of Poverty," *Social Problems,* Vol. 13 (Fall, 1965), p. 141.

[6] G. Leinwand, ed., *Problems of American Society: The Slums* (New York: Washington Square Press, 1968), p. 16.

other hand, a ghetto is described as an area of a city which has acute social disorganization and poverty and whose members are from ethnic or racial groups which live in more or less involuntary segregation.[7]

Generally speaking, the poor live in slums and/or ghettoes. As indicated above, ghettoes tend to be in cities, whereas slums can be found anywhere. Slums are the ghettoes of the city, but they are also the shacks of the migrant workers and share-croppers in the country.

The reason why the criminal justice system should be concerned with poverty, the poor, ghettoes and slums, has been stated quite succintly in a report by the President's Commission on Law Enforcement and the Administration of Justice:

> One of the most fully documented facts about crime is that the common serious crime that worries people most—murder, forcible rape, robbery, aggravated assault, and burglary—happen most often in the slums of large cities. Study after study, in city after city, in all regions of the country, have traced variations in the rates for these crimes. The results, with monotonous regularity, show that the offenses, the victims, and the offenders, are found most frequently in the poorest and most deteriorated and socially disorganized areas.[8]

The idea that slums breed crime and delinquency as well as hopelessness, despair, degradation and disease of the mind and body, is certainly not new, nor is it unfounded.

Slums are composed of drab, dilapidated, shabby buildings. The slum dweller has little reason to feel proud about the outside, or the inside, of his home. Often the home is regarded with shame. This is most important because the children of the slum dweller also see the home as unattractive and consequently not a place to bring friends. This unattractiveness, along with the limited space in most slum homes, cause many children to be out on the streets at an early age and for much of the day. The lack of space in the slum dwelling compared with space in the typical suburban house is documented by the National Advisory Commission on Civil Disorders.[9]

In addition to the immediate family, the slum home is often shared with other relatives or with friends. One room may be shared with brothers, sisters, aunts, uncles, cousins, or maybe even parents. Because

[7] *Report of the National Advisory Commission on Civil Disorders* (Washington, D.C.: U.S. Gov't. Printing Office, 1968), p. 6.

[8] "The Challenge of Crime in a Free Society," A Report by The President's Commission on Law Enforcement and Administration of Justice (Washington, D.C.: U.S. Gov't. Printing Office, 1967), p. 35.

[9] *Report of the National Advisory Commission of Civil Disorders,* p. 258.

of this lack of space, there isn't enough room for privacy, let alone recreation.

A note of interest in regard to overcrowding is that many behavioral scientists feel that mammals, when exposed to overcrowded conditions, respond with uncontrolled aggression. According to the behavioral scientists, a person will react with hostility when a second person intrudes on his "personal space." The problems related to overcrowding and aggression were first suggested by Calhoun.[10]

The children of the slum, in an attempt to gain more room for themselves, are forced to go into the streets. Recreation areas such as parks are at a premium if they exist at all in the slum areas of the community. The streets of these areas, however, abound with criminal activity. Activities such as dope pushing, numbers running, prostitution, pimping, drinking, and drunkenness are apparent to even the youngest child. Life in the slums is harsh for children and adults alike. However, this was endured in the past because it was felt that one could leave the slums behind by getting a good education or by getting a good job. A closer examination of these ideas, with reference to what takes place in actual practice, generally shows something quite different.

EDUCATION

A good education has traditionally been the means by which people have escaped from poverty and the slums, and the educational process has been an important institution as regards the American ideal. However, by and large, schools have not completely succeeded in slum—particularly in slums that can also be designated as ghettoes. This lack of success has caused grievances and resentments by the ghetto minorities. Their grievances are based upon the record of public education for ghetto children. The records show that in the critical verbal skills of reading and writing, minority students, in particular black students, fall farther behind with each year of schooling completed. In 1966, the Department of Health, Education, and Welfare published a report indicating that as a group children from the ghetto are somewhat below children from suburban areas with respect to their entering educational level. By the sixth grade, standard achievement tests indicate that black students are 1.6 grades behind the white suburban student; by the twelfth grade they are 3.3 grades behind the white suburban student who had

[10] J. B. Calhoun, "A 'Behavioral Sink'," *Roots of Behavior,* ed. E. L. Bliss (New York: Harper & Brothers), pp. 295-315.

started school at the same time.[11] As a result of this type experience with school, minority students from the ghetto are three times as likely as the suburban white student to drop out of school. Unfortunately a very high proportion of these drop-outs are not equipped to enter the normal job market. Furthermore, when they do enter the job market they tend to get low-paying, low-skilled jobs.

Another concern regarding the poor in education is the fact that even free public education costs the student money. A student needs to be at least comfortably dressed to attend school. Obviously the clothing needs to be appropriate for the climate in which the child lives. Children of the poor often do not have the bare minimum amount of clothing needed to attend school; and, consequently, they may stay home or take to the street. For a person to learn effectively, his physical needs must also be fulfilled. If a person is hungry, as is often the case with poor children, that person will not be as concerned with learning the abstractions of reading, writing, and arithmetic.[12] There is even some cause to believe that improper diet and undernourishment during the formative years in a child's life may leave that child with permanent brain damage, which manifests itself as mental retardation.[13]

It can be seen that the effects of poverty often suffocate the process of education. Certainly, the American ideal of advancing one's social and economic status by virtue of obtaining a good education is adversely affected by poverty. But if education is felt to move one away from poverty, then employment is felt to have an even greater effect in removing one from the clutches of poverty. Thus, education is thought to have a secondary effect on poverty, whereas employment has a primary effect. An examination of employment should prove useful.

EMPLOYMENT

The federal government has indicated how important employment is in regard to the American ideal. This has been stated in the following manner:

> The capacity to obtain and hold a "good job" is the traditional test of participation in the American society. Steady employment with adequate com-

[11] Department of Health, Education, and Welfare, *Equality of Educational Opportunity* (Washington, D.C.: U.S. Gov't. Printing Office, 1966), p. 20.

[12] G. Leinwand, ed., *Problems of American Society: Poverty and the Poor* (New York: Washington Square Press, 1968), p. 33.

[13] E. Elmer and G. S. Gregg, "Developmental Characteristics of Abused Children," *Pediatrics,* Vol. 40 (October, 1967), pp. 596-602.

pensation provides both purchasing power and social status. It develops the capacities, confidence, and self-esteem the individual needs to be a responsible citizen, and provides a basis for a stable family life.[14]

In the slums and ghettoes there is a chronic unemployment problem. This unemployment is felt to be one of the fundamental causes of the persistent poverty in disadvantaged areas. Surveys conducted in low-income neighborhoods by the Department of Labor in 1966 revealed that the rate of unemployment was approximately three times higher than the unemployment rate of white suburban areas.[15]

Perhaps more important than unemployment is the undesirable nature of many of the jobs open to the poor and particularly to minority poor. Minority poor are often concentrated in the lowest paid and lowest skilled work opportunities. These occupations often involve a great deal of instability and uncertainty; they hold little or no meaningful opportunity for advancement, and they tend to be extremely low status in the eyes of both the employee and the employer. Most times these jobs are monotonous if not unpleasant and exhausting in nature. It is a well-known fact that minority-group members are much more likely to be at or below the poverty level; minority-group men are approximately twice as likely to be unemployed as Caucasian men. Furthermore, when minorities are employed, they often hold low-paying, low-status jobs. Table 7-1 shows this relationship quite well.

Table 7-1 The Social and Economic Conditions of Negroes in the United States *

	Percentage of male workers in each type of occupation, 1965	
Type of occupation	*White*	*Nonwhite*
Professional, technical, and managerial	27	9
Clerical and sales	14	9
Craftsmen and foremen	20	12
Operatives	20	27
Service workers	5	15
Nonfarm laborers	6	20
Farmers and farm workers	7	8

* See also *Report of the National Commission on Civil Disorders* (Washington, D.C.: U.S. Government Printing Office, 1967), p. 124.

14 *Report of the National Advisory Commission on Civil Disorders,* p. 124.

15 *Report of the National Advisory Commission on Civil Disorders,* p. 126.

Note that approximately 27 percent of the white work force is classified as professional, technical, and/or managerial, whereas only 9 percent of the nonwhite work force is found in this category where the highest paid jobs are found. On the other hand, 12 percent of the white labor force is found in the categories of service worker and nonfarm laborer, whereas 36 percent of the nonwhite work force is found in these categories. The categories of service worker and nonfarm laborer represents the lower-paying jobs in the economy.

Slum dwellers often cannot support a family. This is due to the high rate of unemployment or a low-paying job. These low-paying jobs often lack the necessary status to sustain a worker's self-respect or the respect of his family and friends. This respect is further decreased because the women of these slum dwelling families are often forced to work and may be able to earn more money than the men of the family.

Unemployment rates are higher among teen-agers than adults. This is true in all segments of our society. The significant result of this is that young people who are poor and who are not in school will have a great deal of idle time on their hands. The result is usually an increase in criminal behavior. The old adage, "Idle hands are the Devil's workshop," can certainly be substantiated throughout the criminal justice system.

After this brief view of the social problems of poverty, a survey of the social problem of racial and/or ethnic discrimination needs to be undertaken. It will be seen that discrimination in many instances is interrelated to poverty.

RACE AND DISCRIMINATION

The predominant attitude of white Americans toward Americans of ethnic or racial minorities has had its telling effect upon those minorities and upon the American society in general. The trends are most noticeable among black Americans. Although slavery was abolished more than 100 years ago, discriminatory practices are responsible for three mainstays of our present society. These are pervasive discrimination and segregation, black migration to the central city with white exodus from the central city, and the formation of the black ghetto. The exclusion of a great number of black Americans from the benefits of economic progress through discrimination in employment and education has continued up to the present moment. As a result, unemployment rates for black Americans are generally at least double those for white Americans.[16]

Probably as important as unemployment is the underemployment

[16] *Report of the National Advisory Commission on Civil Disorders,* p. 124.

and/or low-status jobs that are open to black Americans. As mentioned, blacks are concentrated in the lowest-skilled and lowest-paying jobs; the jobs held by black Americans often involve low wages, instability, and no guarantee that the job will continue. The job may well be unpleasant and exhausting and present no meaningful advancement possibilities. Furthermore, the status of the job will be low both in the eyes of the employee and the employer.

The reason many black Americans do not qualify for better jobs is because their educational attainment is so low, which in turn can be traced to the school system. The vast majority of inner-city schools are rigidly segregated due to racially segregated neighborhoods and "neighborhood school policies." This of course has the effect of transferring segregation from housing to education. Two reports from the federal government show that inner-city ghetto schools are not only overcrowded but also tend to be the oldest and poorest equipped.[17] Furthermore, the schools attended by disadvantaged black children are commonly staffed by teachers with less experience and lower qualifications than the teachers in middle-class, suburban schools. It is not surprising then that the quality of education offered in ghetto schools is further diminished by the use of materials and curricula which are poorly adapted to the life experiences of the ghetto child. Most educational material is designed to serve middle-class suburban schools, and consequently some of it is irrelevant to children from the ghetto.

Ghettoes were originally formed by black migration from the south to central cities of the north; this movement was coupled with the white exodus from these central cities to the suburban areas. The migration to the central cities followed an old, established, American pattern. In every generation in America, the slums have been the homes of newcomers to the city. The immigrant first settled in the slums after arriving from his home across the seas. The Italians, the Irish, the Germans, the Russians, and the Jews all at one time or another lived in the poor housing of the central city.

The early pattern of blacks settling in the central metropolitan areas resembled that of the immigrant groups coming to the United States from abroad. However, the later phases of black settlement and expansion in metropolitan areas did not follow the pattern of white immigrants. As the whites were absorbed by the larger society, many left their predominantly ethnic neighborhoods and moved to suburban housing. Thereafter, they scattered randomly throughout the suburban area.

Nowhere in urban America has the black population been dispersed

[17] *Report of the National Advisory Commission on Civil Disorders* and *Equality of Educational Opportunity.*

randomly. Indeed, thousands of black families who have attained living standards and cultural levels matching or surpassing many whites have remained predominantly in black neighborhoods. This is true because blacks have been effectively excluded from white residential areas. The effect has been that a good many black Americans have again been segregated into ghetto-type neighborhoods. In regard to the inner city, this concentration of impoverished, black Americans, coupled with the continued exodus of middle-class whites, has burdened the resources of the cities by creating demands for increased services for unmet human needs. As more and more human needs go unmet, more people become less able to advance themselves. The result is a continuation of the poverty cycle and its effects upon crime and delinquency.

Another important factor regarding discrimination is that it tends to adversely affect the attitude of a good number of minority groups toward the criminal justice system. This is quite graphically pointed out in the *Task Force Report.*[18] Generally, the information in this report shows that approximately 66 to 75 percent of the white community believe that police are doing a goob job. On the other hand, approximately 50 percent of the members of the black community feel that police are doing a good job. This percentage difference reflects the dissatisfaction of minority groups with law enforcement and probably the entire criminal justice system. Undoubtedly, this dissatisfaction stems from society's discrimination against minorities. But such dissatisfaction with the criminal justice system weakens the system as a whole. Certainly, efforts to alleviate discrimination and to change negative attitude toward the criminal justice system to positive attitudes would serve the interests of the entire system.

Let us now move from the problems of poverty and discrimination to a consideration of the problem of family disorganization.

FAMILY DISORGANIZATION

Traditionally, family disorganization in itself has not been treated as a social problem. In the past, the results of family disorganization have been treated as problems. Some of these results were desertion, divorce, and delinquency. Probably, at this time in our history, divorce should no longer be considered a social problem. In our present-day society, divorce no longer fits the criterion that the majority of the persons involved must consider the situation a social problem. On the other

[18] The President's Commission on Law Enforcement and Administration of Justice, *Task Force Report: The Police* (Washington, D.C.: U.S. Gov't. Printing Office, 1967), pp. 145-49.

hand, the complete disorganization of family units would certainly have a telling effect on the society s a whole. Consequently, any dysfunction in the family, the smallest of society's units, does have an effect on the larger unit, society itself.

Any dysfunction in society will be felt by the criminal justice system since it is so intimately concerned and involved with society. However, it is police who feel the brunt of domestic disturbances in the society. The police, because they are the front line of the criminal justice system, are often the first to be called to help settle marital disputes. It is no accident that the police are called since marital disputes have a great potential for violence. In fact, domestic disturbances are often associated with such serious crime as homicide and assault.[19]

Unchecked family disturbances are known by all segments of the criminal justice system. Another facet of family disorganization which has affected the criminal justice system is the fact that the family is the basic institution for developing a child's potential. When a family fails to meet the needs that a child has for developing his potential, phrases are applied such as "broken homes," "shiftless adult," "bad household management," "erratic employment habits," "born out-of-wedlock," or "father's whereabouts unknown."[20] The results of these conditions on child are often delinquent behavior.

A closer look at delinquency and family relationships will show this more clearly. If one parent (especially the father of a son) is absent, parental control and authority are reduced, and consequently vulnerability to the influences of delinquent behavior is increased. In cases of divorce, desertion, and birth out of wedlock, the absence of one parent is almost assured. This is not to say that delinquents come only from one-parent families. The fact of the matter is that a one-parent family with stability and harmony is much less likely to produce a delinquent than a two-parent family which is continually at odds.

In an article by Grogan and Grogan,[21] it is shown that significant conflict and tension within a family disrupt wholesome personality development in the children; excessive conflict interferes with the teaching and learning processes involved in socialization. The child reared in such an atmosphere often learns negative values, attitudes, and behavior.

Contrary to popular opinion, not all interfamilial conflict is between the mother and the father. Conflict frequently occurs between the parent

19 *Report of the National Advisory Commission on Civil Disorders,* p. 167.

20 *Report of the National Advisory Commission on Civil Disorders,* p. 167.

21 H. J. Grogan and R. C. Grogan, "The Criminogenic Family—Does Chronic Tension Trigger Delinquency?" *Crime and Delinquency,* Vol. 14 (July, 1968), pp. 220-25.

and child. These conflicts may be just as bitter as conflicts between the parents, but they usually cause more damage to the personality of the growing youth. All families naturally have conflict, but it is chronic conflict and tension which greatly affect personality growth in the child. When there is a high frequency of conflict in a family, discipline suffers.

Social scientists feel that discipline is related to development of interpersonal controls, which allow the individual to make responsible decisions. When these interpersonal controls do not function, the individual will tend to make irresponsible decisions which are often delinquent in nature. Thus, unwise parental discipline tends to be involved in the development of delinquent behavior. Disciplinary practices can be categorized as either exceedingly permissive or exceedingly stern. When the discipline is exceedingly permissive, a child is in charge of his own affairs from a very early age. The child becomes accustomed to making decisions for himself and regards the directions of adults as a challenge to his established independence. On the other hand, strictness which generally amounts to control by force rather than by fair mindedness causes the child to harbor resentment toward the parent until the day he can successfully assert physical mastery of himself. Under this type of disciplinary regime, a child learns that discipline is a matter of power.

An inconsistent mixture of permissiveness and firmness is even more likely to produce a delinquent. This type of mixture is often found in the home where there is internal conflict between parents. Conflicts between parents as well as general family disorganization not only lead to delinquent behavior but may also be connected with child neglect and child abuse. The criminal justice system is well aware of child neglect. It is characterized by abandonment, inadequate adult supervision, irregular meals, lack of medical care, filthy living conditions, or other evidence of parental malfeasance.[22] (See Figure 7-1.) It should be noted that child neglect seems to be highly related to the social problem of poverty; it is related to poverty much more than to child abuse.

Child abuse is a severe form of parental rejection in many cases. Parental affection and/or rejection is an important factor in whether a child becomes an asset or a liability to society as a whole. The President's Commission on Law Enforcement indicates that delinquency correlates more highly with inconsistency of affection from the parents than it does with consistency of discipline. It is generally found that a disproportionately large number of aggressive delinquents have been denied the opportunity to express their feelings of dependence on their parents.[23]

[22] G. R. Wheeler, "Children of the Court: A Profile of Poverty," *Crime and Delinquency*, Vol. 17 (April, 1971), pp. 152-59.

[23] "The Challenge of Crime," p. 64.

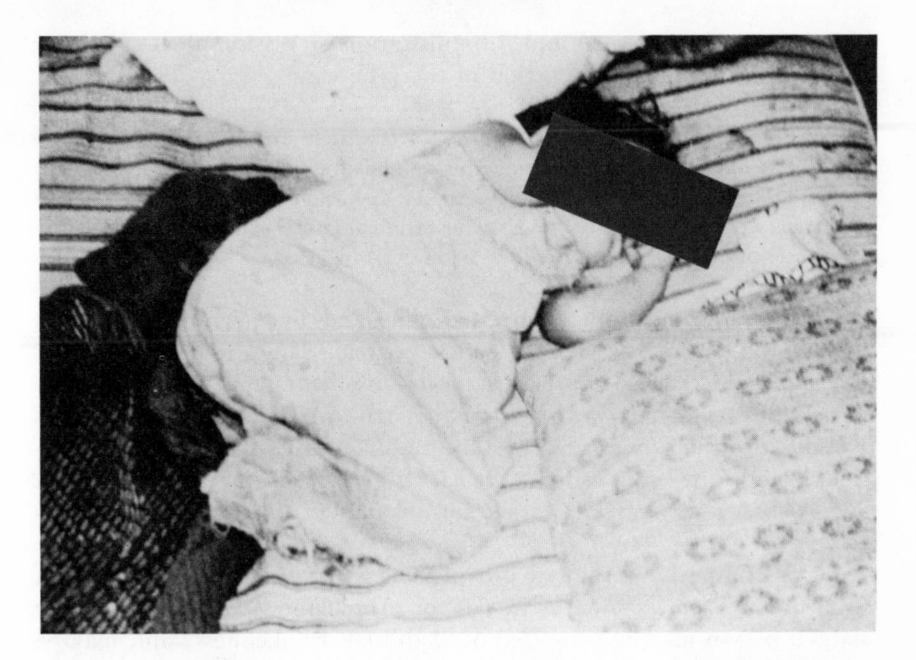

Figure 7-1 Studies have shown that many delinquents were previously known to be dependent children of the juvenile court. Photo courtesy of the Santa Clara County Juvenile Probation Department, San Jose, Ca.

This same source indicates that the strong influence a father has over his son is most significant. When mother-son and father-son relationships are compared, the father-son relationship seems to be more significantly related to the development of delinquent behavior. The importance of this information can be seen when it is remembered that family disorganization is highly related to families without fathers—whether this is due to divorce, desertion, or because the child was born out of wedlock. Although family disorganization has not been specifically designated as a social problem by many social scientists, apparently it has a number of attributes which would indeed make it a social problem. At least, from the point of view of the criminal justice system, it would seem that studying family disorganization as a social problem would be most helpful.

ALCOHOLISM

The criminal justice system's concern with the social problem of alcoholism is summed up best in a statement by the President's Commission on Law Enforcement and Administration of Justice. That statement indicates the size and proportion of the problem.

> Two million arrests in 1965—one of every three arrests in America—were for the offense of public drunkenness. The great volume of these arrests placed an extremely heavy load on the operation of the criminal justice system. It burdens police, clogs lower criminal courts, and crowds penal institutions throughout the United States.[24]

Ordinarily, the alcoholic is arrested time and time again, he poses a major problem for the criminal justice system. The alcoholic is usually referred to the criminal justice system for an offense such as "being drunk in a public place"; however, this is not true in all cases since in some jurisdictions there is no law prohibiting drunkenness. In these jurisdictions, drunkenness that causes a breach of the peace is punishable. Georgia and Alabama, as well as Chicago, are examples of jurisdictions of this sort.

Generally speaking, the law provides for a maximum sentence ranging from five days to six months in jail for drunkenness. However, in some states a person may be convicted of "habitual drunkenness" and may be sentenced to imprisonment for as long as two years. The most common maximum sentence for drunkenness in the United States is thirty days. Once a person is arrested for drunkenness, he is usually placed in a barren cell called a "drunk tank" where he is detained for several hours. The drunk tanks in some cities hold as many as 200 people, whereas others hold only one or two persons.

Offenders charged with drunkenness are generally brought before a magistrate the morning after their arrest, and often they appear in groups as lage as twenty. Usually defendants charged with drunkenness are processed through the court system with haste and are either released or sentenced to jail. In jail the offender is fed and sheltered and released when his time has been served. After the offender serves his brief sentence, he is released. More than likely, however, he returns to society from jail with no money, no job, and no plans. It is no wonder he is often arrested again within a matter of days or even hours of his release.

Most persons in the criminal justice system feel that presently the system is ineffective in its ability to deter drunkenness or to meet the problem of the chronic alcoholic. In most cases, the system merely removes the drunk from public view; in addition, the drunk may be detoxified and forced into a brief period of sobriety. In many cases, he is provided

[24] The President's Commission on Law Enforcement and Administration of Justice, *Task Force Report: Drunkenness* (Washington, D.C.: U.S. Gov't. Printing Office, 1967), p. 1.

with food and shelter and emergency medical treatment. There is a great deal of concern, however, that the system does not meet the underlying social and psychological problems which cause alcoholism.

Up to this point most attention has been given to the chronic alcoholic offender. In an article by Rubington,[25] alcoholic offenders are categorized into three different types. One type is the alcoholic offender who *commits crimes against public property* (essentially the type discussed so far). A second type of alcoholic offender is the one who *commits a crime against persons while under the influence of alcohol.* Under the influence of alcohol, inhibitions are apparently lowered, and a person is no longer able to handle his hostility through internal controls. Consequently the drunken person becomes very aggressive; the result is that such persons are often subject to arrest for drunk and assault charges. A third type of offender is the one who *commits property crimes while under the influence of alcohol.* Often these persons commit forgery and/or check passing while under the influence of alcohol.

Behavior that accompanies the use of alcohol results from a combination of sociocultural, psychological, and situational factors. Insofar as the criminal justice system is concerned, the problem of alcoholism is broader than the "drunk in public" problem. In fact, the problem of public drunkenness is not necessarily handled best by the criminal justice system. Indeed, the President's Commission on Law Enforcement and Administration of Justice recommended that being drunk in public should *not* be a crime. The Commission felt that the application of disorderly conduct statutes would be sufficient to protect the public against criminal behavior stemming from over-indulgence in alcohol.[26] The strongest barrier to making such a change, however, is that in most jurisdictions there are no alternative agencies which could effectively deal with the problem of public drunkenness.

One alternative to the present method of handling drunkenness would be to establish civil detoxification centers. The detoxification centers would replace the drunk tanks which are presently used. Person involved in public drunkenness could be brought to detoxification centers and detained there until they are sober. Once sober, the individual would decide whether to continue treatment for alcoholism. Presently California has enacted such legislation; however, it has not been in operation long enough for any substantial evaluation of its effectiveness.

The social problem of alcoholism will not be solved merely by considering it a "health" problem instead of a crime or by placing the drunk

[25] E. Rubington, "Types of Alcoholic Offenders," *Federal Probation,* Vol. 33 (March, 1969), pp. 28-35.

[26] *Task Force Report: Drunkenness,* p. 4.

in a detoxification center rather than in jail. In fact, there is little reason to believe that the chronic alcoholic offender will change a life pattern of drinking after a few days of sobriety in a detoxification center. Therefore it appears mandatory that any detoxification facilities should be coordinated with after-care agencies. Obviously such programs as Alcoholics Anonymous along with innovative programs not yet tried need to be included in the solution of the problem of alcoholism.

The next social problem to be considered here is the drug addiction problem. Like drunkenness, it is defined as a crime without victims.

DRUGS

In recent years the so-called "drug problem" has been labeled as a major social problem which is undermining the morality of society and destroying many members of the younger generation. The criminal justice system has been painfully aware of this social problem for quite some time. A publication of the federal government indicates this best.

> Organized criminals engaged in drug traffic (are) making high profits. Drug addicts, to support their habits, (are) stealing millions of dollars worth of property every year and contributing to the public's fear of robbery and burglary. The police, the courts, and the jails and prisons, and social agencies of all kinds (are) devoting great amounts of time, money, and manpower (in) attempts to control drug abuse. Worst of all, thousands of human lives (are) being wasted.[27]

Drugs that are involved in abuse are usually placed in two categories. The first category is *narcotics,* and the second category is *dangerous drugs.* The people that abuse these drugs are usually called *addicts* in the case of narcotics and *users* in the case of dangerous drugs. The reason for this is that not all drugs are addictive per se.

At this time there is no clearly defined definition of addiction. However, the medical profession speaks of addiction as physical dependence accompanied by an alteration in the central nervous system which results in illness when the narcotic is abruptly discontinued. Presently the phrase *psychological dependence* is attributed to many drugs that do not cause physical dependence. Since some drugs cause physical dependence and some drugs cause psychological dependence, many persons feel that the problem can be described more accurately by using the term *drug depen-*

[27] The President's Commission on Law Enforcement and Administration of Justice, *Task Force Report: Narcotics and Drug Abuse* (Washington, D.C.: U.S. Gov't. Printing Office, 1967), p. 1.

dence along with a modifying phrase indicating the particular type of drug that causes the dependency.

Narcotics have a highly technical legal definition, but by and large they include opium, morphine, their derivatives, and compounds that are their synthetic equivalents. Some of the opiates have great medical value, the most common of these being morphine and codeine. These two drugs are prescribed for use in approved medical settings; however, misuse or illicit use of these two drugs is not uncommon. The principal opiate derivative for which there is no medical use but which is found most often in illegal drug traffic is heroin. The opiate derivatives are the drugs that generally cause physical dependence. Once a person becomes physically dependent on morphine, or more probably on heroin, they suffer withdrawal sickness when they are unable to use this narcotic.

Persons who are dependent on morphine and heroin usually inject the drug into their system with a hypodermic needle or facsimile thereof. One exception is the addict who has been a serviceman in Southeast Asia; these addicts became drug dependent by smoking cigarettes laced with high-quality heroin. It should be noted that heroin is an illegal drug, and it may not be lawfully imported or manufactured in the United States under any circumstances. Heroin is different from the other opium derivates and their synthetic equivalents since these other drugs are used for medical purposes. The opium derivatives and their synthetic equivalents are classified pharmaceutically as depressants. A depressant relieves anxiety and tension and diminishes the sex and hunger drives as well as other primitive drives.

Another group of drugs manufactured mainly in the United States and sometimes used in the illicit market is the barbiturates, also classed as depressants. Barbiturates such as phenobarbital and secobarbital are manufactured for medical use; however, they are also used for illicit purposes. Since they are relatively inexpensive, barbiturates are often used by teenagers. By and large, barbiturates are taken orally, although it is possible to take them by injection. They are not truly drugs that cause physical dependence, but it is felt that they do cause psychological dependence.

Another group of drugs that causes psychological dependence is amphetamines, which are classified as stimulants. A stimulant causes wakefullness, elevates the mood, and induces a feeling of well-being. This is the basis of their medical value. When prescribed by a physician, they may be used for fatigue, for control of overweight, and in the treatment of mental disorder. There are dozens of amphetamine preparations on the market. They go by the nicknames of "bennies," "dexies," or "speed." A person can develop tolerance to amphetamines, which enables him to ingest or inject larger and larger doses. This is true of the barbiturates and opiate derivatives as well. However, a sudden increase or a dose which is too large may produce bizzare mental effects such as delusions or hallucinations.

Another class of drugs is known as the hallucinogenics because they produce bizzarre mental effects. The hallucinogenic or psychedelic drugs were first hailed as mind-expanding drugs that held a great deal of promise for mankind. The most prominent among these are LSD (lysergic acid diethylamide), mescaline, peyote, and psilocybin.

Different degrees of tolerance to hallucinogens have been reported, and apparently no physical dependence develops. Marijuana is another substance closely related to the hallucinogens wherein no physical dependence develops. There has been a great deal of controversy regarding marijuana and its use. In many states marijuana has been designated a narcotic by the statutes. However, from a pharmacological point of view, this is not truly the case. Because of its designation as a narcotic, possession of marijuana can result in a long prison term. These long sentences are often justified by some persons in the criminal justice system who feel that marijuana leads to the use of addictive drugs such as heroin. The President's Commission on Law Enforcement and Administration of Justice indicates the following:

> There are too many (marijuana) users who do not graduate to heroin and too many heroin addicts with no known prior (marijuana) use, to support such a theory. Moreover, there is no scientific basis for such a theory.

Probably, the social and psychological reasons which make a person predisposed to marijuana use are the same factors which make that person predisposed to heroin use. Further, a person who uses marijuana probably forms personal associations with people who would expose him to heroin if given the opportunity.

There have been some suggestions as to how to deal with the drug problem; and, generally speaking, those suggestions involve diverting the dependent individual from the criminal justice system. This means the *user*—not the person who sells these substances in large amounts. The reason a distinction is made between small quantities and large amounts is that many users sell drugs so they can supply their own habit. Supplying a habit, particularly a habit involving heroin, is often so expensive that a normal person cannot earn enough money in a legitimate manner to keep going. Those people who are dependent on heroin and who do not sell small quantities of it to help supply their own habit usually become involved in theft in order to make enough money to support their habit. Most women who do not sell heroin to support their own habit become involved in prostitution.

The drug problem is complex because it involves a number of sub-

Figure 7-2 No physical dependence develops with the use of marijuana; however, there is much controversy regarding its use and the possibility that it leads to addictive drugs. So far, there is no scientific basis for this theory. Photo courtesy of San Jose Police Department, San Jose, Ca.

stances which affect people in a number of ways. Consequently, solutions to this problem have been hard to come by. In fact, the criminal justice system's ability to change a heroin user into a permanent nonuser has been exceedingly limited. Because of this, a great number of persons in the criminal justice system as well as behavioral scientists feel that drug-dependent persons should be diverted from the criminal justice system.

There has been relatively little diversion of drug-dependent persons from the criminal justice system within the United States. Even the civil commitment statutes allow the state to incarcerate or otherwise supervise the life of the drug-dependent person. In fact, the civil commitment program in California is run by the Adult Authority—the same body that is responsible for maintaining California prisons.

Most arguments against the involvement of the criminal justice system are derived from the basic assumption that drug dependency is a medical problem and should be solved from a medical model. But the medical approach, with the possible exception of the methadone program, has enjoyed no better success than the criminal justice system in dealing with drug-dependent persons. The methadone maintenance program substitutes methadone (which causes physical dependency) for heroin dependency. The benefits of this substitution are that methadone is quite inexpensive, and its intake level can be stabilized so that a person can become engaged in useful employment even though he needs to remain on methadone as the diabetic needs to remain on insulin.

Like alcoholism, the drug problem is referred to as a crime without victims. A third social problem that is often referred to as a crime without victims involves sexual behavior that is deemed illegal by statute.

ILLEGAL SEXUAL BEHAVIOR

The important question regarding illegal sexual behavior is whether presently unlawful behaviors should be legalized. It may be argued that the particular practice forbidden by the law does no harm or that the harm done is not sufficient to warrant prohibition or that the harm done is the consequence of the law itself. Nevertheless, homosexuality and heterosexual relations, particularly prostitution, will be surveyed as problems with which the criminal justice system becomes involved.

Two research reports, now over twenty years old, had the effect of shedding new light on old statutes regarding sexual behavior. These statutes were written by persons who attempted to legislate morality while steeped in puritanical views. The first of these two reports has since become known as the "Kinsey Report." That study indicated that approximately 10 percent of all American men have had fairly extensive experiences with homosexuality. However, it did show that only 4 percent of the total male population were committed to homosexuality.[28] If these figures were truly representative, this would mean that almost one of every twenty male adults is committed to a life of homosexuality. This certainly indicates that a sizeable percentage of the population might be involved in this social problem.

The second research report was done in England for the British government. It is commonly referred to as the "Wolfenden Commission Report." [27] Essentially this report recommended that homosexual behavior between consenting adults in private should no longer be considered a criminal offense in Great Britain. The study found objections to changing the law in Great Britain, however; people felt homosexuality was contrary to the public good on the grounds that (1) it menaced the health of society; (2) it had damaging effects on family life; and (3) a man who indulges in homosexual practices may turn his attention to boys. The

[28] A. C. Kinsey, W. B. Pomeroy, and C. E. Martin, *Sexual Behavior in the Human Male* (Philadelphia, Penn.: W. B. Saunders, 1949).

[29] *Report of the Committee on Homosexual Offenses and Prostitution,* Great Britain, Cmd., 247, Her Majesty's Stationery Office, London, England, 1957.

Commission decided that although homosexuality may be a menace to the health of society, it does not constitute a sufficient reason for making private sexual behavior between consenting adults an offense. The Commission did find that homosexuality has damaging effects upon family life, but these damaging effects would occur whether homosexuality was considered an offense or not. Finally, the Commission came to the conclusion that homosexuals who are involved with adults continue to be involved with adults. On the other hand, pedophiliacs (adults who seek sexual relations with children) constitute a somewhat different problem than homosexuals. In this regard, the Commission indicated that it certainly was not recommending that pedophiliacs or the comparative few persons who are indiscriminate in regard to the age of their partners not be liable to criminal law.

Since the appearance of these two reports, the information continues to suggest that the possibility of altering a confirmed homosexual is quite improbable. Furthermore, homosexuals as a group are becoming an organized, vocal minority. The question of homosexuality in correctional institutions is another facet of the problem which the criminal justice system must deal with. In all probability, homosexuality in correctional institutions has a far greater impact on the criminal justice system than does homosexual acts between consenting adults.

In addition to homosexual behavior, illegal sexual behavior such as prostitution has an impact upon the criminal justice system. Many books and articles have been written about prostitution. It has been called the "oldest profession" and has been of interest from the beginning. Generally speaking, prostitution is defined as the selling of sex outside of marriage as a vocation. An unmarried woman who receives gifts for sexual activity would not be a prostitute as long as this was not her occupational way of life.[30]

In our present society it appears that because of the increasing sexual freedom among women outside of marriage, the profession of prostitution is becoming greatly reduced. However, it seems unlikely that prostitution will disappear from the American society altogether. It is felt that there will always be some persons who, even if the society becomes more permissive, will never be able to get sexual partners, perhaps because of sexual aberrations, age, physical disabilities, or mental disorders.

Presently there seems to be decreasing concern about prostitution. When the public does become concerned it is generally because prostitution has somehow been exposed and linked with business or political practices. It is also at this point that prostitution becomes closest to being a major social problem. The whole problem of illegal sex behavior is

[30] Bell, *Social Deviance,* p. 226.

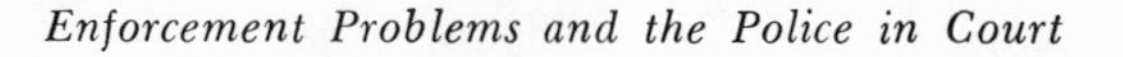

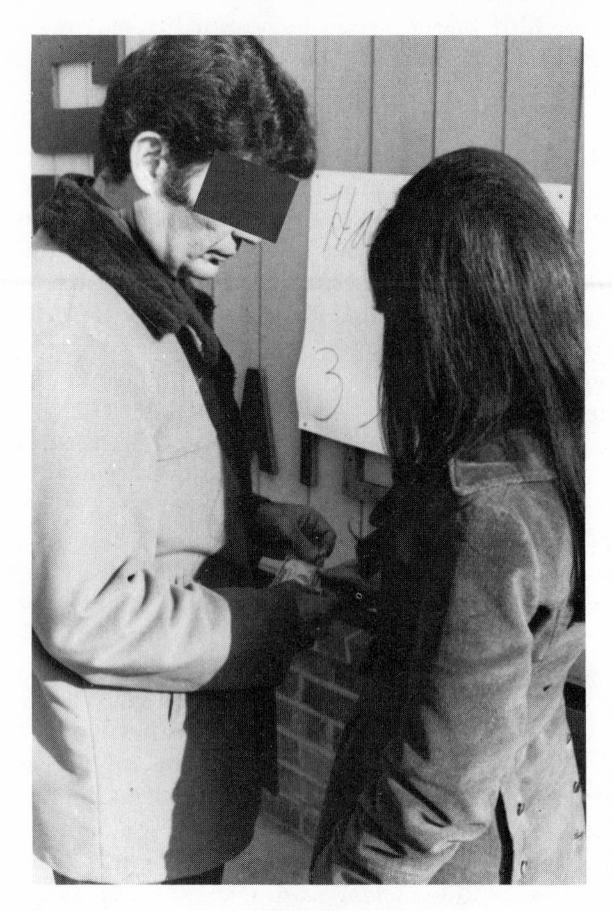

Figure 7-3 The most common type of prostitute is the streetwalker. She is extremely aggressive, not only in procuring customers, but also in responding to attempts by undercover agents in making an arrest. The transfer of money is an important element of the crime. Photo courtesy of Carl Cieslikowski.

related more to how it may corrupt certain individuals within the society than it is to the numbers of individuals involved. The social problem of mental illness could probably cause a more noticeable impact upon the criminal justice system because of its potential to violently disrupt society.

MENTAL ILLNESS

According to Duhl and Leopold, mental illness constitutes a very definite social problem for society. As they have stated,

> Mental illness is so prevalent in our society that it constitutes a social problem simply because of its potential for disrupting the social system. [Furthermore] mental illness has substantially more determinant components . . . than most . . . diseases.[31]

Particularly because of the disruptive potential of the mentally ill, the police are often initially called upon to deal with the problem. But mental illness cuts across the whole of the criminal justice system. Mental illness has an impact when a particular case in court can cost a county government a million dollars to determine whether a murderer was sane or insane. According to one of the definitions of social problems, spending a great deal of tax money may be one of the criteria used in judging whether a problem is indeed a social problem.

Societies in the past were also concerned with justice for the mentally ill. An article by Warren E. Burger in 1964 reflects on this concern quite well.

> For more than 2,000 years, one problem in the administration of justice which has perplexed all organized societies has been the development of some procedural or legal mechanism which would enable society to decide accurately which persons should be punished as willful wrong-doers and which should be excused from the normal legal consequences because of some mental aberration that prevents the act from being a willful act prompted by criminal intent which the law identifies as *mens rea*. We can find this problem discussed in the Talmud, where the law of the ancient Hebrews provided that infants and mentally disordered persons were not to be held accountable for their crimes "because with them only the act is of consequence while the intention is of no consequence." [32]

The article goes on to indicate that it would probably be more self-serving to society and the person pleading mental illness if less concern were given to the court verdict and more concern were given to the proposed treatment of the accused individual. A number of institutions are trying to deal with the offender who quite obviously has severe psychiatric problems. Patuxent Institute in Maryland and the California Medical Facility in Vacaville are two institutions of this type.

There are certainly a number of persons committed to correctional institutions who need many psychiatric services but who receive little if any of these services. The point of concern here is that society and the criminal justice system might well be more concerned with the

[31] L. J. Duhl and R. L. Leopold, "Mental Illness," *Social Problems: A Modern Approach*, ed., H. S. Becker (New York: John Wiley & Sons, 1966), p. 277.

[32] W. E. Burger, "Psychiatrists, Lawyers, and Courts," *Federal Probation*, Vol. 28 (June, 1964), pp. 3-10.

treatment of the person who has psychiatric problems and who is involved in criminal offenses.

Although there are other social problems that are of concern to the criminal justice system, they will not be reviewed here. Rather we will undertake to examine some of the outcomes of the pressures of these social problems.

IMPACT OF SOCIAL PROBLEMS ON CRIMINAL JUSTICE SUBSYSTEMS

During the past ten years the impact of social problems upon the criminal justice system has repeatedly made headlines. This impact has been seen most dramatically in regard to the police.

Social Problems and the Police

The severe social and economic disadvantages of poverty and discrimination were found to be fundamental causes in large outbreaks of disorder in a number of cities in the summer of 1967. These outbreaks occurred in the ghetto areas. Disorders of this magnitude certainly have an impact on the criminal justice system, and police who are in the forefront of the criminal justice system are put in a very trying position. In a number of cases, the police needed help from the National Guard to fulfill their primary function of keeping the peace, protecting persons, and protecting property. Incidents of this kind certainly show that the police cannot operate without the knowledge of social problems and their effects. In response to certain social problems, the police together with other social agencies have formulated innovative programs.

An excellent example is the New York Police Department's experimental Family Crisis Intervention program. This program was established upon varying estimates that the police are involved in interpersonal services up to 90 percent of their working time. Yet ninety-nine or more of their training and professional awards are related to that small portion of time that is devoted to law enforcement.[33] The New York program was organized to develop better police response to marital disputes. The police officers assigned to this project received training in family intervention at the City University of New York; the project was initiated so that police could handle domestic disturbances

[33] M. Bard, "Family Intervention Police Teams as a Community Mental Health Resource," *The Journal of Criminal Law, Criminology, and Police Science,* Vol. 60 (June, 1969), pp. 247-250.

in a much more effective manner. As indicated earlier, domestic disturbances often degenerate into incidents of serious crimes such as assault and homicide. The results of this innovative program seem to indicate that this type of approach to the social problem of family disorganization is more effective than the approaches used in the past.

Ideas about handling social problems are continually being advanced. The National Council of Crime and Delinquency is a professional forum for the expression and discussion of all competent points of view in the fields of prevention and correction of crime and delinquency. Its members are police officers, correctional personnel, and judges. In 1970 the Council made a policy statement regarding crimes without victims. The statement held that crimes without victims should be removed from criminal codes. The most common examples of these kinds of crimes are drunkenness, drug addiction, homosexuality, and other voluntary sexual acts between consenting adults. The suggestion was that these acts no longer be designated as crimes because the criminal justice system is spending enomerous amounts of time and money on them. Significantly draining the capacity of the police, the courts, and corrections to deal effectively with truly criminal conduct.

Social Problems and Courts

The courts by their very nature are best designed to deal with some of the philosophical aspects of social problems. This can be seen quite clearly by reviewing court decisions and legislative enactments over the past 100 years regarding discrimination. The most appropriate place to begin an examination of the history of discrimination in the courts is the Dred Scott decision.[34] This decision made by the Supreme Court in 1857 concerned a Negro slave named Dred Scott who lived with his master for five years in Illinois and the Wisconsin Territory. At that time these areas were free, meaning they had no slavery as did the southern states. The Supreme Court decided that Dred Scott was a Negro slave and therefore not a citizen; the court further decided that, since he was not a citizen, he could not sue in court.

This decision was certainly quite discriminatory. However, this extreme position of discrimination was changed in 1868 when the Fourteenth Amendment to the Constitution was passed. That Amendment stated in part:

> All persons born or naturalized in the United States, and subject to the jurisdiction thereof, are citizens of the United States and of the State where

[34] Dred Scott v. Stanford, 19 HOW 393 (1857).

they reside. No State shall make or enforce any other law which shall abridge the privileges or immunities of citizens of the United States; nor shall any State deprive any person of life, liberty, or property, without due process of law; nor deny to any person within the jurisdiction the equal protection of the law.

This Constitutional Amendment clearly indicated that all people should be treated equal and the law of the land was against discrimination. In practice, however, black people were treated differently than white people. This separate treatment was known as the doctrine of separate but equal rights. In many areas, especially in regard to schools, the doctrine was prevalent, but facilities were far from equal. Indeed, the facilities for black people were quite inferior.

This circumstance of separate but equal rights continued until 1954 when the Supreme Court declared that in regard to public schools the separate but equal rights doctrine was unconstitutional. This decision came in the case of *Brown* v. *Board of Education*.[35] The Court felt that the separate but equal rights doctrine had been used to segregate public schools and that segregation was unconstitutional. Specifically, this decision was concerned with the Board of Education in Topeka, Kansas. Similar cases regarding Virginia, Delaware, and South Carolina were decided at the same hearing. Since that time the Supreme Court has actively led this country toward a fuller understanding of the ideal set forth in the Constitution. Through various decisions, the Supreme Court has made a great impact on equalizing the chances for justice.

Because minority group members are often poorer than members of the white majority, Supreme Court decisions regarding poor people have often served to further eliminate discrimination. A case in point is *Gideon* v. *Wainwright*.[36] This case was decided by the Supreme Court in 1963. A man named Gideon was on trial for a felony; he asked the court to appoint a lawyer for him, but the judge refused. When the Supreme Court reviewed the case, they responded by stating that legal assistance is the right of anyone charged with a crime and is fundamental to a fair trial. As a consequence of this ruling, we now have public defenders in the United States. The public defender's office is composed of attorneys who are available to defend indigent persons charged with criminal acts. Thus, it can be seen that the Supreme Court can have a great impact on social problems. Court decisions and court treatment surrounding the issues of fair housing, fair employment practices, and *de facto* segregation will certainly have an impact upon the social problems of poverty and discrimination.

Until decisions were handed down concerning school desegregation,

[35] Brown v. Board of Education, 307 U.S. 483 (1954).

[36] Gideon v. Wainwright, 372 U.S. 33S (1963).

many social scientists felt that the courts' effect on social problems was not very great. However, during the past twenty years, it has become obvious to most social scientists that court decisions indeed have an effect upon social problems. The concept that social problems can be changed by the courts has gained much prominence, and many people feel that social problems can best be solved there. The great increase in class-action suits is mute testimony to this type of thinking. As long as this idea prevails, courts will continue to feel the pressures of social problems in this secondary way. Obviously, the courts will continue to feel the primary pressure of social problems as long as these issues are considered problems that must be dealt with by the criminal justice system.

Social Problems and Corrections

The municipal and county jails as well as correctional institutions (or perhaps more properly detention facilities), are continually being impeded by the problem of drunkenness. Through court actions and the police, violators are separated out according to the severity of their offenses. As a result, persons coming to the attention of the correctional process tend to be the ones who are most deeply involved in social problems.

One article regarding homosexuals is a good illustration of the fact that corrections generally deals with only the top of the iceberg.[37] The authors state that present knowledge concerning sexual behavior and development indicates that homosexual acts are somewhat common in the life of males throughout our society. However, only a small percent of the male population can be classified as exclusively homosexual, even though in sheer numbers they represent a large group. Only a small fraction of these persons is ever likely to be formally charged in court, let alone found guilty and placed in the correctional system. Furthermore, the typical cases which appear in court are not incidents where homosexual acts occurred between consenting adults in private. Rather these cases can be classified as (1) adult homosexual acts in public places and (2) homosexual relations with children and youths.

To a large extent, corrections has been cognizant of the fact that it is expected to deal with the hard-core problems. Professionals in the field of corrections have long recognized the link between poverty and crime and a further link between lack of job skills and poverty. Corrections has reacted to this by attempting to initiate job programs in correctional institutions. Another approach has been the work-furlough program; here, the person committed to a correctional institution is

[37] A. K. Gigeroff, J. W. Mohr, and R. E. Turner, "Sex Offenders on Probation: Homosexuality," *Federal Probation,* Vol. 33 (March, 1969), pp. 36-39.

allowed to leave the institution each day to work at a job in the community. Still another approach has been to encourage probation and parole personnel to spend much of their time acting as an employment bureau for their clients. As in all parts of the criminal justice system, corrections feels the impact of social problems and tries to ameliorate these social problems within the framework of its own operation. Obviously, social problems still remain with the society and new and better methods of dealing with these problems still need to be formulated and put into effect.

SOCIAL PROBLEMS AND INNOVATIONS

In the past, the responsibility for formulating new programs and methods of dealing with social problems was more or less left up to government and philanthropic organizations. The government responded by passing legislation when a great deal of pressure was brought to bear. Philanthropic organizations have traditionally been in the forefront of dealing with social problems; at this time in our history, however, many legislators seem to be much more open to suggestions for solutions to the problems. Knowing that no one person can understand all of the intricacies of the problems of our present-day society, the legislative and executive branches of governments have established committees and commissions of people knowledgeable in the particular areas of concern. These persons are called upon to make reports or to testify so that more appropriate legislation can be drafted and enacted.

Persons in the criminal justice system represent people who have expertise regarding social problems in the criminal justice system. This expertise should be contributed so that it can be brought to bear upon the social problems. If government refuses to listen to the individual expert, then professional organizations of the criminal justice system should impress their knowledge upon the appropriate governmental branches. The passive role of enforcing a "bad" law without actively attempting to change that law is not in the best interest of the criminal justice system. The people in the criminal justice system must actively seek to solve social problems. If they do not, at least half of their expertise will be lost to society.

SUMMARY

This chapter has been concerned with social problems and the criminal justice system. As a starting point, a number of definitions of social problems were reviewed. All the definitions shared a great number of points in common; yet each authority emphasized different facets of the concept of social problems.

Examples of social problems that conform to these definitions were reviewed. These were poverty, discrimination, family disorganization, drunkenness, drug abuse, and illegal sex activities. The impact of certain selected social problems on the criminal justice system was also reviewed. The problems of poverty and discrimination were reviewed in reference to the police.

Social problems and how the courts attempt to solve them were also surveyed. Particular emphasis was given to the courts' attempts to deal with the social problem of discrimination.

The criminal justice system and its relation to the social problem of drunkenness was a concern throughout much of this chapter; the impact of drunkenness upon corrections was also reviewed. The problem of homosexuality as it affects the correctional system was viewed from several perspectives within the chapter.

Finally, it was emphasized that the professionals within the criminal justice system need to bring their expertise to bear upon social problems. Concern with social problems and their solutions is indeed an obligation of the criminal justice system.

QUESTIONS

1. Why is the criminal justice system concerned with social problems?
2. How are poverty and discrimination related?
3. What are "crimes without victims"?
4. Give an example of a social problem affecting the police.
5. Give an example of a social problem affecting the courts.
6. Give an example of a social problem affecting corrections.
7. Give reasons for or against the criminal justice system actively trying to influence the legislature regarding social problems.

ANNOTATED REFERENCES

BELL, R.R. *Social Deviants.* Homewood, Ill.: The Dorsey Press, 1971. This is an excellent text regarding social deviants and social problems. The information and point of view presented in this text are well worth the consideration of a student of the criminal justice system.

BERNARD, J. *Social Problems at Midcentury.* New York: Holt, Rinehart and Winston, 1957. This text on social problems is almost twenty years old;

however, it is worth considering because it defines and realistically deals with social problems.

LEINWAND, G., ed. *Problems of American Society: The Slums.* New York: Washington Square Press, 1968. This is a concise little paperback that gives a quick and accurate account of the homes of the poor.

———. *Problems of American Society: Poverty and the Poor.* New York: Washington Square Press, 1968. This is another concise little book which gives much information about the state of poverty and a good accounting of what it means to be poor.

KINSEY, A. C.; POMEROY, W. B.; and MARTIN, C. E. *Sexual Behavior in the Human Male.* Philadelphia, Penn.: W. B. Saunders 1949. This was one of the first serious research attempts regarding the sexual behavior in man. Although it is over twenty years old it is considered a classic in its field.

President's Commission on Law Enforcement and Administration of Justice. *The Challenge of Crime in a Free Society.* Washington, D.C.: U.S. Gov't. Printing Office, 1967. This report is the summation of a number of reports about the different problems of the administration of justice. As such, it sets forth a number of recommendations regarding the idea of administration of justice and regarding social problems that are involved in the administration of justice.

———. *Task Force Reports: Drunkenness.* Washington, D.C.: U.S. Gov't. Printing Office, 1967. This is part of the supporting material for *The Challenge of Crime in a Free Society.* This report regarding drunkenness and the effects of this social problem on the criminal justice system basically sets forth certain tenets of this problem.

———. *Task Force Report: Narcotics and Drug Abuse.* Washington, D.C.: U.S. Gov't. Printing Office, 1967. This is part of the supporting material for *The Challenge of Crime in a Free Society.* This report regarding narcotics and drug abuse sets forth very basic information that is important to the student of the criminal justice system.

Report of the National Advisory Commission on Civil Disorders. Washington, D.C.: U.S. Gov't. Printing Office, 1968. This is a comprehensive study of several riots in a number of large cities in the summer of 1967. It gives an extensive report on conditions within the ghetto.

8

The Prosecution

Various theories on human behavior and the social problems relating to behavior were discussed in the two preceding chapters. The topic of prosecution and defense is presented from this perspective of behavior. As regards the vital role of prosecution-defense in the criminal justice system, a discussion of *evidence* alone could fill many volumes. The focus of this chapter and the next will be merely on clarifying what prosecution-defense "does."

PROSECUTION DEFINED

Some agreement on what prosecution is might be useful before dealing with what prosecution does. *Webster's New World Dictionary* gives the generally accepted definition of *prosecution* as: "the instituting and carrying on of criminal proceedings in court." This definition is succinct and accurate but falls somewhat short of the requirements suggested in Chapter 1 for a functional system. Some embellishment of this definition is therefore in order. It might be interesting to look at American, leisure-time radio and TV programs for further elaborations of the definition. When programmed entertainment entered the home mainly by radio, one program that enjoyed much success was a weekly half-hour show called *Mr. District Attorney*. Devout followers of the program would hear, prior to every weekly episode, the echo-chambered voice of "Mr. District Attorney" presenting the program's version of the role of prosecution in criminal justice:

> And it shall be my duty as District Attorney, not only to prosecute to the limit of the law, all persons accused of crime in this county, but to defend with equal vigor the rights and privileges of all its citizens.

If we, for the moment, ignore the fact that most prosecutors spend as much or more time dismissing or reducing charges as they do "prosecuting to the limit of the law," then it becomes possible to focus on "defending with equal vigor." As a practical matter, Mr. District Attorney simply cannot "prosecute to the limit of the law *all* persons accused of crime"; he can't even prosecute *most* accused persons to the limit of the law. Such prosecution cannot be carried on if for no other reason than there are too many accusations, too little evidence, and too few prosecutors.

Even though Mr. District Attorney cannot prosecute every accused person, he can "defend with equal vigor the rights and privileges of all citizens." The chapter that follows deals with this vital role of defense in the criminal justice system. If the criminal justice system is to provide the "justice" reflected in the system's name, the prosecutor must also concern himself with "defending rights and privileges." A prosecutor concerned with nothing more than "winning" (where a "win" is defined as a *conviction*) may in the long run cause as many problems as he solves in the criminal justice PROCESS.

For the purposes of this chapter, then, the definition of *prosecution* is modified to: "instituting and carrying on criminal proceedings in cases where such prosecution clearly serves the best interest of justice, *after* careful consideration of the rights and privileges of all concerned." Having considered what prosecution is, we can now examine the function of prosecution. And since much (if not most) of determining what "serves the best interest of justice" will depend upon "criminal evidence," consideration of evidence provides a basis for examining the function of prosecution.

CRIMINAL EVIDENCE

In 1967 the President's Commission on Law Enforcement and Administration of Justice made the following comment:

> The cases decided at the trial are only a small fraction of the total of cases, but they are most important to the process because they set standards for the conduct of all cases. The trial decides the hard legal issues and reviews the rules or claims of official abuse. Trial procedures have evolved over centuries and in general have proven that they can resolve disputed cases effectively. Unlike the administrative proceedings in the pretrial stage, court pro-

ceedings are continually being studied by lawyers and are now receiving intensive scrutiny from other groups.[1]

The prosecution in a society that presumes the innocence of an accused person until there is *proof* of guilt has the task of assessing the adequacy of evidence before bringing the criminal issue before the court. The prosecution has the additional responsibility of considering evidence of innocence as well.

Figure 8-1 The prosecutor pleading his case before the court. Photo courtesy of the Santa Clara County Public Information Office, San Jose, Ca.

Since judges and juries do not witness the crimes that will be tried, the prosecution has considerable responsibility in ascertaining whether the evidence available would convince a judge or jury of the accused person's guilt. The "hard legal issues" decided by a trial more often than not evolve into a system of persuasion—*persuasion* becoming the first major consideration in a prosecutors assessment of criminal evidence.

PERSUASION

Proof of guilt or innocence depends on many things. A most crucial consideration in proving or persuading is the nature of the evidence it-

[1] President's Commission on Law Enforcement and Administration of Justice, *The Challenge of Crime in a Free Society* (Washington, D.C.: U.S. Gov't. Printing Office, 1967), p. 137.

self; but in terms of *persuasion,* the prosecution frequently turns to *logic.* To understand the nature of criminal evidence, then, some consideration must be given the concept of logic.

Persuasion and Logic

From a legal point of view, *logic* is simply a method of reasoning. The method can be either *inductive,* or it can be *deductive.* In either case, a "logical conclusion" is sought. In other words, to be persuasive the prosecutor must frequently be logical—whether his logic is inductive or deductive.

With the deductive method, one reasons from something that is general to something that is specific. For example, one might conclude that a specific defendent is accused, since the general observation is that all defendents are accused. In contrast, the inductive method is simply the reverse of deductive reasoning; one reasons from specifics to the general. The "logical conclusion" or goal sought in both methods remains the same—to persuade.

Proposition: The Introduction of Logical Persuasion

The prosecutor begins with a statement. In terms of pure logic, the statement such as "He is guilty" may or may not be true. Such an assertion is called a *proposition.*

The criminal court trial always begins with two propositions: "He is guilty," and "He is innocent." [2] Some propositions can be proven or disproven merely with the passage of time; an example would be the proposition that it will rain tomorrow. But from the prosecutor's viewpoint, the mere passage of time rarely proves or disproves or even clarifies the two propositions of guilt or innocence. Thus, other steps are needed to *persuade.* The prosecutor's job is to determine whether the evidence necessary to take the additional steps is available. In relation to guilt and innocence, evidence that leads to a "logical conclusion" is called for. Such evidence affords persuasion through *inference.*

An example of inference might be drawn from the typical jury process. A jury which is told that "some defendents are guilty" has a *proposition* from which they may logically *infer* that "some defendants are not innocent." [3] This can be inferred because the existence of any guilty de-

[2] 23 American Law Review 2nd, 1397; Also see: Lilienthal v. U.S., 97 U.S. 237.

[3] 91 American Law Review 2nd, 1252.

fendants establishes the existence of at least that many defendants who are not innocent.[4] But this does not logically infer that "some defendants are innocent" because, in the absence of other evidence, the *proposition* could mean all defendants, not just some defendants, are guilty.

Although such reasoning is confusing at times, a great deal of continuity can be gained by the prosecutor assessing available evidence in such terms. The likelihood of persuading a jury is determined in this manner. Consider, for example, that the jury is told by a defendant's attorney that the proposition "some defendants are not guilty" holds the possibility that all defendents could logically be innocent. The prosecutor's use of logic then determines his assessment of the evidence available.

Logical Evidence and Proof

The prosecutor must distinguish between *evidence* and *proof*. This distinction is made in terms of the persuasiveness of the two fundamental propositions of guilt and innocence. Not all evidence proves because it does not reach an adequate stage of persuasiveness. But even though all evidence does not prove, all proof is obviously evidence.

Providing that the jury is confronted with enough evidence to be persuaded that crimes are law violations, and that law violations are indeed social problems, the jury can then infer that crimes are also social problems. This *inference* is indeed strong enough to suggest the "logical conclusion" that "crimes are social problems." [5]

The presuasive quality of evidence can be enhanced with various true stories or perhaps hypothetical cases. These stories and hypothetical cases are frequently similar enough to the actual situation that they may be considered *analogous*. Analogies are simply point-by-point comparisons of one thing to another in an effort to imply still further similarities. For example, a jury might be told of a case having all of the characteristics of the accused situation, but in the story the person described is definitely guilty. The point of analogy is of course the inference that the initial similarity extends beyond the positive knowledge available in the trial. The vague implications of this approach to evidence raise the question of how much persuading is necessary. Put another way, the prosecutor must judge how many analogies equal one eyewitness.

4 18 American Law Review 2nd, 1319.

5 162 American Law Review 505.

Degrees of Evidence

Inasmuch as proof requires evidence but not all evidence actually proves, the job of the prosecution is to determine if there is enough evidence to prove. Consideration of the *degree* of evidence is therefore necessary. In general terms, the amount of evidence needed to prove will depend on the type case. Although somewhat unrelated to prosecution, it might be noted that various civil courts use the *preponderence-of-evidence* standard in which an attorney producing as little as 51 percent of the evidence theoretically "wins" over the attorney presenting only 49 percent of the persuasion.[6]

In contrast to various civil courts, the standard for criminal court is to establish guilt beyond reasonable doubt. This standard places upon the prosecution the responsibility of presenting enough evidence to persuade a jury that there is no reasonable doubt of guilt.[7] The various ramifications of criminal evidence will be discussed in the context of this responsibility—a responsibility of awesome dimensions in a free society of ever-increasing individual rights.

Enough Evidence for Particular Proof

Evidence which is sufficient to persuade the court that there is proof of guilt beyond a reasonable doubt comes from three sources: (1) circumstantial evidence including testimony;[8] (2) witness evidence other than circumstantial evidence;[9] and (3) any evidence of confessions or admissions.[10] In most instances the category of confessions eliminates the need for other kinds of evidence in persuading the court. Certain exceptions will be discussed later in this chapter in terms of *admissibility;* but insofar as "logical persuasion" is concerned, a prosecutor draws mainly from the categories of witnesses and circumstantial evidence.

Circumstantial Evidence

The task of the prosecutor in trying to determine if he has sufficient evidence is simply to consider the two propositions of guilt or innocence.

[6] 34 AMERICAN LAW REVIEW 942. Also: 152 AMERICAN LAW REVIEW 626.

[7] Hem v. U.S., 268 U.S. 178.

[8] 4 AMERICAN LAW REVIEW 1509. Also: 156 AMERICAN LAW REVIEW 625.

[9] Roberts v. Carlson 142 Nebraska 851.

[10] 17 AMERICAN LAW REVIEW 1276. Also 38 AMERICAN LAW REVIEW 113.

Furthermore, innocence is only related to these issues when evidence of guilt is produced, since all persons are assumed innocent until proven guilty in a free society. The issue of which proposition is to be accepted is resolved with a "valid confession"; but without a confession the issues should be decided on the basis of the persuasive quality of the evidence available.

Evidence can be *anything* that proves logically persuasive. This being true, a great deal of evidence in the criminal court is "circumstantial evidence." [11] Many complicated rules govern the kinds of evidence known as circumstantial. The key rule, however, is that evidence be *relevant* [12] to the issue before the court; *all* evidence is subject to this relevance stand—not just circumstantial evidence.

The relevancy of the evidence can best be determined through contrast with a concept known in law as *materiality* of evidence.

> The materiality of evidence depends on what specific issue is to be proven in the court. If the evidence presented tends to prove anything other than the specific issue, it is considered "immaterial"—therefore unacceptable to the court.
>
> *Relevancy,* on the other hand, deals with the relationship between evidence and "facts" in general. In this sense, evidence that is immaterial could be considered relevant.
>
> An example might be evidence showing a defendant was seen in a bar with a lady who is not his wife, in order to show that he and his wife are separated. Now, if this defendant is accused of burglary, evidence that he has been seen in a bar with anther woman is not *material* to this trial, but may indeed be relevant to the issue of whether or not he is separated from his wife.[13]

Circumstantial evidence, when material and relevant, might be thought of in terms of the inferences that can be drawn from the circumstances presented. The circumstances of a defendant's fingerprints on a murder weapon can indeed form the basis for the *proposition* that the defendant is guilty. Ownership of the weapon might reinforce this proposition, or it might lead to the alternate proposition that the defendant is innocent—depending on the *circumstances.* If in addition to the fingerprints there is admissible evidence that the defendant was at the scene, there begins to emerge the basis for the logical conclusion that the defendant is guilty.

But most circumstances have alternate explanations, and so more

[11] State v. Buck 88 *Kansas* 114.

[12] 63 American Law Review 595.

[13] 3 American Law Review 1038.

evidence is needed to prove guilt—at least in a court system requiring proof beyond a reasonable doubt. The actual evidence depicting circumstances takes many forms and has endless variety. Generally, however, it is presented as either the testimony of witnesses or as *exhibits*.

Circumstances and Witnesses. When circumstances are presented by testimony, the criminal court usually requires the witness to have observed everything to which his testimony refers. The so-called hearsay testimony often referred to in motion pictures depicting court process *is* acceptable but only under very special conditions—conditions usually relating to the expertise of witnesses available to the prosecutor.[14]

An example of admissible hearsay evidence might be a physician offering an opinion as to the time of death or a psychiatrist giving "expert testimony" on the defendant's knowledge of right and wrong. Under other special circumstances, police officers are acknowledged as experts in certain areas and are therefore able to testify to matters not directly observed.[15] An example might be an officer's testimony regarding a vehicle's speed at impact in an accident. Even though the officer did not observe the collision, his experience in measuring skidmarks on arrival at the accident scene constitutes a reasonable degree of expertise. Another occasional example is the policeman's expert testimony on a defendant's sobriety even though the officer did not witness alcohol being consumed. Further, hearsay evidence is always admissible if not objected to.

Exhibits and Circumstantial Evidence. When a prosecutor seeks to use *exhibits*[16] as persuasion of circumstances, the approach has even greater variety than in the case of testimony. Hardly a year passes without extremely significant discoveries from the science of criminalistics—a major source of circumstantial evidence used by prosecutors. Fingerprints, ballistics, chemical analysis, photography, and graphology are but a few types of exhibits.

The stated purpose of criminalistics is to furnish recognition, identification, and evaluation of physical evidence by applying the natural sciences to the criminal justice system. Insofar as the prosecutor is concerned, criminalistics serves to persuade. This, of course, contrasts with the law enforcement use of criminalistics in apprehending suspected law violators.

The crime laboratory, when staffed with well-trained technicians and appropriate equipment, has proven efficient in both law enforcement

[14] 10 AMERICAN LAW REVIEW 2nd, 1037.

[15] E. Eldefonso, A. Coffey, and R. Grace, *Principles of Law Enforcement* (New York: Wiley & Sons, 1968), Chapter 4.

[16] 28 AMERICAN LAW REVIEW 2nd, 1142.

and prosecution. The crime laboratory has provided the prosecution with persuasive exhibits ranging from spectographic, serological, toxicological, metalurgical, and radiological analysis.

Evidence and Scientific Experiment

The prosecutor also has scientific experiments available for persuading the jury as to the guilt of an accused person—providing, of course, that the scientific experiment is from a recognized science.[17] Traditionally the court expects the experiment used to be completely acceptable among scientists in general. On special occasions, however, courts have ruled on "scientific experiment evidence" solely on the basis of the relevant conclusions produced. In other words, if the evidence is relevant, courts have held that this evidence is admissable, whether or not it is acceptable among scientists in general.[18]

Scientific experiments might range from determining the average travel time between points, to researching the time it takes to make a firearm inoperable by holding it under water.[19] Prosecution interest in such experiments is frequently connected to evidence originally gathered by law enforcement.[20]

PRESERVATION OF EVIDENCE

Since the nature of evidence is persuasive, anything that tends to weaken the persuasive quality of evidence becomes an important consideration for the prosecutor. This consideration is in part responsible for the many rules designed to "preserve" evidence until the time of trial. What is meant by the technical term *preservation* is the retention of the persuasive quality of evidence.

Recalling that judges and juries do not witness the crimes being tried, we recognize that a defendant's guilt is largely a matter of proof—proof assessed by the prosecutor in determining whether to prosecute. One thing a prosecutor must consider is the degree of accuracy that the evidence reflects. In some cases the evidence is gathered in such a way that there is an inherent question as to how well it has been protected or preserved. (This is also known as "proof of the chain.") The follow-

[17] 8 American Law Review 18, and 85 American Law Review 479.

[18] 78 American Law Review 2nd, 364, 2.

[19] 8 American Law Review 26.

[20] 76 American Law Review 2nd 365, 72 (chemical); see also: 63 ALR 2nd, 1151 (ballistics); 28 *ALR* 2nd, 185, 10 (visibility); 66 *ALR* 2nd, 548, 3 (alcohol).

ing example, though exaggerated for purposes of illustration, reflects in part some of the problems of protecting and preserving evidence:

> Officer A arrests a suspected narcotics peddler in the early morning and, before going off duty, places on the desk of a narcotics detective an envelope containing what Officer A believes to be heroin. This evidence has a note instructing the narcotics detail to have the contents analyzed.
>
> Officer B makes a similar arrest on another patrol beat and follows the same procedure—using the same narcotic detective's desk.
>
> On arriving at work the narcotics detective finds the janitor picking the two envelopes up from the floor where they had been allegedly pushed by the dusting cloth of the cleaning lady.
>
> Nothing more is thought of the situation until the crime lab declares the contents of one envelope to be baking soda, the contents of the other envelope to be heroin.
>
> An investigator for the prosecutor's office then determines that the janitor is the brother of Officer A's suspect, and the cleaning lady to be the wife of Suspect B.
>
> Further discovery is made that the cleaning lady is divorcing Suspect B.

The prosecutor must now wonder whether the janitor changed the contents of one of the envelopes to protect his brother. Perhaps, the cleaning lady switched the envelopes after learning what the janitor had done because of guilt feelings over divorcing Suspect B; or perhaps she inserted heroin in a soda filled envelope to ensure Suspect B's conviction prior to the divorce. The prosecutor must wonder also if the janitor misjudged the cleaning lady's motives and made an inappropriate switch himself. Or for that matter, did someone completely unknown tamper with the evidence that had been left completely unprotected on the detective's desk?

Of course, a little common sense would prevent all of the implied problems from developing in the first place. These problems, nevertheless, represent very real *kinds* of difficulties encountered in protecting and preserving evidence. In regard to the importance of knowing the many rules for preserving evidence, one fact emerges: The quality of the evidence is no greater than how well it has been preserved. Since the function of the evidence is to persuade, evidence of marginal quality becomes virtually valueless to the prosecutor.

EYEWITNESS

The testimony of witnesses who have allegedly observed the actual commission of crime is subject to many of the same complicated rules governing *circumstantial* evidence. In terms of *materiality* and *relevance,* however, the testimony of eyewitnesses can be greatly simplified. Of course the laws and procedures that apply to eyewitnesses are essentially the same as those applying to all witnesses. The eyewitness has been selected here for clarity.

Exhibits and testimony about circumstances frequently evoke lengthy legal discussions regarding the immateriality or relevance of such evidence. But the eyewitness testimony relating to an observed crime is rarely challenged on the grounds of either materiality or relevance. When the testimony of an eyewitness is challenged, it is usually in terms of how competent or how valid the testimony may be. These questions, when raised, deal with the credibility of an eyewitness. Efforts to challenge the credibility of a witness is known as *impeachment.*[21] Impeachment is based on an assertion that, for one reason or another, the witness cannot be believed.

Impeachment does not necessarily imply that the witness lies; in many instances it simply means that the witness's perception and/or memory are not reliable. Attempts to impeach any witness, but particularly the eyewitness,[22] are actually efforts to reverse the persuasion of the evidence being offered. Attempts to impeach should be based on examples of unreliability. For example, the nearsighted witness testifying to incidents allegedly observed at some distance without his glasses may be challenged as unreliable. Observations supposedly made in poor lighting (as in the case of identifying a suspect) are also frequently challenged.

Impeachment might also include exploring the relationship between the defendant and the witness in terms of matters that would motivate particular styles of testimony. Financial matters, accumulated anger, and other motivational factors are often introduced into the court process is an effort to *impeach* a witness. A prosecutor must anticipate this when determining whether available witnesses will ultimately persuade of guilt or innocence.

ADMISSIBILITY

Although the range of appropriate evidence available to prosecutors varies widely in different jurisdictions, there is nonetheless some consistency in the rules for determining what evidence can be admitted. Rules governing the types of evidence that a prosecutor might use are

[21] 154 American Law Review 167, S. Also see: 19 *ALR* 2nd, 1153, 36.

[22] 71 American Law Review 2nd, 464, 8.

more often than not measured against the two standards already discussed: *relevance* and *materiality*. In addition to these two standards, there are complex rules systems and controls that have been created by Supreme Court interpretations of the Constitution.[23]

In light of the many complicated rules involved in admissibility, even a valid confession requires considerable scrutiny on the part of the prosecutor before making the decision to utilize this as part of his persuasive approach. For even an apparently valid confession may not be admissable for a wide variety of reasons that are often very technical. An example would be "privileged communication" which allows a defendant to confess to his clergyman or psychiatrist without being in jeopardy of repeating the confession in testimony. A few of the restrictions on confessions might be considered.

Confessions

In general, a "valid" confession for the prosecutor to use is a confession *freely* given, with the defendant's knowledge of his *right* not to incriminate himself, and with his knowledge of his right to legal counsel prior to confession. The problems arising here customarily relate to the question of how freely a confession was given. It would seem that concern with this freedom motivates at least some Supreme Court decisions; the following summary begins with freedom concepts and moves into concerns with confessions.

> In 1914, the United States Supreme Court ruled in the *Weeks* v. *United States* a case in which a confession was obtained in violation of the Fourth Amendment. In 1963, the Supreme Court ruled on the appeal case of *Gideon* v. *Wainwright*. The effect of the ruling was that new trials could be demanded by anyone convicted of crime who did not have legal counsel. Moving closer to the field of law enforcement, a 1964 decision was handed down in the case of *Escobedo* v. *Illinois*. This decision, based on a 5-4 majority, ensured the constitutional right of an indigent by providing legal counsel at the time of interrogation. Moving to specific concerns with confessions, in June of 1966, a ruling was handed down in *Miranda* v. *Arizona* (again by a 5-4 majority) with the effect of providing legal counsel as soon as the interrogated person is considered a specific suspect in an investigation.

[23] E. L. Barrett, Personal Rights, Property Rights, and the Fourth Amendment," *Supreme Court Review* (Chicago: University of Chicago Press, 1961), p. 65. See also: C. R. Sowle, ed., *Police, Power and Individual Freedom* (Springfield, Ill.: Thomas, 1962); W. H. Parker, "Birds Without Wings," International Association of Chiefs of Police, *The Police Yearbook, 1965* (Washington, D.C.: 1965). Also refer to Appendix A in this volume for important excerpts of sections of the United States Constitution related to police work.

Confessions then must not only conform to the many complicated rules of evidence (any of which can serve as the basis to reject evidence and possibly terminate the trial) but must also be given "freely" enough to avoid violation of the constitutional rights granted by the Supreme Court's interpretation of the Constitution. The confession, however, even when freely offered (in the total absence of threats, promises, or implied inducements) is no more acceptable than the level of the defendant's understanding of his "right" at the time the confession was made. (Refer to Appendix B for pertinent court decisions relating to police work.)

Perhaps here, in the area of confessions, as no where else in the process of accumulating and assessing persuasive evidence, the prosecution has assumed an increasingly significant role in the criminal justice system. It would appear that the future holds even more significant responsibilities for prosecution in this area. The late lawyer and criminologist, Paul W. Tappan, succinctly stated the paradoxical dilemma: "Only

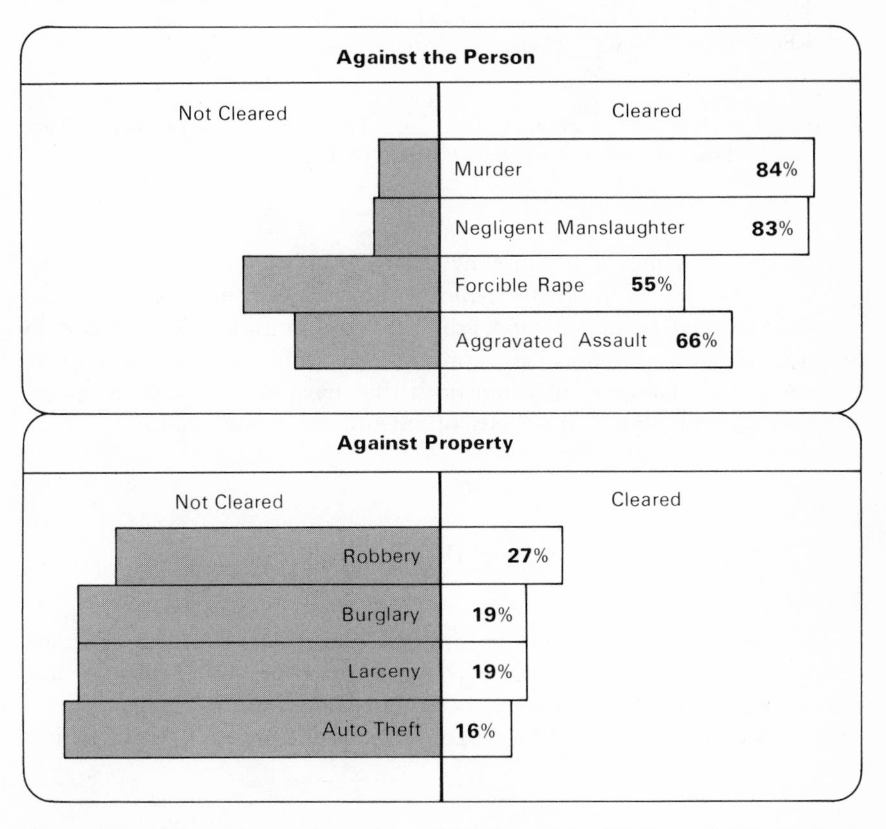

Figure 8-2 Crimes cleared by arrest, 1971. From the *Uniform Crime Report,* 1971, p. 32.

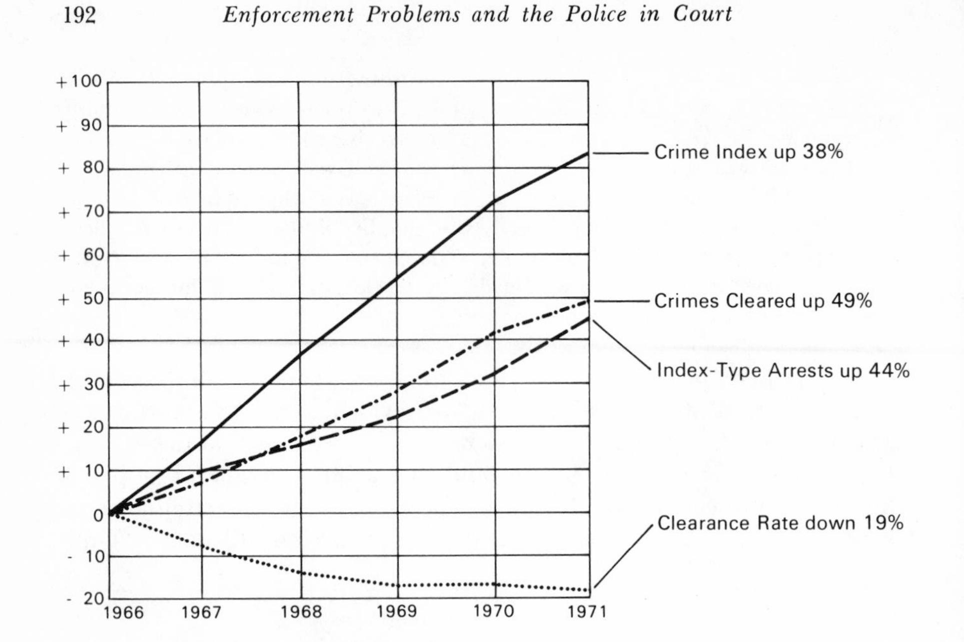

Figure 8-3 Crime and crimes cleared, 1966–71 (percent change over 1966). From the *Uniform Crime Report,* 1971, p. 33.

a minority of crimes result in conviction. *This is largely because of the failure of the police to discover, and prosecutors to convict, persons who have committed crimes against property.* Any considerable increase in the effectiveness of police and prosecution would appear to require *abandonment* of important protections that have been devised to guard suspects against abusive methods of investigation and trial." [24]

POLICE ROLE IN PROSECUTION

The law enforcement process and the prosecution process overlap considerably. The actual police role in the court room process has already been covered. However, the specific relationship between police and prosecution deserves further consideration. One manner in which

[24] P. Tappan, *Crime, Justice and Corrections* (New York: McGraw-Hill, 1960), pp. 366-67. (Italics added.)

this overlapping responsibility might be presented is to review a verbatim response given by an anonymous prosecutor to the question of what a district attorney would like from police:

1. The first and most important quality is *complete honesty* regarding the facts of his case and his views concerning prosecution and possible disposition and reasons. Many officers consult us, state the facts, and then add: "I don't think it is a violation." We appreciate that and we will go along in nine out of ten cases; and if we don't, we will point out why.

   Maybe his views regarding prosecution and possible disposition come from reasons that have nothing to do with the facts in the case. So what! None of us is perfectly logical all of the time.

   Example: A 77-year-old woman went through a stop sign. She is still in the hospital after four months. Should she be prosecuted?

   She should not drive a car; her own family says so—so we make a deal. We will not prosecute provided that she does not drive again and that the family will see the agreement is enforced.

   Example: A man ran into the rear of a truck, killing his wife and putting himself in the hospital for six months. Should he be prosecuted?

   This is an interesting question, and there may be a difference in your answer and mine. I don't think he should be prosecuted.

2. I like an officer who is completely honest in saying so if he thinks *he might have made a mistake* in what he did in any part of his investigation or even in the arrest.

   In 1967 it was suggested to the California Highway Patrol and all traffic officers in the county that in prosecutions for Section 502 of the Vehicle Code we be very cautious. "Be sure he's under the influence before you bring him in—then no reductions. *And* if you think you have made a mistake, come to me—I'll take care of it."

   One officer of the Highway Patrol—a very conscientious officer—came to me one day and said: "In this case I might have made a mistake regarding intoxication when I arrested the man for 501." Upon talking to the defendant about the facts of the case, he had no hesitation whatever in saying: "Oh, I was drunk as hell." We let the case go for 502. We like the conduct of that officer because it is basically honest.

3. Conversely, we do not like the conduct of an officer who has *no good reason to substantiate* his request that a 502 be dropped after *he* files it. Especially if we find out later that:
   a. The officer sold the defendant a Cadillac (between the date of arrest and the trial); or
   b. It was the officer's day off, and he asked that the case be dismissed just because it was his day off and he brought neither his report nor the blood evidence because he thought it would be dismissed.

   In both these cases, the defendants were tried and found guilty.

4. We like officers *who will listen to our side.* When the officer wants to prosecute for burglary or bad checks, sometimes we prefer to make it petty theft because we have actually tried cases in which the defendants are obviously guilty but jurors have found them "not guilty" and when asked simply say: "You filed too serious a charge; if you had made it petty theft, we would have found him guilty."

5. I like an officer who has *no exaggerated idea* that just because he has carried a gun for years he is a gun expert. It just isn't so. If he thinks so, ask him the number of riflings in the gun he now carries and the direction in which they turn. (Ninety-five out of 100 can't tell you.)

   I like the officer who, when questioned in detail about guns, says: "I'm sorry, sir. I'm not a gun expert," and leaves the subject to one who is an expert.

6. I like an officer who *learns from experience.* That same officer was asked one day about photography and the difference between hue and tone. He got a little fouled up. Then he was asked what color is black, and about that time he threw in the towel.

   I like a witness who says: "I don't know anything about photography; I just held the camera up and clicked it and this is what I got." *You don't have to be an expert, and I like an officer who makes no claim to being what he is not.*

7. I like an officer who *will admit he made a mistake.*

   A star witness for the prosecution in a murder case was the brother of the deceased. He was brought from jail in Fresno where he was held on a narcotics charge, and we were very uncertain as to how the jury would receive his testimony. But on cross-examination the defendant's attorney pointed his finger at him and said harshly: "Isn't it a fact that you started a fight at the Cherry Inn just two weeks before," and the witness gave the finest answer that he could give: "I'm sorry, sir. I did." From there on the jury took everything he said, hook, line and sinker.

8. I like officers who are friends and do *not suffer from jealousy and bitterness.*

   We have seen information withheld from us by certain officers because they were bitter and jealous as a result of the arrest having been made by other officers.

9. I like an officer who knows and understands that I expect to judge his conduct in the *light of all the circumstances,* and before I criticise him I propose to know all the facts respecting what he did and the pressure under which he was working.

   It is easy for a district attorney and others to criticize an officer. We can think about what was done for a day, a week, or a month. The officer has to act on the spot at the instant. And so in one case when I was asked, "Why don't you chew-out the officer," the answer was: "Because I'm not too sure I would have done any better myself under the same circumstances."

10. I like an officer who is a *human being and who understands* or at least thinks that I'm a human being. I'm affected by the same things that affect other people.

    Once I cited a man in for stealing $500 from his employer, and when he sat down he said: "I did it. I knew I was stealing when I took it. I'm guilty; I'll plead guilty if you charge me. There's nothing else I can do, but I have a wife, and three kids. I've never been in trouble in my life before. I've got to repay the money—if you'll just give me a little time."

    And to date I'm proud that I did not prosecute this man because he is a respectable businessman in our community.

    I think of the case of the man who came into the office at 8:15 one morning. He told about stealing from his employer—writing bum checks and a number of other things. Then he said: "Liquor is my trouble. I understand that they've good doctors at San Quentin. Would you please send me up there?"

    There are many people in the world who would think that police officers and district attorneys would have a field day in such a case. Instead, this man was sent to the state hospital for a week; the doctor said there was nothing wrong with him. He was prosecuted for petty theft; he served two months in the county jail; and today he is working for one of the largest corporations in the United States, making more money than I make.

    I like an officer who, in a shoplifting case, after looking into the circumstances and the background of the accused, finds things that make him say: "The family has promised to watch her very carefully, and I don't thnk we'll have any more trouble. If it is O.K. with you, I'll turn her over to her family."

    I like such an officer because if he does that, I'm sure he is a human being.

11. I like officers *who are not auditors.* Auditors have single track, narrow-gauge minds that are completely mathematical and not human. In their work, one and one always makes two, but when we're dealing with human beings that is not always so.

12. I don't like an officer *who is a "yes" man.* If he thinks I'm wrong, I expect him to tell me so and argue it out. Discussion and argument is the best way to reach a correct conclusion.

    I have a particular affection for one of the officers on the highway patrol, and I'm sure that the only reason is that whenever he comes in I know I'm in for a good argument. Whether it be on the subject of yielding a right-of-way or on the subject of county permits for overloading, there is bound to be a good argument.

    If an officer thinks one of the deputies in our office is wrong, he is welcome to come and see me. We don't claim our deputies know it all any more than I do. If I think one of them is wrong, I don't mind saying so—just as they'll tell me if they think I'm wrong.

13. I like an officer who understands *that he and I are on the same ball team; that his job is my job; that he is my police officer and I am his district attorney; that when he does something that is good and nice I'm proud of him and I'm proud to say so;* and that when he does something that is not good and not nice, I'm ashamed.

    It is a great satisfaction to me that in the last ten years there has been a great improvement in the officers in our county. It gives me a very pleasant feeling to have citizens relate to me the things they have done and then add: "You know, that officer was so nice about it; I sure felt like a heel."

14. I like an officer who understands that he is going *to be accused of improper conduct.* (It is part of the business.) The best defense is sometimes a strong offense. And if the accusations are made to me, I would like to talk to him about it. He's presumed to be innocent just like anybody else, and I know from sheer experience that 98 out of 100 accusations against officers are false. If I can find the accusation to be false, I'll be happy; if it be true, I should like some mitigation.

    One investigator in our office is there entirely as a result of complaints made against him by citizens. The first time they complained I paid no attention. (I'm used to it.) The second time, very much the same —like water off a duck's back. The third time I was getting tired of listening so I asked the officer to come up. His conduct and his answers to the accusations caused me to say: "Next time I need an investigator he's my man." Frequently the best way to judge a man is to see how he acts under the fire of accusation.

15. I like an officer who realizes that *I'm going to be accused of this and that and who'll give me the same benefit of same reasonable doubt, and if there's any question he wants to ask about it let him ask me—we'll discuss it fully.* I have been accused of selling out many times—I know that—but by the same caliber of people who in one breath say I sold out, and in the next breath (and sometimes in the next case) say I paid witnesses to testify for the prosecution.

16. *I like officers to know that they can ask me and the deputies in our office about their cases and their dispositions any time, and we'll tell them.* We should do that anyway. We will not get the impression that they are nosy, because it is the officer's case and he is entitled to know.

17. I like an officer who can *take a licking when he does not have it coming; one who can lose a good case and not moan;* one who is *big enough to understand that maybe the court or the jury sees qualities and characteristics in the defendant that we can't see;* one who *understands* that even though a guilty man goes free, we are still administering justice and that justice is not only just what we think it is but that sometimes others have a different idea.

    I like a man *who can lose a good case and then proceed to work hard and efficiently and well on the preparation of the next case.*

18. I like an officer who will *not* close the case just as soon as the defendant

says: "I did it." We have been fooled too many times by defendants changing their minds, and when we're put on our proof we are short.

I like an officer who, after the defendant says: "I did it," will say to the defendant: "Prove it," and then gather up all the proof and preserve it.

19. I like an officer who can take the witness stand and by *his conduct and his manner* and by his answers make a cold chill of pride run down my spine that tells me something like this: "That's a real police officer. He's my police officer and I'm proud of him and all he's done in this case."

    I like an officer who by *his conduct and his manner* and the handling of himself in the courtroom and on the witness stand forces me to express my pride to the jury, because that same cold chill of pride that runs down my spine can also affect people on the jury, and if it does, I've got them in the palm of my hand.

20. To have officers like that—who have these qualifications—is one of the finer compensations of being a district attorney. The salary I get is only a small part of my pay. *The big dividends are in the form of many satisfactions of duties well done, and if my officers have done their duties well it makes it so easy for me to do mine.*

SUMMARY

In this chapter we isolated the specific function of prosecution in the criminal justice system. The role of prosecution includes not only the instituting of criminal proceedings in court but also the consideration of rights and privileges of persons accused of crime.

The practical problems of dismissing and reducing charges is a realistic problem, but this chapter stressed the major role of assessing available evidence. The entire concept of evidence has been cast in terms of *persuasion*—with the prosecution judging the degree to which evidence is persuasive. Persuasion of guilt beyond a reasonable doubt is the yardstick. The prosecutor's responsibility is to judge whether sufficient evidence is available to provide such persuasion; he does this before determining whether the matter is to be presented in court.

The persuasive value of presenting evidence has been viewed in terms of "logical conclusions" arrived at through logical presentation. Also, a distinction has been made between *evidence* and *proof*. The distinction here is in the degree of persuasion. Proof exists when sufficient logical evidence is offered to *persuade*. When logical evidence is insufficient, *proof* had not been established. Put another way, all proof is evidence, but not all evidence is proof.

The logical concepts of proposition, inferences, and syllogism have been discussed as a background for considering the degree of evidence. Other related matters such as admissibility and circumstantial evidence were also discussed.

The problem of protecting and preserving evidence was presented in relation to the prosecution's responsibility to *persuade.* Eyewitnesses, credibility, impeachment, and other related matters were also covered. The subject of *admissibility* of evidence has been viewed in the context of Constitutional rights defined through Supreme Court interpretations of the Fourth Amendment.

Finally, the overlapping responsibilities of prosecution and police have been examined.

QUESTIONS

1. If one role of the prosecution is instituting criminal proceedings against an accused person, what is the other role presented in this chapter?
2. Distinguish between the nature of any particular evidence and the *logic* of its presentation.
3. Discuss the value of a prosecutor evaluating the availability of evidence "logically."
4. What has *persuasion* got to do with the prosecutor's responsibility?
5. How does *evidence* differ from *proof?*
6. For what reasons do prosecutors concern themselves with the United States Constitution?
7. Discuss the Constitution and admissibility of evidence.
8. What is meant by *preservation* of evidence? How does preservation relate to *persuasion?*
9. In what ways do the police and the prosecution overlap in terms of a prosecutor's evaluation of available evidence?

ANNOTATED REFERENCES

Bahm, A. J. *Logic for Beginners.* Boston: Student Outlines, 1960. This 91-page booklet is an ideal resource for clarifying the fundamentals of *logic* as applied to presentation of evidence.

Cataldo, B. F.; Gilliam, C. W.; Kempin, F. D.; Stockton, J. M.; and Weber, C. M. *Introductory Cases on Law and the Legal Process.* New York: John Wiley & Sons, 1968. The sections pertaining to due process and fair trial are particularly relevant to the concept of prosecution.

Eldefonso, E.; Coffey, A.; and Grace, R. *Principles of Law Enforcement.* New York: John Wiley & Sons, 1968. Chapters 4 and 11 of this text clarify the relationship of investigative effort to evidence in general.

Morgan, E. M. *Basic Problems of Evidence.* The Joint Commission on Continuing Legal Education of American Law Institute and the American Bar Association, 1963. An excellent coverage of the title subject.

Tappan, P. W. *Crime, Justice and Correction.* New York: McGraw-Hill, 1960. Part II, "The Administration of Justice," surveys the entire criminal justice process.

Witkins, B. E. *California Evidence.* 2nd ed. San Francisco: Bancroft-Whitney, 1966. Although addressed in part to California law, this publication nonetheless affords outstanding coverage of the concept of evidence in general.

9

The Defense

The vital roles played in the criminal justice system by both prosecution and defense require at least a cursory review of the functions of both parts of the system. Needless to say, many volumes have already been written on the role of defense. Here, we shall merely highlight the important aspects.

THE CONCEPT OF DEFENSE

The first half of the criminal court process is prosecution, and the other half of the process is defense. Unlike any other segment of the criminal justice process, the defense is not bound to the overall system except through the rules, procedures, and laws affecting the system. Put another way, the rationale for "system continuity" as presented in Chapter 1 does not apply to the defense in the same manner as it applies to all other system segments. Inleed, except for certain mutually recognized interpretations of "justice," the *defense* has virtually no identity tends to reduce the system's efficiency.

In spite of these essential differences, the defense nevertheless has a vital role in the criminal justice system. This observation raises the question: Why is it vital to have a segment of the criminal justice process which seems radically opposed to the immediate results sought by other segments? The answer to this question has to do with "certain mutually recognized interpretations of justice."

EFFICIENCY VERSUS EFFECTIVENESS

In order to clarify the vital role of defense, it would be useful to distinguish between *efficiency* and *effectiveness.* A system might be both efficient and effective; it might be neither; or a system might be either effective or efficient.

If the *output* as discussed in Chapter 1 is the result of reducing the number of crimes and the number of criminals in society, then *effectiveness* is the reduction itself. In other words, the system is effective to the degree that numbers of crimes and criminals are reduced. *Efficiency,* on the other hand, may be nothing more than getting all the work done on time—whether or not the work produces results. Put another way, *efficiency* may produce results, or it may not produce results. Efficiency might even produce bad results.

Hopefully, efficiency does lead to effectiveness in the criminal justice system—at least in most cases. In the case of defense, however, the nature of its function reduces efficiency in order to increase effectiveness. Understanding this seeming paradox is vital to comprehending the real measure of success of the American approach to criminal justice. To clarify possible confusion, some consideration must be given to *how* effectiveness is achieved. How does the criminal justice process reduce crime and the number of criminals?

It must first be noted that at least a part of justice system effectiveness comes from large numbers of potential criminals believing that the system is efficient—that the system gets the work done. But equally important in a free society is the concept of justice—a belief that the system is also fair.

Millions upon millions of dollars are continually spent in the United States, along with long protracted periods of time, all to insure that the criminal trial is both fair and just. With very few exceptions, criminal trials would be far more efficient without all of the elaborate defense procedures, and certainly they would be far less expensive. Many feel that improvements in the overall system would save a great deal of money and time, but few seriously argue that reducing the defense role in the system would be in the interest of justice or fairness.

To the degree that effectiveness is more important than efficiency, and that justice is part of effectiveness, *defense* is vital to the *criminal justice system.* Mistakes and miscarriages of justice are far too expensive a price to pay for efficiency—regardless of the rarity of such mistakes. The certainty that all possible measures are taken to prevent mistakes is the vital role played by an efficient defense.

CRIMINAL DEFENSES

It should be noted that many Western civilizations have been faced with the problem of crime long before the causes of crime were studied. This, of necessity, caused the criminal law and its specific defenses to evolve primarily in terms of "self-determinism." (See Chapter 4.) Reducing or diminishing an individual's responsibility for a criminal act was slow to develop. Indeed, in this area the primary concern of defense is related to *intent* rather than to relieving an offender of responsibility. That is, one's ability to form an *intent* to violate the law may in some instances be considered relevant, even though environmental stress and psychological tension in no way excuse violating the law.

LACK OF CAPACITY[1]

When a criminal defense hinges on the question of *capacity*, one of the following issues is customarily cited as the specific basis:

1. *Insanity:* Most jurisdictions distinguish between insanity at the time of the trial and insanity at the time of the alleged crime. Confusions sometimes arise in that a person judged insane at the time of the trial cannot be held criminally responsible until such time as he is sufficiently "sane" to "appreciate" the punishment for the crime—even though evidence indicates he was "sane" at the time of the criminal act.

   In determining insanity at the time of the criminal act, virtually all courts used the legal test known as the M'Naghten Rule.[2] In effect, this 1843 precedent causes the court to attempt to ascertain if the accused at the time of the act was "laboring under such a defect of reason or from disease of the mind as not to know the nature and quality of the act which he was doing, or if he did know it, then he did not know what he was doing was wrong."

   Many of the widely publicized legal entanglements in criminal trials in which the defense of insanity is used hinge on the distinctions of *nature and quality* along with the interpretation of the words *right and wrong.*

   Usually, in some criminal court jurisdictions, there are additional insanity defense pleas far more directly related to behavioral science explanations of crime causes. Two of the better known of these variations

[1] 75 American Law Review 265, 1ALR 965, 973, 3.

[2] 45 American Law Review 2nd, 1451; 45 ALR 2nd 1452, 3. (M'Naghten was supplemented by the "irrestable impulse" doctrine, 1 ALR Fed 965).

are the "irrestable impulse"[3] and the "delusion defense."[4] When such defenses are invoked, the psychiatric and sociological considerations invariably became a great deal more involved than simply, ascertaining the question of "right and wrong" (refer to the M'Naghten Rule).

2. *Idiocy:* When using the question of capacity as a defense in a criminal trial, most jurisdictions distingush between the category of idiot and insane. Idiots are deemed to be those persons who never had "mental capacity" in the first place, whereas an insane person "lost" his capacity through mental disease.[5] The impact of behavioral science on this particular criminal defense is usually related to determining what degree of feeble-mindedness is necessary to establish idiocy. Such distinctions as "morons" or "imbeciles" are often cited in these psychological classifications.
3. *Intoxication and Narcosis:* In the majority of criminal court jurisdictions, the voluntary use of alcohol or narcotics is not permitted as a defense regardless of how much one's capacity is inhibited by intoxication or narcosis. In some instances, however, the specific issue of *intent* to commit a criminal act can be somewhat mitigated by intoxication.[6] As an example of such mitigation, a completely inebriated person presumably could not form the required premeditation and deliberation to commit first-degree murder even though he would be convictable of involuntary manslaughter since no *intent* is required in the latter.
4. *Mistake of Fact:* Most jurisdictions permit a defense in which the accused person's *intent* was motivated by variations in facts.[7] This is technically not a defense, but an example of such mistake of fact presented in a court might be the following: A man and woman walking down the street are attacked by a vicious dog. The man, woman, and dog are entangled in a struggle on the ground when a well-meaning passerby surmises that a girl and her dog are being attacked by a rapist. With such mistaken fact, the girl's benefactor slays the supposed rapist, only to find himself accused of murder. The important point in mistakes of fact is that they defend only against the presence of intent.
5. *Consent:* In jurisdictions that define a *crime* as an act performed "without consent of the victim," proof of the victim's consent is customarily permitted as a defense.[8] Examples of situations of this nature are such

[3] 70 American Law Review 663, 70 ALR 675.

[4] 74 American Law Review 266; see also the Durham Test explained in 1 ALR Fed 965, 979, 4.

[5] 44 American Law Review 586 (mental incompetence).

[6] 22 American Law Review 3rd, 1228 (1st degree murder).

[7] Technically, mistake of fact is not a defense from strict liability of offense; for the reason of its functional use, see 61 American Law Review 1158.

[8] 52 American Law Review 2nd, 1181.

crimes as rape and certain forms of theft. Of course, such a criminal defense is invalid where further evidence indicates that such consent was induced through some form of intimidation.

This particular form of criminal defense, along with those to follow, are clearly less related to the causal factors of the behavioral sciences.

6. *Entrapment:* When a person accused of crime is able to prove that he was in some way induced to commit an illegal act and had no intention of doing so, the law customarily permits a criminal defense known as entrapment.[9] This is not to say that every person responding to an offer to commit a crime is entitled to plead entrapment. An undercover police officer successfully purchasing narcotics from a suspected seller has not entrapped the defendant. The actual test is determining whether or not the crime originated in the mind of the defendant. As discussed elsewhere in this text, this introduces certain aspects of the defendant's previous conduct.
7. *Coercion and Duress:* In much the same manner as entrapment reduces the accused person's responsibility for a criminal act, evidence of coercion or duress is also acceptable in criminal defenses in most jurisdictions. Such evidence customarily needs to demonstrate that the accused person acted under fear of immediate physical harm or threat of future injury to himself or his property.

   Coercion and duress as a defense become complicated on the issue of severity—the degree of intimidation involved.[10]
8. *Justification:* The term *justification* when used in the legal context acquires a technically different meaning than the "psychological and environmental justifications" reviewed in Chapter 4. Although the criminal defense known as *justification* is frequently related to the term *justifiable homocide,* there are generally three technical categories of justification: (a) defense of property;[11] (b) defense of another or other persons;[12] and (c) defense of self.[13]

   Law enforcement agencies become involved in the various forms of "defense of property" more often than not through one's "defense of habitation" (the owner or occupant defending his dwelling). Another instance frequently involving the law enforcement segment of the criminal justice process is an intended victim resisting force in a robbery.

   The category of "defense of others" is permitted in criminal court under certain conditions but only insofar as the defendant exerted the degree of force which he might have exercised in defense of himself. The similarity

[9] 69 American Law Review 2nd, 1439, 3.

[10] 40 American Law Review 2nd, 910, 2 (wife coercion by husband, 4ALR 277, 71ALR 1118).

[11] 25 American Law Review 547, 32 ALR 1541.

[12] 46 American Law Review 904 (officer arrest).

[13] 53 American Law Review 486.

between this cateogry of defense and the previously discussed mistake-of-fact defense is noteworthy.

The most common form of justification in the criminal justice system is the category of "self-defense." This relates to the legal provision that "one is privileged to use whatever force is reasonably necessary to prevent a physical invasion of his person by another where he knows or reasonably believes that such invasion is imminent." The degree of force legally available in defending one's self is restricted by the degree of force that is imminent. One could not kill another in self-defense unless it was reasonable to assume that one was about to be killed. The law customarily imposes a "duty to retreat" which in effect requires one to make every effort to avoid the assault before acting in self-defense.

9. *Double Jeopardy:*[14] When a defendant is placed on trial for an offense for which he has already been tried by another court *having jurisdiction,* that defendant is permitted to plead a defense known as "former jeopardy." Numerous legal technicalities complicate the actual plea in this particular defense and relate to the manner in which the original trial was terminated.

As an example, a trial terminated by dismissing a jury *without* consent of the accused permits the accused to claim a "double jeopardy" at any subsequent trial for the same offense. Conversely, if a convicted defendant successfully appeals or motions for a new trial, he cannot then claim that the first trial was former jeopardy.

DEFENSE AND BEHAVIOR SCIENCE

A number of other considerations dealing with *defense* may also be considered. Even though the law itself does not provide defenses beyond those already discussed in this chapter, defense attorneys are increasingly making use of behavioral approaches toward mitigating the severity of the offender's *intent* to commit a crime. Put another way, defense tactics increasingly include a behavioralistic explanation of an offender's conduct in order to mitigate the self-determined implications discussed early in Chapter 4. A brief consideration of some of these possible uses of behavioral science might be useful.

Consider for example *sociology.* Utilizing the implications of cultural approach, a defense might contend that an offender exposed to cultural patterns where there is conflict between legitimate and illegitimate means is grossly influenced by that environment, and therefore his *intent* to commit crime is partially mitigated. "Differential association" could

[14] American Law Review 3rd, 874 (former jeopardy is basis of *habeas corpus*); see also: 8 ALR 2nd 285 and 21 ALR 2nd 1158.

similarly be cast in the role of mitigating an offender's intent. The discussion of families in Chapter 4 is also readily adaptable to forming an influence on an offender's *intent* to commit crime. Indeed virtually every consideration discussed under the subtitle "Social Approach" is adaptable to this kind of defense.

The "psychological approach" has virtually boundless implications in terms of an offender's *intent*.[15] To whatever degree such considerations are permissible in the criminal trial, possibilities exist in the id, ego, and superego, along with the various body shapes and biochemical influences already discussed. Certainly the heredity factors presented are at least as germane as the other causative considerations.

Probably the most significant consideration in relating criminal defense to the behavioral sciences is the concept of *intent*. The paradox of "determinism" and "self-determinism" forever impinges in a justice system in a free society. Simply stated, if in fact behavioral science explanations of the cause of crime serve as a defense, then people are neither responsible or accountable for the crimes they commit. The alternative extreme, that of complete "self-determinism," promises to regress justice thousands of years to the point where offenders were summarily executed without regard to mitigating circumstances. The American criminal justice system finds itself somewhere in between these extremes. As continuing adjustments are made, criminal defense continues to play a vital role.

DEFENSE AND PROSECUTION

Procedurally, there is a great deal in common between defense and prosecution. As seen in the preceding chapter, the prosecution concerns itself with *persuasion*. Adequate defense also requires great understanding of the principles of persuasion—proof, logic, inductive or deductive reasoning, and so forth. Like the prosecution the defense must be concerned with syllogisms, inferences, and many other tools of the logician. Both defense and prosecution must be expert in proof, evidence, and the wide range of related matters. Court procedures and methods are also of mutual concern.

Certainly, materiality and relevance of evidence concern defense as much as prosecution. Witnesses, exhibits, and the preservation of evidence are equally related to criminal defense and prosecution. Also the procedures to impeach witnesses, evidence admissibility, confessions, and a host of legal technicalities influencing the decision to employ any

[15] P. Tappan, *Contemporary Corrections* (New York: McGraw-Hill, 1951), p. 21.

of these variables are of mutual concern. In short, virtually all that was discussed on prosecution relates directly to the defense.

Criminal defense, to be *effective* in the justice system, must bring to bear *similar levels of skills and knowledgeability* as brought forth by the prosecution. Indeed, in order to assure a continuation of the very best prosecution possible, the defense must be *at least* as skilled in the judicial process as the prosecution.

Figure 9-1 Probably one of the most controversial cases in the criminal justice process was the trial of Angela Davis. Ms. Davis was found innocent of all charges against her—murder, kidnapping, and conspiracy—stemming from the August 7, 1970, Marin County Courthouse escape attempt. Ms. Davis is shown leaving the courtroom with her attorney and an officer of the court. Photo courtesy of the *San Jose Mercury News,* San Jose, Ca.

SUMMARY

In this chapter criminal defense was introduced as a vital segment of the criminal justice process. A distinction was made between *efficiency* and *effectiveness,* and the role of defense has been presented as part of the effectiveness of the criminal justice system. Despite being a crucial part of the effectiveness of the system, however, the nature of defense tends to reduce the system's efficiency.

Fairness and justice are the areas of effectiveness which relate to the crucial defense role. Time and money might be saved through increased efficiency in the system, but such savings could not in any way impinge upon the role of defense without impairing the effectiveness of the system.

Various criminal defenses have been presented. The relationship of the behavioral sciences to "mitigation" was reviewed in terms of sociology, psychology, and other theoretical frameworks. These relationships hinge on the concept of *intent* to commit crime.

Finally, after acknowledging the gross differences between prosecution and defense, we also reviewed some similarities. Prosecution and defense use overlapping procedures and identical skills.

QUESTIONS

1. Relate criminal defense to the process of the criminal justice system.
2. Contrast efficiency and effectiveness as they both relate to criminal defense.
3. What are the criminal defenses?
4. How does the "mitigation" approach of the behavioral sciences relate to criminal defenses? To intent?
5. Discuss the relationship between any criminal defense and sociology. And psychology.
6. Discuss differences between prosecution and defense.
7. What are the specific areas in which prosecution and defense require identical expertise?
8. Why is defense crucial to justice?

ANNOTATED REFERENCES

Chapman, S. and St. Johnston, T. *The Police Heritage in England and America.* East Lansing: Michigan State University Press, 1962. This booklet covers many of the significant variables in the criminal law that link police and defense.

Coffey, A.; Eldefonso, E.; and Hartinger, W. *Human Relations: Law Enforcement in a Changing Community.* Englewood Cliffs, N.J.: Prentice-Hall, 1971. Chapter 3 explores in depth the areas in which the effectiveness of justice depends upon belief in fairness.

GERMANN, A.; DAY, T.; and GALLATI, R. *Introduction to Law Enforcement.* Springfield, Ill.: Thomas, 1962. Chapter 2 elaborates the relationship of the individual to society for the reader concerned with effective versus efficient justice.

SULLIVAN, J. *Introduction to Police Science.* New York: McGraw-Hill, 1966. Chapters 6 and 7 provide perspective for the concept of consistency in criminal law application.

TAPPAN, P. *Crime, Justice and Correction.* New York: McGraw-Hill, 1960. Chapter 13, entitled "Justice and Efficiency," presents that subject in a different perspective than adopted in this chapter.

PART FOUR

Scope of Juvenile and Adult Corrections

All societies seek to prevent what is perceived as illegal and antisocial behavior. If a society fails to do so in an individual case, it will evoke controls. In primitive societies these controls may be strict retribution or elaborate taboos, but in present day Western society's police power is used in the final attempt to control the offender. There is more or less general agreement within the society regarding prevention and control—at least more so than about what is to be done after a crime is committed. When prevention and control have failed, responsibility shifts to that portion of the criminal justice system known as corrections.

W. HARTINGER, E. ELDEFONSO, A. COFFEY
Corrections: A Component of the Criminal Justice System

10

The Justice System and Juveniles

Figures from the Federal Bureau of Investigation and the Children's Bureau indicate that 64 percent of the arrests for auto theft, 52 percent of the arrests for burglary, 47 percent of the arrests for theft, and 26 percent of the arrests for robbery are juveniles.[1] About two million youths commit delinquent acts during a year; yet approximately three-fourths of these cases are dealt with directly by the police and the family without involving the courts. This is because police use a large amount of discrepancy in how they handle juveniles; as a consequence, only one-fourth of the juvenile offenders end up in the correctional process. This is significant since police do not have the discretion to deal with adults in a like manner.

Data indicate that approximately 28 percent of the clientele within the correctional system are juveniles.[2] This suggests that almost three out of every ten persons handled within the system are being handled under the Juvenile Court Law. Certainly, this proportion of the correctional population is large enough to cause concern. It is large enough, in fact, to merit an investigation of the unique system by which this population is handled. The system, known as the Juvenile Court Law,

[1] U.S. Department of Health, Education and Welfare, *Juvenile Court Statistical Series* (Washington, D.C.: U.S. Gov't. Printing Office, 1969). See also: Federal Bureau of Investigation, *Uniform Crime Reports* (Washington, D.C.: U.S. Gov't. Printing Office, 1970).

[2] President's Commission on Law Enforcement and Administration of Justice, *Task Force Report: Corrections* (Washington, D.C.: U.S. Gov't. Printing Office, 1967), p. 193.

came about because of humanistic concerns for youth who were being handled as adult criminals.

The juvenile court concept has never been completely understood by the majority of the citizens of the United States. This difficulty in understanding seems to revolve around the fact that the juvenile courts were conceived to serve two functions—the first being judicial (deciding whether the alleged offense was committed by the minor before the court); the second being correctional (providing a service designed to rehabilitate the youth). The juvenile justice system, as differentiated by statute from the criminal justice system, is approximately seventy-five years old in the United States. However, the separate and different handling of children involved in criminal conduct has been in practice for a longer period of time. At this point, a historical perspective of the handling of juveniles might be helpful.

FOUNDATIONS OF JUVENILE COURT LAW

Under English common law, the forerunner of our present-day law, a child below the age of seven was felt to be incapable of forming criminal intent—the concept of *doli capax*. For youths between the ages of seven and fourteen, juries were asked to determine upon the evidence whether an offense was committed with intelligence and capacity and an understanding of the unlawful character of the crime. This, of course, meant that youths over the age of seven were often placed in jail—some even were committed to prison. Obviously, these youths were subjected to the crudest form of treatment. This condition stirred educators, philanthropists, and others concerned with humanistic endeavors to try to rectify the situation. The following description should give the reader some understanding of the time and the impetus of the movement which led to the present-day juvenile court system.

> Although the 19th Century movement for reform and treatment of children was a natural enough development in the humanizing of the criminal law, it well may have been accelerated and intensified by social conditions then prevailing. Both industrialization and immigration were bringing people into the cities by the thousands, with resulting overcrowding, disruption of family life, increase in vice and crime, and all the other destructive factors characteristic of rapid urbanization. Truancy and delinquency rose rapidly, and civic-minded men and women worried about the exposure of children to tobacco, alcohol, pornography, and street life in general. With the growing concern over emotional influences came the desire to rescue children and restore them to a healthful, useful life. In addition throughout the 19th Century there was a rising concern about official treatment of

> children—the growth of what has been called the spirit of social justice. The ascending social sciences, with their optomistic claims to diagnose and treat the problems underlying deviants, seemed to provide the ideal tool for implementing the dual roles of treating wayward children humanely and offsetting their deleterious surroundings. Philanthropic men and women such as the members of the Chicago Women's Club, emancipated intellectual femininists like the Hull House Group, and professional penologists and reformers joined forces to achieve recognition of the greater vulnerability and salvagability of children—first in establishing separate institutions for youth and substituting noninstitutional supervision whenever feasible, then in adapting physically separate court proceedings, and finally in altering the very philosophy underlying judicial handling of children.[3]

It can be seen that the time was right for reforms to take place. These reforms started with changes in correctional institutions available for the placement of children and youth involved in criminal activities. The first institution of this sort was the New York City House of Refuge founded in 1825. This institution was under the direction of an organization known as the Society for Reformation of Juvenile Delinquents. This society received authority from the State of New York to manage the House of Refuge. The purpose was to separate children from adult offenders and give them corrective treatment rather than punishment.[4]

The House of Refuge in New York was followed by similar institutions in Boston and Philadelphia. Even so, many large-city magistrates continued to send youths to crowded jails because they felt that thirty days stay in jail was far better for such youth than several years imprisonment in a house of refuge.

The houses of refuge were important since they began a trend whereby separate correctional institutions for youth would be the accepted fact. In 1847 the State of Massachusetts set up the first state reform school for youths aimed at teaching discipline and an honest trade and instilling dedication to advancement through hard work. The institution that was to be most copied was the Girls' Reform School opened in 1854 in Lancaster, Massachusetts. This was an institution based on the cottage or family plan. Most juvenile correctional institutions since that time have been patterned after this particular plan.

A second development in corrections which had an impact on the method by which juveniles would be handled in the criminal justice system was probation. Beginning in Massachusetts in 1880, probation was used as a substitute for confinement and reflected the growing belief in

[3] President's Commission on Law Enforcement and Administration of Justice, *Task Force Report: Juvenile Delinquency and Youth Crime* (Washington, D.C.: U. S. Gov't. Printing Office, 1967), pp. 2-3.

[4] *Task Force Report: Juvenile Delinquency and Youth Crime,* p. 3.

Figure 10-1 Students returning to their cottages for the evening activities program at the Federal Youth Center, Morgantown, West Virginia. Photo courtesy of Public Information Department, Federal Bureau of Prisons, Washington, D.C.

application of the social sciences to treatment and supervision as a means of preventing further criminal or delinquent behavior.

During the latter part of the nineteenth century attention shifted somewhat to an attempt to change the court process. These changes were the forerunners of the present-day juvenile court law.

> Awareness of the brutality of incarcerating children with adult criminals led to efforts to separate them before and during trial as well. In 1861, the Mayor of Chicago was authorized to appoint a commission to hear and decide minor charges against boys between six and seventeen years, and to place them on probation or in a reformatory, power which the judges received in 1867. In 1869, a Massachusetts statute provided for the presence in court of an agent of the state in cases where the child might be committed to a state reformatory: The agent was also charged with finding foster homes in suitable cases and paying subsequent visits to them. A law of 1870 required separate hearings of childrens cases in Suffolk County (Boston) and authorized a representative of the Commonwealth to investigate cases, attend trials, and protect childrens interests. The separate trial statute was extended throughout the Commonwealth in 1872, followed in 1877 with provisions for separate sessions, dockets and court records in juvenile cases. New York established separate trials, dockets, and records in 1892. Rhode Island in 1898 instituted segregated facilities for children under 16 years awaiting trial, separate arraignment and trials, special dockets and records,

and presence at juvenile proceedings of public and private agents to protect the interest of the child.[5]

Although these modifications regarding procedures by which youth were to be handled were of importance, the juvenile court law concepts specifically began when the Illinois Legislature passed a Juvenile Court Act in April, 1899. Under this concept, delinquents were to be treated as "wayward children" in the first state-wide court created for the treatment of children. The Juvenile Court Act passed in Illinois did not specifically create a new court, but rather it included most of the features that have come to be distinguished as the juvenile court. The original act and the amendments to it brought together under one jurisdiction cases of neglect, dependency, and delinquency. Delinquency was felt to include youngsters involved in criminal law violations as well as youngsters that were involved in immoral associations and incorrigibility. Juvenile court hearings were to be informal and not open to the public. Also, juvenile court records were to be confidential. Youths were to be detained in facilities separate from adults. In short, the process used to deal with youths was not the same process that was used to deal with adult criminals.

By 1911, twenty-two states had adopted juvenile court acts similar to that of the State of Illinois; by 1925, forty-six of the forty-eight states had enacted legislation that created juvenile courts. There are now juvenile courts in all jurisdictions within the United States including the District of Columbia. There are approximately 2,700 courts that hear cases regarding youths under juvenile court theory. The juvenile court act as first developed in Illinois was in many respects the reflection of an idea which was already widespread.[6] The philosophical underpinnings for acceptance of the idea of a juvenile court was fairly well accepted by the time the legislation was first enacted. What this philosophy was, and is, will be examined so that a better understanding of juvenile courts can be ascertained.

PHILOSOPHY OF JUVENILE COURT LAW

Under the old common law, a child under seven years of age was considered incapable of forming criminal intent. The philosophy of the juvenile court law has since extended this original concept. Obviously,

[5] *Task Force Report: Juvenile Delinquency and Youth Crime,* p. 3.

[6] *Task Force Report: Juvenile Delinquency and Youth Crime,* p. 3.

criminal courts designated for adults are not the proper courts to deal with youngsters who may be older than seven but are still not able to make adult decisions. Philosophically, there appears to be at least two reasons why adult criminal courts are inappropriate for minors. The first reason is that youths before the court may be in need of protection due to their own social circumstances. Second, they may also need protection from incurring severe criminal penalties because they were unable to fully comprehend the consequences of their actions.

In an effort to deal with these problems in a more astute manner, there was developed a philosophy regarding intercession into the lives of minors who violate the law. In essence, the idea behind juvenile court law is that the state is enabled to step in and exercise guardianship over a youth who violated the law. Most often, there are social and psychological conditions that lead to a youth's law violations. Consequently, the juvenile court law was devised as a means whereby such youths could be treated in a setting where they are not considered criminals. In fact, they are not legally charged wih crime. Instead youths who are found to be involved in criminal acts are declared wards of the state or court so that they can receive a particular kind of care.[7] This care may include custody and discipline that approximates as nearly as possible that which should have been given by the minor's parents.

The function of protecting the juvenile when the youth's own parents have not done so is a function called *parens patriae.* This Latin phrase, as used in the juvenile court law, means that the juvenile court acts for the state and, to the extent that the minor's real parents have defaulted, assumes the minor's parental responsibilities.[8]

Generally speaking, the philosophy of juvenile court law has also had its impact on proceeding. From a philosophical point of view, the proceedings in juvenile court cases tend to be governed by the principles of chancery, or equity, in the matter of disposition of the case. The concept of *equity* is such that the court is allowed a much more flexible, more equitable manner of handling disposition than would be possible if the matter were handled under the concept of criminal law. For example, in states where the criminal law is codified, there might be a prescribed sentence for a particular criminal act. A minor found to have been involved in that particular act is not subject to the criminal penalties prescribed. Rather, the minor under the concept of equity is regarded as a ward of the state or court who needs guidance and protection rather

[7] R. Pound, "The Juvenile Court and the Law," *Crime and Delinquency,* Vol. 10 (1964), pp. 490-504.

[8] U.S. Children's Bureau, *Standards for Specialized Courts Dealing With Children,* Publication No. 346 (Washington, D.C.: U.S. Gov't. Printing Office, 1954).

than punishment. Consequently, the disposition of the court is the one which the court feels would be the best prescribed plan available for rehabilitating the minor.

The philosophy of the juvenile court law is also much broader than the philosophy of the criminal courts in that juvenile courts have generally been endowed with jurisdictions broad enough to include all cases in which a minor violates laws or ordinances; they also include those minors who are in need of protection and supervision because they are so-called "wayward youth." It should be noted that the philosophy of juvenile court also encompasses intervention in cases where children have been abandoned, neglected, or cruelly treated by their parents or guardians.

These philosophical concepts suggest there is a certain framework or standard through which the juvenile court should operate. This standard, according to the U.S. Children's Bureau [9] should include: (1) broad jurisdiction in cases of youth under 18 years of age who require court action or protection because of their acts or circumstances; (2) a judge chosen because of his special qualifications for juvenile court work, with legal training, understanding of social problems, and knowledge of child development; (3) private court hearings rather than public court hearings; (4) informal court procedure which still conforms to the rules of evidence; and (5) detention in separate facilities for youth. These detention facilities should be used only if the following conditions exist:

1. The minor is in need of proper and effective parental care or control and has no parent, guardian, or responsible relative; or has no parent, guardian, or responsible relative willing to exercise, or capable of exercising, such care or control; or has no parent, guardian, or responsible relative actually exercising such care or control.
2. The minor is destitute or is not provided with the necessities of life, or he is not provided with a home or suitable place of abode.
3. The minor is provided with a home which is an unfit place for him by reason of neglect, cruelty, or depravity of either of his parents, or of his guardian, or other persons in whose custody or care he is.
4. Continued detention of the minor is a matter of immediate and urgent necessity for the protection of the minor or the person or property of another.
5. The minor is likely to flee the jurisdiction of the court.
6. The minor has violated an order of the juvenile court.
7. The minor is physically dangerous to the public because of a mental or physical deficiency, disorder, or abnormality.[10]

[9] *Standards for Specialized Courts. . . .*

[10] Section 628, California Juvenile Court Law.

Further elements of the standard juvenile courts should follow are: (6) a well-qualified probation staff, with limited caseloads; (7) resources available for individualized and specialized treatment (psychological, psychiatric, and medical facilities available to the clientele being serviced by the juvenile court); (8) an adequate record-keeping system which provides for both social and legal records that are safeguarded from indiscriminate public inspection; and (9) youths brought before the juvenile court defined not as criminals but as delinquents.

With some understanding of the ideals behind juvenile courts, an examination of how they function in comparison to criminal courts may give a better picture of their operation.

JUVENILE COURTS COMPARED WITH CRIMINAL COURTS

Comparing juvenile courts to criminal courts needs to be done in a realistic manner so one does not get an unfavorable picture of the juvenile court or an unrealistic and unfavorable picture of the criminal courts.[11] First, one must note that juvenile courts vary a great deal from one jurisdiction to the next. Indeed, they vary so much that in a strict sense it may be incorrect to speak of juvenile courts or the juvenile court system as being uniform throughout the country. However, there are some fundamental characteristics of juvenile and criminal courts that can be compared. The first of these comparisons might well be the purpose for which courts take action.

In a criminal court, the purpose for a trial is to determine if there is sufficient evidence to convict the person accused. On the other hand, in juvenile court the purpose of the court hearing is first to ascertain whether the youth did indeed commit the act for which he is appearing before the court. Upon ascertaining that he did commit the act, the court's principle objective is the welfare of the youth, his protection, guidance, and rehabilitation.

A second characteristic that can be compared is the matter of procedure. In criminal courts, the trial is usually a public one; a jury is used unless it is waived in accordance with law. In the juvenile court, the hearing is private, and in only nine states is there jury trial. However, in many states where the alleged delinquent may be permitted to have a jury trial usually no jury is used. Furthermore, in juvenile cases a probation officer is present in court. Also a different vocabulary regarding legal matters is used in juvenile courts. For example, instead of a com-

[11] P. W. Tappan, *Juvenile Delinquency* (New York: McGraw-Hill, 1949), p. 179.

plaint the youth is brought before the court upon a *petition.* Instead of warrants the juvenile court uses *summonses.* The prejudicial stage or the initial hearing commonly referred to as the *detention hearing* is the first stage of the court's involvement rather than the arraignment. The juvenile court involves a finding of involvement at the jurisdictional hearing rather than a finding of guilt as in the criminal trial. After ascertaining involvement, there is a dispositional hearing instead of a sentencing.

Often the physical surroundings of juvenile court are less imposing than the regular criminal courtroom; the judge may sit at a desk or table instead of behind the bench.[12]

The results of criminal courts tend to be somewhat different than the results of juvenile courts. In criminal court if a defendant is convicted, he is sentenced for punishment as prescribed by the law. The judge does not have broad discretionary powers in the exercise of his authority to sentence the convicted person. The emphasis is on the crime rather than on the needs of the person who committed the crime. In the juvenile court if a youth is adjudged delinquent, the court has broad discretionary powers to provide for the youth's care and rehabilitation. Generally speaking, the court emphasizes the youth's needs as a person and considers what would be the best plan to change the youth's behavior to a more acceptable pattern.[13]

Armed with these comparisons, a view of the day-to-day operation of the juvenile court should be of more interest to the reader.

OPERATION OF THE JUVENILE COURT

In 1966, there were 2,671 juvenile courts in the United States and Puerto Rico.[14] The structure of each court and its position or status within each jurisdiction may vary a great deal. Some are separate, independent courts, although these are relatively few. Most are part of superior, county, municipal, circuit, district, common pleas, or probate courts. In a few jurisdictions, family courts have been created to deal both with domestic relations and the problems of delinquency, dependency, and neglect. Generally speaking, no matter where the juvenile court is placed in the operational scheme, the judge assigned to hear cases often operates his court quite independently of other court operations.

12 *Task Force Report: Juvenile Delinquency* . . . , p. 3.

13 R. G. Caldwell, *Criminology* (New York: Ronald Press, 1965), pp. 389-91.

14 *Task Force Report: Juvenile Delinquency* . . . , p. 77.

Even though there may be some differences among states and, in some instances, within states, there seems to be some common ground upon which all juvenile courts agree. For one, there is general agreement as to what constitutes a delinquent youngster. The definition of a *delinquent* as used in the juvenile court encompasses all youths who have committed an act which would be considered a crime if committed by an adult. However, the term also includes youths who have committed violations of specific acts that apply only to minors—for example, acts against use of alcohol or violation of truancy ordinances. Finally, a delinquent youth may also be considered beyond control, ungovernable, incorrigible, and so forth.

Under the latter two definitions of delinquency, adults would not be brought before a court. However, approximately 25 percent of the youths brought before juvenile courts fall into these two categories of violating laws designed for minors or of being "incorrigible".[15] There is growing concern over the handling of the so-called "incorrigible" youth in the juvenile court system. Up to this point in time, however, it appears that, although referral to juvenile court may not be the ideal, it is the most viable alternative. In many instances there is no other social agency willing or able to deal effectively with youth of this sort.[16]

In some states the jurisdiction of the juvenile court is concurrent with that of the criminal court in serious offenses. In other states major offenses such as capital crimes are excluded from the juvenile court jurisdiction. Traditionally, age has served the purpose of limiting the population subject to juvenile court jurisdiction. This is because age is an objective and readily ascertainable criteria. It does not take into account individual differences in maturity, past and present behavior, and other factors such as criminal sophistication when deciding on adult or juvenile court handling of a given minor. Presently, the upper ages vary from 16 to 21 from state to state. Most probably, since the enactment of the Twenty-sixth Amendment, 18 will be the upper age limit.

Age may not be the best indicator of who should be handled in juvenile court. Because of this, approximately forty states provide for waivers or transfer from the juvenile court to the adult court, giving the juvenile court some discretion and flexibility in exercising its jurisdiction. It should be noted, however, that the waiver laws vary greatly. Nearly half attach no conditions to the judge's exercise of discretion. In a num-

[15] W. H. Sheridan, "Juveniles Who Commit Noncriminal Acts: Why Treat in a Correctional System," *Federal Probation*, Vol. 31 (March, 1967), pp. 26-30.

[16] E. Schepses, "Delinquent Children and Wayward Children," *Federal Probation*, Vol. 32 (June, 1968), pp. 42-46.

ber of states, the waiver is authorized for any offense, but only for a minor above a specific age. In approximately ten states, a waiver is permitted without regard to age, but only for specific offenses.

In any discussion of the operation of the juvenile court today, one must examine the overall effects of this court process in stemming youthful crime. A statement by the President's Commission on Law Enforcement and Administration of Justice indicates that the juvenile court movement has not run as well as was originally hoped.

> Studies conducted by the commission, legislative inquiries in various states, and reports by informed observers compel the conclusion that the great hopes originally held for the juvenile court have not been fulfilled. It has not succeeded significantly in rehabilitating delinquent youth, in reducing or even stemming the tide of juvenile criminality, or in bringing justice and compassion to the child offender. To say that juvenile courts have failed to achieve their goals is to say no more than what is true of criminal courts in the United States. But failure is most striking when hopes are highest.[17]

Perhaps the difficulty is the philosophy and ideal that the juvenile court should lead "errant youths" to the paths of "righteousness." The truth of the matter is that a split exists between theory and practice. Professor Francis Allan has observed this most succinctly:

> In a great many cases the juvenile court must perform functions essentially similar to those exercised by any court adjudicating cases of persons charged with dangerous and disturbing behavior. It must re-assess the norms and standards of the community when confronted by serious deviant conduct and it must protect the security of the community by such measures as it has at its disposal, though the available means may be unsatisfactory when viewed either from the standpoint of the community interests or of the welfare of the child.[18]

Ever since the establishment of juvenile courts over seventy years ago, they have been severely criticized by both friend and foe alike. However, there was little change until the mid-1960s. At this time, legal scholars and social reformers became increasingly distressed with the juvenile court failures. Consequently, Supreme Court decisions have somewhat changed the nature of the juvenile court.

[17] *Task Force Report: Juvenile Delinquency . . .* , p. 7.

[18] President's Commission on Law Enforcement and Administration of Justice, *The Challenge of Crime in a Free Society* (Washington, D.C.: U.S. Gov't. Printing Office, 1967), p. 80.

THE EFFECT OF SUPREME COURT DECISIONS

In 1966, the Supreme Court recognized that the juvenile court system had some faults. In the first of a number of decisions subsequently affecting the juvenile court, the Supreme Court clearly indicated that the informality of juvenile court proceedings did not entitle the juvenile court to disregard fundamental procedural guidelines. The ruling on the particular case in point, *Kent* v. *United States,*[19] indicated that the District of Columbia juvenile court was in error when it waived jurisdiction over a 16-year-old, thereby releasing him to the adult criminal court without granting him a hearing on that waiver. The Supreme Court further held that any juvenile who was to have such a hearing must have certain procedural safeguards, including counsel who has access to social records and a judicial statement for the reasons underlying the waiver decision.

One year later, in 1967, the Supreme Court in its now famous ruling *In re Gault* indicated that fundamental due process guarantees must apply to the adjudication phase of juvenile court proceedings. The Supreme Court held that when a juvenile faces possible commitment to an institution certain procedural safeguards are guaranteed to him by the Fourteenth Amendment due process clause. The safeguards mentioned were: (1) advance notice of the charges, including particular allegations of wrongful conduct; (2) notice of the minor's right to counsel and the availability of court appointed counsel if the minor is indigent; (3) warning to the minor of his privilege against self-incrimination and the subsequent right to remain silent; (4) admonishment of the minor's right to confront and cross-examine any witnesses that might testify against him; and finally (5) a record of the juvenile court's proceedings or a statement of the grounds for the court's decision made available if that particular matter is appealed.

In effect, this decision established that a juvenile proceeding can no longer be considered a civil matter; in reality the commitment of adults and juveniles are indistinguishable in terms of loss of liberty. Furthermore, if the punishment is similar, in the sense that liberty is restrained, then due process safeguards afforded at criminal trials apply equally to juvenile proceedings.[20]

In 1970, the Supreme Court again expanded the due process rights of the accused juvenile in a case known as *In re Winship.*[21] Again the court

[19] Kent v. United States, 383 US 541 (1966).

[20] In re Gault, 381 U.S. (1967).

[21] In re Winship, 397 U.S. 358 (1970).

compared delinquency and criminal proceedings in regard to the extent that each potentially threatened the defendant's liberty; the Supreme Court felt that, in order for the allegations of the petition to be found true, the matter should meet the standard of proof "beyond a reasonable doubt." Before this time, the amount of proof needed resembled that accepted in civil trials—that is, a preponderance-of-evidence standard was used. (Preponderance of evidence is, of course, a lower standard of proof.) At this hearing, the Supreme Court did indicate that their ruling was not to affect the informality, flexibility, or speed with which the fact finding in a juvenile matter takes place.

This particular concept seems to have been enlarged in a case known as *McKeiver* v. *Pennsylvania*.[22] The Supreme Court held that a trial by jury is not constitutionally required in state court proceedings. The court denied that the jury is "a necessary component of accurate fact finding" and expressed concern that the jury might impair the juvenile court operation. In fact Justic Blackmun pointed out that juries were not used in probate, deportation proceedings, or military trials; and yet the judicial system in these areas functioned effectively. Furthermore, Justice Blackmun felt that a jury trial, if incorporated into juvenile court proceedings, threatened to convert juvenile proceedings into full-scale criminal adversary proceedings, thereby negating the need for a separate system. It should be noted, however, that in at least eleven states jury trials are allowed in juvenile cases under limited circumstances.[23]

One final consideration which finds a parallel in both the criminal court and the juvenile court is bail. Bail in juvenile court up to this time is a matter of state law and is provided for in nine states—Arkansas, Colorado, Georgia, Massachusetts, Michigan, North Carolina, South Dakota, and West Virginia.[24] In the other states it is generally felt that adjudging a person to be a delinquent of the juvenile court is not a conviction of crime, and consequently the proceedings are not criminal in nature. Therefore, it follows that the provision in the Constitution regarding bail in criminal matters does not apply to a noncriminal proceeding.

As can be seen from the foregoing discussion, procedural matters in the juvenile court are quite comparable in most cases to procedural matters in the criminal courts. Obviously, then, the benefits of juvenile

[22] McKeiver v. Pennsylvania, 403 U.S. 528 (1971).

[23] N. L. Nathanson, "Jury Trial—Juvenile Court," *The Journal of Criminal Law, Criminology and Police Science,* Vol. 62 (December, 1971), pp. 497-504.

[24] E. Eldefonso, *Youth Problems and Law Enforcement* (Englewood Cliffs, N.J.: Prentice-Hall, 1972), p. 57.

court are to be found elsewhere than in the adjudicative phase of the juvenile court hearing. It is generally held that the juvenile court's unique benefits consist mainly of discretionary intake procedures that permit disposition without adjudication and the dispositional hearing which allows flexible sentencing.

DISPOSITION OTHER THAN ADJUDICATION

The whole juvenile court movement was devised for handling juveniles differently from adult offenders. One of the most significant places where this occurs is in the early stages of the juvenile justice system—that portion of the system from apprehension to the time of formal hearing and disposition. Methods used during this stage are referred to as "police station adjustments"; they are planned diversions of delinquents from the court system and/or the "unofficial" handling of cases referred to the juvenile court. These are prejudicial handling methods that have acquired recognized status in the juvenile justice system.

Some have argued that the juvenile justice system is too severe in labeling a youth delinquent and that this label harms the youth and may reinforce his pattern of delinquent behavior. Undoubtedly pressures based on this kind of thinking have been responsible for the development of prejudicial dispositions in the juvenile system. In all stages of law enforcement regarding juveniles, there is the use of discretionary authority. To a certain extent, this is also true with adults, since not every adult wrongdoer is brought to trial for his misconduct. The case for using discretion in the practice of criminal justice can be justified on the following basis:

> First, in many cases in which technically the law has been violated, application of the full criminal process is too severe, and there is a need to mediate between general formulated laws and the human values in particular cases. . . . Even the most careful of legislative draftsmen is not likely to achieve a completely unambiguous definition of criminal conduct.
>
> A second argument for discretion in administering criminal justice arises from the tendency of legislatures to overcriminalize human conduct or to reach ends other than crime prevention through a penal code. The appetites and pursuits of many men bring them into technical conflict with the law, yet scarcely disturb the public order as it is commonly viewed. Criminal procedure is a mighty weapon to use against bingo and private poker games . . . and numerous other forms of conduct prescribed by law.
>
> A third point in favor of discretion is plainly practical. Sheer volume demands the use of screening devices in law enforcement. Official agencies are undermanned, underbudgeted, and overloaded; of necessity they must select

for attention the cases that appear to them most pressing. The natural tendency appears to be to concentrate on major crimes, although there are exceptions, and some choices are open to question.[25]

For some or all of these reasons, every community uses informal handling of the delinquent. Still, informal handling is insufficently understood by the public; this is mainly because concern about the operation of the juvenile justice system has focused on the formal system. In many jurisdictions, however, the informal procedures are more significant in the overall control of delinquency than the formal system.

Prejudicial handling can and is made at three important contact points. The first of these contact points occurs between the victim of the delinquent act and the perpetrator of that act. An example would be the store owner who admonishes the youth caught in the act of theft but who does not refer the matter to any law enforcement agency.

The second important contact point occurs when the matter comes to the attention of a law enforcement agency. Dispositions available to the police are: release to the parents, release with a reprimand, release with conditions such as payment of restitution, release with a referral to a social agency, or referral to the juvenile court. Reportedly, on a national scale, prejudicial handling by the police occurs in 45 to 50 percent of all juvenile referrals.[26]

A third point where prejudicial adjustments are made occurs in the juvenile court or its arm, the juvenile probation department. Data indicate that on a national scale approximately 50 percent of the juveniles referred to juvenile court are disposed of prejudicially.[27] The options open to the juvenile court and/or the juvenile probation department are: outright dismissal, referral to another community agency, informal supervision by the juvenile probation staff, or petitioning for a court hearing.

There is a great temptation to use prejudicial handling as a means of alleviating the workload in the judicial system. This should be guarded against. The rationale for prejudicial handling should be based upon the possibilities for greater flexibility, efficiency, and humanity in the formal system. There are certain guidelines that should be kept in mind; these are:

1. Prejudicial disposition should be made as early as possible in the stages of official agency contact;

[25] *Task Force Report: Juvenile Delinquency* . . . , p. 10.
[26] *Task Force Report: Juvenile Delinquency* . . . , p. 12.
[27] *Task Force Report: Juvenile Delinquency* . . . , p. 14.

2. They should be based on stated criteria that are shared with and rigorously reviewed by all delinquency-control authorities within the community; and
3. Whenever attempts are undertaken to render guidance or expert control (as distinguished from screening without further action), the prejudicial handling agencies should be alert to cohesive possibilities, and the dispositions it can render should be effectively restricted.[28]

At this point we will turn our attention away from the prejudicial handling of juveniles and back to the system's method of dealing with them. We will examine certain facilities or practices which are important and/or different from the mainstream criminal justice methods of handling similar problems.

DETENTION FACILITIES FOR JUVENILES

In the criminal justice system, jails are often used as facilities to detain those accused of crimes pending their trials. This same function of detaining juveniles awaiting a juvenile court hearing is accomplished by the detention home and/or juvenile hall. Although in many ways juvenile halls are similar to jails, they are also different in many respects. Some discussion of these homes is in order.

Figure 10-2 After questioning and finger printing (if this process is necessary), the minor is subsequently admitted to juvenile hall. Photo courtesy of Sgt. Frank Furnaw, Campbell Police Department, and Michael Johnson, Santa Clara County Juvenile Probation Department, San Jose, Ca.

[28] *Task Force Report: Juvenile Delinquency . . .*, pp. 18-19.

Detention homes were first created after the juvenile court acts made provisions for segregating minors from adults charged with crime. The first detention facilities were private homes converted for detaining minors. In some jurisdictions the work house, the county infirmary, and portions of hospitals were pressed into use as detention facilities. It wasn't until after World War II that institutions were built around the unit concept, where groups of youths of similar ages and problems were placed in the same sleeping and living accommodations. These facilities were constructed within enclosed areas resembling large English boarding schools and became known as juvenile halls. This type of construction was started in the western states.

Because juvenile courts deal with neglected and abused children as well as with delinquent youths, there has been some confusion in regard to housing these youth before court hearings. Obviously, two distinct types of temporary care facilities are needed. The first type for delinquent children can be described in the following manner:

> Detention for the juvenile court is a temporary care of children in physically restricted facilities pending court disposition or transfer to another jurisdiction or agency. If detention is used properly, these are children who have committed delinquent acts and for whom secure custody is required for their own or the community's protection.
>
> Any temporary care facility with locked outer doors, a high fence or wall, and screens, bars, detention sashes, or other window obstruction design to deter escape is a detention facility whether or not it needs [National Council of Crime and Delinquency] standards. If a substantil part of the building is used for the detention purposes, as defined, it is a detention facility no matter how flimsy these restricting features might be.[29]

The facilities for neglected and abused children are called shelters and are defined in the following manner:

> Shelter is the temporary care of children in physically *unrestricted* facilities, usually pending return to their own homes or placement for longer term care. While its main use is for dependent and abused children, it may also be properly used for children apprehended for delinquent behavior who need temporary care but not secure custody. For example, children picked up for delinquent acts may require shelter care if their home is not fit for their return and they are not likely to run away. But detention care should never be used for dependent and neglected children.[30]

[29] *Standards and Guides for the Detention of Children and Youth* (New York: National Council on Crime and Delinquency, 1961), pp. 1-2.

[30] *Standards and Guides* . . . , p. 2.

By and large the juvenile court laws within the different states encompass this philosophy of detention. This separate means of handling juveniles, then, is part of the difference between the criminal justice system and the juvenile system.

The dispositional aspects of handling adults and juveniles on probation and in institutions show still more differences between the two systems. Juvenile probation and institutions for juveniles will be examined next.

JUVENILE PROBATION

Juvenile probation permits a youth to remain within the community under the supervision and guidance of a probation officer. Probation generally involves a judicial finding that the youth's behavior has been such that the court thought intervention necessary. Furthermore, the court generally imposes conditions which impinge upon the freedom of the youth placed on probation. Arrangements are made for the youth to meet the conditions set forth by the court, a determination is made of the degree to which the youth meets these conditions.

The goals of juvenile probation are threefold, and they include: (1) preventing a repitition of the youth's delinquent behavior; (2) preventing the youth from a long-term involvement in deviant or criminal behavior; and (3) assisting the youth to achieve his potential as a productive citizen. As can be seen, the central goals of juvenile probation are directed toward the delinquent youth and his family. The Juvenile Probation Department, an arm of the juvenile court, tries to accomplish these goals. The Juvenile Probation Department generally performs three primary functions; these are intake and screening, social studies and diagnosis, and supervision and treatment.

Intake and Screening

The intake and screening process is something unique to juvenile probation and is not, strictly speaking, part of the adult probation function. The scope and jurisdiction of the juvenile court is defined by statute. Consequently, many juvenile probation departments must engage in a preliminary examination or screening to determine if the youths referred meet the legal criteria for court intervention. This examination includes contacts with the youth, the family, and the referring source.

Often the juvenile probation department must decide, or participate in deciding, whether a youth should be admitted to, continue in, or released from a detention facility pending the disposition of his case in juvenile court. Removal of a youth from his home and family and holding that youth in a detention facility, no matter how temporary, constitutes an intervention into the youth's and family's life of no small magnitude. In some cases, detention may be necessary and indeed helpful. In other cases, detention may not be useful, and it may even be somewhat damaging. This is particularly so where facilities are overcrowded, and supervision and care in the detention facility is below standard.

Social Studies and Diagnosis

The juvenile court can exercise a tremendous amount of power when it makes a decision. Certainly, removing a youth from his family's control for a period ranging from several weeks so several years demonstrates this power. Decisions of this nature obviously have an impact on the future of the individuals involved and therefore must be made on the basis of careful and competent social studies and diagnoses.

Any careful social study and diagnosis includes an examination of the influences of the members of the family and other significant persons in the youth's life (for instance, his peers and their influences on his attitudes and behavior). The neighborhood where the youth and his family reside, the school, and the youth's adjustment to school also need to be examined. A competent diagnostic study must further try to evaluate the value system of the youth brought to the court's attention. The youth's perception and feelings about his antisocial behavior, his family, and his life situation must be evaluated.

All the information must be brought together in a meaningful report that will give some insight into the youth's personality, problems, and environmental situations. Once this diagnosis and study are made, a supervision and treatment approach regarding the youth can be initiated.

Supervision and Treatment

Good probation involves much more than merely giving a youth "another chance." Therefore, a course of supervision and treatment for the youth placed on probation should be set into motion. The major elements of such supervision and treatment are surveillance, casework services, and counseling.

Surveillance has been a part of probation from the onset. It is still most important because without surveillance the service of probation cannot be rendered. This is true because surveillance is a matter of keeping in touch with the youth, his parents, his school, and other persons involved and concerned about his adjustment. If contact is not maintained, then services cannot be rendered. Furthermore, surveillance when properly used is a method of helping a youth become aware of his responsibilities and the demands that life makes upon him as a member of the society; it is not just a veiled threat. Hopefully, it provides the youth with the assurance that society is aware and interested in him to the extent that it does not want a repeat of the self-defeating behavior that brought him to the court in the first place.

Casework services can and should be provided when needed in probation supervision. The juvenile probation officer first needs to determine the extent of the problem confronting the youth and his family. The problem may be alleviated somewhat by the use of available community services and/or agencies. The officer then must try to organize these services so that they can be utilized in an effective manner. It should be noted that this is extremely complicated, particularly when dealing with the so-called "hard-core" problem family.

The counseling aspect of supervision ties service and surveillance together in a manner that helps the family understand and face problems. The family and youth need to be counseled and encouraged to mobilize their energies toward solving problems rather than toward engaging in self-defeating, nonproductive behavior.

The dispositions that can be made in the juvenile justice system emphasize returning the youth to his family. However, as mentioned, the juvenile court does have the power—upon finding a youth to be delinquent, dependent, or neglected—to remove him from the family's control for a period of time. Once removed, the youth needs to be placed somewhere. The placement facilities available to the juvenile court are also part of the juvenile correctional system and therefore need some examination.

PLACEMENTS FOR THE JUVENILE COURT

By and large the juvenile court operates on a philosophy that can be paraphrased in the following manner: "The least amount of restraint necessary in the rehabilitation plan for a minor should be the plan used." As regards placement, the least amount of restraint is the placement of the youth in a foster home. Foster home placements have long been one of the most commonly used alternatives for institutionalization used by the juvenile court. Over 40 percent of the juvenile courts and juvenile departments utilize foster home placement, and a sizable proportion of institutional release plans incorporate the placement of the youth released from an institution into a foster home.

The foster home has several advantages if the youth placed there does not require the controls of an institution. Foster home placements keep the youth in the community where he must eventually work out his future. Furthermore, they tend to leave less sense of stigma or criminal identity than do juvenile correctional institutions. Finally, foster homes are far less expensive than the institutionalization of a youth.[32]

There are three kinds of institutional placements that juvenile courts routinely use for placing delinquent youths. These are private institutions, public institutions administered by the state, and public institutions administered by municipal- and county-level governments. An examination of each of these types of institutions should clarify the differences.

Private institutions have handled delinquents from the time that youths were first segregated from adult criminals. The New York City House of Refuge, a private institution, was essentially the first institution in the United States built specifically to deal with delinquents. Private institutions still are significant since probably one-fourth to one-fifth of the juveniles institutionalized in the United States are placed in private facilities.[33]

Giving a physical description of a private institution is almost an impossible task, since private institutions may house several hundred youths or they may be responsible for housing only six to eight youths. Many so-called group foster homes are licensed as private institutions rather than as foster homes. Many half-way houses are essentially private institutions. Many people feel the advantages of private institutions are that they can handle delinquents in small groups and with more individualized programs which may be more conducive to rehabilitation than large, overcrowded, and understaffed public training schools.[34]

Locally Operated Juvenile Training Facilities

Locally operated juvenile correctional facilities may be found in sixteen states.[35] The State of California has utilized the concept of local juvenile correctional institutions more than any other state. The probable reason for this is that California has paid monies to the counties for operating local juvenile correctional facilities. The institutions that are so subsi-

32 *Task Force Report: Corrections . . .* , p. 40.

33 D. G. Blackburn, "Institutions for Juvenile Delinquents—A Review of Recent Developments." *NPPA Journal,* Vol. 4 (January, 1958), pp. 12-21.

34 H. J. Palmieri, "Private Institutions," *NPPA Journal,* Vol 4 (January, 1958), pp. 51-56.

35 U.S. Department of Health, Education and Welfare, *Statistics on Public Institutions for Children,* Children's Bureau Statistical Series 81 (Washington, D.C.: U.S. Gov't. Printing Office, 1965).

dized are generally referred to as camps. The original concept which stimulated the building of these local facilities was a forestry camp that developed a program of work including fire suppression and reforestation. Since 1935, the different county jurisdictions have experimented with and modified the camp concept. Presently, there is at least one institution that is far more secure than the typical camp, and there is at least one institution that is coeducational. Several facilities are for delinquent girls.

One advantage of the locally operated juvenile correctional facility is the tendency toward smaller populations than those of state facilities. In California the law specifies that there can be no more than one hundred youth placed in a facility of this type at any one time.[36]

A second advantage of the locally operated facility is that the agency responsible for supervising the younger (most generally the juvenile probation department) as well as the committed youth can maintain ongoing contact with the youth's family.

State Operated Juvenile Correctional Institutions

In 1967 there were 220 state operated juvenile institutions in the fifty states, Puerto Rico, and the District of Columbia. Within these facilities 86 percent of the youths committed to juvenile correctional facilities operated by government bodies were being housed.[37] By and large, commitment to a state facility is the most serious action that can be taken for any minor being handled within the juvenile justice system.

Almost without exception, youths committed to juvenile correctional facilities are released from the facility and returned to the community. The length of stay for youths committed to state training facilities generally ranges from four to twenty-four months; the median length of stay is approximately nine months. If the institution is to perform is function, it must make an impact in that amount of time upon a youth who probably has had a much longer time in which to establish a delinquent pattern. Because these facilities are often unable to accomplish this end, a great deal of criticism has been directed toward them. There has been so much criticism that in at least one state, Massachusetts, the traditional juvenile correctional facilities have been phased out; most of the youths who need placement in a juvenile correctional facility are now being handled in group homes. Youths who present extreme danger to persons are being committed to private and public psychiatric hospitals for care and treatment.[38]

[36] Section 886 California Juvenile Court Law, p. 886.

[37] *Task Force Report: Corrections* . . . , p. 145.

[38] National Council on Crime and Delinquency, *NCCD News,* Vol. 51, No. 2 (1972), p. 2.

As regards state operated institutions, the critical difference between the criminal justice system and the juvenile justice system is that the juvenile system expects to return these youths to the community in a rather short period of time. Consequently, it becomes quite obvious that, in order to insure some semblance of safety in the community, these committed youths need to have their delinquent behavior patterns changed. In this area, juvenile institutions have been much more willing to experiment with new treatment programs than have adult institutions. It should also be noted that juvenile correctional institutions tend to have more professional staff. The objective behind this seems to be that diverting a teen-ager from a life of crime is of great economic value to society. With more professional persons available, it follows that many new programs could be tried in the juvenile justice system.

SUMMARY

Statistics show that a significant minority of criminal law violators are handled in a system auxiliary to the criminal justice system. This is generally called the juvenile court system. The one criteria that assures that the criminal law violator will be handled under the juvenile court law is a youthful age. The method of handling juveniles has evolved over the years. It began with the understanding that children do not have the maturity and decision-making ability of adults. True evolution in the juvenile justice system began with the separation of adults from juveniles in correctional institutions. Up to 1825, juvenile law violators were housed with adult law violators in correctional institutions. However, with the advent of the New York City House of Refuge under a private philanthropic organization, provisions began to be made for real changes in handling juveniles. Following this initial breakthrough a number of juvenile correctional facilities were built. Slowly provisions in the statutes were made so that juveniles could also be handled differently in the court process. However, a completely separate system did not come into being until 1899 with the enactment of the Juvenile Court Law in Illinois. Soon after its enactment in Illinois, the other states followed suit.

The changes brought on by juvenile court laws came about because of the philosophy that juveniles could not make adult decisions. Because juveniles could not make adult decisions, they needed protection, care, and rehabilitation—rather than punishment for criminal behavior. Also, because the juvenile law violator needed care, a new court procedure was devised.

One of the cornerstones of the new procedure was the doctrine of *parens patrai*. This was a doctrine which put the state in the position of a helpful parent, interested in the needs of the juvenile violator. Diagnosis of the juvenile's familial, social, psychological, and behavioral circumstances were emphasized in deciding how to rehabilitate the minor.

In the first sixty-seven years after the initial enactment of the juvenile court law, the emphasis was on care and rehabilitation. This emphasis left something to be desired in regard to the individual rights of the accused juvenile. Consequently, the Supreme Court intervened in the precedent-setting cases of *Kent, Gault,* and *Winship* to assure certain rights to accused juveniles. These were: (1) the right to have a full procedural hearing in a case; (2) the right to be informed of the allegations of the wrongful conduct; (3) the right to counsel; (4) the right to know about the privilege against self-incrimination; (5) the right of appeal from juvenile court judgments; and (6) the right to have the allegations proved beyond a reasonable doubt.

These procedural changes did not affect the rehabilitative trust of the juvenile court law. Provisions for handling juveniles prejudically still remain. More than 50 percent of the juvenile law violators referred to the police are handled at that level. From 45 to 50 percent of the juveniles referred to the juvenile court are also handled without a formal court hearing.

For youths who are processed through court, rehabilitation is the aim, rather than punishment. Because of this, the probation process has been expanded in juvenile court over the years. Also the philosophy of the juvenile court regarding the separation of youthful law violators from adult law violators has never changed. Therefore, placement, the alternative to probation, has continued to segregate adult criminals from youths who violate the law.

Obviously, foster home placement is utilized only with youths. It is, however, widely used as a dispositional plan by the juvenile courts. When the juvenile court considers institutionalizaton, it must consider private institutions as well as public institutons. In the juvenile correctional field, the first correctional institutions for youths were private; further, private institutions continue to be important placements for delinquent youths.

Public institutions are under the control of the state or the local government. Most are under the control of the state government. One of the most important aspects of these institutions is that they ofen tend to be involved in new developments and new correctional programs. The juvenile institutions seem to have more innovative ideas than do adult institutions.

Discussed throughout this chapter is the fact that shortly after a juvenile is arrested until the time of the final disposition of that matter, the treatment of the juvenile is different from the adult so arrested. This difference in treatment is due to the juvenile justice system more commonly known as the juvenile court law.

QUESTIONS

1. What does *doli capax* have to do with the juvenile court law?
2. What does *parens patrai* mean?
3. Of what importance was the New York City House of Refuge to the development of the juvenile justice system?
4. What is the importance of the Supreme Court's decision entitled *in re Gault?*
5. What are the procedural differences between the juvenile court and the criminal court?
6. What is the significance of the prejudicial handling of juveniles?
7. Why is there separate facilities for juvenile criminal law violators?
8. Why is probation important to the juvenile justice system?

ANNOTATED REFERENCES

ELDEFONSO, E. *Youth Problems and Law Enforcement.* Englewood Cliffs, N.J.: Prentice-Hall, 1972. This small volume contains a great deal of information regarding the youthful offender. As such, it is a handy little reference.

"Juvenile Due Process in the Lower Courts." *The Journal of Criminal Law, Criminology and Police Science.* Vol. 62, (September, 1971), pp. 335–349. This article written by students at Northwestern University School of Law contains a great deal of information regarding some of the upper court decisions on juvenile court law.

NATHANSON, N. L. "Jury Trials—Juvenile Court." *The Journal of Criminal Law, Criminology and Police Science.* Vol. 62 (December, 1971), pp. 497–504. This is an excellent review of the Supreme Court decisions that have shaped some of the more recent changes in the juvenile court law.

POUND, R. "The Juvenile Court and the Law." *Crime and Delinquency.* Vol. 10 (1964), pp. 490–504. This article is a useful philosophical perspective of the juvenile court law.

———. "The Juvenile Court in the State Service." *Crime and Delinquency.* Vol. 10 (1964), pp. 516–531. Again Roscoe Pound, the great legal scholar, took a philosophical look at the juvenile court. His thoughts on the matter are worthy of consideration.

President's Commission on Law Enforcement and Administration of Justice. *Task Force Report: Juvenile Delinquency and Youth Crime.* Washington, D.C.: U.S. Gov't. Printing Office, 1967. This report is a most useful description of the youthful offender and the juvenile court system. It covers the history, philosophy, and legal and social implications of this problem.

11

Correctional Institutions

The criminal justice system is concerned with when and how criminal sanctions will be imposed. With few exceptions and from a practical standpoint, the most severe sanctions are commitment and placement of an offender in a correctional institution. The exception to this has been the imposition of the death penalty, which may be a thing of the past by virtue of the Supreme Court decision of *Furman* v. *Georgia*.[1] From a practical standpoint, however, use of the death penalty has recently been nonexistent; 1967 was the last year that anyone was legally executed in the United States. In that year, there were two executions,[2] while there were approximately 77,850 persons in state and federal institutions.[3] In 1935, the year of the highest number of legal executions in the United States, there were 199 executions. Even this, if one is only concerned with numbers and is not thinking of human tragedy, was a fraction of the percent of the total number of persons handled by the criminal justice system.

By tracing the history of legal sanctions, one can get a better perspective on how the sanctions came about and how they are used in the criminal justice system today. The main emphasis of this historical survey will be the legal sanctions of correctional institutionalization.

[1] Furman v. Georgia 33L Ed 2d 346 (1972).

[2] U.S. Department of Justice, "Capital Punishment 1930–1968," *National Prisoner Statistics,* No. 45 (August, 1969), p. 30. Washington, D.C.

[3] U.S. Department of Justice, "Prisoners in State and Federal Institutions for Adult Felons: 1967," *National Prisoner Statistics,* No. 44 (July, 1969), p. 31.

SHORT SURVEY OF CORRECTIONAL HISTORY

When governments accepted the responsibility of imposing sanctions on criminal behavior, actions of retribution were removed from the family, friends, and neighbors of the victim. Up to that point in time, the whole criminal justice system was based on the power of the accused versus the power of the accusers. When governments interceded, the bare beginnings of a criminal justice system began to emerge. With this emergence, the very beginnings of detention and correctional facilities also emerged.

Placing a person who commits a serious criminal act in prison became the general practice and means of dealing with this type of behavior during the nineteenth century. Before that time, other methods such as capital punishment, corporal punishment, fines, and banishment were the accepted means of dealing with criminals.

The present-day correctional institution is the outgrowth of many different values and procedures. Consequently, no one single doctrine is responsible for the evolution of the correctional institution. Instead these institutions are founded in religious and ethical beliefs, military traditions, political and administrative expediencies, and humanitarian concerns. Because the present correctional system is the outgrowth of these many doctrines, an examination of these will help explain why certain social concepts and standards are accepted today.

Religious philosophies and practices have had their impact on the methods society uses to deal with criminal behavior. An example of this is the Judaic doctrine of "an eye for an eye, and a tooth for a tooth." In prehistoric times, retribution for a wrong often went beyond the original wrong; therefore, the "eye for an eye" philosophy was an attempt at restraining retributive punishment.

Probably the next great influence that religion had on the correctional system happened during medieval times after the collapse of the Roman Empire. At that time the Catholic Church assumed control of many peoples and territories. During this period, any secular ruler in Europe had to have the blessings of the Pope. Obviously, the Church was the most important agent of social control; it enforced Canon Law, and secular rulers supported the decrees of the Church. During this period ecclesiastical prisons were built to supplement other places of confinement such as dungeons. In fact, the word *penitentiary* comes from the practice of placing a person in solitary confinement in the ecclesiastical prisons so the offender could do penance for his sins. In general, these prisoners were treated better than prisoners in civil confinement; the ecclesiastical prisoners' sentences tended to be shorter, and they could hope for a pardon on special holy days.

Saying that the prisoners of the church had shorter sentences implies that prisoners of the civil authorities served a sentence. By and large, this was not so. Confinement to a dungeon, a prisoner's cage, or a public jail known as a gaol was for detention purposes while awaiting the trial. The sentence was usually one of capital or corporal punishment. The duration of detention might have been for years at the prisoner's expense.

In England from the middle of the sixteenth century until the seventeenth century, there developed a number of places to deal with prostitutes and beggars; they were locked up, whipped, and made to work. These places were called houses of correction. Later these houses were assimilated into the jail system. Thus, the idea of work as part of the prison program was begun. Furthermore, as capital and corporal punishment decreased, the houses of correction began to be used more and more.

With the discovery of America, new methods of handling some criminals came into being. This method came to be known as *transportation* because the convicted criminal was transported to America in lieu of capital or corporal punishment. However, after the Revolutionary War, transportation to the American Colonies was no longer possible for England. (England also utilized Australia as a place for transporting criminals.) The use of transportation further changed the pattern of thinking about crimes punishable by death.

The next great advancement in corrections occurred in Colonial America. In 1682, William Penn, the founder of the Commonwealth of Pennsylvania, set forth a charter that retained the death penalty only for the crime of homicide. All other crimes were punished by imprisonment at hard labor. The aim was clemency and rehabilitation. Although these laws were set aside after Penn's death in 1718, they affected society's thinking about how to deal with the criminal. These thoughts again came forward after the Revolutionary War. Once again, Pennsylvania was the leader in reestablishing prisons and prison sentences in lieu of capital and corporal punishment.[4]

Probably the first true penitentiary in the United States was the Walnut Street Jail in Philadelphia. In 1790, after enactment of the Pennsylvania Reform Acts, a cell block of three tiers of eight cells was erected in that jail for the confinement of hardened criminals. This cell block in the Walnut Street Jail became the penitentiary for the State of Pennsylvania

[4] The American Correctional Association, *Manual of Correctional Standards* (New York: The American Correctional Association, 1966), pp. 10-11.

because it accepted prisoners for commitment from several counties in that state. Apparently establishing correctional institutions for the placement of long-term prisoners during the latter part of the eighteenth century and the early part of the nineteenth century was not intended only as a substitute for capital and corporal punishment but was also intended to have an impact upon the unwholesome conditions existing in jails of the time. These unwholesome conditions included confinement of men, women, and children who were forced to sleep indiscriminately on filthy floors. Neglect and brutality were rather standard practices; idleness was also common to the jails of the time. In fact it was not uncommon for alcoholic beverages to be sold under the auspices of the jail system itself.[5]

Two new prisons were erected to combat the evils of jails. The first of these two prisons was the New York State Prison at Albany which opened in 1819; the second was the Eastern Penitentiary in Philadelphia which opened in 1829. The difference between these two prisons was that the prisoners in Philadelphia worked and lived in separate cells with individual exercise yards, while the New York prisoners lived in separate cells but worked together in shops. In both these prisons, silence was enforced.

Most American prisons soon adopted the work pattern established in the New York State Prison at Albany. By and large most American prisons opened during the nineteenth century were patterned after the New York State Prison at Albany; the United States was in the midst of the Industrial Revolution, and individual craft type manufacturing was being replaced by large assembly-line factories.

The next most significant change in the penal system came about in the decade between 1870 and 1880. During this ten-year period, the State of Massachusetts and the State of Indiana opened separate institutions for women prisoners. Also, during this period the reformatory at Elmira, New York opened. The change in the names of correctional institutions from penitentiaries or prisons to reformatories indicates a significant change in attitude regarding the handling of prisoners. The opening of Elmira represents this change. The *reformatory,* as the word implies, was to reform persons convicted of crime rather than strictly punish them as implied by the word *penitentiary.* Elmira Reformatory was concerned with education as a mass treatment program. As a second part of this rehabilitation program, Elmira began using parole systematically for the first time in the United States.[6]

Unfortunately, education for all persons committed to correctional

[5] *Manual of Correctional Standards,* p. 10-11.

[6] *Manual of Correctional Standards,* p. 11.

facilities apparently does not provide a very good answer for rehabilitating all who are convicted of crimes. Mass education does not take into account the individual differences and motivations for criminal and/or delinquent behavior.

Parole was granted on the basis of how a prisoner responded to the educational program. However, these programs neither tested nor trained the inmates adequately for release back into the community. Although many states emulated the program at Elmira (which admittedly left a deal to be desired), many institutions were still operating under a strictly punitive philosophy. In fact, the punitive philosophy was predominant policy and practice in American prisons well into the twentieth century. Correctional training and treatment up to 1930 was truly marked by the exploitation of prison labor, as well as by the use of corporal punishment such as floggings.

The major development in correctional institutions from the 1930s to the present time has been the concern with classificaton systems—in other words, concern for individualizing training and treatment. Primarily the individualization has corresponded to the degree of custody utilized in regard to the inmate. Not all prisoners need confinement in maximum-security units. As a consequence of this understanding, the number of minimum- and medium-security institutions has steadily increased during the past forty years. Another development has been institutions designed for specific types of offenders, such as mentally defective and/or mentally ill inmates. Other institutions are essentially medical centers.

The historical uses of correctional institutions have led to the shaping of our present-day correctional institution. We shall look at this institution next.

PRESENT-DAY CORRECTIONAL INSTITUTIONS

Present-day correctional institutions can be viewed along several lines. The most common way to classify correctional institutions is according to the level of government responsible for their operation. A second way institutions can be classified is according to the amount of security involved in their operation. Third, the institutions can be classified in regard to the type of treatment and/or lack of treatment programs offered. An examination of the levels of government responsible for correctional facilites will be made first.

Level of Governmental Jurisdiction

Correctional institutions are responsible for large amounts of money and for a great number of people; yet their administration is quite fragmented. Correctional facilities are run by all fifty states, the District of Columbia, Puerto Rico, the federal government, and many of the municipalities of this nation.[7] Furthermore, each level of government seems to act independently of other levels of government. The result of this is that the federal government has no control over a state government's operation of correctional facilities. State governments in turn have little control over county and/or city governments in their operation of county and city jails. This approach to the administration of correctional institutions is more or less unique to the United States. In most other industrial countries, correctional institutions and almost all other activities of corrections are the responsibility of the central government.

There has been a trend in recent years toward integrating correctional institutions and agencies within the individual state. Up to this time, each institution seemingly has had a board of governors and/or an administrative board which was only responsible for that one particular institution. Presently, however, various correctional systems can be place in three major categories. These may be described as:

(1) those that use boards to manage their correctional programs;
(2) those that have placed corrections in some larger, existing department;
(3) those that administer corrections in an independent department.[8]

Experience has shown that these different methods of administering correctional programs are not equally effective. The least effective method of administering institutions is when local boards control individual institutions. Placing corrections in a larger existing department is generally an improvement and makes for a more effective administration. An example of this would be when the state department of corrections is combined with the department of mental health to make one large department. There is a possible drawback, however, when the larger department's primary interest is focused on functions other than corrections; this may mean that the causes of corrections would be served rather poorly.

Most populous states operate best with a single chief administrator. The administrator in this situation can be expected to be quite familiar with correctional problems and with methods of handling his designated function.

The administration of correctional institutions to be found within the several states range from having separate administrative boards for each

[7] President's Commission on Law Enforcement and Administration of Justice, *Task Force Report: Corrections* (Washington, D.C.: U.S. Gov't. Printing Office, 1967), p. 5.

[8] G. Heyns, "Patterns of Corrections," *Crime and Delinquency*, Vol. 13 (July, 1967), p. 422.

institution to having all correctional services organized and administered within a single department.[9] The absence of well-balanced correctional programs, when viewed from the amazing circumstances of their fragmented administrative arrangements, should not surprise the general public. Indeed, most of the administrative methods of governing correctional institutions have been enacted into the statutes in a more or less "patchwork" pattern. This again is evidence of the unscientific and unsystematic methods by which the tenets of corrections have been formulated.

The majority of the people in the United States have seen the outside of a municipal or county jail. Consequently, they may feel they have some familiarity with what a correctional institution is. On this assumption, we shall continue our examination of correctional institutions with a look at jails.

Local Institutions–Jails

Jails are probably the oldest of the correctional institutions used for detaining criminal law violators. Originally the function of the jail was for the detention of persons charged with a crime before trial. Later jails began to be used for serving short sentences, and they now continue to serve this dual purpose.

The jail is the first step in the detention and supervision of most people charged with a crime—whatever the disposition of the charges from acquittal through probation through institutional placement. Consequently, the greatest variety and number of offenders can be found in jails.

According to the President's Commission, there were 3,473 jails and local correctional institutions in the United States in 1967. These detention facilities for unconvicted persons are often the worst of all correctional institutions, and they are often operated under maximum-security conditions. This primary concern with security shapes the routine of the institution, and it may hamper the person being detained in his efforts to arrange for his trial defense. It may also hamper his efforts to maintain contact with the community. Programs of any sort in most local correctional institutions and in jails leave a great deal to be desired. Work programs tend to be minimal; educational programs are minimal or nonexistent; and rehabilitation programs are often nonexistent. Yet, constructive activities and employment tend to be the best assurance against the unwholesome atmosphere of the jail.

Local correctional institutions have some things in common with

[9] *Task Force Report: Corrections,* pp. 199-200.

state and federal correctional institutions, but there are also some very distinct differences. These need to be examined for a better understanding of correctional institutions per se. Let us now look at the security which correctional institutions afford.

CORRECTIONAL INSTITUTIONS AND SECURITY

The primary responsibility of all correctional institutions is custody and control of the inmates. This is prescribed for by statute and is an expectation of the general public. This concept may deviate from what some liberal psychologists, sociologists, and psychiatrists would advocate, but it is obvious that any correctional institution which ignores the custody and control concept will not function for long. Programs and institutions for rehabilitation can only operate effectively where there is a modicum of control. Hence, institutions have been and will continue to be concerned with the security they offer. (Figure 11-1 presents an aerial view of a correctional facility.)

Most prisons were built during the nineteenth century and were pat-

Figure 11-1 Security has been a primary responsibility of all correctional institutions. This maximum security facility has a wall around its perimeter with armed guards stationed in protected towers. Photo courtesy of Philip D. Guthrie, Chief of Community Relations and Information, California State Department of Corrections.

terned after the "Auburn System." Obviously these institutions were maximum-security facilities. This means they were built with the idea of making it difficult, if not impossible, for prisoners to escape. Durng the last forty years, however, it became apparent that not all inmates are in need of confinement in maximum-security institutions. An important consideration here is that maximum-security institutions are unbelievably expensive, whereas less secure facilities, although still quite expensive, are somewhat less costly for the state. Partly bcause of this, a system of classification according to degrees of custody was begun. Presently this system is utilized to rate institutions on a range from maximum security to medium security to minimum security. The definitions of these degrees of security are set forth in the *Manual of Correctional Standards.*[10]

Maximum-Security Institution

The typical maximum-security institution is enclosed by a brick or stone wall from 18 to 25 feet high. A double fence, with the inner fence being from 12 to 14 feet high and the outer fence being from 8 to 12 feet high, may be substituted for the wall. The distance between the inner and outer fence is from 16 to 20 feet; and both fences are topped with barbed wire. When a greater degree of security is desired, a third fence about 50 feet inside the double fence may be constructed. Certainly this provides an ample buffer area around the prison compound. Armed guards located in well-protected towers are found around all maximum-security institutions. These towers are strategically located around the perimeter of the institution.

A large percent of the inmates in this type of institution are housed in interior cell blocks of the Auburn variety. Ideally, each cell will house one prisoner and will be equipped with complete plumbing and sanitary facilities. Most of the prisons and penitentiaries built in the United States before World War I were maximum security in nature. Fewer maximum-security institutions have been built since that time—the reason being that many inmates could be handled in less secure and, consequently, less expensive facilities.

Medium-Security Institutions

Normally a medium-security institution has a double fence. The inner fence is from 12 to 14 feet high, and the outer fence is approxi-

[10] *Manual of Correctional Standards,* 1966.

mately 12 feet high. These fences will be from 16 to 20 feet apart and both will be topped with barbed wire. The buildings within this wire perimeter will be at least 35 feet from the inner fence. The fence perimeter will have personnel to guard it, and the cells within this institution will be outside type. A unit not exceeding 150 cells may be a building with interior cell blocks for difficult inmates assigned to the institution. Still other inmates may be housed in honor rooms, squad rooms, and/or dormitories. Dormitory housing is a compromise between individual rooms with a corresponding large building cost and a number of people housed together with a much smaller cost in construction. Medium-security facilities can and do house many more prisoners in any one state than do maximum-security facilities.

Minimum-Security Institutions

Minimum-security institutions operate without fixed posts or armed guards; these institutions may or may not have a fence around their perimeter. Smaller institutions in remote areas tend not to be enclosed. On the other hand, minimum-security institutions in heavily populated areas or larger minimum-security institutions are usually fenced in. By and large, inmates in minimum-security facilities live in dormitories. Again, even though individual cells or rooms are generally preferred to dormitories, the expense is prohibitive. Obviously, these dormitories are supervised by institutional personnel. Consequently, a group dormitory is planned so that sight supervision is possible with the least amount of personnel. If the dormitory is poorly planned for supervision, additional personnel may be needed. In such cases, the low cost of construction is offset by high operational expenditures.

Camps. As indicated, most correctional institutions attempt to segregate prisoners into facilities that are either more or less restrictive. The camp facility is generally the least restrictive of those operating in the correctional system. This type of facility has flourished because its construction cost is much less than that of more secure facilities. Through the use of good classification procedures, inmates who are not in need of close security can be selected and assigned to camps. Where guards and other means of restraint are unnecessary, inmates can be supervised by unarmed officers and/or personnel. The segregation of minimum-security inmates from the general prison population has had many beneficial effects. One of these benefits is that the construction of camps can be accomplished much faster and much more economically than can the construction of other correctional institutions. Further, inmates in the camps can be used in conservation programs and environmental protection projects. A number of states use camp inmates for fighting forest fires, for reforestation, and for the construction of roads or other public facilities such as parks.

One criticism of correctional institutions is that they do not have sufficient work to keep inmates occupied. Most penologists know that idleness leads to problems within the institution. Camps are seldom concerned with this problem of idleness because their inmates can be kept busy most of the time. Generally speaking, camps have more wholesome settings than do other correctional institutions. Camp inmates can live in a setting which has fewer regulations and restrictions than do other facilities. A camp or farm is much more desirable because it has a tendency to ease tensions, and it affords opportunities for physical work which may be helpful to the inmate when he wants to enter the productive labor force. Furthermore, in most camps or farms, it is possible for an inmate to receive some slight pay for his labor, he may therefore have an opportunity to save some money for his release.

An investigation published in 1967 reported results on 350 institutions and 40 satellite facilities.[11] The 390 institutions were located in the fifty states, the District of Columbia, and Puerto Rico. These institutions were classed into the following types. Fifty-five were maximum-security institutions; 124 were medium-security institutions; and 103 were minimum-security institutions. Sixty-eight were designated as mixed security institutions. When the 40 satellite institutions were considered, then it was learned that of the 390 institutions, 148 were camps or farms. It seems apparent therefore that corrections is using the camp type institution quite extensively.

Let us now turn our attention from matters of security and administration to a discussion of some specific characteristics of the inmate. We shall first look at institutions for juveniles and for women.

Institutions for Juveniles and for Women

There is at least one training school for juveniles in each state. (The exception is Massachusetts which is attempting to do away with juvenile institutions.) In most states, training schools are administered by the state government. The purpose of the training schools is to change relatively hardened delinquents into law-abiding citizens. Although these are relatively long-term facilities, the average length of stay of the inmates is short when compared with inmates of adult state correctional institutions.

Besides the movement during the nineteenth century to construct

[11] *Task Force Report: Corrections*, pp. 179-80.

institutions specifically for juveniles, there was also a movement to construct institutions specifically for women. These institutions have contributed to the correctional system and as such should be reviewed here. Approximately one hundred years ago, women were housed in the same institutions as men. When women were separated from men in these institutions, notable contributions to the progress of corrections began to be made. As a matter of fact, some women's institutions are rated among the best correctional institutions in the country. One of the main reasons for this is that women superintendents generally are willing to experiment with new methods and techniques. Probably women superintendents tend to feel less pressure from public opinion because they have smaller populations. Furthermore, women inmates tend to escape less frequently and to commit less violent acts.[12]

Women's institutions have developed educational programs that go beyond vocational and academic training and attempt to provide a social education. Also, women's institutions have tended to do away with the mass treatment in custody that is typical of men's prisons. Women are usually housed in cottages in open type institutions. This is true despite the fact that a high percentage of women are serving very long sentences, and supposedly they should therefore present a much higher escape risk. Women's institutions have demonstrated that effective treatment within an institution involves much more than safe custody while developing vocational skills and stimulating wholesome leisure-time interests. Somehow women's institutions have been able to create a social milieu which has a much more rehabilitative effect than that of men's institutions.[13]

Besides institutions for juveniles and institutions for women, special institutions have been developed which represent an even newer concept in the history of corrections. Most of these special institutions are found in the most populous states. One of these institutions is the reception and classification center.

RECEPTION-CLASSIFICATION CENTERS

The reception-classification center is based on the idea that, after an offender has been adjudicated in the court, the decision as to his placement in a state facility should be left to specialists in the correctional field. The reception-classification center is important in the individualized study, treatment, and training offered inmates. This holds true

[12] M. A. Elliott, *Crime in Modern Society* (New York: Harper & Bros., 1952), p. 706.
[13] *Manual of Correctional Standards.*

even though a court may have made a careful study of the offender before sentencing. Most judges, however, are not acquainted with the various institutions and programs to which an inmate can be assigned. The reception-classification center is a correctional institution under the direction of a single administrator where psychiatrists, physicians, dentists, psychologists, social workers, counselors, teachers, and chaplains can work as a team to ascertain an inmate's limitations, strengths, and attitudes. Through their diagnostic and preliminary treatment programs these centers can divert a significant number of offenders back to the community much sooner than would occur under other circumstances. This represents a great savings in money as regards the institutionalizational cost for the individual.

Another quite specific problem of institutionalization pertains to inmates who present a severe psychiatric problem. We shall look at psychiatric correctional institutions next.

PSYCHIATRIC CORRECTIONAL INSTITUTIONS

Persons in the field of corrections have noted for quite some time that there has been a need for specialized medical institutions for inmates with psychiatric problems. An institution of this sort serves the need of accepting and helping defective persons who are unwilling or unable to adjust within the more conventional correctional institution. There is agreement that offenders of this type should be placed in a psychiatric facility. However, there is disagreement as to who should direct and control institutions responsible for these inmates. Some persons feel that these institutions should be under the direction of the state department of mental health, whereas other persons feel that the institutions should be under the direction of the state department of corrections.

Persons in the field of corrections generally feel that placing inmates in mental hospitals operated by the department of mental health tends to cause undue problems. The reasons for this is that mental hospitals tend to decrease security and custody, which makes these institutions essentially minimum-security facilities. Correctional personnel indicate that many of the inmates in need of these psychiatric facilities represent such a danger to society that more rigorous security is advisable. Consequently, the alternative of a prison/medical hospital is generally preferred by correctional personnel. The purpose of an institution of this nature is to receive, segregate, confine, and treat certain inmates in the correctional system. Chief among the inmates housed in a facility of this nature would be persons who are mentally ill, mentally defective, epileptic, strongly addicted, abnormal sex offenders, or inmates with chronic disorders or conditions.[14]

Approximately 6 percent of the prison population could be diagnosed as psychotic or borderline psychotic, although this 6 percent may be found sane as far as the courts are concerned. Nonetheless, this approximate 6 percent of the prison population is very much in need of psychiatric treatment and represents the main thrust of the psychiatric correctional institutions.

Blending the knowledge of the correctional field with knowledge from the mental health field to formulate an institutional program is a difficult task. This is true whether the institution with this program is to function under the department of corrections, department of mental health, or a combination of the two. Obviously, the institution will have a successful program when persons in corrections and mental health agree that inmates committed to such facilities need to be withheld from society to receive psychiatric treatment until they are sufficiently rehabilitated to be released back into the community.[15] Let us now take a look at this important variable of the programs of correctional institutions.

INSTITUTIONAL PROGRAMS

Institutional programs revolve around work, education, treatment, and leisure-time activities. These different programs will be examined in turn. However, it should be noted that most institutional programs are devised to fit within the requirements of custody and control.

Work Programs

Penologists, prison administrators, and the general public feel that inmates should work while in a correctional institution. Penologists and prison administrators recognize that work programs are useful in building morale as well as in maintaining high levels of security and discipline. This holds true because work tends to reduce tension and unrest. It is generally felt that work activities tend to reactivate and inculcate

[14] J. W. Stahl, "Caged or Cured: Classification and Treatment of California Felons at the California Medical Facility," *The Journal of Criminal Law, Criminology and Police Science,* Vol. 56 (June, 1965), pp. 174-89.

[15] H. M. Boslow and S. H. Manne, "Mental Health in Action-Treating Adult Offenders at Patuxent Institution," *Crime and Delinquency,* Vol. 12 (January, 1966), pp. 22-28.

certain attitudes, skills, and habit patterns that are helpful in the rehabilitation of offenders; particularly helpful is the carry-over effect that work programs have upon the inmate when he is released back into the community.[16] The type of work programs that are in use in correctional institutions can be classified as: (1) maintenance, (2) industrial programs, (3) farming, and (4) forestation and conservation.

Figure 11-2 Inmates may learn a trade while in a correctional institution. Photo courtesy of Philip D. Guthrie, Chief of Community Relations and Information, California Department of Corrections.

Maintenance. Maintenance work involves care of the inmate population and the upkeep of the institution. Often maintenance in a correctional institution is also related to the operating cost of that institution. Obviously, the more maintenance work that can be performed by inmates, the lower the cost of inmate care. However, maintenance work, like other employment of inmates, should be used to provide vocational training opportunities for those inmates who are assigned to this type of program.

Industrial Work Programs. Since the enactment of the Hawes-Cooper

[16] *Manual of Correctional Standards.*

Act in 1934 and the Ashurst-Sumner Act in 1935, prison industries have been limited in the distribution and sale of goods manufactured in prison. The market for prison products is limited to governmental agencies. Even so, of all the work activities in correctional institutions, the industrial program probably has the greatest potential for vocational training of inmates. If an industrial work program is well planned and diversified in its operation, it probably is quite useful in the rehabilitation of committed offenders.

There are a number of industries within correctional institutions. Even so a large number of men in the prison system lead a rather idle existence rather than engaging in a meaningful work program that will be useful to them upon their release back to the community.

Farming. Farming as a work program has been used in correctional facilities for many years. However, our change from a rural, agrarian society to an industrial society has brought about a change in the vocational training value of this activity. This does not mean that farming activities have no value, but it does mean that the value as regards vocational training is limited. However, there are advantages in allowing inmates to work outdoors, probably in a freer institutional work program. Furthermore, any work assignment wherein a person learns good work habits may have some intrinsic value.

Forestation and Conservation. A number of correctional facilities operate programs of forestation and conservation. Work of this nature is generally in rural mountain areas. Employment in forestation and conservation, like farming, probably does not hold great opportunities for vocational training. However, this too may have intrinsic value in teaching inmates good working habits.

It is generally agreed that work programs in correctional institutions could be of great value to inmates. However, all too often there is not enough work, and consequently many inmates remain idle or do meaningless work while assigned to exceedingly large maintenance crews. To combat this, some correctional institutions have become involved in imaginative work programs known as work furloughs.

Work Furlough Programs

Work furlough has many other names; some of these are: work release; day parole; private prerelease work; extramural, private employment; day work; daylight parole; free labor; free work; and intermittent jailing. Work furlough refers to the release of inmates from confinement during certain times of the day. Usually this release is for the purpose of employment outside the correctional institution. The inmate returns to confinement at the close of the work day and upon the completion of his civilian job.[17]

Most work furlough programs are for persons convicted of misdemeanors and placed in county correctional facilities (county jails). If the inmate is eligible for work furlough, or if he already has a job, he may be allowed to continue in this employment. Work furlough programs were used in twenty-eight states in their state correctional institutions and in twenty-eight states in their county and municipal correctional institutions in 1968. There is still a small percentage of inmates involved in programs of this nature; and a broader use of such programs would also seemingly be quite beneficial to the correctional portion of the criminal justice system.

Educational Programs

Inmates have often been deprived in many areas. Nowhere is this more evident than in academic and vocational education. Often inmates have failed to conform to basic public school requirements, and consequently they have low academic or vocational aptitudes. If an inmate is to be reintegrated successfully into the community, then his skills, either academically or vocationally, generally need to be improved.

Because many inmates have been failures in the school setting, the problem is to make learning a more relevant and rewarding experience. As a matter of course, most juvenile correctional institutions provide a program of academic and vocational training. Vocational and academic training programs in adult correctional institutions at the state level have waxed and waned through the years. However, these programs have tended to remain part of the total institutional experience in most facilities within the states. In fact, indications are that learning a trade or preparing for a better job when released from prison is one of the first interests of most inmates.[19] Originally most education in correctional institutions was of the academic type; in addition to academic educational programs, however, there is a need for a variety of vocational training programs. These vocational training programs need to be integrated with the work program to include actual job experience.

In most good educational programs within correctional institutions an inmate can receive credit toward graduation from school. Indeed,

[17] S. E. Grupp, "Work Release and the Misdemeanant," *Federal Probation,* Vol. 29 (June, 1965), pp. 6-12.

[18] E. H. Johnson, "State Work-Release Programs," *Crime and Delinquency,* Vol. 16, No. 4 (October, 1970), pp. 417-26.

[19] *Task Force Report: Corrections,* p. 183.

correctional institutions generally come closer to providing an educational program for inmates than they do to providing a treatment program for these same inmates.

Treatment Programs

Most people feel that correctional institutions should provide programs to change an offender's criminal attitude and behavior. Further, these programs should be under the guidance of psychiatrists, psychologists, sociologists, and social workers. However, evidence suggests that there is a shortage of behavioral scientists to work in corrections.[20] Because of this shortage, behavioral scientists are often used in training custodial and other operation personnel in counseling techniques. Consequently, much counseling in correctional institutions is done by "lay" personnel. There is evidence to suggest that counseling of this type tends to have an impact on reducing inmate return to criminal behavior.[21]

Professional behavioral scientists are used much more frequently in their professional capacity in institutions concerned with classification, screening, and diagnosis. Institutions of this sort would be reception-classification centers and institutions for mentally disturbed offenders.

Recreational Programs

Correctional administrators believe that a well-run recreational program is an important part of the total institutional correctional program. Recreation is important in relieving the monotony of institutional life and is a release for pent-up energies which otherwise might be used destructively.[22]

Important to a good recreational program is trained leadership. Money, equipment, and facilities are also important to the complete recreational program within the correctional institution. In addition, a good institutional recreational program should make motion pictures, radio, and television available to the inmates. Athletics, arts and crafts, literary activities, drama, and music should also be part of the activities in which inmates can participate.

Well-run recreational programs as well as well-run treatment, educa-

[20] *Task Force Report: Corrections,* p. 51.

[21] *Task Force Report: Corrections,* p. 52.

[22] *Manual of Correctional Standards,* p. 335.

tional, and work programs are all factors that make for the effective correctional institution.

The foregoing descriptions of programs for work, education, treatment, and leisure-time activity should give the reader some idea of what a correctional institution is like. However, one should not assume that correctional institutions do not present problems to the criminal justice system. Indeed, some outstanding problems of correctional institutions remain.

PROBLEMS OF CORRECTIONAL INSTITUTIONS

The President's Commission on Law Enforcement and Administration of Justice made the following statement about correctional institutions:

> For a great many offenders . . . corrections does not correct. Indeed, experts increasingly are coming to feel that conditions under which many offenders are handled, particularly in institutions, are often a positive deterrent to rehabilitation.
>
> Life in many institutions is at best barren and futile, at worst unspeakingly brutal and degrading. To be sure, the offenders in such institutions are incapacitated from committing further crimes while serving their sentences, but the conditions in which they live are the poorest possible preparation for their successful re-entry into society and often merely reinforces in them a pattern of manipulation or destructiveness.[23]

This statement is certainly a sobering one. It is particularly sobering when one recalls that commitment to a correctional institution tends to be the most stringent sanction that the criminal justice system can impose. However, if institutions for the commitment of felons are felt to leave a great deal to be desired, then by comparison jails theoretically used for the commitment of misdemeanants tend to be *very* undesirable.

Jails, for quite some time have been used for safekeeping and supposedly for the correction of certain offenders. However, in many cases jails become little more than enforced meeting places for society's antisocial and derelict persons. In the course of an offender's confinement to jail, he may be forced to wait in a drunken or sober condition in a vomit-befouled drunk tank. For that matter, he may be thrown nude into a totally dark isolation cell. While in jail, he may be exposed to

[23] President's Commission on Law Enforcement and Administration of Justice, *The Challenge of Crime in a Free Society* (Washington, D.C.: U.S. Gov't. Printing Office, 1967), p. 159.

drugs and rackets. It is possible he may become the victim of homosexual rape and/or beatings.[24]

The President's Commission on Law Enforcement and Administration of Justice describes these institutions in the following manner:

> No part of corrections is weaker than the local facilities that handle persons awaiting trial and serving short sentences. Because their inmates do not seem to present a clear danger to society, the response to their needs has usually been one of indifference. Because their crimes were considered petty and the sentences they serve are relatively short, the correctional system gives them low status. Many local jails and misdemeanant institutions are administered by the Police or County Sheriffs, authorities whose experience and main concern are in other fields. Most facilities lack well-developed recreational and counseling programs, sometimes even medical services. The first offender, the innocent awaiting trial, sometimes juveniles, and women are imprisoned with confirmed criminals, drunks and mentally disturbed or retarded.[25]

The great majority of the clientele of the correctional system—indeed, the majority of the clientele of the whole criminal justice system—have contact with the jail. It is surprising, then, that some of the problems of the jail have not been alleviated. Possibly part of the reason for this revolves around the feeling that corrections has not been geared as part of the criminal justice system. Here in the United States our greatest concern has been to make every effort to safeguard a person's right in the criminal justice system up to the time he or she is convicted of a crime. After conviction, society's concern with a person's rights seems to wane considerably.

The concern from the public as regards the convicted offender wanes even though it might be in the best interest of the public to be more informed about the situation. The reason for this is that approximately 61 percent of the adults convicted of a criminal act are placed on probation back in the community. Approximately 16⅔ percent of the convicted adults are placed in county jails to be released within a year's time. Only 22 percent of the adults convicted of crime are placed in state institutions.[26]

It should be noted that large numbers of convicted offenders are returned to the community from state and federal correctional institutions each year. In fact, most adult offenders are released from these correctional institutions and returned to the community. Whether this

[24] "Justice on Trial," *Newsweek* (March 8, 1971), pp. 16-19.

[25] *The Challenge of Crime in a Free Society,* p. 178.

[26] *The Challenge of Crime in a Free Society,* p. 193.

is through the parole process or through the expiration of the criminal law violator's sentence, the important fact is that return to the community occurs in a great majority of the cases. Although most adult criminal law violators are released sooner or later from correctional institutions, almost all juveniles under commitment are released from juvenile correctional institutions.

From the statistics we see that approximately 39 percent of the adults are referred to correctional institutions. Furthermore, a great majority of these persons are released and returned to the community later in their life. This suggests that these severe sanctions are probably imposed from some theoretical rationale.

RATIONALE FOR IMPOSING THE SANCTION OF IMPRISONMENT

The choice between probation or imprisonment, the selection of the appropriate degree of security, and determining the correct timing for release from incarceration are decisions that must be made within the framework of the criminal justice system. In some cases these decisions must be made by courts, and in other cases these decisions must be made by correctional administrators and/or parole boards. However, these decisions are concerned with very similar issues, which are:

1. The degree of threat to the public posed by the individual (significant clues will be provided by the nature of the present offense and the length of any prior record);
2. The nature of the response to any earlier correctional programs;
3. The kind of personal stability and responsibility evidenced in his employment record, residential pattern, and family support history;
4. The kind of personal deficiencies apparent, including educational and vocational training needs;
5. The personal psychological characteristics of the offender that determine how he perceives the world and his relationship to it.[27]

Several pieces of data indicate that in general corrections has done a fairly adequate job in making these selections. In research reported by Scarpitti and Stephenson, the data indicate that persons placed on probation tend to come from more stable, and far less deprived backgrounds. The persons assigned to probation tend to have more positive educational histories, and their delinquent and criminal careers tend to be shorter. They have had fewer offenses and official court appearances.

[27] *Task Force Report: Corrections,* p. 14.

Psychological test information indicated that persons placed on probation tend to be less delinquently oriented, less antisocial, and better adjusted than persons placed in correctional facilities. The data indicated quite clearly that "bad risks," or the persons most likely to continue to be involved in criminal or delinquent behavior, were the ones most likely to be placed in correctional institutions.[28]

Another pertinent collection of data indicates that persons placed in state correctional institutions often represent a great threat to other people. For example, in a California study, 25.5 percent of the male inmate population had been convicted of armed robbery; 9.5 percent of this population had been convicted of homicide; 6.1 percent were convicted of felonious assault; and 3.2 percent were convicted of forcible rape.[29]
Over 44 percent of the prison population in California had been committed for serious offenses against the person, and consequently they could be considered potentially dangerous as far as their behavior is concerned.

The data indicate that by and large the criminal justice system tends to invoke the most severe sanctions against persons who are potentially quite dangerous and against persons who seemingly have not changed their criminal behavior patterns, although they have been exposed to a number of correctional programs. This seems to imply that the criminal justice system has built within it a conflict of interest. This conflict of interest is between preserving the personal liberty of the individual while safeguarding the greatest common good of the other members of society. The criminal justice system is involved in evaluating and deciding whether to institutionalize the person convicted of a criminal law violation. The public's concern at the beginning of the criminal justice process is generally with the protection of the individual freedom involved in this delicate balance.

CONFLICT BETWEEN FREEDOM AND ORDER

In the criminal justice system the balance between freedom and order means that the rights of defendants and those convicted of criminal law violations must be weighed against the optimum protection of the community. These rights come in conflict most strikingly at three points—

[28] F. R. Scarpitti and R. M. Stephenson, "The Study of Probation Effectiveness," *The Journal of Criminal Law, Criminology and Police Science*, Vol. 59 (September, 1968), pp. 361-69.

[29] State of California, Department of Corrections, *Progress Report—1967–68*, p. 12.

at the time of trial, at the sentencing hearing, and (if an individual is incarcerated) at the time of a parole release hearing. Milton Burdman has pointed out this conflict most succinctly in the following manner:

1. Adversary proceedings with legal representation are valuable in reaching findings as to probable guilt in courts of law.
2. Adversary proceedings with legal representation are appropriate but less useful to assist the court in arriving at disposition once guilt is established.
3. In the correctional process, considering the number and variety of decisions to be made, the adversary method with legal representation and hearings is not desirable; in fact, it may even reduce effectiveness on quality and decision making:
   a. Once a person is committed to a correctional department, the issue is no longer absolute liberty but mainly one of degrees of freedom—e.g., minimum or maximum security, working release, etc. The adversary process in these decisions would be an excessively cumbersome intervention.
   b. The collarity of judgment factors upon which decisions are made to increase or restrict relative freedom would not be enhanced by the adversary process.
   c. Major abuses can be remedied through the exercise of writ to the court.
   d. The balance between freedom and order can be best maintained by a strong system for objective decision making depending upon professional, mature personnel, careful administrative review, and deteached independent review of major decisions.[30]

The conflict between personal freedom and the protection of society has perhaps been exploited to some extent. However, all members of the criminal justice system should remember that central to the evaluation of these two opposing rights is the identification of certain criteria in the criminal law violator. It is necessary to identify those persons who are dangerous or who are habitual offenders posing serious threats to the community's safety. These offenders include persons who are so grossly unstable as to erupt periodically into assaultive behavior. Furthermore, it includes those persons whose long-term exposure to criminal attitudes has produced a genuine commitment to criminal values. For persons who meet these criteria, it becomes apparent that institutionalization is necessary. It may be that the reason for institutionalization is that our knowledge of human behavior and the method for changing it are insufficient to the challenge posed by persons with these ingrained attitudes.

[30] M. Burdman, "The Conflict Between Freedom and Order," *Crime and Delinquency,* Vol. 15 (July, 1969), p. 372.

SUMMARY

This chapter has been concerned with the correctional system and its correctional institutions. Obviously, correctional institutions tend to be the most severe sanctions that the criminal justice system can impose upon the criminal law violators. This has come about through the elimination of capital and corporal punishment and the accompanying historical development of places of incarceration. Imprisonment as a sanction against criminal law violation did not come into being until the development of the idea that restricting one's freedom was a method of punishing and a method by which one could show penitence.

Historically, the development of prisons as we know them today can be traced to William Penn and the colony he founded in Pennsylvania. The progress in prisons was then shifted to the State of New York by virtue of New York's State Prison at Auburn and later the Elmira Reformatory for men.

The present nature of correctional institutions was also examined in this chapter. The level of government responsible for the administration of correctional institutions was discussed. Here in the United States the different correctional institutions are the responsibility of federal, state, and local governments. This is quite different from other industrial countries where corrections is usually administered at the national level.

Correctional institutions have been rated according to how much security they offer. Basically, these institutions are categorized into maximum-, medium-, and minimum-security institutions. A maximum-security facility is concerned with keeping inmates within the confines of that institution. The primary concern of such an institution revolves around security. Medium-security institutions are still quite concerned with keeping inmates inside the institution, but the physical restraints to insure this security certainly are not quite as elaborate as the ones in maximum-security institutions.

Institutions classed as minimum security operate without guard-posts, or armed guards. Very often they do not have a fence around them. A classic example of minimum-security institutions is the camp. Camps are characteristically small institutions that operate around a work program such as forestation, fire suppression, road building, or farming. Camps can be operated by any level of government.

Another concern of institutions is the nature of the clientele committed to them. Certain institutions are concerned with operating for women prisoners only; some are concerned only with juveniles; and still others are concerned with the reception and classification of newly committed inmates. Within corrections. it is generally believed that one of the keys to having a good correctional program within the state is to provide for an orderly diagnosis of offenders and to classify them into appropriate treatment categories. Therefore, special institutions concerned with reception and classification has increased a great deal.

With improved diagnosis it has become apparent that there is also a need for special medical and/or mental health type institutions. Consequently, there has been an increase in correctional institutions that specialize in performing psychiatric type services. There is some evidence to suggest that 6 percent of the persons committed to correctional facilities are in need of psychiatric care.

This chapter also reviewed programs offered by correctional institutions. These programs generally can be classed as work programs, educational programs, treatment programs, and leisure-time activity programs.

The work programs when properly conducted perform two functions. The first is to keep the inmates from being completely idle. The second function is to train inmates in some type of salable job skill which they can use after their release from the correctional institution.

The educational program includes providing academic training for inmates as well as vocational training. When properly utilized, vocational training in an institution is often tied in with a work program. Together, the work and vocational training programs can train inmates for job opportunities upon their release from the institution.

The third program of treatment, generally, has been developed with nonprofessional personnel. The results that have been obtained using lay personnel in counseling capacities have been quite good. Institutions where few lay personnel are utilized are those institutions that are a cross between a prison and psychiatric hospital.

Finally, leisure-time activities are generally concerned with keeping inmates from being idle. Idleness tends to cause problems in the correctional institution; therefore the concern with leisure-time activity as regards these institutions is certainly very real.

The general criticism of correctional institutions is that they do not correct but rather tend to educate the inmate in more sophisticated ways of committing criminal acts. Jails, furthermore, have been singled out as an example of the poorest type of correctional institution within the whole criminal justice system.

Understanding who should be and who is committed to correctional institutions is also important. Persons who present a threat to the person or those who have been involved in a number of correctional programs and have not profited from them are generally regarded as those who should be committed to institutions.

With the knowledge that correctional institutions are probably the severest sanctions that the criminal justice system can impose upon the individual, it becomes apparent that the system must be concerned with balancing the individual's right to freedom against society's right to protection. Some discussion and some ideas as to how to balance these two concerns were set forth for the consideration of the reader.

QUESTIONS

1. What is the relationship between correctional institutions and the criminal justice system?
2. Why is the State of Pennsylvania important to the development of present-day prisons?
3. How did Elmira Reformatory change the concept of corrections?
4. What is meant by maximum, medium, and minimum security as far as correctional institutions are concerned?
5. What relationship is there between the administration of a correctional institution and level of government?
6. What significance does the work program have to correctional institutions?
7. What is the significance of the educational program to corrections?
8. Of what significance is the treatment program to correctional institutions?
9. What are some of the criticisms of the correctional institutions?
10. What does the conflict between individual freedom and protection of society have to do with correctional institutions?

ANNOTATED REFERENCES

American Correctional Association. *Manual of Correctional Standards.* New York: The American Correctional Association, 1966. This manual describes directions and the standards that are expected in correctional institutions. This is a very excellent source book for someone involved with standards in the corrections field.

HARTINGER, W.; ELDEFONSO, E.; and COFFEY, A. *Corrections: A Component of the Criminal Justice System.* Pacific Palisades, Calif.: Goodyear Publishing, 1973. This is a text concerned with the correctional system and its part in the total criminal justice system.

President's Commission on Law Enforcement and Administration of Justice. *A Challenge of Crime in a Free Society.* Washington, D.C.: U.S. Gov't. Printing Office, 1967. This is a condensation of several of the task force reports of the Commission on Law Enforcement and Administration of Justice.

———. *Task Force Report: Corrections.* Washington, D.C.: U.S. Gov't. Printing Office, 1967. This report contains information regarding correctional institutions in the United States. The report was compiled for the President's Commission on Law Enforcement and Administration of Justice, and as such it included many noted people in the field of criminal justice.

SCARPITTI, F. R. and STEPHENSON, R. N. "The Study of Probation Effectiveness." *The Journal of Criminal Law, Criminology and Police Science.* Vol. 59, pp. 361-69. This study compares persons on probation and persons in a correctional institution. The results of this study indicate that probation is an effective treatment agent for persons who are less delinquent or criminally involved and come from stable family backgrounds. More severely disturbed delinquents or criminals do not do well on probation.

12

Community-Based Correctional Programs

The final chapter of this text is concerned with corrections in the community. The reason for emphasizing corrections within the community is two-fold: first, the majority of the correctional clientele are in the community. Fifty-four percent are on probation, while 13 percent are on parole or after-care supervision.[1] The following statement sums this up quite well:

> With two-thirds of the total correctional caseloads under probation or parole supervision today, the central question is no longer whether to handle offenders in the community but how to do so safely and successfully.[2]

The second reason for concentrating on corrections in the community is that more than 95 percent of the persons placed in correctional institutions are released and returned to the community.[3] True, not all releases are placed under that branch of community corrections called parole, but they are still released from the institution to the community.

In order for the criminal justice system to be effective in its function of deterring crime, community corrections must be utilized to the utmost.

[1] President's Commission on Law Enforcement and Administration of Justice, *Task Force Report: Corrections* (Washington, D.C.: U.S. Gov't. Printing Office, 1967).

[2] President's Commission on Law Enforcement and Administration of Justice, *The Challenge of Crime in a Free Society* (Washington, D.C.: U.S. Gov't. Printing Office, 1967), p. 165.

[3] R. G. Caldwell, *Criminology* (New York: Ronald Press, 1965), p. 653.

To examine community corrections a definition of the process of probation and parole supervision is needed. *Probation* is defined as: "a legal status granted by a court whereby a convicted person is permitted to remain in the community subject to conditions specified by the court." [4] *Parole* is defined as: "a method of releasing an offender from an institution prior to the completion of his maximum sentence, subject to conditions specified by the paroling authority." [5]

With these functions in mind, an examination for the reasons of the extensive use of the community correctional process would be most useful.

REASONS FOR COMMUNITY CORRECTIONS

The idea that probation and parole form a correctional process is justified by the fact that these correctional programs share with other correctional programs the characteristics of being a form of criminal law sanctions. This view is emphasized by the following statement:

> Restriction of freedom is punishment, no matter whether it is imposed by physical confinement (jail or prison) or by surveillance of movement within the community (probation or parole).[6]

The fact that probation and parole have punitive connotations truly puts them in their perspective in the total criminal justice system. As such, their advantages as an alternative to institutionalization should be examined. From the public viewpoint as well as from the viewpoint of the practitioners in the criminal justice system, there has been disenchantment with extensive use of correctional institutions as a means of solving the crime problem in the United States. Consequently, there has been a growing emphasis on community correctional programs. Basically there are five reasons for the use of community correctional programs rather than institutionalization. Each of these reasons will be discussed in term.

The first reason is that institutionalization may have a derogatory effect upon a person committed to such a facility. Offenders of all types are confined together in correctional institutions; often, because of the lack of staff, offenders are handled indiscriminately without much con-

[4] "Corrections in the United States," *Crime and Delinquency,* Vol. 13 (January, 1967), p. 266.

[5] "Corrections in the United States," p. 269 .

[6] J. Robinson and G. Smith, "The Effectiveness of Correctional Programs," *Crime and Delinquency,* Vol. 17 (January, 1971), p. 79.

tact with the correctional staff. The inmate has contact with other inmates who tend to develop an "inmate subculture" that is detrimental, especially to the newcomer. Within the inmate subculture, the aggressive inmates tend to be the leaders, and they consequently superimpose their cultural (generally antisocial ideas) upon other inmates. This inmate subculture and its ideas are imposed upon the inmates whether the correctional staff approves or disapproves. Even the best supervised correctional institutions tend to have an inmate code seemingly developed because of the criminal background of the majority of the inmates. Attitudes toward authority tend to be hostile. This hostility tends to make inmates less receptive to academic or vocational education as well as to any counseling or therapy programs that might be offered.[7]

Frequently in poorly run institutions and at times even in the best run institutions, violence, corruption, rackets, and coerced homosexuality may take place. Old prison buildings tend to be physically inadequate and are sometimes overcrowded. Generally, their construction is such that they are not suited for the present-day philosophy, ideals, and therapy programs that penologists feel to be rehabilitative.[8]

It is generally unwise to commit an unsophisticated young law violator to a correctional institution where negative influences may have an effect. Yet, some type of correctional plan may be deemed necessary, and the community correctional program of probation may then be the most appropriate.

A second reason for the use of community correctional programs is the apparent success of some of these programs. The reason for this success may well be the ability of the courts and probation departments to eliminate the potential failures from probation status by institutionalizing them. The following statement characterizes this success:

> Various studies have sought to measure the success of community treatment. One summary analysis of 15 different studies of probation outcome indicate that from 60 to 90 percent of the probationers studied completed terms without revocation. In another study, undertaken in California, 11,638 adult probationers who were granted probation during 1956–1958 were followed up after seven years. Of this group almost 72 percent completed their probation term without revocation.
>
> These findings were not obtained under controlled conditions, nor were they supported by data which distinguished among the types of offenders who succeeded or among the types of services that were rendered. But they are the product of a variety of probation services administered at different

[7] A. M. Kirkpatrick, "Prisons Produce People," *Federal Probation,* Vol. 26 (December, 1962), pp. 26-33.

[8] *The Challenge of Crime in a Free Society,* p. 163.

times and places and provide some evidence that well planned and administered community programs can be successful in reducing recidivism. These findings, combined with the data from the national survey of corrections showing that probation and parole services are characteristically poorly staffed and more often poorly administered, suggest that improvement in quality of community treatment should be a major goal.[9]

The third reason for placing the criminal law violator in a community correctional program is to help the family function as a unit. Ultimately, the rehabilitation of an individual may depend more upon the support and concern of the family than on any other one factor. Certainly, when a member of the family is forcibly separated from the family via institutionalization, the everyday support and concern of the family will be absent. Also, some antisocial activity is precipitated by faulty family relationships. These faulty relationships can often best be resolved by providing resources such as counseling while the family is still a unit.

A fourth argument for the use of community corrections is economic. The cost of institutionalizing all persons convicted of criminal law violations might well be prohibitive. The reason for this treatment has to do with the following statistics. About 80 percent of the total budget spent on corrections in a year's time is spent on institutionalization. The cost of institutionalizing an adult in a state facility is approximately six times as much as the cost of placing that person on parole. It costs about fourteen times more to institutionalize an adult than it does to handle that person on probation.[10] Approximately two-thirds of the correctional population are in the community correctional program, where the cost is only 20 percent of the total correctional budget. According to these figures, institutionalizing our total correctional population would mean a necessary increase in the criminal budget by as much as 175 percent.

Other economic factors that come to bear, particularly when the breadwinner of the family is institutionalized. These factors are the increase in welfare assistance necessary to support the breadwinner's family when he or she is institutionalized.

The fifth reason for the use of community corrections is the social behavioral theory that re-integrating the offender within the community may be more successful than removing him. The underlying premise for this new direction in corrections is that crime is not only a symptom of individual failure but also a symptom of failure and disorganization

[9] *The Challenge of Crime in a Free Society,* p. 166.

[10] *Task Force Report: Corrections,* p. 193.

of the community. These community failures in a sense deprive the offender of contact with social institutions which are responsible for developing law-abiding conduct. These social institutions are sound family life, good schools, and a reasonably sound means of earning a living—to name but a few. When a person is unable to come into contact with reasonably sound social institutions of this sort, antisocial behavior such as crime is often a consequence.

The task of community corrections therefore includes building or rebuilding sound ties between the community and the criminal law violator. Integration or re-integrating the criminal law violator into community life means restoring family ties, obtaining employment, and finding educational opportunities so that the individual may be able to function in an acceptable manner within our society. Obviously, this requires efforts to change the individual, but it also may require some mobilization and change of our community institutions. Furthermore, all of these efforts to change the criminal law violator must be undertaken without surrendering the deterrent and control role that has always been and will continue to be the cornerstone of corrections. The control and deterrent effects of corrections are particularly important in relation to the criminal law violator who presents a danger to the community when unsupervised.[11]

These five justifications for the use of community corrections may be even better understood when community corrections is more closely examined.

COMMUNITY CORRECTIONS—PROBATION

More than one-half of the offenders who are involved in the correctional process are placed on probation.[12] This supervision in the community subject to the authority of the court is generally felt to be valuable in a great number of cases. In fact, data available indicate that probation offers one of the most significant prospects for effective correctional programs. It is apparent that there must be at least two components in the probation process if that process is to work effectively. The first of these components is a screening-diagnostic method to select those who will profit from probation; those who need a more restrained correctional program will not be placed on probation. The second is a good supervision program which can effectively assist in the rehabilitation of the criminal law violator.

[11] *Task Force Report: Corrections,* p. 7.

[12] *Task Force Report: Corrections,* p. 27.

Let us now look at various other aspects of probation—its history, presentence investigation, casework services, and administrative structure.

History of Probation

Probation is a rather recent innovation of the criminal justice system. It is generally thought to have originated about the year 1841 with a Boston shoemaker named John Augustus who got the municipal court of Boston to defer sentences and entrust the care of defendants to him. The court, after entrusting the care of the defendant to John Augustus, would defer sentence and await the outcome of this trust before making a final disposition of the matter. During his lifetime, nearly 2,000 defendants were entrusted to Augustus' care. Most of those so entrusted were charged with drunkenness and/or vagrancy.

In 1878, Massachusetts passed the first statute regarding probation. The statute authorized the mayor of Boston the option of annually appointing a member of the police department to act as a probation officer. Two years later, the power to appoint probation officers was granted to all cities and towns in the State of Massachusetts. This power of appointment was given by Massachusetts to the lower courts in 1891 and to the Superior Court judges in 1898.

Interestingly enough, the first statute authorizing courts to grant probation wasn't passed until 1898 (by the State of Vermont). That statute made probation a condition added to suspending the execution of the sentence of the court. The idea of probation grew rapidly. Seventeen years later, in 1915, there were thirty-three states that had legislation authorizing adult probation.

However, it was forty-two more years (until 1957) before all the states and territorial jurisdictions had passed legislation enabling probation.

Along with developments regarding the legal basis for probation, there was also a refinement of the process of defining the duties and responsibilities of the probation officer. Also there was the formation of criteria for granting probation along with the authorization of the conditions of probation and probation revocation. The presentence investigation coupled with a report to the court based on that investigation was implemented during this period. The casework method was also adapted to probation services.[13]

The two major concerns of the probation process *are diagnosis and casework services.* The diagnostic process is presently more involved in

[13] *Task Force Report: Corrections,* pp. 169-70.

the presentence report, which has become a valuable service performed by probation departments.

Presentence Investigation

An analytical presentence study of the criminal law violator can produce much more meaningful insight for the court than the information generated in the heat of a trial. For that matter, it can produce much more meaningful information than the so-called "practical" recommendation agreed to by the prosecuting attorney, the defense attorney, and the judge. This practice is known as *plea bargaining* and may leave something to be desired. Much more fair to all parties involved—particularly society and the criminal law violator—is an unbiased and fair presentation of the total picture of the defendant—his problems, needs, attitudes, feelings, responses, outlook, degree of ability to communicate, and other personal characteristics. These must be presented fairly in a good presentence report.[14]

The presentence report is one of the basic working documents in judicial and correctional administration. The report, when it includes a recommendation for disposition, assists the court in imposing judgment consistent with the court's dual responsibility to society and the criminal law violator. The report should assist the probation officer assigned to supervise the criminal law violator placed on probation. Furthermore, it should assist the correctional institution in classification and treatment programs as well as in release planning if the criminal law violator is committed. The report could very well help the parole board in its consideration regarding parole.[15]

The report should contain a description of the referring offense. This information can be obtained from the police reports or the arresting agency. Also, for clarity's sake if possible, statements of the witnesses and codefendants should be obtained. Obviously, a statement from the defendant regarding the offense should also be a part of the presentence report. A more thorough picture of the offense and the precipitating factors surrounding it may well be most useful in evaluating the defendant. An article like David Zoellner's points this out quite succinctly:

> A "battery" may be either a slap in the face, or a rather brutal beating. A theft may represent a symptom of kleptomania, a calculated, mercenary

[14] R. M. Smith, "A Probation Officer Looks at Disparities in Sentence," *Federal Probation,* Vol. 26 (December, 1962), pp. 19-23.

[15] R. M. Carter, "It Is Respectfully Recommended . . . ," *Federal Probation,* Vol. 30 June, 1966), pp. 38-42.

act, or may even be a symptom of sexual maladjustment. The defendant who steals ladies lingerie, for example, may in one case intend to sell it, and in another case to slash it with a knife [or to sleep in it].[16]

The defendant's prior record needs to be incorporated into any presentence report. Whereas an arrest record from the Federal Bureau of Investigation or a state department of criminal statistics or identification may give a record of the defendant's prior arrests and convictions, it still does not give a complete picture of his difficulties. To clarify these difficulties the probation officer may have to include a check with local police as well as a check with records from other courts regarding the defendant.

The presentence report must be concerned with the family of the defendant. Next to the defendant himself, the best source of information about him tends to be his family. In many cases, the family feels they must present the defendant in a favorable light. Nevertheless, certain family-supplied information may be quite revealing.

Also included in the presentence report should be a statement regarding the neighborhood and home where the defendant has been living. Certainly the defendant who lives in a rat-infested apartment in a ghetto experiences different pressures than the individual who lives in the typical middle-class home found in a suburban area.

A good presentence report discusses the defendant's employment and/or school record. The importance of this is that students spend from one-fourth to one-fifth of their time in school, and someone in the work force spends at least that much time in his employment. How the defendant adjusted in these situations certainly should give some information that might well be useful in formulating a correctional treatment plan.

The defendant's health also needs to be reported—particularly if it might have some bearing on his behavior and adjustment. Generally speaking this means some kind of evaluation of the defendant's personality.

Usually the probation officer can provide substantial information regarding the defendant's intelligence and emotional make-up when there are psychological or psychiatric summaries available. When there is no information of this nature available, the probation officer should appraise personality factors within the limitations of his training. He should review material obtained during his interview with the defendant and information supplied by community sources. Certainly, a rough estimation of the defendant's intellectual ability can be made by evaluating his

[16] D. Zoellner, "Writing the Evaluative Section for Probation Court Reports," *Journal of the California Probation, Parole, and Correctional Association,* Vol. 2 (Fall, 1965), pp. 21-22.

vocabulary level, his general mode of communications, and by analyzing how successful he has been in handling jobs and/or projects requiring certain abilities.

The probation officer can make some estimation as to how the defendant handles his emotions and feelings in an interview situation. The probation officer can form some impression of how the defendant handles psychological defenses and how adequate these psychological defenses are. Finally, the probation officer should be able to make some evaluation of the defendant's interpersonal relationships, he might want to note the extent to which the defendant is able to form close personal relationships.[17]

Because much of the information in the presentence report will be obtained from the defendant, a great deal of care needs to be taken in interviewing the defendant. John Manson addresses himself to this particular problem:

> Probation officer's contacts with the defendant are generally the most important assessment tool in the presentence work. From these contacts we not only obtain the necessary biographic material but also have the opportunity to assess personality strengths and weaknesses which help us to predict future behavior. Rarely, if ever, can the probation officer feel comfortable dictating his report without re-interviewing the defendant. The second interview enables the defendant to clarify and explain information obtained from other sources which may be in conflict with information provided by the defendant. The second interview may help the probation officer to resolve these difficulties or to lend proper weight to them in his evaluation of the defendant.[18]

The entire presentence report, and most particularly its evaluation portion, should clearly lead to the recommendations. If the recommendations are to appear reasonable and valid, there must be evidence that full consideration was given to all the avenues which are open to the court in making a disposition. This means that if there are two or three possibilities which might logically be considered by the court, the presentence report should deal with all these possibilities in an explicit manner. This is of particular importance when the defendant and his attorney are setting forth a plan that is at variance with the plan being set forth by the probation officer. Also, it is particularly important when a recommendation and plan are rather unusual in nature.

In presenting the plan of action that will be recommended, it is im-

[17] J. R. Manson, "Studying the Offender Before the Court," *Federal Probation,* Vol. 33 (June, 1969), pp. 17-21.

[18] Manson, "Studying the Offender . . . ," pp. 19-20.

portant to show some connection between the apparent causal factors and the remedial measures that are being recommended. Obviously, besides being pertinent to the problem, the plan should be realistic in terms of the sources that are actually available to the defendant.

The report should not be a furtive intent to "sell" the court on a plan. The recommendations should proceed logically from the evaluation set forth in the presentence report.[19]

The diagnosis involved in formulating the presentence report is one of the essential functions of probation services. This is true because the ability to pick criminal law violators who would succeed in probation programs has been demonstrated; success ratio of those persons placed on probation supervision is quite high. The ability to separate the potential successes from the potential failures may well be one of the most distinguishing characteristics of good probation services.[20]

Casework Services

Probation was initiated as a humanitarian measure. Early pioneers in the field of corrections simply wished to keep first offenders and minor recidivists from being exposed to the corrupt effects of jails or prisons. However, as probation services continued to expand, there was increasing demand for professionally trained people to deal with the criminal law violator who had been placed on probation. With the development of social casework, there was a corresponding demand for casework services in the correctional field.

At the heart of the philosophy of correctional casework is the concept of social control and social treatment. These two concepts when thought of in terms of correctional casework are not mutually exclusive. Traditionally, it has been felt that through treatment, control could be established in the casework situation. Many practitioners of the "helping professions" feel that there is an irreconcilable conflict between the use of casework techniques and the use of authority. This has been the topic of many debates and journal articles; to some extent, the conflict remains unresolved and will probably continue to remain so.

A different method of reviewing correctional casework might be helpful in understanding the definition used here. Most all definitions of social casework focus on the process by which an individual is helped to become a more effectively functioning individual within his social environ-

[19] Zoellner, "Writing the Evaluative Section. . . . ," pp. 20-24.

[20] F. R. Scarpitli and R. M. Stephenson, "The Study of Probation Effectiveness," *Journal of Criminal Law, Criminology, and Police Science,* Vol. 59 (September, 1968), pp. 361-69.

ment. The emphasis is on the individual and his motivation to solve the problem. Social control, on the other hand, is essentially a method of constraining or restraining by force. In the case of correctional casework, this restraining or constraining is done by the legal authority of the court.

The philosophical underpinnings of the process of establishing conditions of probation are certainly ones of social control. Certainly, a client of the criminal justice system who is instructed not to associate with certain people, not to drive, or not get married, is being restrained by virtue of social control.

Many persons feel that the motivation to improve or to resolve problems must come from within the client. They feel that casework is not effective unless it is desired and voluntarily requested by the client. Somehow the client must be willing to deal with his problems if the problems are to be resolved at all. On a number of occasions, however, correctional clients have been ordered to participate in therapy and somehow to profit by this therapy. The assumption must then be that motivation for therapy was developed after being ordered into the program. This concept has been stated very well:

> While it is true that effective casework is not something done *to* or *for* the client, but *with* him, it is also true that sometimes it is a matter of some action which "gets his attention" or "holds him still" long enough for him to recognize that there *is* motivation from within; he may only need to make way for it to begin to function. Or, it may be necessary, through restraint and constraint, to structure action until the validity of it can be understood and accepted for itself as a way of life.
>
> In this initial stage of the correctional treatment process, one need not necessarily be complicated in the design of his casework methods and techniques. He may need only to set, and enforce, behavioral limits—to inform his client "you can go this far, but no further"; to say, "No! You can't do that." [21]

If the offender is unsuccessful in his adjustment to the pressures and demands of society, he often needs to have the feeling of success, even if it is first arrived at through coercion.

It is generally felt that three general principles must be applied for probation casework to succeed. These principles are:

1. The needs, problems, capacities, and limitations of the individual probationer must be considered in planning and carrying out supervision;

[21] C. T. Mangrum, "The Function of Coercive Casework in Corrections," *Federal Probation,* Vol. 35 (March, 1971), p. 28.

2. Legal requirements and conditions must be applied for the best interests of the offender and the community;
3. The goal of supervision is to help the offender understand his own problems and enable him to deal adequately with them.[22]

In any event, for probation supervision to succeed the probation officer needs to interpret to the probationer his status and responsibility.

The two broad services that probation is to perform—diagnosis and casework supervision—obviously need to be in some kind of administrative structure. The discussion of this structure may well disclose some of the problems of probation.

Administrative Structure

According to the *Task Force Report: Corrections,* the extent to which probation is used in the United States varies from place to place; consequently its administrative systems are also rather diverse. All fifty states and territories have legislation authorizing probation. Of the 3,082 counties and districts that make up these states, 91 percent have some type of probation service.

However, in fourteen states adult probation is a county-operated system, whereas in thirty-seven states it is a state-wide system operated by a state agency. This latter group includes seventeen states in which there is some combination of county and state services. The state agency provides minimum service to the courts upon request in three states; in fourteen states a varied number of counties from one to seven provide the service locally, while the state agency provides service for the remaining counties. Nine of those states which have retained the county as the governmental body responsible for probation are among the most densely populated states in the nation. Furthermore, in these states the adult probation departments are generally administered by the court. In only one of these fourteen states are a few of the probation departments responsible to the county government.

Of the thirty-two states where adult probation is a state operated system, thirty are administered by agencies that are also responsible for adult paroles. Of the remaining seven states where a state agency administers probation as a separate program, one has a probation board; one has a department of probation; one has a bureau within the department of corrections; two have a probation commission; and two have an office of court administration.

22 *Manual of Correctional Standards* (New York: The American Correctional Association, 1966), p. 532.

The essential ingredients of an effective probation department are (1) that it is established on a sound legal basis, (2) that it has insightful and conscientuous leadership, and (3) that it has good financial support. If these essential ingredients are present, the organizational and administrative form under which probation operates is usually not that important.[23] There are, however, quite a number of persons in the correctional field who feel that probation services should be in an agency supervised by the state government.[24]

PAROLE

The difference between parole and probation is that probation deals with the criminal law violator in the community before commitment to a correctional institutional program, *while parole deals with some criminal law violators upon release from the institution.* Not all persons released from a correctional institution are under parole supervision. Persons are released from correctional institutions under one of four procedures. These procedures are *by pardon, by discharge at the completion of sentence, by mandatory or conditional release, or by parole.* When someone is pardoned, they no longer are under any restrictions of the correctional system, and obviously, they are not under any parole supervision. Persons discharged from a correctional institution at the completion of their sentence are also no longer under the jurisdiction of the correctional system. On the other hand, persons who are released by mandatory or conditional release and those released on parole are under parole supervision. Essentially, *parole* is a method of releasing an offender from a correctional institution prior to the completion of his sentence and subject to certain conditions. *Mandatory* or *conditional release* is defined as follows:

> Mandatory or conditional release—[is] the release, as prescribed by law, of a prisoner who has served his term of commitment less "good time" or "work time" credit, under parole conditions and under supervision until the expiration of the maximum term for which he was sentenced.[25]

Some discussion of how parole came about may be of some interest to the reader at this point.

23 *Task Force Report: Corrections,* pp. 171-72.

24 *Task Force Report: Corrections,* p. 172; and *Manual of Correctional Standards,* p. 513.

25 *Task Force Report: Corrections,* p. 269.

Correctional History

The idea of parole can be traced back to the identure and transportation of convicts during the 1700s. Indenture was the method whereby a convict was placed with an employer to work and live rather than being placed in prison. Transportation was a method of dealing with convicts in England during the seventeenth and eighteenth centuries. With this method, some convicts were allowed to go to America or Australia in lieu of going to prison. They were transported from England to these countries, and this process consequently became known as Transportation.

It wasn't until 1876 that the concept of parole received its first official recognition. This was at the Elmira Reformatory in New York State. Since that time the growth of parole services has been continuous, although uneven. Parole has expanded in the adult field more rapidly than it has in the juvenile field. The selection of inmates for parole is determined by many things including the legislature, the courts, and administrative boards.[26]

Institutional Release

Approximately two-thirds of the persons leaving correctional institutions during the year leave either on parole or on a conditional release status where parole supervision is part of the release plan. Almost all of the remaining one-third who leave prison during a particular year do so at the expiration of their sentence. As early as 1939, at a National Parole Conference in Washington, President Roosevelt said the following about parole:

> We know from experience that parole, when it is honestly and expertly managed, provides better protection for society than does any other method of release from prison.[27]

The objectives of a parole system when it is well managed can be summarized as follows:

1. Release of each person from confinement at the most favorable time, with appropriate consideration to requirements of justice, expectations of subsequent behavior, and cost.

[26] *Task Force Report: Corrections,* pp. 185-86.

[27] *Manual of Correctional Standards,* p. 531.

2. The largest possible number of successful parole completions.
3. The smallest possible number of new crimes committed by released offenders.
4. The smallest possible number of violent acts committed by released offenders.
5. An increase of general community confidence in parole administration.[28]

According to the *Task Force Report: Corrections,* the release procedures for parole are determined by several factors. One of these factors is the legislature which establishes the limits wherein the courts and the parole board are to operate. A second consideration regarding the parole release procedure has to do with the judgment the courts make defining the boundaries of the parole board's discretion. Finally, the parole board may be involved in term setting.

In forty-three states the parole board has full and exclusive power to grant and revoke parole. In the other states, the board has advisory or limited authority in this area. The most important function of parole boards, at least in the forty-three states where they have exclusive power to grant or revoke parole, is the conducting of parole hearings where these decisions are made. Generally the board meets at the correctional institutions where revocation and release hearings are conducted. At these hearings the inmate makes a personal appearance. (Presently there is before the Supreme Court two cases—*Morrissey* v. *Brewer* and *Midgett* v. *Cox*—which should shed a great deal of light upon whether legal counsel at parole hearings is a constitutional guarantee.)

The hearings range from formal to quite informal. Consequently, the information presented at the hearings may be unverified comments on the one hand, or detailed accommodations of data on the other hand.[29] Once the inmate is granted parole supervision in the community begins.

Correctional Casework

Correctional casework with parolees should begin long before an inmate is a parolee. A good parole program and good parole casework have a prerelease program that prepares the parolee but also prepares the community to receive the parolee when he is released from the correctional institution. During the prerelease period, arrangements should be made so that, upon leaving the correctional institution, the parolee will have adequate clothing and a suitable place to live. Arrangements should also be made so that the parolee will have money for food and

[28] *Task Force Report: Corrections,* p. 185.
[29] *Task Force Report: Corrections.*

other incidental expenses. Attempts should be made to obtain suitable employment for the parolee, which may be done in conjunction with the state department of employment.

Generally speaking, inmates need to be prepared to accept the difficulties of readjusting to society upon their release from a correctional institution. Therefore a counseling program (individual or group) is often very helpful in resolving some of the inmates' feelings regarding release from the institution and return to the community.

Society's responsibility for accepting the parole back into the community is mainly vested in the parole officer. The parole officer is likely to be concerned with the personal and social factors that led to the commission of the parolee's crime as well as any character or attitudinal abnormalities that may have to be dealt with. It can be surmised that most all of the casework techniques utilized in probation supervision are also appropriately used in parole supervision. If there is a difference, it is that persons on parole tend to be more recalcitrant than persons on probation. Because of this, there tends to be a major emphasis on how a parole officer exercises controls. The rules and conditions established by the paroling authority tend to be somewhat more stringent than those established by courts for probationers. However, it is important to recognize that parole rules are not ends in themselves; rather, they are meant to be tools that will assist the officer in supervising the parolee in such a manner as to prevent further crime.

Parole services are administered in a manner somewhat different from probation services. Some description of these administrative services may be of interest to the reader.

Correctional Administration

There are two dominant patterns of administration in the parole field. In one, parole decision making and the administration of parole is vested in the institution. This type of administrative design is to be found in juvenile institutions. The second pattern of administration is through an autonomous group. In the adult field, every state has an identifiable and separate parole authority.

Two types of administrative structures are used in the parole field. In one, the parole executive is responsible to the parole board. This form of administrative structure is found in thirty-one states and territorial jurisdictions. The other type of administrative structure is where the parole executive is responsible to the department with general administrative responsibility for the correctional program. This type administrative structure is found in twenty states and territories.

As indicated previously, in thirty-seven states, probation and parole are administered jointly by one state agency. In fourteen states (usually with large populations), parole is operated as a separate service from probation.[30]

Besides traditional probation and parole, there has been a tendency in the past ten years to experiment with placing criminal law violators in programs that are more restrictive than traditional probation and parole, but yet not as restrictive as traditional correctional institutional placement.

ALTERNATIVES TO INSTITUTIONALIZATION—SPECIAL PROGRAMS

A number of experimental community programs have been set up in various parts of the country in the past several years. These programs although somewhat different in content and structure offer greater supervision and guidance than the traditional probation and/or parole programs. These programs offer a set of alternatives between regular probation and parole supervision and commitment or recommitment to a correctional institution. These programs provide more guidance than is commonly offered in probation services, and they also tend to enrich parole supervision.

Placing a criminal law violator in one of these experimental programs, by and large, costs a great deal less than committing him to a correctional institution. Most of the data suggest that these programs are at least as effective in reducing recidivism as are traditional correctional programs.

Many of these experimental programs have been conducted with a population that is traditionally younger than the populations found in adult correctional institutions. However, it is felt that some of the ideas from these programs can be adapted to adults. Placing the criminal law violator on an extremely small caseload with intensive supervision and counseling is an example of a community-based correctional program. (See Figure 12-1.)

Other new programs that have had an impact are halfway houses, residential community treatment centers, and work-release programs. The work-release program is certainly not a new one; it was first used in Wisconsin in 1913. Since that time, the program has grown and has

[30] *Task Force Report: Corrections,* p. 218.

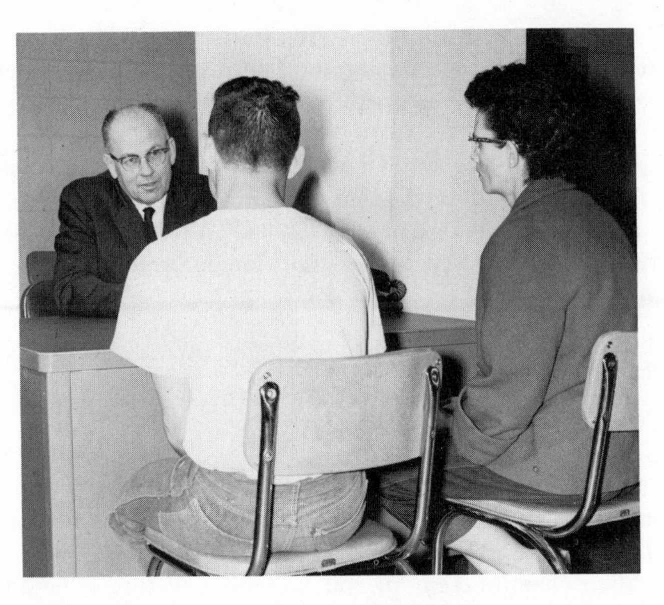

Figure 12-1 Frequent counseling and close supervision are some of the aspects of experimental community-based correctional programs. Here, a criminal law violator and a member of his family are receiving counseling services. Photo courtesy of the Santa Clara County Public Information Office, San Jose, Ca.

been accepted in the field of corrections; at least twenty-eight states have statutes authorizing the use of this program.[31]

The residential community treatment center is an adaption of the work-release program. As a prerelease center, it performs many of the functions of work-release; however it has the advantage of being based in the community. The residents in this facility have access to community services and are still able to receive support from the staff at the facility.

Early experiences with youths at centers of this sort have indicated that re-entry into the community is greatly facilitated. They have been so successful that there is the possibility of using these facilities as intermediate centers for short-term care of persons who might otherwise be committed to traditional correctional institutions.

Many people in the correctional field consider the halfway house an alternative to institutional placement; as such. halfway houses are con-

[31] E. H. Johnson, "State Work-Release Programs," *Crime and Delinquency,* Vol. 16 (October, 1970), pp. 417-26.

sidered part of community treatment programs. They serve as an alternative between probation and the correctional institution; they can also be used as a place where an institutional inmate can be released in order to ease the stress of the transition from incarceration to freedom. The halfway house is a "semi-institution" where a probationer or parolee has officially been placed, but where he can also associate with the "free" community more or less as a free person. The significance of the halfway house in the correctional field is just beginning to be understood. Its use will probably continue to grow in the next decade.

Extensive casework services, work-release, community treatment centers, and halfway houses are all examples of new correctional treatment programs. As such they are alternatives to present correctional programs, but the development of alternatives requires that certain things take place. First, administrators and legislators must become aware of these programs so that enabling legislation can be passed and so that administrators will be willing to set up programs of this sort. A second concern is manpower. These new programs need more skilled correctional personnel to operate them.

Problems regarding the administration of new programs also exist. Few people have had the experience necessary to operate some of the programs effectively. It is apparent that with these new correctional programs in operation, there will be a need to form liaisons with other agencies such as welfare. Also, to make a community correctional program operate at its maximum efficiency, the community itself should become involved in the rehabilitative process.[32]

CORRECTIONS AND THE CRIMINAL JUSTICE SYSTEM

Recently there has been a great deal of criticism of the courts, apparently because the public assumes that court decisions are capable of significantly reducing the incidence of crime. Although these beliefs are undeniably misconceptions, they do reflect the public's frustration at the apparent failure of society as a whole to reduce crime. In the criminal justice process, it is only the correctional system—not the courts or the police—that has the capacity, even though a very small one, to rehabilitate and reform the criminal law violator. This being so, it appears somewhat strange that so many courts and so many correction officials still fail to realize that the criminal law violator will participate

[32] *Task Force Report: Corrections,* pp. 38-44.

in his own rehabilitation only when correctional administration is fair, honest, carefully thought out, and amply financed.

It may be that there is little we can do to rehabilitate most criminal law violators. Perhaps, any chance they might have had for rehabilitation in a healthy environment is gone long before they are brought to the attention of the criminal justice process. Nonetheless, corrections can at least present them with a model of fairness and honesty in its decision making regarding their welfare.[33]

Figure 12-2 A juvenile and her parents before a judge in juvenile court. Photo courtesy of the Santa Clara County Juvenile Probation Department, San Jose, Ca.

Suggestions have been made, of course, for improving the criminal justice system. A task force on probation and parole made some suggestions, and some of those suggestions that seem to apply are:

1. There should be increased contact between probation, parole, and other law enforcement personnel.
2. The gathering and use of statistical data should be improved throughout the criminal justice system.
3. Criminal statistics should be evaluated to determine the factors which affects them so early response to problems can be initiated.
4. Courts should continue to evaluate their sentencing policies to better

[33] M. Meltsner, "The Future of Corrections: A Defense Attorney's View," *Crime and Delinquency*, Vol. 17 (July, 1971), pp. 266-70.

balance the protection of society against the rehabilitation potential of the criminal law violator.

5. Case loads for probation, parole, and correctional institutions in many cases should be reduced to a more realistic figure.
6. There should be an in-depth study of the effects of plea bargaining on the whole of the criminal justice system and society itself.[34]

The 184th General Assembly of the United Presbyterian Church also had some thoughts on what should be done about problems of the criminal justice system. These thoughts were set forth for public debate searching for practical answers and constructive action:

1. Victimless crimes should be removed from criminal codes.
2. Alternatives to the justice system should be used to handle noncriminal behavior by juveniles (truancy, running away, drinking and smoking, etc.).
3. Practices of discrimination based on racial, ethnic, religious, or political identification should be eliminated from the criminal justice system.
4. Unconvicted defendants must not be incarcerated solely because they are indigent.
5. Unconvicted defendants who must be incarcerated for specific reasons must be afforded all constitutional protections.
6. All nonconvicted defendants must be brought to trial within a reasonable length of time.
7. Alternatives to incarceration must be developed at all levels of government.
8. Persons who must be imprisoned should have the advantage of the richest possible training and treatment programs, but courts should not sentence persons to prison and parole boards should not retain them in prison solely because of that training or treatment.
9. Persons sentenced to institutional care should be given, within 90 days of admission, a definite release date based exclusively on the nature of the offense and the pattern of their criminal history.
10. Human, civil, religious, and political rights of offenders, except the right of movement and the right to vote and hold public office while in prison, should not be abrogated by any judicial, legislative, or administrative act in criminal cases.[35]

[34] *Report to the Attorney General—Task Force on Probation and Parole,* Mimeographed report to the Attorney General of California, 1972, pp. 35-41.

[35] "Church Seeks Reforms," *Crime and Delinquency,* Vol. 19 (January, 1973), pp. 109-10.

SUMMARY

This chapter was concerned with community-based corrections. By and large, community-based corrections are the processes of probation and parole. It is quite important for the criminal justice system to be concerned with probation and parole since two-thirds of the persons involved in the correctional process are on probation and parole. Furthermore, over 95 percent of the criminal law violators who are placed in correctional institutions are sooner or later released from those institutions and returned to society. This means that, if crime is to be dealt with effectively, it must be dealt with through community correctional programs.

Probation was examined as a separate entity of the criminal justice system. The origin of probation can be traced to a shoemaker who lived in the nineteenth century in Boston, Massachusetts. Since the time of John Augustus, commonly known as the "father of probation," this type of correctional program has come into use in all fifty states and territories. Part of this success of probation is related to the ability of the probation department and the court to predict who will succeed on probation. The instrument or tool that is used most successfully in this prediction process is the presentence report.

The presentence report and the obligation of the probation department to do a presentence investigation so that the best correctional plan can be recommended to the court were discussed. We also reviewed the importance of casework supervision.

Casework supervision was discussed from the standpoint of its coercive nature. It is felt that casework services should be offered to the client without coercion, but many times coercion is needed among correctional clientele.

The administrative systems found in probation were reviewed next. Generally speaking, large states tend to have probation departments that are operated from a local base, while the states with smaller populations tend to have a state agency in charge of probation.

Attention was then shifted to parole. Parole, which originated in Europe, is a system of release from correctional institutions before one's sentence is complete. The word *parole,* itself, is from a French word which means to "give one's word." Consequently, the idea of parole is that the parolee gives his word that he will abide by certain rules and regulations until his sentence expires. Parole officially became a part of the correctional system with the opening of Elmira Reformatory in New

York in 1876. Some discussion was also presented in regard to who makes the decision when someone should be paroled. This discussion emphasized parole boards and their responsibilities.

It has long been felt that good parole services begin with good casework services while the criminal law violator is still within the correctional institution. From the correctional institution, casework services with the parolee resembles casework services afforded persons on probation. If there is a difference between the two, it is in regard to the rules a parolee is expected to follow. These tend to be more stringent. Also, a parole client is usually much more recalcitrant than is a probation client.

Finally, the administration of parole services was examined. It was learned that all adult parole services are administered from agencies independent of the correctional institution. By and large, it is felt that this separation is in the best interests of the parolee.

Some mention has also been made of newer methods in community corrections. It was noted that many of the new methods in community corrections were started with juveniles. The one exception to this is the work-furlough program which was started with adults in 1913 in Wisconsin. A second type of community program that has been used with adults as well as juveniles is the small, concentrated caseload approach. A third type of new development is the community correctional center. Data from the few centers that have been in operation suggest that this type of approach might be most useful.

It was pointed out that, in the complete criminal justice system, only corrections truly has an opportunity to change the criminal law violator. Therefore, to do something about crime—which, by the way, is the job of the entire criminal justice system—a much more concentrated effort needs to be made in the correctional area.

QUESTIONS

1. What is probation?
2. What is parole?
3. What does coercive casework mean?
4. Why should the criminal justice system be concerned with community corrections?
5. What is a presentence report?
6. What does the parole board do?
7. Who is administratively responsible for adult probation in most states?
8. What are some of the new community correctional programs?

ANNOTATED REFERENCES

"Corrections in the United States." *Crime and Delinquency.* Vol. 13 (January, 1967). This is the research that the National Council of Crime and Delinquency did for the federal government. The information was used in reports made by the President's Commission on Law Enforcement and Administration of Justice.

MANGRUM, C. T. "The Function of Coercive Casework in Corrations." *Federal Probation.* Vol. 35 (March, 1971), 17-21. This is an excellent article regarding casework services as they are used in the correctional field.

MANSON, J. R. "Studying the Offender Before the Court." *Federal Probation.* Vol. 33 (June, 1969), pp. 17-21. This article gives a good rundown on the diagnostic process involved in making presentence reports.

MELTSNER, M. "The Future of Correction: A Defense Attorney's View." *Crime and Delinquency.* Vol. 17 (July, 1971), pp. 266-70. This is an excellent article regarding the correctional process as it is related to the whole of the criminal justice system.

Selected Readings in the Criminal Justice System

CORRECTIONS

BARNES, H., and TEETER:, N. *New Horizons in Criminology.* Englewood Cliffs, N.J.: Prentice-Hall, 1959.

CRESSY, DONALD. *The Prison.* New York: Holt-Rinehart-Winston, 1961.

DRESSLER, DAVID. *Probation and Parole.* New York: Columbia University Press, 1961.

ELDEFONSO, EDWARD, *Issues in Corrections: A Book of Readings.* Beverly Hills, Ca.: Glencoe Press, 1973.

EVRARD, FRANKLIN. *Successful Parole.* Springfield, Ill., Charles C. Thomas, 1971.

EYMAN, J. *Prisons for Women.* Springfield, Ill.: Charles C. Thomas, 1971.

HARTINGER, WALTER, ELDEFONSO, EDWARD, and COFFEY, ALAN. *Corrections: A Component of the Criminal Justice System.* Pacific Palisades, Ca.: Goodyear Publishing Co., 1973.

KAY, BARBARA, and VEDDER, CLYDE. *Probation and Parole.* Springfield, Ill.: Charles C. Thomas 1971.

KEVE, PAUL. *Imaginative Programming in Probation and Parole.* Minneapolis: University of Minnesota Press, 1967.

NEWMAN, CHARLES. *Sourcebook on Probation, Parole and Pardons.* 3rd ed. Springfield, Ill.: Charles C. Thomas, 1970.

TAPPAN, PAUL. *Crime, Justice and Corrections.* New York: McGraw-Hill, 1960.

VEDDER, CLYDE, and KAY, BARBARA. *Penology.* Springfield, Ill.: Charles C. Thomas, 1969.

CRIME

DE RIVER, J. PAUL. *Crime and the Sexual Psychopath.* Springfield, Ill.: Charles C. Thomas, 1950.

———. *The Sexual Criminal.* Springfield, Ill.: Charles C. Thomas, 1956.

FLAMMANG, C. *The Police and the Unprotected Child.* Springfield, Ill.: Charles C. Thomas, 1970.

FONTANA, VINCENT. *The Maltreated Child.* Springfield, Ill.: Charles C. Thomas, 1971

MACDONALD, JOHN M. *Homicidal Threats.* Springfield, Ill.: Charles C. Thomas, 1968.

———. *The Murderer and His Victim.* Springfield, Ill.: Charles C. Thomas, 1961.

———. *Rape: Offenders and Their Victims.* Springfield, Ill.: Charles C. Thomas, 1971.

ROEBUCK, JULIAN. *Criminal Typology.* Springfield, Ill.: Charles C. Thomas, 1971.

SILVING, HELEN. *Constituent Elements of Crime.* Springfield, Ill.: Charles C. Thomas, 1967.

WINSLOW, ROBERT. *Crime in a Free Society.* Belmont, Calif.: Dickenson Publishers, 1968.

CRIMINALISTICS

ARTHER, RICHARD. *The Scientific Investigator.* Springfield, Ill.: Charles C. Thomas, 1970.

BATES, BILLY. *Typewriting Identification.* Springfield, Ill.: Charles C. Thomas, 1971.

CONWAY, JAMES. *Evidential Documents.* Springfield, Ill.: Charles C. Thomas, 1959.

EVANS, W. E. D. *The Chemistry of Death.* Springfield, Ill.: Charles C. Thomas, 1963.

FIELD, ANNITA. *Fingerprint Handbook.* Springfield, Ill.: Charles C. Thomas, 1971.

KIRK, P., and BRADFORD, L. *The Crime Laboratory.* Springfield, Ill.: Charles C. Thomas, 1965.

KREMA, VACLAV. *The Identification and Registration of Firearms.* Springfield, Ill.: Charles C. Thomas, 1971.

INVESTIGATION

ARONS, HARRY. *Hypnosis in Criminal Investigation.* Springfield, Ill.: Charles C. Thomas, 1967.

MERKLEY, DONALD K. *The Investigation of Death.* Springfield, Ill.: Charles C. Thomas, 1957.

MOTTO, CARMINE. *Undercover.* Springfield, Ill.: Charles C. Thomas, 1971.

RIEDER, ROBERT. *Law Enforcement Information Systems.* Springfield, Ill.: Charles C. Thomas, 1971.

WALL, PATRICK. *Eye Witness Identification in Criminal Cases.* Springfield, Ill.: Charles C. Thomas, 1971.

JUVENILES

AMOS, W., and WELLFORD, C. *Delinquency Prevention.* Englewood Cliffs, N.J.: Prentice-Hall, 1967.

ELDEFONSO, EDWARD. *Law Enforcement and the Youthful Offender,* 2nd ed. New York: John Wiley & Sons, 1973.

———, *Youth Problems and Law Enforcement.* Englewood Cliffs, N.J.: Prentice-Hall, Inc., 1972.

KENNY, JOHN, and PURSUIT, DAN. *Police Work with Juveniles and the Administration of Juvenile Justice.* Springfield, Ill.: Charles C. Thomas, 1971.

VEDDER, CLYDE. *Juvenile Offenders.* Springfield, Ill.: Charles C. Thomas, 1971.

LAW

COHEN, STANLEY. *A Law Enforcement Guide to United States Supreme Court Decisions.* Springfield, Ill.: Charles C. Thomas, 1971.

ELDEFONSO, E.; COFFEY, A.; and SULLIVAN, J. *Police and the Criminal Law.* Pacific Palisades, Calif.: Goodyear Publishers, 1972.

NORDSTROM, NILS. *The Rights and Rewards of the Medical Witness.* Springfield, Ill.: Charles C. Thomas, 1962.

POLSON, C. J. *The Essentials of Forensic Medicine.* Springfield, Ill.: Charles C. Thomas, 1965.

SLOVENKO, RALPH. *Sexual Behavior and the Law.* Springfield, Ill.: Charles C. Thomas, 1971.

WRIGHT, EDWARD. *Practical Municipal Law.* Springfield, Ill.: Charles C. Thomas, 1971.

POLICE

BASSIOUNI, M.C. *The Law of Dissent and Riots.* Springfield, Ill.: Charles C. Thomas, 1971.

BRODIE, THOMAS. *Bombs and Bombings.* Springfield, Ill.: Charles C. Thomas, 1971.

COFFEY, A.; ELDEFONSO, E.; and HARTINGER, W. *Human Relations: Law Enforcement in a Changing Community.* Englewood Cliffs, N.J.: Prentice-Hall, 1971.

COFFEY, A.; ELDEFONSO, E.; and HARTINGER, W. *Police-Community Relations.* Englewood Cliffs, N.J.: Prentice-Hall, 1971.

ELDEFONSO, E.; COFFEY, A.; and GRACE, R. *Principals of Law Enforcement.* New York: John Wiley & Son, 1968.

ELDEFONSO, EDWARD. *Readings in Criminal Justice.* Beverly Hills, Ca.: Glencoe Press, 1973.

LEONARD, V. A. *Police Crime Prevention.* Springfield, Ill.: Charles C. Thomas, 1971.

MOMBOISSE, RAYMOND. *Riots, Revolts and Insurrections.* Springfield, Ill.: Charles C. Thomas, 1970.

PATRICK, CLARENCE. *The Police, Crime, and Society.* Springfield, Ill.: Charles C. Thomas, 1971.

WESTON, PAUL. *The Police Traffic Control Function.* Springfield, Ill.: Charles C. Thomas, 1971.

Appendixes

A

Sections of the United States Constitution Significant to Police Work

ARTICLE I (LEGISLATIVE DEPARTMENT)

Section 7: Mode of Passing Laws

[*Special Provision as to Revenue Laws*] All bills for raising revenue shall originate in the House of Representatives, but the Senate may propose or concur with amendments as on other bills.

[*Laws, How Enacted*] Every bill which shall have passed the House of Representatives and the Senate, shall, before it becomes a law, be presented to the President of the United States; if he approves, he shall sign it, but if not, he shall return it, with his objections, to that House in which it originated, who shall enter the objections at large on their journal, and proceed to consider it. If, after such consideration, two-thirds of that House shall agree to pass the bill, it shall be sent, together with objections, to the other House, by which it shall likewise be reconsidered, and if approved by two-thirds of that House it shall become a law. But in all such cases the votes of both Houses shall be determined by yeas and nays; and the names of the persons voting for and against the bill shall be entered on the journal of each House respectively. If any bill shall not be returned by the President within ten days (Sundays excepted) after it shall have been presented to him, the same shall be a law, in like maner as if he had signed it, unless the Congress, by their adjournment, prevent its return, in which case it shall not be a law.

[*Same Rules Apply to Resolutions*] Every order, resolution, or vote, to which the concurrence of the Senate and the House of Representatives may be necessary (except on a question of adjournment), shall be presented to the President of the United States; and, before the same shall take effect, shall be approved by him, or disapproved by him, shall be repassed by two thirds of the Senate and House of Representatives, according to the rules and limitations prescribed in the case of a bill.

Section 8: Powers Granted to Congress

[*Coin*] To coin money, regulate the value thereof and of foreign coins, and fix the standard of weights and measures.

[*Counterfeiting*] To provide for the punishment of counterfeiting the securities and current coin of the United States.

[*Courts*] To constitute tribunals inferior to the Supreme Court.

[*Piracies*] To define and punish piracies and felonies committed on the high seas, and offenses against the laws of nations.

[*Federal District and Other Places*] To exercise exclusive legislation, in all cases whatsoever, over such district (not exceeding ten miles square) as may, by cession of particular States, and the acceptance of Congress, become the seat of government of the United States, and to exercise like authority over all places purchased by the consent of the Legislature of the State in which the same shall be, for the erection of forts, magazines, arsenals, dockyards, and other needful buildings.

[*Make Laws to Carry Out Foregoing Powers*] To make all laws which shall be necessary and proper for carrying into execution the foregoing powers, and all other powers vested by this Constitution in the Government of the United States, or in any department, or officer thereof.

Section 9: Limitations on Powers Granted to the United States

[*Habeas Corpus*] The privilege of the writ of habeas corpus shall not be suspended, unless when, in cases of rebellion or invasion, the public safety may require it.

[*Ex Post Facto Law*] No bill of attainder or ex post facto law shall be passed.

[*Direct Taxes*] No capitation, or other direct, tax shall be laid, unless in proportion to the census or enumeration hereinbefore directed to be taken.

ARTICLE III (JUDICIAL DEPARTMENT)

Section 1: One Supreme Court—Other Inferior Courts

[*Courts—Terms of Office and Salary of Judges*] The judicial power of the United States shall be vested in one Supreme Court, and in such inferior courts as the Congress may from time to time ordain and establish. The judges, both of the supreme and inferior courts, shall hold their offices during good behavior, and shall, at stated times, receive for their services a compensation which shall not be diminished during their continuance in office.

Section 2: Jurisdiction of United States Courts

[*Cases That May Come Before United States Courts*] The judicial power shall extend to all cases, in law and equity, arising under this Constitution, the laws of the United States, and treaties made, or which shall be made under their authority; to all cases affecting ambassadors, other public ministers, and consuls; to all cases of admiralty and maritime jurisdiction; to controversies to which the United States shall be a party; to controversies between two or more States (between a state and citizens of another State–restricted by the Eleventh Amendment; between citizens of different States; between citizens of the same State claiming lands under grants of different States; and between a State, or the citizens thereof, and foreign states, citizens or subjects.

[*Jurisdiction of Supreme and Appellate Courts*] In all cases affecting ambassadors, other public ministers, and consuls, and those in which a State shall be a party, the Supreme Court shall have original jurisdiction. In all other cases before mentioned the Supreme Court shall have appellate jurisdiction, both as to law and fact, with such exceptions and under such regulations as the Congress shall make.

[*Trial of Crimes*] The trial of all crimes, except in cases of impeachment, shall be by jury; and such trial shall be held in the State where said crimes shall have been committed; but when not committed within any State, the trial shall be put at such place or places as the Congress may, by law, have directed. (Extended by the Fifth, Sixth, Seventh, and Eighth Amendments.

Section 3: Treason

[*Treason Defined*] Treason against the United States shall consist only in levying war against them, or in adhering to their enemies, giving them aid and comfort.

[*Conviction*] No person shall be convicted of treason, unless on the testimony of two witnesses to the same overt act, or on confession in open court.

[*Punishment*] The Congress shall have power to declare the punishment of treason; but no attainder of treason shall work corruption of blood, or forfeiture except during the life of the person attained.

ARTICLE IV (THE STATES AND THE FEDERAL GOVERNMENT)

Section 2: Citizens—Fugitives

[*Interstate Privileges of Citizens*] The citizens of each State shall be entitled to all the privileges and immunities of citizens in the several States. (Extended by the Fourteenth Amendment.)

[*Fugitives From Justice*] A person charged in any State with treason, felony, or other crime, who shall flee from justice and be found in another State shall, on demand of the executive authority of the State from which he fled, be delivered up, to be removed to the State having jurisdiction of the crime.

[*Fugitives From Service*] No person held to service or labor in one State, under the laws thereof, escaping into another, shall in consequence of any law or regulation therein, be discharged from such service or labor, but shall be delivered up on claim of the party to whom such service or labor may be due. (Superseded, as to slaves, by the Thirteenth Amendment.)

AMENDMENTS

ARTICLE I (RESTRICTIONS ON POWERS OF CONGRESS)

Section 1: Further Protection of Citizens' Rights

[*Freedom of Religion, Speech and Press*] Congress shall make no law respecting an establishment of religion, or prohibiting the free exercise thereof, or abridging the freedom of speech or of the press; or the right of the people peaceably to assemble, and to petition the Government for a redress of grievances.

ARTICLE II (RIGHT TO BEAR ARMS)

Section 1: Security of States

[*State Militia*] A wellregulated militia being necessary to the security of a free State, the right of the people to keep and bear arms, shall not be infringed.

ARTICLE III (BILLETING OF SOLDIERS)

Section 1: In Peace—In War

[*By Consent or Law Only*] No soldier shall, in time of peace, be quartered in any house without the consent of the owner; nor in time of war, but in a manner to be prescribed by law.

ARTICLE IV (SEIZURES, SEARCHES, AND WARRANTS)

Section 1: Respect for Privacy and Property

[*Rights and Regulations*] The right of the people to be secure in their persons, houses, papers, and effects, against unreasonable searches and seizures shall not be violated, and no warrants shall issue but upon reasonable cause, supported by oath or affirmation, and particularly describing the place to be searched and the person or things to be seized.

ARTICLE V (CRIMINAL PROCEEDINGS, CONDEMNATION OF PROPERTY)

Section 1: Capital Crimes—Compensation

[*Grand Jury Indictment*] No person shall be held to answer for a capital or otherwise infamous crime, unless on a presentment or indictment of a Grand Jury, except in crimes arising in the land or naval forces, or in the militia, when in actual service in time of war or public danger; nor shall any person be subject for the same offense to be twice put in jeopardy of life or limb; nor shall be compelled in any criminal case to be a witness against himself; nor be deprived of life, liberty, or property, without due process of law; nor shall private property be taken for public use without just compensation.

ARTICLE VI (MODE OF TRIAL IN CRIMINAL PROCEEDNGS)

Section 1: Right to Speedy Trials

[*Witnesses*] In all criminal proceedings the accused shall enjoy the right to a speedy and public trial, by an impartial jury of the State and district wherein the crime shall have been committed, which district shall have previously ascertained by law, and to be informed of the nature and cause of the accusation; to be confronted with the witnesses against him; to have compulsory process for obtaining witnesses in his favor, and to have assistance of counsel for his defense.

ARTICLE VIII (BAILS–FINES–PUNISHMENTS)

Section 1: In Moderation

[*Safeguard Against Excessiveness*] Excessive bail shall not be required, nor excessive fines imposed, nor cruel and unusual punishments inflicted.

ARTICLE IX (CERTAIN RIGHTS NOT DENIED TO THE PEOPLE)

Section 1: Constitutional Interpretation

[*Respect for Others' Rights*] The enumeration in the Constitution of certain rights shall not be construed to deny or disparage others retained by the people.

ARTICLE XIII (SLAVERY)

Section 1: Involuntary Servitude

[*Abolition–Exception*] Neither slavery nor involuntary servitude, except as a punishment for crime whereof the party shall have been duly convicted, shall exist within the United States, or any place subject to their jurisdiction.

ARTICLE XIV (CITIZENSHIP, REPRESENTATION, AND PAYMENT OF PUBLIC DEBT)

Section 1: Citizenship

[*Equal Protection*] All persons born or naturalized in the United States and subject to the jurisdiction thereof, are citizens of the United States and of the States wherein they reside. No State shall make or enforce any laws which shall abridge the privileges or immunities of citizens of the United States; nor shall any State deprive any person of life, liberty, or property, without due process of law, nor deny to any person within its jurisdiction the equal protection of the laws.

B

Case Law: Excerpts of Selected United States Supreme Court Decisions

ESCOBEDO V. *ILLINOIS*

The critical question in this case is whether, under the circumstances, the refusal by the police to honor petitioner's request to consult with his lawyer during the course of an interrogation constitutes a denial of "the Assistance of Counsel" in violation of the Sixth Amendment to the Constitution as "made obligatory upon the States by the Fourteenth Amendment," *Gideon* v. *Wainwright,* and thereby renders inadmissible in a state criminal trial any incriminating statement elicited by the police during the interrogation.

On the night of January 19, 1960, petitioner's brother-in-law was fatally shot. At 2:30 A.M. that morning, petitioner was arrested and interrogated. Petitioner made no statement to the police . . . was released at 5 P.M. that afternoon pursuant to a state court writ of habeas corpus obtained by . . . a lawyer.

On January 30, Benedict DiGerlando, who was then in police custody and who was later indicted for the murder along with petitioner, told the police that petitioner had fired the fatal shots. Between 8 and 9 P.M. that evening, petitioner and his sister, the widow of the deceased, were arrested and taken to police headquarters. En route to the police station, the police . . . "told defendant that DiGerlando had named him as the one who shot" the deceased. Petitioner testified, without contradiction, that the "detectives had us pretty well, up pretty tight, and we might as well admit to this crime," and that he replied, "I am sorry but I would like to have advice from my lawyer." A police officer testified that although petitioner was not formally charged "he was in custody" and couldn't "walk out the door."

Shortly after petitioner reached police headquarters, his retained lawyer arrived. The lawyer described the ensuing events in the following terms: ". . . I went to the Detective Bureau at 11th and State. The first person I talked to was the Sergeant on duty at the Bureau Desk . . . I asked the Sergeant (on duty) for permission to speak to my client, Danny Escobedo . . . The Sergeant made a call to the Bureau lockup and informed me that the boy had been taken from the lockup to the Homicide Bureau. This was between 9:30 and 10:00 in the evening. Before I went anywhere, he called the Homicide Bureau and told them there was an attorney waiting to see Escobedo. He told me I could not see him. Then I went upstairs to the Homicide Bureau. There were several Homicide Detectives around and I talked to them. I identified myself as Escobedo's attorney and asked permission to see him. They said I could not. . . . The police officer told me to see Chief Flynn who was on duty. I identified myself to Chief Flynn and asked permission to see my client. He said I could not. The door was open and I could see through the office. . . . I waved to him and he waved back and then the door was closed by one of the officers at Homicide. There were four or five officers milling around the Homicide Detail that night. As to whether I talked to Captain Flynn any later that day, I waited around for another hour or two and went back again and renewed request to see my client. He again told me I could not. . . . I filed an official complaint with Commissioner Phelan of the Chicago Police Department. I had a conversation with every police officer I could find. I was told at Homicide that I couldn't see him and I would have to get a writ of habeas corpus."

Petitioner testified that during the course of the interrogation he repeatedly asked to speak to his lawyer and that the police said that his lawyer "didn't want to see" him. The testimony of the police officers confirmed these accounts in substantial detail.

Nothwithstanding repeated requests by each, petitioner and his retained lawyer were afforded no opportunity to consult during the course of the entire interrogation. At one point, as previously noted, petitioner and his attorney came into each other's view for a few moments but the attorney was quickly ushered away. A police officer testified that he had told the lawyer that he could not see petitioner until "we were through interrogating" him.

It is undisputed that during the course of the interrogation Officer

Montejano, who "grew up" in petitioner's neighborhood, who knew his family, and uses "Spanish language [when necessary in] police work," conferred alone with petitioner. Petitioner testified that the officer said to him "in Spanish that my sister and I could go home if I pinned it on Benedict DiGerlando," that "he would see to it that we could go home and be held only as witnesses, if anything, if we made a statement against DiGerlando." Petitioner testified that he made the statement in issue because of this assurance. Officer Montejano denied offering any such assurance.

Petitioner moved both before and during trial to suppress the incriminating statement, but the motions were denied. Petitioner was convicted of murder and he appealed the conviction.

[The Supreme Court of Illinois, on rehearing, found the confession voluntary and affirmed the conviction.]

In *Massiah* v. *United States,* this Court observed that "a Constitution which guarantees a defendant the aid of counsel at . . . trial could surely vouchsafe no less to an indicted defendant under interrogation by the police in a completely extra-judicial proceeding. Anything less . . . might deny a defendant effective representation by counsel at the only stage when legal aid and advice would help him."

The interrogation here was conducted before petitioner was formally indicted. But in the context of this case, that fact should make no difference. When petitioner requested, and was denied, an opportunity to consult with his lawyer, the investigation had ceased to be a general investigation of "an unsolved crime." *Spano* v. *New York*. Petitioner had become the accused, and the purpose of the interrogation was to "get him" to confess his guilt despite his constitutional right not to do so. At the time of his arrest and throughout the course of the interrogation, the police told petitioner that they had convincing evidence that he had fired the fatal shots. Without informing him of his absolute right to remain silent in the face of this accusation, the police urged him to make a statement. As this Court observed many years ago;

"It cannot be doubted that, placed in the position in which the accused was when the statement was made to him that the other suspected person had charged him with a crime, the result was to produce upon his mind the fear that, if he remained silent, it would be considered an admission of guilt, and therefore render certain his being committed for trial as the guilty person, and it cannot be conceived that the converse impression would not also have naturally arisen that, by denying, there was hope of removing the suspicion from himself." *Bram* v. *United States*. Petitioner, a layman, was undoubtedly unaware that under Illinois law an admission of "mere" complicity in the murder plot was legally as damaging as an admission of firing the fatal shots. The "guiding hand of counsel" was essential to advise petitioner of his rights in this delicate situation. *Powell*

v. *Alabama.* This was the "stage when legal aid and advice" were most critical to petitioner. *Massiah* v. *United States.* It was a stage surely as critical as was the arraignment in *Hamilton* v. *Alabama* and the preliminary hearing in *White* v. *Maryland.* What happened at this interrogation could certainly "affect the whole trial," *Hamilton* v. *Alabama,* since rights "may be as irretrievably lost, if not then and there asserted, as they are when an accused represented by counsel waives a right for strategic purposes." It would exalt form over substance to make the right to counsel, under these circumstances, depend on whether at the time of the interrogation, the authorities had secured a formal indictment. Petitioner had, for all practical purposes, already been charged with murder.

It is argued that if the right to counsel is afforded prior to indictment, the number of confessions obtained by the police will diminish significantly, because most confessions are obtained during the period between arrest and indictment, and "any lawyer worth his salt will tell the suspect in no uncertain terms to make no statement to police under any circumstances." *Watts* v. *Indiana.* This argument, of course, cuts two ways. The fact that many confessions are obtained during this period points up its critical nature as a "stage when legal aid and advice" are surely needed. The right to counsel would indeed be shallow if it began at a period when few confessions were obtained. There is necessarily a direct relationship between the importance of a stage to the police in their quest for a confession and the criticality of that stage to the accused in his need for legal advice. Our Constitution, unlike some others, strikes the balance in favor of the right of the accused to be advised by his lawyer of his privilege against self-incrimination.

We have learned from history that no system of criminal justice can, or should, survive if it comes to depend for its continued effectiveness on the citizens' abdication through unawareness of their constitutional rights. No system worth preserving should have to *fear* that if an accused is permitted to consult with a lawyer, he will become aware of, and exercise, these rights. If the exercise of constitutional rights will thwart the effectiveness of a system of law enforcement, then there is something very wrong with that system.

We hold, therefore, that where, as here, the investigation is no longer a general inquiry into an unsolved crime but has begun to focus on a particular suspect, the suspect has been taken into police custody, the police carry out a process of interrogations that lends itself to eliciting incriminating statements, the suspect has requested and been denied an opportunity to consult with his lawyer, and the police have not effectively warned him of his absolute constitutional right to remain silent, the accused has been denied the "Assistance of Counsel" in violation of the Sixth Amendment to the Constitution as "made obligatory upon the

States by the Fourteenth Amendment," *Gideon* v. *Wainright,* and that no statement elicited by the police during the interrogation may be used against him at a criminal trial.

Nothing we have said today affects the powers of the police to investigate "an unsolved crime," *Spano* v. *New York,* by gathering information from witnesses and by other "proper investigative efforts." *Haynes* v. *Washington.* We hold only that when the process shifts from investigatory to accusatory—when its focus is on the accused and its purpose is to elicit a confession—our adversary system begins to operate, and, under the circumstances here, the accused must be permitted to consult with his lawyer.

The judgment of the Illinois Supreme Court is reversed and the case remanded for proceedings not inconsistent with this opinion.

Reversed and remanded.

GAULT V. ARIZONA

This is an appeal under 28 U.S.C.Sec. 1257 (2) from a judgment of the Supreme Court of Arizona affirming the dismissal of a petition for a writ of habeas corpus. The petition sought the release of Gerald Francis Gault, petitioners' 15-year-old son, who had been committed as a juvenile delinquent to the State Industrial School by the Juvenile Court of Gila County, Arizona. The Supreme Court of Arizona affirmed dismissal of the writ against various arguments which included an attack upon the constitutionality of the Arizona Juvenile Code because of its alleged denial of procedural due process rights to juveniles charged with being "delinquents." The court agreed that the constitutional guarantee of due process of law is applicable in such proceedings. It held that Arizona's Juvenile Code is to be read as "impliedly" implementing the "due process concept." It then proceeded to identify and describe "the particular elements which constitute due process in a juvenile hearing." It concluded that the proceedings ending in commitment of Gerald Gault did not offend these requirements. We do not agree, and we reverse. We begin with a statement of the facts.

On Monday, June 8, 1964, at about 10 A.M., Gerald Francis Gault and a friend, Ronald Lewis, were taken into custody by the Sheriff of Gila County. Gerald was then still subject to a six months' probation order which had been entered on February 25, 1964, as a result of his having been in the company of another boy who had stolen a wallet from a lady's purse. The police action on June 8 was taken as the result of a verbal complaint by a neighbor of the boys, Mrs. Cook, about a telephone call made to her in which the caller or callers made lewd or indecent remarks.

It will suffice for purposes of this opinion to say that the remarks or questions put to her were of the irritatingly offensive, adolescent, sex variety.

At the time Gerald was picked up, his mother and father were both at work. No notice that Gerald was being taken into custody was left at the home. No other steps were taken to advise them that their son had, in effect, been arrested. Gerald was taken to the Children's Detention Home. When his mother arrived home at about 6 o'clock, Gerald was not there. Gerald's older brother was sent to look for him at the trailer home of the Lewis family. He apparently learned then that Gerald was in custody. He so informed his mother. The two of them went to the Detention Home. The deputy probation officer, Flagg, who was also superintendent of the Detention Home, told Mrs. Gault "why Jerry was there" and said that a hearing would be held in Juvenile Court at 3 o'clock the following day, June 9.

Officer Flagg filed a petition with the Court on the hearing day, June 9, 1964. It was not served on the Gaults. Indeed, none of them saw this petition until the habeas corpus hearing on August 17, 1964. The petition was entirely formal. It made no reference to any factual basis for the judicial action which it initiated. It recited only that "said minor is under the age of 18 years and in need of the protection of this Honorable Court (and that) said minor is a delinquent minor." It prayed for a hearing and an order regarding "the care and custody of said minor." Officer Flagg executed a formal affidavit in support of the petition.

On June 9, Gerald, his mother, his older brother, and Probation Officers Flagg and Henderson appeared before the Juvenile Judge in chambers. Gerald's father was not there. He was at work out of the city. Mrs. Cook, the complainant was not there. No one was sworn at this hearing. No transcript or recording was made. No memorandum or record of the substance of the proceedings was prepared. Our information about the proceedings and the subsequent hearing on June 15, derives entirely from the testimony of the Juvenile Court Judge, Mr. and Mrs. Gault and Officer Flagg at the habeas corpus proceeding conducted two months later. From this, it appears that at the July 9 hearing, Gerald was questioned by the judge about the telephone call. There was conflict as to what he said. His mother recalled that Gerald said he only dialed Mrs. Cook's number and handed the telephone to his friend, Ronald. Officer Flagg recalled that Gerald had admitted making the lewd remarks. Judge McGhee testified that Gerald "admitted making one of these (lewd) statements." At the conclusion of the hearing, the judge said he would "think about it." Gerald was taken back to the Detention Home. He was not sent to his own home with his parents. On June 11 or 12, after having been detained since June 8, Gerald was released and driven home. There is no explanation in the record as to why he was kept in the Detention Home or why he was released. Mrs. Gault received a note signed by Officer Flagg. It was on plain paper, not letterhead. Its entire text was as follows:

"Mrs. Gault: Judge McGhee has set Monday, June 15, 1964, at 11:00 A.M. as the date and time for further Hearings on Gerald's delinquency /s/ Flagg."

At the appointed time on Monday June 15, Gerald, his father and mother, Ronald Lewis and his father, and Officers Flagg and Henderson were present before Judge McGhee. Witnesses at the habeas corpus proceeding differed in their recollections of Gerald's testimony at the June 15 hearing. Mr. and Mrs. Gault recalled that Gerald again testified that he had only dialed the number and that the other boy had made the remarks. Officer Flagg agreed that at this hearing Gerald did not admit making the lewd remarks. But Judge McGhee recalled that "there was some admission again of some of the lewd statements." Again, the complainant, Mrs. Cook, was not present. Mrs. Gault asked that Mrs. Cook be present "so she could see which boy had done the talking, the dirty talking over the phone." The Juvenile Judge said "she didn't have to be present at that hearing." The judge did not speak to Mrs. Cook or communicate with her at any time. Probation Officer Flagg had talked to her once—over the telephone on June 9.

At this June 15 hearing, a "referral report" made by the probation officers was filed with the court, although not disclosed to Gerald or his parents. This listed the charge as "Lewd Phone Calls." At the conclusion of the hearing, the judge committed Gerald as a juvenile delinquent to the State Industrial School "for the period of his minority (that is, until 21), unless sooner discharged by due process of law." An order to that effect was entered. It recites that "after a full hearing and due deliberation the Court finds that said minor is a delinquent child, and that said minor is of the age of 15 years."

No appeal is permitted by Arizona law in juvenile cases. On August 3, 1964, a petition for a writ of habeas corpus was filed with the Supreme Court of Arizona and referred by it to the Superior Court for hearing.

At the habeas corpus hearing on August 17, Judge McGhee was vigorously cross-examined as to the basis for his actions. He testified that he had taken into account the fact that Gerald was on probation. He was asked "under what section of . . . code you found the boy delinquent?"

His answer is set forth in the margin. In substance, he concluded that Gerald came within ARS Sec. 8-201-6(a) which specified that a "delinquent child" includes one "who has violated a law of the state or an ordinance or regulation of a political subdivision thereof." The law which Gerald was found to have violated is ARS Sec. 13-377. This section of the Arizona Criminal Code provides that a person who "in the presence of or hearing of any woman or child . . . uses vulgar, abusive or obscene language, is guilty of a misdemeanor. . . ." The penalty specified in the Criminal Code, which would apply to an adult, is $5 to $50, or imprisonment for not more than two months. The judge also testified that he acted under ARS Sec. 8-201-6(d) which includes in the definition of a "delinquent child" one who, as the judge phrased it, is "habitually involved in immoral matters."

Asked about the basis for his conclusion that Gerald was "habitually involved in immoral matters," the judge testified, somewhat vaguely, that two years earlier on July 2, 1962, a "referral" was made concerning Gerald "where the boy had stolen a baseball glove from another boy and lied to the Police Department about it." The judge said there was "no hearing" and "no accusation" relating to this incident "because of lack of material foundation." But it seems to have remained in his mind as a relevant factor. The judge also testified that Gerald had admitted making other nuisance phone calls in the past which, as the judge recalled the boy's testimony, were "silly calls, or funny calls, or something like that."

The Superior Court dismissed the writ, and appellants sought review in the Arizona Supreme Court. That court staed that it considered appellants assignments of error as urging (1) that the Juvenile Code ARS Sec. 8-201 to Sec. 8-239, is unconstitutional because it does not require that parents and children be apprised of the specific charges, does not require proper notice of a hearing, and does not provide for an appeal; and (2) that the proceedings and order relating to Gerald constituted a denial of due process of law because of the absence of adequate notice of the charge and the hearing; failure to notify appellants of certain constitutional rights including the rights to counsel and to confrontation, and the privilege against self-incrimination; the use of unsworn hearsay testimony; and the failure to make a record of the proceedings. Appellants further asserted that it was error for the Juvenile Court to remove Gerald from the custody of his parents without a showing and finding of their unsuitability, and alleged a miscellany of other errors under state law.

The Supreme Court handed down an elaborate and wide-ranging opinion affirming dismissal of the writ and stating the court's conclusions as to the issues raised by appellants and other aspects of the juvenile process. In their jurisdictional statement and brief in this Court, appellants do not urge upon us all of the points passed upon by the Supreme Court of Arizona. They urge that we hold the Juvenile Code of Arizona invalid on its face or as applied in this case because, contrary to the Due Process Clause of the Fourteenth Amendment, the juvenile is taken from the custody of his parents and committed to a state institution pursuant to proceedings in which the Juvenile Court has virtually unlimited discretion, and in which the following basic rights are denied:

1. Notice of the charges
2. Right to counsel
3. Right to confrontation and cross-examination
4. Privilege against self-incrimination
5. Right to a transcript of the proceedings
6. Right to appellate review

Notice of Charges

Appellants allege that the Arizona Juvenile Code is unconstitutional or alternatively that the proceedings before the Juvenile Court were constitutionally defective because of failure to provide adequate notice of the hearings. No notice was given to Gerald's parents when he was taken into custody on Monday, June 8. On that night, when Mrs. Gault went to the Detention Home, she was orally informed that there would be a hearing the next afternoon and was told the reason why Gerald was in custody. The only written notice Gerald's parents received at any time was a note on plain paper from Officer Flagg delivered on Thursday or Friday, June 11 or 12, to the effect that the judge had set Monday, June 15, "for further hearings on Gerald's delinquency."

A "petition" was filed with the court on June 8 by Officer Flagg reciting only that he was informed and believed that "said minor is a delinquent minor and that it is necessary that some order be made by the Honorable Court for said minor's welfare." The applicable Arizona statute provides for a petition to be filed in Juvenile Court, alleging in general terms that the child is "neglected, dependent, or delinquent." The statute explicitly states that such a general allegation is sufficient, "without alleging the facts." There is no requirement that the petition be served and it was not served upon, given, or shown to Gerald or his parents.

The Supreme Court of Arizona rejected appellants claim that due process was denied because of inadequate notice. It stated that "Mrs. Gault knew the exact nature of the charge against Gerald from the day he was taken to the detention home." The court also pointed out that the Gaults appeared at the two hearings "without objection." The court held that because "the policy of the juvenile law is to hide youthful errors from the full gaze of the public and bury them in the graveyard of the forgotten past," advance notice of the specific charges or basis for taking the juvenile into custody and for the hearing is not necessary. It held that the appropriate rule is that "the infant and his parent or guardian will receive a petition only reciting a conclusion of delinquency. But no later than the initial hearing by the judge, they must be advised of the facts involved in the case. If the charges are denied, they must be given a reasonable period of time to prepare."

We cannot agree with the court's conclusion that adequate notice was given in this case. Notice, to comply with due process requirements, must be given sufficiently in advance of scheduled court proceedings so that reasonable opportunity to prepare will be afforded, and it must "set forth the alleged misconduct with particularity." It is obvious, as we have discussed above, that no purpose of shielding the child from the public stigma of knowledge of his having been taken into custody and scheduled for hearing is served by the procedure approved by the court below. The "initial hearing" in the present case was a hearing on the merits. Notice at that time is not timely; and even if there were a conceivable purpose served by the deferral proposed by the court below, it would have to yield to the requirements that the child and his parents or guardian be notified, in writing, of the specific charge or factual allegations to be considered at the hearing, and that such written notice be given at the earliest practicable time, and in any event sufficiently in advance of the hearing to permit preparation. Due process of law requires notice of the sort we have described—that, notice which would be deemed constitutionally adequate in a civil or criminal proceeding. It does not allow a hearing to be held in which a youth's freedom and his parents' right to his custody are at stake without giving them timely notice, in advance of the hearing, of the specific issues that they must meet. Nor, in the circumstances of this case, can it reasonably be said that the requirements of notice was waived.

Right to Counsel

Appellants charge that the Juvenile Court proceedings were fatally defective because the court did not advise Gerald or his parents of their right to counsel, and proceeded with the hearing, the adjudication of delinquency and the order of commitment in the absence of counsel for the child and his parents or an express waiver of the right thereto. The Supreme Court of Arizona pointed out that "there is disagreement (among the various jurisdictions) as to whether the court must advise the infant that he had a right to counsel." It noted its own decision in *State Dept. of Public Welfare* v. *Barlow* (1965), to the effect "that the parents of an infant in a juvenile proceeding cannot be denied representation by counsel of their choosing." It referred to a provision of the Juvenile Code which it characterized as requiring "that the probation officer shall look after the interests of neglected, delinquent and dependent children," including representing their interest in court.

The court argued that "The parent and the probation officer may be relied upon to protect the infant's interests." Accordingly it rejected the proposition that "due process requires that an infant has a right to counsel." It said that juvenile courts have the discretion, but not the duty, to allow such representation; it referred specifically to the situation in which the Juvenile Court discerns conflict between the child and his parents as an instance in which this discretion might be exercised. We do not agree. Probation officers, in the Arizona scheme, are also arresting officers. They initiate proceedings and file petitions which they verify, as here, alleging the delinquency of the child; and they testify, as here, against the child. And here the probation officer was also superintendent of the Detention Home. The probation officer cannot act as counsel for the child. His role in the adjudicatory hearing, by statute and in fact, is as arresting officer and witness against the child. Nor can the judge represent the child. There is no material difference in this respect between adult and juvenile proceedings of the sort here involved. In adult proceedings, this contention has been foreclosed by decisions of this Court. A proceeding where the issue is whether the child will be found to be "delinquent" and subjected to the loss of his liberty for years is comparable in seriousness to a felony prosecution. The juvenile needs the assistance of counsel to cope with problems to law, to make skilled inquiry into the facts, to insist upon regularity of the proceedings, and to ascertain whether he has a defense and to prepare and submit it. The child "requires the guiding hand of counsel at every step in the proceedings against him." Just as in *Kent* v. *United States,* we indicated our agreement with the United States Court of Appeals for the District of Columbia Circuit that the assistance of counsel is essential for purposes of waiver proceedings, so we hold now that it is equally essential for the determination of delinquency, carrying with it the awesome prospect of incarceration in a state institution until the juvenile reaches the age of 21.

During the last decade, court decisions, experts, and legislatures have demonstrated increasing recognition of this view. In at least one-third of the States, statutes now provide for the right of representation by retained counsel in juvenile delinquency proceedings, notice of the right, or assignment of counsel, or a combination of these. In other States, court rules have similar provisions.

The President's Crime Commission has recently recommended that in order to assure "procedural justice for the child," it is necessary that "Counsel . . . be appointed as a matter of course wherever coercive action is a possibility, without requiring any affirmative choice by child or parent." As stated by the authoritative "Standards for Juvenile and Family Courts," published by the Children's Bureau of the United States Department of Health, Education, and Welfare:

> "As a component part of a fair hearing required by due process guaranteed under the 14th Amendment, notice of the right to counsel should be required at all hearings and counsel provided upon request when the family is financially unable to employ counsel."

This statement was "reviewed" by the National Council of Juvenile Court Judges at its 1965 Convention and they "found no fault" with it. The New York Family Court Act contains the following statement:

> "This act declares that minors have a right to the assistance of counsel of their own choosing or of law guardians in neglect proceedings under Article Three and in proceedings to determine juvenile delinquency and whether a person is in need of supervision under Article Seven. This declaration is based on a finding that counsel is often indispensable to a practical realization of due process of law and may be helpful in making reasoned determinations of fact and proper orders of disposition."

The Act provides that "At the commencement of any hearing" under the delinquency article of the statute, the juvenile and his parent shall be advised of the juvenile's "right to be represented by counsel chosen by him or his parent . . . or by a law guardian assigned by the court. . . ." The California Act (1961) also requires appointment of counsel.

We conclude that the Due Process Clause of the Fourteenth Amendment requires that in respect of proceedings to determine delinquency which may result in commitment to an institution in which the juvenile's freedom is curtailed, the child and his parent must be notified of the child's right to be represented by counsel retained by them, or if they are unable to afford counsel, that counsel will be appointed to represent the child.

At the habeas corpus proceeding, Mrs. Gault testified that she knew that she could have appeared with counsel at the juvenile hearing. This knowledge is not a waiver of the right to counsel which she and her juvenile had, as we have defined it. They had a right expressly to be advised that they might retain counsel and to be confronted with the need for specific consideration of whether they did or did not choose to waive the right. If they were unable to afford to employ counsel, they were entitled in view of the seriousness of the charge and the potential commitment, to appointed counsel, unless they chose waiver. Mrs. Gault's knowledge that she could employ counsel is not an "intentional relinquishment or abandonment" of a fully known right.

Confrontation, Self-Incrimination, Cross-Examination

Appellants urge that the writ of habeas corpus should have been granted because of the denial of the rights of confrontation and cross-examination in the Juvenile Court hearings, and because the privilege against self-incrimination was not observed. The Juvenile Court Judge testified at the habeas corpus hearing that he had proceeded on the basis of Gerald's admissions at the two hearings. Appellants attack this on the ground that the admissions were obtained in disregard of the privilege against self-incrimination. If the confession is disregarded, appellants argue that the delinquency conclusion, since it was fundamentally based on a finding that Gerald had made lewd remarks during the phone call to Mrs. Cook, is fatally defective for failure to accord the rights of confrontation and cross-examination which the Due Process Clause of the Fourteenth Amendment of the Federal Constitution guarantees in state proceedings generally.

Our first question, then, is whether Gerald's admission was improperly obtained and relied on as the basis of decision, in conflict with the Federal Constitution. For this purpose, it is necessary briefly to recall the relevant facts.

Mrs. Cook, the complainant, and the recipient of the alleged telephone call, was not called as a witness. Gerald's mother asked the Juvenile Court Judge why Mrs. Cook was not present and the judge replied that "she didn't have to be present." So far as appears, Mrs. Cook was spoken to only once, by Officer Flagg, and this was by telephone. The judge did not speak with her on any occasion. Gerald had been questioned by the probation officer after having been taken into custody. The exact circumstances of this questioning do not appear but any admissions Gerald may have made at this time do not appear in the record. Gerald was also questioned by the Juvenile Court Judge at each of the two hearings. The judge testified in the habeas corpus proceeding that Gerald admitted making "some of the lawd statements . . . (but not) any of the more serious lewd statements." There was conflict and uncertainty among the witnesses at the habeas corpus proceeding–the Juvenile Court Judge, Mr. and Mrs. Gault, and the probation officer–as to what Gerald did or did not admit.

We shall assume that Gerald made admissions of the sort described by the Juvenile Court Judge, as quoted above. Neither Gerald nor his parents was advised that he did not have to testify or make a statement, or that an incriminating statement might result in his commitment as a "delinquent."

The Arizona Supreme Court rejected appellant's contention that

Gerald had a right to be advised that he need not incriminate himself. It said: "We think the necessary flexibility for individualized treatment will be enhanced by a rule which does not require the judge to advise the infant of a privilege against self-incrimination."

In reviewing this conclusion of Arizona's Supreme Court, we emphasize again that we are here concerned only with proceedings to determine whether a minor is a "delinquent" and which may result in commitment to a state institution. Specifically, the question is whether, in such a proceeding, an admission by the juvenile may be used against him in the absence of clear and unequivocal evidence that the admission was made with knowledge that he was not obliged to speak and would not be penalized for remaining silent. In light of *Miranda* v. *Arizona* (1966), we must also consider whether, if the privilege against self-incrimination is available, it can effectively be waived unless counsel is present or the right to counsel has been waived.

It has long been recognized that the eliciting and use of confessions or admissions or admissions required careful scrutiny. Dean Wigmore states:

> "The grounds of distrust of confessions made in certain situations is, in a rough and indefinite way, judicial experience. There has been no careful collection of statistics of untrue confessions, nor has any great number of instances been even loosely reported . . . but enough have been verified to fortify the conclusion, based on ordinary observation of human conduct, that under certain stresses a person, especially one of defective mentality or peculiar temperament, may falsely acknowledge guilt. This possibility arises wherever the innocent person is placed in such a situation that the untrue acknowledgement of guilt is at the time the more promising of two alternatives between which he is obliged to choose; that is, he chooses any risk that may be in falsely acknowledging guilt, in preference to some worse alternative associated with silence.
>
> The principle, then, upon which a confession may be excluded is that it is, under certain conditions, testimonially untrustworthy. . . . (T)he essential feature is that the principle of exclusion is a testimonial one, analogous to the other principles which exclude narrations as untrustworthy. . . ."

The privilege against self-incrimination is, of course, related to the question of safeguards necessary to assure that admissions or confessions are reasonably trustworthy, that they are not the mere fruits of fear or coercion, but are reliable expressions of the truth. The roots of the privilege are, however, far deeper. They tap the basic stream of religious and political principle because the privilege reflects the limits of the individual's attornment to the state and—in a philosophical sense—insists upon the equality of the individual and the State. In other words, the privilege has a broader and deeper thrust than the rule which prevents the use of confessions that are the product of coercion because coercion is thought to carry with it the danger of unreliability. One of its purposes is to prevent the State, whether by force or by psychological domination, from overcoming the mind and will of the person under investigation and depriving him of the freedom to decide whether to assist the State in securing his conviction.

It would indeed be surprising if the privilege against self-incrimination were available to hardened criminals but not to children. The language of the Fifth Amendment, applicable to the States by operation of the Fourteenth Amendment, is unequivocal and without exception. And the scope of the privilege is comprehensive.

With respect to juveniles, both common observation and expert opinion emphasize that the "distrust of confessions made in certain situations" is imperative in the case of children from an early age through adolescence. In New York, for example, the recently enacted Family Court Act provides that the juvenile and his parents must be advised at the start of the hearing of his right to remain silent. The New York statute also provides that the police must attempt to communicate with the juvenile's parents before questioning him, and that a confession may not be obtained from a child prior to notifying his parents or relatives and releasing the child either to them or to the Family Court.

The authoritative "Standards for Juvenile and Family Courts" concludes that, "Whether or not transfer to the criminal court is a possibility, certain procedures should always be followed. Before being interviewed (by the police), the child and his parents should be informed of his right to have legal counsel present and to refuse to answer questions or be fingerprinted if he should so decide."

Against the application to juveniles of the right to silence, it is argued that juvenile proceedings are "civil" and not "criminal," and therefore the privilege should not apply. It is true that the statement of the privilege in the Fifth Amendment, which is applicable to the States by reason of the Fourteenth Amendment, is that no person "shall be compelled in any criminal case to be a witness against himself." However, it is also clear that the availability of the privilege does not turn upon the type of proceeding in which its protection is invoked, but upon the nature of the statement of admission and the exposure which it invites. The privilege may, for example, be claimed in a civil or administrative proceeding, if the statement is or may be inculpatory.

It would be entirely unrealistic to carve out of the Fifth Amendment all statements by juveniles on the ground that these cannot lead to "criminal" involvement. In the first place, juvenile proceedings to determine "delinquency," which may lead to commitment to a state institution, must be regarded as "criminal" for purposes of the privilege against self-incrimination. To hold otherwise would be to disregard substance because of the feeble enticement of the "civil" label-of-convenience which has been attached to juvenile proceedings. Indeed, in over half of the States, there is not even assurance that the juvenile will be kept in separate institutions, apart from adult "criminals." In those States, juveniles may be placed in or transferred to adult penal institutions after having been found "delinquent" by a juvenile court. For this purpose, at least, commitment is a deprivation of liberty. It is incarceration against one's will, whether it is called "criminal" or "civil." And our Constitution guarantees that no person shall be "compelled" to be a witness against himself when he is threatened with deprivation of his liberty—a command which this Court has broadly applied and generously implemented in accordance with the teaching of the history of the privilege and its great office in mankind's battle for freedom.

In addition, apart from the equivalence for this purpose of exposure to commitment as a juvenile delinquent and exposure to imprisonment as an adult offender, the fact of the matter is that there is little or no assurance in Arizona, as in most if not all of the States, that a juvenile apprehended and interrogated by the police or even by the juvenile court itself, will remain outside of the reach of adult courts as a consequence of the offense for which he has been taken into custody. In Arizona, as in other States, provision is made for juvenile courts to relinquish or waive jurisdiction to the ordinary criminal courts. In the present case, when Gerald Gault was interrogated concerning violation of a section of the Arizona Criminal Code, it could not be certain that the Juvenile Court Judge would decide to "suspend" criminal prosecution in court for adults by proceeding to adjudication in Juvenile Court.

It is also urged, as the Supreme Court of Arizona here asserted, that the juvenile and presumably his parents should not be advised of the juvenile's right to silence because confession is good for the child as the commencement of the assumed therapy of the juvenile court process, and he should be encouraged to assume an attitude of trust and confidence toward the officials of the juvenile process. This proposition has been subjected to widespread challenge on the basis of current reappraisals of the rhetoric and realities of the handling of juvenile offenders.

In fact, evidence is accumulating that confessions by juveniles do not aid in "individualized treatment," as the court put it, and that compelling the child to answer questions, without warning or advice as to his right to remain silent, does not serve this or any other good purpose. In light of the observations of Wheeler and Cottrell, and others, it seems probable that where children are induced to confess by "paternal" urgings on the part of officials and the confession is then followed by disciplinary action, the child's reaction is likely to be hostile and adverse—the child may well feel that he has been led or tricked into confession and that despite his confession, he is being punished.

Further, authoritative opinion has cast formidable doubt upon the reliability and trustworthiness of "confessions" by children. The recent decisions of the New York Court, in the matters of Gregory W., and Gerald S., deals with a dramatic and, it is to be hoped, extreme example. Two 12-year-old Negro boys were taken into custody for the brutal assault and rape of two aged domestics, one of whom died as the result of the attack. One of the boys was schizophrenic and had been locked in the security ward of a mental institution at the time of the attacks. By a process that may best be described as bizarre, his confession was obtained by the police. A psychiatrist testified that the boy would admit "whatever he thought was expected so that he could get out of the immediate situation." The other 12-year-old also "confessed." Both confessions were in specific detail, albeit they contained various inconsistencies. The Court of Appeals, in an opinion by J. Keating, concluded that the confessions were products of the will of the police instead of the boys. The confessions were therefore held involuntary and the order of the Appellate Division affirming the order of the Family Court adjudging the defendants to be juvenile delinquents was reversed.

A similar and equally instructive case has recently been decided by the Supreme Court of New Jersey. In the interests of Carlo and Stasilowicz, supra. The body of a 10-year-old girl was found. She had been strangled. Neighborhood boys who knew the girl were questioned. The two appellants, aged 13 and 15, confessed to the police, with vivid detail and some inconsistencies. At the Juvenile Court hearing, both denied any complicity in the killing. They testified that their confessions were the product of fear and fatigue due to extensive police grilling. The Juvenile Court Judge found that the confessions were voluntary and admissible. On appeal, in an extensive opinion by J. Proctor, the Supreme Court of New Jersey reversed. It rejected the State's argument that the constitutional safeguard of voluntariness governing the use of confessions does not apply in proceedings before the Juvenile Court. It pointed out that under New Jersey court rules, juveniles under the age of 16, accused of commiting a homicide are tried in a proceeding which "has all of the appurtenances of a criminal trial," including participation by the county prosecutor, and requirements that the juvenile be provided with counsel, that a stenographic record be made, etc. It also pointed out that under New Jersey law, the confinement of the boys after reaching age 21 could be extended until they had served the maximum sentence which could have been imposed on an adult for such a homicide, here found to be second degree murder carrying up to 30 years imprisonment. The court concluded that the confessions were involuntary, stressing that the boys, contrary to statute, were placed in the police station and there interrogated; that the parents of both boys were not allowed to see them while they were being interrogated; that inconsistencies appeared among the various statements of the boys and with the objective evidence of the crime; and that there were protracted periods of questioning. The court noted the State's contention that both boys were advised of their constitutional rights before they made their statements, but it held that this should not be given "significant weight in our determination of voluntariness." Accordingly, the judgment of the Juvenile Court was reversed.

We conclude that the constitutional privilege against self-incrimination is applicable in the case of juveniles as it is with respect to adults. We appreciate that special problems may arise with respect to waiver of the privilege by, or on behalf of, children, and that there may well be some differences in technique—but not in principle—depending upon the age of the child and the presence and competence of parents. The participation of counsel will, of course, assist the police, juvenile courts and appellate tribunals, in administering the privilege. If counsel is not present for some permissible reason when an admission is obtained, the greatest care must be taken to assure that the admission was voluntary, in the sense not only that it has not been coerced or suggested, but also that it is not the product of ignorance of rights or of adolescent fantasy, fright or despair.

The "confession" of Gerald Gault was first obtained by Officer Flagg out of the presence of Gerald's parents, without counsel and without advising him of his right to silence, as far as appears. The judgment of the Juvenile Court was stated by the judge to be based on Gerald's admission in court. Neither "admission" was reduced to writing, and, to say the least, the process by which the "admissions" were obtained and received must be characterized as lacking the certainty and order which are required of proceedings of such formidable consequences. Apart from the "admission," there was nothing upon which a judgment or finding might be based. There was no sworn testimony. Mrs. Cook, the complainant, was not present. The Arizona Supreme Court held that "sworn testimony must be required of all witnesses, including police officers, probation officers and others who are part of, or officially related to, the juvenile court structure." We hold that this is not enough. No reason is suggested or appears for a different rule in respect to sworn testimony in juvenile courts than in adult tribunals. Absent a valid confession adequate to support the determination of the Juvenile Court, confrontation and sworn testimony by witnesses available for cross-examination were essential for a finding of "delinquency" and an order committing Gerald to state institution for a maximum of six years.

The recommendations in the Children's Bureau "Standards for Juvenile and Family Courts" are in general accord with out conclusions. They state that testimony should be under oath and that only competent material and relevant evidence under rules applicable to civil cases should be admitted in evidence. The New York Family Court Act contains a similar provision.

As we said in *Kent* v. *United States* (1966), with respect to waiver proceedings, "there is no place in our system of law for reaching a result of such tremendous consequences without ceremony. . . ." We now hold that, absent a valid confession, a determination of delinquency and an order of commitment to a state institution cannot be sustained in the absence of sworn testimony subjected to the opportunity for cross-examination in accordance with our law and constitutional requirements.

Appellate Review and Transcript of Proceedings

Appellants urge that the Arizona statute is unconstitutional under the Due Process Clause because, as construed by its Supreme Court, "there is no right of appeal from aid because the proceedings are confidential and any record must be destroyed after a prescribed period of time. Whether a transcript or other recording is made, it [the Supreme Court of Arizona] held, is a matter for the discretion of the juvenile court.

This Court has not held that a State is required by the Federal Constitution "to provide appellate courts or a right to appellate review at all." In view of the fact that we must reverse the Supreme Court of Arizona's affirmance of the dismissal of the writ of habeas corpus for other reasons, we need not rule on this question in the present case or upon the failure to provide a transcript or recording of the hearings—or, indeed, the failure of the juvenile court judge to state the grounds for his conclusion. As the present case illustrates, the consequences of failure to provide an appeal, to record the proceedings, or to make findings or the state the grounds for the juvenile's court's conclusion may be to throw a burden upon the machinery for habeas corpus, to saddle the reviewing process with the burden of attempting to reconstruct a record, and to impose upon the juvenile judge the unseemly duty of testifying under cross-examination as to the events that transpired in the hearings before him.

For the reasons stated, the judgment of the Supreme Court of Arizona is reversed and the case remanded for further proceedings not inconsistent with this opinion. *It is so ordered.*

GIDEON V. *WAINWRIGHT*

Petitioner was charged in a Florida state court with having broken and entered a poolroom with intent to commit a misdemeanor. This offense is a felony under Florida law. Appearing in court without funds and without a lawyer, petitioner asked the court to appoint counsel for him, whereupon the following colloquy took place:

"The Court: Mr. Gideon, I am sorry, but I cannot appoint Counsel to represent you in this case. Under the laws of the State of Florida, the only time the Court can appoint Counsel to represent a Defendant is when that person is charged with a capital offense. I am sorry, but I will have to deny your request to appoint Counsel to defend you in this case."

"Defendant: The United States Supreme Court says I am entitled to be represented by Counsel." Put to trial before a jury, Gideon conducted his defense about as well as could be expected from a layman. The jury returned a verdict of guilty, and the petitioner was sentenced to serve five years in the state prison. Later, petitioner filed in the Florida Supreme Court, his habeas corpus petition . . . on the ground that the trial court's refusal to appoint counsel for him denied his rights "guaranteed by the Constitution and the Bill of Rights by the United States Government." Treating the petition for habeas corpus as properly before it, the State Supreme Court denied all relief. Since 1942, when *Betts* v. *Brady* was decided by a divided Court, the problem of a defendant's federal constitutional right to counsel in a state court has been a continuing source of controversy and litigation in both State and Federal courts. To give this problem another review here, we granted certiorari. . . . Since Gideon was proceeding *in forma pauperis,* we appointed counsel to represent him and requested both sides to discuss in their briefs and oral arguments, the following:

"Should this Court's holding in *Betts* v. *Brady* be reconsidered?" The facts upon which Betts claimed that he had been unconstitutionally denied the right to have counsel appointed to assist him are strikingly like the facts upon which Gideon here bases his federal constitutional claim. Like Gideon, Betts sought release by habeas corpus, alleging that he had been denied the right to assistance of counsel in violation of the Fourteenth Amendment. Betts was denied any relief, and on review, this Court affirmed. It was held that a refusal to appoint counsel for an indigent defendant charged with a felony did not necessarily violate the Due Process Clause of the Fourteenth Amendment, which for reasons given the Court deemed to be the only applicable federal constitutional provision. The Court said:

". . . asserted denial [of due process] is to be tested by an appraisal of the totality of facts in a given case. That which may, in one setting, constitute a denial of fundamental fairness, shocking to the universal sense of justice, may, in other circumstances, and in the light of other considerations, fall short of such denial."

Treating due process as "a concept less rigid and more fluid than those envisaged in other specific and particular provisions of the Bill of Rights," the Court held that refusal to appoint counsel under the particular facts and circumstances in the Betts case was not so "offensive to the common and fundamental ideas of fairness" as to amount to a denial of due process. Since the facts and circumstances of the two cases are so nearly indistinguishable, we think *Betts v. Brady* holding if left standing would require us to reject Gideon's claim that the Constitution guarantees him the assistance of counsel. Upon full reconsideration we conclude that *Betts v. Brady* should be overruled.

The Sixth Amendment provides, "In all criminal prosecutions, the accused shall enjoy the right . . . to have the Assistance of Counsel for his defense." We have construed this to mean that in federal courts counsel must be provided for defendants unable to employ counsel unless the right is competently and intelligently waived. Betts argued that this right is extended to indigent defendants in state courts by the Fourteenth Amendment. In response the Court stated that, while the Sixth Amendment laid down "no rule for the conduct of the states, the question recurs whether the constraint laid by the amendment upon the national courts expresses a rule so fundamental and essential to a fair trial, and so, to due process of law, that it is made obligatory upon the states by the Fourteenth Amendment." In order to decide whether the Sixth Amendment's guarantee of counsel is of this fundamental nature, the Court in Betts set out and considered "[r]elevant data on the subject . . . afforded by constitutional and statutory provisions subsisting in the colonies and the states prior to the inclusion of the Bill of Rights in the national Constitution, and in the constitutional, legislative, and judicial history of the states to the present date." On the basis of this historical data the Court concluded that "appointment of counsel is not a fundamental right, essential to a fair trial."

We think the Court in Betts had ample precedent for acknowledging that those guarantees of the Bill of Rights which are fundamental safeguards of liberty immune from federal abridgement are equally protected against state invasion by the Due Process Clause of the Fourteenth Amendment.

We accept *Betts* v. *Brady's* assumption, based as it was on our prior cases, that a provision of the Bill of Rights which is "fundamental and essential to a fair trial" is made obligatory upon the States by the Fourteenth Amendment. We think the Court in Betts was wrong, however, in concluding that the Sixth Amendment's guarantee of counsel is not one of these fundamental rights. Ten years before *Betts* v. *Brady,* this Court, after full consideration of all the historical data examined in Betts, had unequivocally declared that "the right to the aid of counsel is of this fundamental character." *Powell* v. *Alabama.* While the Court at the close of its Powell opinion did by its language, as this Court frequently does, limit its holding to the particular facts and circumstances of that case, its conclusions about the fundamental nature of the right to counsel are unmistakable.

The fact is that in deciding as it did—that "appointment of counsel is not a fundamental right, essential to a fair trial"—the Court in *Betts* v. *Brady* made an abrupt break with its own well-considered precedents. In returning to these old precedents, sounder we believe than the new, we but restore constitutional principles established to achieve a fair system of justice. Not only these precedents but also reason and reflection require us to recognize that in our adversary system of criminal justice, any person hailed into court, who is too poor to hire a lawyer, cannot be assured a fair trial unless counsel is provided for him. This seems to us to be an obvious truth. Governments, both state and federal, quite properly spend vast sums of money to establish machinery to try defendants accused of crime. Lawyers to prosecute are everywhere deemed essential to protect the public's interest in an orderly society. Similarly, there are few defendants charged with crime, few indeed, who fail to hire the best lawyers they can get to prepare and present their defense. That government hires lawyers to prosecute and defendants who have the money hire lawyers to defend are the strongest indications of the widespread belief that lawyers in criminal courts are necessities, not luxuries. The right of one charged with crime to counsel may not be deemed fundamental and essential to fair trials in some countries, but it is in ours. From the very beginning, our state and national constitutions and laws have laid great emphasis on procedural and substantive safeguards designed to assure fair trials before impartial tribunals in which every defendant stands equal before the law. This noble idea cannot be realized if the poor man charged with crime has to face his accusers without a lawyer to assist him.

The Court in *Betts* v. *Brady* departed from the sound wisdom upon which the Court's holding in *Powell* v. *Alabama* rested. Florida, supported by two other States, has asked that *Betts* v. *Brady* be left intact. Twenty-two states, as friends of the Court, argue that Betts was "an anachronism when handed down" and that it should now be overruled. We agree.

The judgment is *reversed* and the cause is remanded to the Supreme Court of Florida for further action not inconsistent with this opinion. It is so ordered.

MAPP V. *OHIO*

Appellant stands convicted of knowingly having had in her possession and under her control certain lewd and lascivious books, pictures, and photographs in violation of . . . Ohio's Revised Code. The Supreme Court of Ohio found that her conviction was valid though "based primarily on the introduction of evidence of lewd and lascivious books and pictures unlawfully seized during an unlawful search of defendant's home. . . ."

. . . May 23, 1957 . . . police officers arrived at appellant's residence . . . pursuant to information that "a person . . . hiding in the home . . . was wanted for questioning in connection with a recent bombing, and that there was a large amount of policy paraphernalia being hidden in the home." . . . Officers knocked on the door and demanded entrance but appellant, after telephoning her attorney, refused to admit them without a search warrant.

. . . The officers again sought entrance some three hours later when four or more additional officers arrived on the scene. . . . Miss Mapp did not come to the door immediately. . . . One of the several doors . . . was forcibly opened and the policemen gained admittance. Meanwhile, Miss Mapp's attorney arrived, but the officers, having secured their own entry . . . would permit him neither to see Miss Mapp nor to enter the house. Miss Mapp . . . demanded to see the search warrant. A paper, claiming to be a warrant, was held up by one of the officers. She grabbed at the "warrant" and placed it in her bosom. A struggle ensued in which the officers recovered the piece of paper and as a result of which they handcuffed appellant because she had been "belligerent" in resisting their official rescue of the "warrant" from her person. . . . Appellant, in hand-cuffs, was then forcibly taken upstairs to her bedroom where the officers searched a dresser, a chest of drawers, a closet, and some suit cases . . . and some personal papers belonging to the appellant. The search spread to the rest of the second floor . . . The basement of the building, and a trunk therein were also searched. The obscene materials, for possession of which she was ultimately convicted, were discovered in the course of that widespread search.

> . . . "There is, in the record, considerable doubt as to whether there ever was any warrant for the search of the defendant's home." The Ohio Supreme Court . . . found determinative the fact that the evidence had not been taken "from the defendant's person by the use of brutal or offensive physical force against defendant."

The State [of Ohio] says that even if the search were made without authority, or otherwise unreasonably, it is not prevented from using the unconstitutionally seized evidence at trial, citing *Wolfe* v. *Colorado* . . . on this appeal . . . it is urged once again that we review that holding.

Seventy-five years ago, in *Boyd* v. *United States* (1886), considering the Fourth and Fifth Amendments as running "almost into each other" on the facts before it, this Court held that the doctrines of those Amendments "apply to all invasions on the part of the government and its employees of the sanctity of a man's home and the privacies of life. . . . It is not the breaking of his doors and the rummaging of his drawers, that constitutes the essence of the offense; but it is the invasion of his indefeasible right of personal security, personal liberty and private property. . . ."

. . . This Court, in the year 1914 [in *Weeks* v. *United States*], "for the first time" held that "in a federal prosecution, the Fourth Amendment barred the use of evidence secured through illegal search and seizure." This Court has ever since required of federal law officers a strict adherence to that command which the Court has held to be clear, specific, and constitutionally required. . . . It meant, quite simply, that "conviction by means of unlawful seizures and enforced convictions . . . should find no sanction in the judgments of the courts. . . ." In *Olmstead* v. *United States,* in unmistakable language [the Court] . . . related the *Weeks* Rule:

> "The striking out of the *Weeks* case and those which followed it was a sweeping declaration that the Fourth Amendment, although not referring to or limiting the use of evidence in courts, really forbade the introduction if obtained by officers through a violation of the Amendment."

In McNabb v. United States

"(A) Conviction in a federal court, the foundation of which is evidence obtained in disregard of liberties deemed fundamental by the Constitution cannot stand. [*Boyd* v. *United States*] . . . [*Weeks* v. *United*

States] . . . This Court has, on Constitutional grounds, set aside convictions, both in the federal and state courts, which were based upon confessions 'secured by protracted and repeated questionings of ignorant and untutored persons, and those in whose minds the power of the officers was greatly magnified' . . . or 'who have been unlawfully held incommunicado without advice of friends or counsel'. . . ."

Moreover, our holding is not only the logical dictate of prior cases, but it also makes very good sense. . . . Presently a federal prosecutor may make no use of evidence illegally seized, but a State's attorney across the street may, although he supposedly is operating under the enforcible prohibitions of the same Amendment. Thus the State, by admitting evidence unlawfully seized, serves to encourage disobedience to the Federal Constitution which it is bound to uphold. Moreover, as was said in Elkins, ". . . healthy Federalism depends upon the avoidance of needless conflict between State and Federal courts."

The ignoble short-cut to conviction left open to the State tends to destroy the entire system of constitutional restraints upon which the liberties of the people rest. Having once recognized that the right to privacy embodied in the Fourth Amendment is enforcible against the States, . . . we can no longer permit that right to remain an empty promise. Because it is enforcible in the same manner and to like effect as other basic rights secured by the Due Process Clause, we can no longer permit it to be revokable at the whim of any police officer, who in the name of law enforcement itself, chooses to suspend its enjoyment. Our decision, founded on reason and truth, gives to the individual no more than that which the Constitution guarantees him, to the police officer no less than that to which honest law enforcement is entitled, and, to the courts that judicial integrity so necessary in the true administration of justice. . . .

Reversed and remanded.

MIRANDA V. *ARIZONA*

The Miranda case [also: *Vignera* v. *New York, Westover* v. *United States,* and *Stewart* v. *California*] deals with the admissibility of statements obtained from an individual who is subjected to custodial police interrogation, and the necessity for procedures which assure that the individual is accorded his privilege against self-incrimination. Without specific concentration on the facts of this case, the Supreme Court of the United States, in an opinion by WARREN, Ch. J., expressing the views of five members of the Court, laid down the governing principles, the most important of which is that, as a constitutional prerequisite to the admissibility of such statements, the suspect must, *in the absence of a clear, intelligent waiver of the constitutional rights involved, be warned prior to questioning that he has a right to remain silent, that any statement he does make may be used as evidence against him, and that he has a right to the presence of an attorney, either retained or appointed.*

On March 13, 1963, petitioner, Ernesto Miranda, was arrested at his home and taken in custody to a Phoenix police station. He was there identified by the complaining witness. The police then took him to "Interrogation Room No. 2" of the detective bureau. There he was questioned by two police officers. The officers admitted at trial that Miranda was not advised that he had a right to have an attorney present. Two hours later, the officers emerged from the interrogation room with a written confession signed by Miranda. At the top of the statement was a typed paragraph stating that the confession was made voluntarily, without threats or promises of immunity and "with full knowledge of my legal rights, understanding any statement I make may be used against me."

At his trial before a jury, the written confession was admitted into evidence over the objection of defense counsel, and the officers testified to the prior oral confession made by Miranda during the interrogation. Miranda was found guilty of kidnapping and rape. He was sentenced to 20 to 30 years' imprisonment on each count, the sentences to run concurrently.

On appeal, the Supreme Court of Arizona held that Miranda's constitutional rights were not violated in obtaining the confession and affirmed the conviction. In reaching its decision, the court emphasized heavily the fact that Miranda did not specifically request counsel.

The cases before us raise questions which go to the roots of our concepts of American criminal jurisprudence: the restraints society must observe consistent with the Federal Constitution in prosecuting individuals for crime. More specifically, we deal with the admissibility of statements obtained from an individual who is subjected to custodial police interrogation and the necessity for procedures which assure that the individual is accorded his privilege under the Fifth Amendment to the Constitution not to be compelled to incriminate himself.

We dealt with certain phases of this problem recently in *Escobedo* v. *Illinois.* There . . . law enforcement officials took the defendant into custody and interrogated him in a police station for the purpose of obtaining a confession. The police did not effectively advise him of his right to remain silent or of his right to consult with his attorney. Rather, they confronted him with an alleged accomplice who accused him of having perpetrated a murder. When the defendant denied the accusation and said "I didn't shoot Manuel, you did it," they handcuffed him and took him to an interrogation room. There, while handcuffed and standing, he was questioned for four hours until he confessed. During this interrogation, the police denied his request to speak to his attorney, and they prevented his retained attorney, who had come to the police station, from consulting with him. At his trial, the State, over his objection, introduced the confession against him. We held that the statements thus made were constitutionally inadmissible.

This case has been the subject of judicial interpretation and spirited legal debate since it was decided two years ago. Both state and federal courts, in assessing its implications, have arrived at varying conclusions. A wealth of scholarly material has been written tracing its ramifications and underpinnings.

We start here, as we did in Escobedo, with the premise that our holding is not an innovation in our jurisprudence, but is an application of principles long recognized and applied in other settings. We have undertaken a thorough re-examination of the Escobedo decision and the principles it announced, and we reaffirm it. That case was but an explication of basic rights that are enshrined in our Constitution—that "No person . . . shall be compelled in any criminal case to be a witness against himself," and that "the accused shall . . . have the Assistance of Counsel"—rights which were put in jeopardy in that case through official overbearing. These precious rights were fixed in our Constitution only after centuries of persecution and struggle.

". . . While the admissions or confessions of the prisoner, when voluntarily and freely made, have always ranked high in the scale of incriminating evidence, if an accused person be asked to explain his apparent connection with a crime under investigation, the case with which the questions put to him may assume an inquisitorial character, the temptation to press the witness unduly, to browbeat him if he be timid or reluctant, to push him into a corner, and to entrap him into fatal contradictions, which is so painfully evident in many of the earlier state trials, notably in those of Sir Nicholas Throckmorton, and Udal, the Puritan minister, made the system so odious as to give rise to a demand for its total abolition. The change in the English criminal procedure in that particular seems to be founded upon no statute and no judicial opinion, but upon a general and silent acquiescence of the courts in a popular demand. But, however adopted, it has become firmly embedded in English, as well as in American jurisprudence. So deeply did the iniquities of the ancient system impress themselves upon the minds of the American colonists that the States, with one accord, made a denial of the right to question an accused person a part of their fundamental law, so that a maxim, which in England was a mere rule of evidence, became clothed in this country with the impregnability of a constitutional enactment."

In stating the obligation of the judiciary to apply these constitutional rights, this Court declared in *Weems* v. *United States,* (1910): ". . . our contemplation cannot be only of what has been but of what may be. Under any other rule a constitution would indeed be as easy of application as it would be deficient in efficacy and power. Its general principles would have little value and be converted by precedent into impotent and lifeless formulas. Rights declared in words might be lost in reality. And this has been recognized. The meaning and vitality of the Constitution have developed against narrow and restrictive construction."

This was the spirit in which we delineated, in meaningful language the manner in which the constitutional rights of the individual could be enforced against overzealous police practices. It was necessary in Escobedo, as here, to insure that what was proclaimed in the Constitution had not become but a "form of words," *Silverthorne Lumber Co.* v. *United States,* (1920), in the hands of government officials. And it is in this spirit, consistent with our role as judges, that we adhere to the principles of Escobedo today.

. . . the prosecution may not use statements, whether exculpatory or inculpatory, stemming from custodial interrogation of the defendant unless it demonstrates the use of procedural safeguards effective to secure the privilege against self-incrimination. By custodial interrogation, we mean questioning initiated by law enforcement officers after a person has been taken into custody or otherwise deprived of his freedom of action in any significant way. As for the procedural safeguards to be employed, unless other fully effective means are devised to inform accused persons of their rights of silence and to assure a continuous opportunity to exercise it, the following measures are required. Prior to any questioning, the person must be warned that he has a right to remain silent, that any statement he does make may be used as evidence against him, and that he has a right to the presence of an attorney, either retained or appointed. The defendant may waive effectuation of these rights, provided the waiver is made voluntarily, knowingly and intelligently. If, however, he indicates in any manner and at any stage of the process that he wishes to consult with an attorney before speaking there can be no questioning. Likewise, if the individual is alone and indicates in any manner that he does not wish to be interrogated, the police may not question him. The mere fact that he may have answered some questions or volunteered some statements on his own does not deprive him of the right to refrain from answering any further inquiries until he has consulted with an attorney and thereafter consents to be questioned.

The constitutional issue we decide in each of these cases is the admissibility of statements obtained from a defendant questioned while in custody or otherwise deprived of his freedom of action in any significant way. In each, the defendant was questioned by police officers, detectives, or a prosecuting attorney in a room in which he was cut off from the outside world. In none of these cases was the defendant given a full and effective warning of his rights at the outset of the interrogation process. In all the cases, the questioning elicited oral admissions, and in three of them, signed statements as well which were admitted at their trials. They all thus share salient features—incommunicado interrogation of individuals in a police-dominated atmosphere, resulting in self-incriminating statements without full warnings of constitutional rights.

An understanding of the nature and setting of this in-custody interrogation is essential to our decisions today. The difficulty in depicting what transpires at such interrogations stems from the fact that in this country they have largely taken place incommunicado. From extensive factual studies undertaken in the early 1930s, including the famous Wickersham Report to Congress by a Presidential Commission, it is clear that police violence and the "third degree" flourished at that time. In a series of cases decided by this Court long after these studies, the police resorted to physical brutality—beating, hanging, whipping—and to sustained and protracted questioning incommunicado in order to extort confessions. The Commission on Civil Rights in 1961 found much evidence to indicate that "some policemen still resort to physical force to obtain confessions." The use of physical brutality and violence is not, unfortunately, relegated to the past or to any part of the country. Only recently in Kings County, New York, the police brutally beat, kicked and placed lighted cigarette butts on the back of a potential witness under interrogation for the purpose of securing a statement incriminating a third party. *People* v. *Portelli,* (1965).

The examples given above are undoubtedly the exception now, but they are sufficiently widespread to be the object of concern. Unless a proper limitation upon custodial interrogation is achieved—such as these decisions will advance—there can be no assurance that practices of this nature will be eradicated in the foreseeable future. The conclusion of the Wickersham Commission Report, made over 30 years ago, is still pertinent:

"To the contention that the third degree is necessary to get the facts, the reporters aptly reply in the language of the present Lord Chancellor of England (Lord Sankey): "It is not admissible to do a great right by doing a little wrong. . . . It is not sufficient to do justice by obtaining a proper result by irregular or improper means." Not only does the use of the third degree involve a flagrant violation of law by the officers of the law, but it involves also the dangers of false confessions, and it tends to make police and prosecutors less zealous in the search for objective evidence. As the New York prosecutor quoted in the report said, 'It is a short cut and makes the police lazy and unenterprising.' Or, as another official quoted remarked: 'If you use your fists, you are not so likely to use your wits.' We agree with the conclusion expressed in the report, that:

> "The third degree brutalizes the police, hardens the prisoner against society, and lowers the esteem in which the administration of justice is held by the public."

Again we stress that the modern practice of in-custody interrogation is psychologically rather than physically oriented. As we have stated before, "Since *Chambers* v. *Florida,* this Court has recognized that coercion can be mental as well as physical, and that the blood of the accused is not the only hallmark of an unconstitutional inquisition." *Blackburn* v. *Alabama,* (1960). Interrogation still takes place in privacy. Privacy results in secrecy and this in turn results in a gap in our knowledge as to what in fact goes on in the interrogation rooms. A valuoble source of information about present police practices, however, may be found in various police manuals and texts which document procedures employed with success in the past, and which recommend various other effective tactics. These texts are used by law enforcement agencies themselves as guides. It should be noted that these texts professedly present the most enlightened and effective means presently used to obtain statements through custodial interrogation. By considering these texts and other data, it is possible to describe procedures observed and noted around the country.

The officers are told by the manuals that the "principal psychological factor contributing to a successful interrogation is *privacy*—being alone with the person under interrogation." The efficacy of this tactic has been explained as follows:

> "If at all practicable, the interrogation should take place in the investigator's office or at least in a room of his own choice. The subject should be deprived of every psychological advantage. In his own home he may be confident, indignant, or recalcitrant. He is more keenly aware of his rights and more reluctant to tell of his indiscretions or criminal behavior within the walls of his home. Moreover his family and other friends are nearby, their presence lending moral support. In his own office, the investigator possesses all the advantages. The atmosphere suggests the invincibility of the forces of the law."

To highlight the isolation and unfamiliar surroundings, the manuals instruct the police to display an air of confidence in the suspect's guilt and from outward appearance to maintain only an interest in confirming certain details. The guilt of the subject is to be posited as a fact. The interrogator should direct his comments toward the reasons why the subject committed the act, rather than court failure by asking the subject whether he did it. Like other men, perhaps the subject has had a bad family life, had an unhappy childhood, had too much to drink, had an unrequited desire for women. The officers are instructed to minimize the moral seriousness of the offense, to cast blame on the victim or on society. These tactics are designed to put the subject in a psychological state where his story is but an elaboration of what the police purport to know already—that he is guilty. Explanations to the contrary are dismissed and discouraged.

The texts thus stress that the major qualities an interrogator should possess are patience and perseverance. One writer describes the efficacy of these characteristics in this manner:

> "In the preceding paragraphs emphasis has been placed on kindness and stratagems. The investigator will, however, encounter many situations where the sheer weight of his personality will be the deciding factor. Where emotional appeals and tricks are employed to no avail, he must rely on an oppressive atmosphere of dogged persistence. He must interrogate steadily and without relent, leaving the subject no prospect of surcease. He must dominate his subject and overwhelm him with his inexorable will to obtain the truth. He should interrogate for a spell of several hours, pausing only for the subject's necessities in acknowledgment of the need to avoid a charge of duress that can be technically substantiated. In a serious case, the interrogation may continue for days, with the required intervals for food and sleep, but with no respite from the atmosphere of domination. It is possible in this way to induce the subject to talk without resorting to duress or coercion. The method should be used only when the guilt of the subject appears highly probable."

The manuals suggest that the suspect be offered legal excuses for his actions in order to obtain an initial admission of guilt. Where there is a suspected revenge-killing, for example, the interrogator may say:

> "Joe, you probably didn't go out looking for this fellow with the purpose of shooting him. My guess is, however, that you expected something from him and that's why you carried a gun—for your own protection. You knew him for what he was, no good. Then when you met him he probably started using foul, abusive language and he gave some indication that he was about to pull a gun on you, and that's when you had to act to save your own life. That's about it, isn't it, Joe?"

Having then obtained the admission of shooting, the interrogator is advised to refer to circumstantial evidence which negates the self-defense explanation. This should enable him to secure the entire story. One text notes that "Even if he fails to do so, the inconsistency between the subject's original denial of the shooting and his present admission of at least doing the shooting will serve to deprive him of a self-defense 'out' at the time of trial.

When the techniques described above prove unavailing, the texts recommend they be alternated with a show of some hostility. One ploy often used has been termed the "friendly-unfriendly" or the "Mutt and Jeff" act:

> ". . . In this technique, two agents are employed. Mutt, the relentless investigator, who knows the subject is guilty and is not going to waste any time. He's sent a dozen men away for this crime and he's going to send the subject away for the full term. Jeff, on the other hand, is obviously a kindhearted man. He has a family himself. He has a brother who was involved in a little scrape like this. He disapproves of Mutt and his tactics and will arrange to get him off the case if the subject will cooperate. He can't hold Mutt off for very long. The subject would be wise to make a quick decision. The technique is applied by having both investigators present while Mutt acts out his role. Jeff may stand by quietly and demur at some of Mutt's tactics. When Jeff makes his plea for cooperation, Mutt is not present in the room."

The interrogators sometimes are instructed to induce a confession out of trickery. The technique here is quite effective in crimes which require identification or which run in series. In the identification situation, the interrogator may take a break in his questioning to place the subject among a group of men in a line-up. "The witness or complainant (previously coached, if necessary) studies the line-up and confidently points out the subject as the guilty party." Then the questioning resumes "as though there were now no doubt about the guilt of the subject." A variation on this technique is called the "reverse line-up:"

> "The accused is placed in a line-up, but this time he is identified by several fictitious witnesses or victims who associated him with different offenses. It is expected that the subject will become desperate and confess to the offense under investigation in order to escape from the false accusations."

The manuals also contain instructions for police on how to handle the individual who refuses to discuss the matter entirely, or who asks for an attorney or relatives. The examiner is to concede him the right to remain silent. "This usually has a very undermining effect. First of all, he is disappointed in his expectation of an unfavorable reaction on the part of the interrogator. Secondly, a concession of this right to remain silent impresses the subject with the apparent fairness of his interrogator."

After this psychological conditioning, however, the officer is told to point out the incriminating significance of the suspect's refusal to talk:

> "Joe, you have a right to remain silent. That's your privilege and I'm the last person in the world who'll try to take it away from you. If that's the way you want to leave this, O.K. But let me ask you this. Suppose you were in my shoes and I were in yours and you called me in to ask me about this and I told you, 'I don't want to answer any of your questions.' You'd think I had something to hide, and you'd probably be right in thinking that. That's exactly what I'll have to think about you, and so will everybody else. So let's sit here and talk this whole thing over."

Few will persist in their initial refusal to talk, it is said, if this monologue is employed correctly.

In the event that the subject wishes to speak to a relative or an attorney, the following advice is tendered:

> "[T]he interrogator should respond by suggesting that the subject first tell the truth to the inerrogator himself rather than get anyone else involved in the matter. If the request is for an attorney, the interrogator may suggest that the subject save himself or his family the expense of any such professional service, particularly if he is innocent of the offense under investigation. The interrogator may also add, 'Joe, I'm only looking for the truth, and if you're telling the truth, that's it. You can handle this by yourself.'"

From these representative samples of interrogation techniques, the setting prescribed by the manuals and observed in practice becomes clear. In essence, it is this: To be alone with the subject is essential to prevent distraction and to deprive him of any outside support. The aura of confidence in his guilt undermines his will to resist. He merely confirms the preconceived story the police seek to have him describe. Patience and persistence, at times relentless questioning, are employed. To obtain a confession, the interrogator must "patiently maneuver himself or his quarry into a position from which the desired objective may be attained." When normal procedures fail to produce the needed result, the police may resort to deceptive stratagems such as giving false legal advice. It is important to keep the subject off balance, for example, by trading on his insecurity about himself or his surroundings. The police then persuade, trick, or cajole him out of exercising his constitutional rights.

Even without employing brutality, the "third degree" or the specific stratagems described above, the very fact of custodial interrogation exacts a heavy toll on the individual liberty and trades on the weakness of individuals. This fact may be illustrated simply by referring to three confession cases decided by this Court in the Term immediately preceding our Escobedo decision. In *Townsend* v. *Sain,* (1963), the defendant was a 19-year-old heroin addict, described as a "near mental defective." The defendant in *Lynumn* v. *Illinois,* (1963), was a woman who confessed to the arresting officer after being importuned to "cooperate" in order to prevent her children from being taken by relief authorities. This Court as in those cases reversed the conviction of a defendant in *Haynes* v. *Washington,* (1963), whose persistent request during his interrogation was to phone his wife or attorney. In other settings, these individuals might have exercised their constitutional rights. In the incommunicado police-dominated atmosphere, they succumbed.

In the cases before us today [*Miranda, Vignero, Westover,* and *Stewart*] given this background, we concern ourselves primarily with this interrogation atmosphere and the evils it can bring.

. . . In these cases [*Miranda,* et al.], we might not find the defendants' statements to have been involuntary in traditional terms. Our concern for adequate safeguards to protect precious Fifth Amendment rights is, of course, not lessened in the slightest. In each of the cases, the defendant was thrust into an unfamiliar atmosphere and run through menacing police interrogation procedures. The potentiality for compulsion is forcefully apparent, for example, in *Miranda,* where the indigent Mexican defendant was a seriously disturbed individual with pronounced sexual fantasies, and in *Stewart,* in which the defendant was an indigent Los Angeles Negro who had dropped out of school in the sixth grade. To be sure, the records do not evince overt physical coercion or patent psychological ploys. The fact remains that in none of these cases did the officers undertake to afford appropriate safeguards at the outset of the interrogation to insure that the statements were truly the product of free choice.

It is obvious that such an interrogation environment is created for no purpose other than to subjugate the individual to the will of his examiner. This atmosphere carries its own badge of intimidation. To be sure, this is not physical intimidation, but it is equally destructive of human dignity. The current practice of incommunicado interrogation is at odds with one of our Nation's most cherished principles—that the individual may not be compelled to incriminate himself. Unless adequate protective devices are employed to dispel the compulsion inherent in custodial surroundings, no statement obtained from the defendant can truly be the product of his free choice.

From the foregoing, we can readily perceive an intimate connection between the privilege against self-incrimination and police custodial questioning.

We reverse. From the testimony of the officers and by the admission of respondent, it is clear that Miranda was not in any way apprised of his right to consult with an attorney and to have one present during the interrogation, or was his right not to be compelled to incriminate himself effectively protected in any other manner. Without these warnings the statements were inadmissible. The mere fact that he signed a statement which contained a typed-in clause stating that he had "full knowledge" of his "legal rights" does not approach the knowing and intelligent waiver required to relinquish constitutional rights. . . .

McKEIVER AND TERRY V. *PENNSYLVANIA* *IN RE BARARA AND* *BURRUS,* ET AL., PETITIONERS

These cases raised the issue whether the due process clause of the Fourteenth Amendment affords the right to trial by jury in state juvenile delinquency proceedings. In *McKeiver and Terry,* it involved separate proceedings against two boys, 15 and 16 years old, respectively, in the Juvenile Branch of the Court of Common Pleas of Philadelphia County, Pennsylvania, charging as acts of juvenile delinquency conduct by the juvenile in one case which constituted felonies under Pennsylvania law, and conduct amounting to misdemeanors in the second case. The trial judge in each case denied a request for jury trial, and adjudged the juvenile as delinquent on the respective charges, one of the juveniles being put on probation and the other being committed to an institution. The Superior Court of Pennsylvania affirmed both orders without opinion. Consolidating the appeals in both cases, the Supreme Court of Pennsylvania affirmed, holding that there was no constitutional right to a jury trial in the juvenile court. In Burrus, a group of children, ranging in age from 11 to 15 years, were charged by juvenile petitions in the District Court, Hyde County, North Carolina, with various acts amounting to misdemeanors under state law, which acts arose out of a series of demonstrations protesting school assignments and a school consolidation plan. Consolidating the several cases into groups for hearing, the trial judge excluded the general public over counsel's objection in all but two of the cases; denied a request for jury trial in each case; and entered a custody commitment order in each case, declaring the juvenile a delinquent and placing each juvenile on probation after suspending the commitments. The cases were consolidated into two groups for appeal, and the Court of Appeals of North Carolina affirmed in each instance. Consolidating the cases into a single appeal, the Supreme Court of North Carolina deleted that portion of each order relating to the commitment, but otherwise affirmed, holding that a juvenile was not constitutionally entitled to a jury in delinquency proceedings.

On appeal in the Pennsylvania case, and on certiorari in the North

Carolina proceedings, the United States Supreme Court affirmed in each instance. A majority of the court, although not agreeing upon an opinion, agreed that the due process clause of the Fourteenth Amendment did not assure the right to jury trial in the adjudicative phase of a state juvenile court delinquency proceeding.

WINSHIP V. *NEW YORK*

Mr. Justice Brennan delivered the opinion of the Court.

Constitutional questions decided by this Court concerning the juvenile process have centered on the adjudicatory stage at "which a determination is made as to whether a juvenile is a 'delinquent' as a result of alleged misconduct on his part, with the consequence that he may be committed to a state institution." *In re Gault,* 387 U.S. 1, 13 (1967). Gault decided that, although the Fourteenth Amendment does not require that the hearing at this stage conform with all the requirements of a criminal trial or even of the usual administrative proceeding, the Due Process Clause does require application during the adjudicatory hearing of "the essentials of due process and fair treatment." Id., at 30. This case presents the single, narrow question whether proof beyond reasonable doubt is among the "essentials of due process and fair treatment" required during the adjudicatory stage when a juvenile is charged with an act which would constitute a crime if committed by an adult.

Section 712 of the New York Family Court Act defines a juvenile delinquent as "a person over seven and less than sixteen years of age who does any act which, if done by an adult, would constitute a crime." During a 1967 adjudicatory hearing, conducted pursuant to 742 of the Act, a judge in New York Family Court found that appellant, then a 12-year-old boy, had entered a locker and stolen $112 from a woman's pocket-book. The petition which charged appellant with delinquency alleged that his act, "if done by an adult, would constitute the crime or crimes of Larceny." The judge acknowledged that the proof might not establish guilt beyond a reasonable doubt, but rejected appellant's contention that such proof was required by the Fourteenth Amendment. The judge relied instead on 744 (b) of the New York Family Court Act which provides that "[a]ny determination at the conclusion of [an adjudicatory] hearing that a [juvenile] did an act or acts must be based on a preponderance of the evidence." During a subsequent dispositional hearing, appellant was ordered placed in a training school for an initial period of 18 months, subject to annual extensions of his commitment until his 18th birthday—six years in appellant's case. The Appellate Division of the New York Supreme Court, First Judicial District, affirmed without opinion, 291 N.Y.S. 2d 1005 (1968). The New York Court of Appeals then affirmed by a four-to-three vote, expressly sustaining the constitutionality of 744 (b) 24 N.Y. 2d 196, 247 N.E. 2d 253 (1969). We noted probable jurisdiction, 396 U.S. 885 (1969). *We reverse.*

I

The requirement that guilt of a criminal charge be established by proof beyond a reasonable doubt dates at least from our early years as a Nation. The "demand for a higher degree of persuasion in criminal cases was recurrently expressed from ancient times, [though] its crystallization into the formula 'beyond a reasonable doubt' seems to have occurred as late as 1798. It is now accepted in common law jurisdictions as the measure of persuasion by which the prosecution must convince the trier of all the essential elements of guilt." McCormick, Evidence, 321, at 681-682 (1954); see also 9 Wigmore, Evidence, 2497 (3d ed. 1940). Although virtually unanimous adherence to the reasonable-doubt standard in common-law jurisdictions may not conclusively establish it as a requirement of due process, such adherence does "reflect a profound judgment about the way in which law should be enforced and justice administered." *Duncan* v. *Louisiana,* 391 U.S. 145, 155 (1968).

Expressions in many opinions of this Court indicate that it has long been assumed that proof of a criminal charge beyond a reasonable doubt is constitutionally required. See, for example, *Miles* v. *United States,* 103 U.S. 304, 312 (1880); *Davis* v. *United States,* 160 U.S. 469, 488 (1895); *Holt* v. *United States,* 218 U.S. 245, 253 (1910); *Wilson* v. *United States,* 232 U.S. 563, 569-570 (1914); *Brinegar* v. *United States,* 338 U.S. 160, 174 (1949); *Leland* v. *Oregon,* 343 U.S. 790, 795 (1952); *Holland* v. *United States,* 348 U.S. 121, 138 (1954); *Speiser* v. *Randall,* 357 U.S. 513, 525-526 (1958). Cf. *Coffin* v. *United States,* 156 U.S. 432 (1895). Mr. Justice Frankfurter stated that "[i]t is the duty of the Government to establish . . . guilt beyond a reasonable doubt. This notion—basic in our law and rightly one of the boasts of a free society—is a requirement and safeguard of due process of law in the historic, procedural content of 'due process.' " *Leland* v. *Oregon,* supra, at 802-803 (dissenting opinion). In a similar vein, the Court said in *Brinegar* v. *United States,* supra, at 174, that "[g]uilt in a criminal case must be proved beyond a reasonable doubt and by evidence confined to that which long experience in the common-law tradition, to some extent embodied in the Constitution, has crystallized into rules of evidence consistent with that standard. These rules are historically grounded rights of our system, developed to safeguard men from dubious and unjust convictions, with resulting forfeitures of life, liberty and property." *Davis* v. *United States,* supra, proceeding where the issue is whether the child will be found to be 'delinquent' and subjected to the loss of his liberty for years is comparable in seriousness to a felony prosecution." Id., at 36.

Nor do we perceive any merit in the argument that to afford juveniles the protection of proof beyond a reasonable doubt would risk destruction of beneficial aspects of the juvenile process. Use of the reasonable-doubt standard during the adjudicatory hearing will not disturb New York's policies that a finding that a child has violated a criminal law does not constitute a criminal conviction, that such a finding does not deprive the child of his civil rights, and that juvenile proceedings are confidential. Nor will there be any effect on the informality, flexibility, or speed of the hearing at which the fact finding takes place. And the opportunity during the post-adjudicatory or dispositional hearing for a wide-ranging review of the child's social history and for his individualized treatment will remain unimpaired. Similarly, there will be no effect on the procedures distinctive to juvenile proceedings which are employed prior to the adjudicatory hearing.

The Court of Appeals observed that "a child's best interest is not necessarily, or even probably, promoted if he wins in the particular inquiry which may bring him to the juvenile court." 24 N.Y. 2d, at 199, 247 N.E. 2d, at 255. It is true, of course, that the juvenile may be engaging in a general course of conduct inimical to his welfare which calls for judicial intervention. But that intervention cannot take the form of subjecting the child to the stigma of a finding that he violated a criminal law and to the possibility of institutional confinement on proof insufficient to convict him were he an adult.

We conclude, as we concluded regarding the essential due process safeguards applied in Gault, that the observance of the standard of proof beyond a reasonable doubt "will not compel the States to abandon or displace any of the substantive benefits of the juvenile process." Gault, supra, at 21.

Finally, we reject the Court of Appeals' suggestion that there is, in any event, only a "tenuous difference" between the reasonable-doubt and preponderance standards. The suggestion is singularly unpersuasive. In this very case, the trial judge's ability to distinguish between the two standards enabled him to make a finding of guilt which he conceded he might not have made under the standard of proof beyond a reasonable doubt. Indeed, the trial judge's action evidences the accuracy of the observation of commentators that "the preponderance test is susceptible to the misinterpretation that it calls on the trier of fact merely to perform an abstract weighing of the evidence in order to determine which side has produced the greater quantum, without regard to its effect in convincing his mind of the truth of the proposition asserted." Dorsen and Reznek, supra, at 26-27.

III

In sum, the constitutional safeguard of proof beyond a reasonable doubt is as much required during the adjudicatory stage of a delinquency proceedings as are those constitutional safeguards applied in Gault—notice of charges, right to counsel, the rights of confrontation and examination, and the privilege against self-incrimination. We therefore hold, in agreement with Chief Judge Fuld in dissent in the Court of Appeals, "that, where a 12-year-old child is charged with an act of stealing which renders him liable to confinement for as long as six years, then, as a matter of due process . . . the case against him must be proved beyond a reasonable doubt." 24 N.Y. 2d, at 207, 247 N.E. 2d, at 260.

Reversed.

FURMAN V. GEORGIA

This Supreme Court case involved three different cases of persons sentenced to death: *Furman* v. *Georgia, Jackson* v. *Georgia,* and *Branch* v. *Texas.*

In the three cases people convicted in state courts were subsequently sentenced to death after a trial by jury. Under the state laws in these cases, the courts had the discretion of imposing the death penalty. One of the persons had been convicted of murder; the other two of rape. All three were members of an ethnic minority—a fact important to one justice.

The Supreme Court by a five-to-four majority held that the imposition of the death sentence in these cases constituted cruel and unusual punishment. Specifically the justices indicated the following:

Justice Brennan stated that the Eighth Amendment to the Constitution's prohibition against cruel and unusual punishment was not limited to punishments which were considered cruel and unusual at the time the Eighth Amendment was adopted. He stated that a punishment was cruel and unusual if it did not comply with the idea of human dignity. Further, he stated that, since this punishment is a denial of human dignity, when a state arbitrarily subjects a person to an unusually severe punishment which society indicates it does not regard as acceptable, and which cannot be shown to be of any penal purpose more effective than a significantly less drastic punishment, then death is a cruel and unusual punishment.

Justice Douglas stated that it is cruel and unusual to apply the death penalty selectively to minorities whose members are few, who are outcasts, and who are unpopular. However, society is willing to see these minorities suffer the death penalty, yet it does not apply the same penalty across all borders. Because of this discriminatory application of the laws authorizing the discretionary imposition of the death penalty, such laws are unconstitutional in their operation.

Justice Marshall stated that the death penalty violated the Eighth Amendment because it was excessive and because it was morally unacceptable to the people of the United States.

Justice Stewart stated that the persons in these cases were a capriciously selected random few, who were sentenced to death. Further, the Eighth and Fourteenth Amendments did not permit the infliction of the death sentence under legal systems which permitted it to be so freakishly and wantonly imposed. Also, he stated that it is unnecessary to decide whether the death penalty is unconstitutional in all circumstances as regards to the Eighth and Fourteenth Amendments.

Justice White stated that as the laws involved in the present cases were administered, the death penalty was so infrequently imposed that the threat of execution was of little value to criminal justice. Furthermore, he stated that it was unnecessary to decide whether the death penalty was unconstitutional per se, or whether there was any system of capital punishment which could comply with the Eighth Amendment.

Chief Justice Burger joined by *Justices Blackmun, Powell,* and *Rehnquist* dissented, stating that the constitutional prohibition against cruel and unusual punishment could not be construed to bar the death penalty. Further, they stated that none of the opinions supporting the Court's decision could be maintained when viewed from the perspective of the affirmative references to capital punishment in the Constitution. The prevailing precedents of the Supreme Court and the duty of the Court to avoid encroachment on the powers conferred upon the state and federal legislatures justified not interceding in these cases.

Furthermore, they stated that the Eighth Amendment was not concerned with the process by which a state determined that a particular punishment was to be imposed in a particular case, nor did the Eighth Amendment speak to the power of legislatures regarding the conferring of sentencing discretion to juries.

Index

AUTHOR INDEX

SUBJECT INDEX